AMERICAN ROULETTE

AMERICAN ROULETTE

HOW I TURNED THE ODDS UPSIDE DOWN—
My Wild Twenty-Five-Year Ride Ripping Off the World's Casinos

Richard Marcus

Thomas Dunne Books
St. Martin's Press ♏ New York

The names and identifying characteristics of persons in this book have been changed, as have dates, places, and other details of events depicted.

THOMAS DUNNE BOOKS.
An imprint of St. Martin's Press.

www.stmartins.com

ISBN 0-312-29139-6

First Edition: September 2003

10 9 8 7 6 5 4 3 2 1

For Stephanie, who's even more fun than the casinos

CONTENTS

Prologue   1

Savannah   4

Las Vegas   30

Initiation   74

The Wheel   96

On the Road   119

The Back Room   132

The Blackjack Move   143

Brainstorm   150

Joe Classon and the Pioneers   161

The Classon Pastposting Team   179

The Mix-Up   205

On the Boardwalk   214

Cat-and-Mouse   223

The Other Side of the Road   241

Passage of Rites   266

The Gay and Not So Gay Nineties
(A Casino Revolution)   277

Balls   282

Pat and the Chocolate Chip Cookie   303

An Irishman in France   322

Taking Savannah to the Ball   333

The End   362

AMERICAN ROULETTE

Prologue

THE LAST TIME YOU WALKED THROUGH A CROWDED GAMBLING CASINO
in full swing, I'm sure you noticed hordes of men gathered around
the craps tables, cheering and hollering as the dice tumbled across
the layout. You must have seen all those well-behaved women with
painted fingernails at the blackjack tables, playing their hands with
religious adherence to every system, every strategy, every hunch that
numbers and fate twist the brain into believing. You couldn't have
missed all those couples, perhaps a bit unruly, feverishly spreading
their chips over their favorite numbers on the roulette tables, counting only on pure luck. And of course the temporary mindlessness of
the masses glued to their stools in front of the blipping, clinking, and
clanking slot machines. Have you ever asked yourself if any of these
gamblers actually win? In the long run?

Of course they don't. You don't need me to tell you that Las
Vegas and Atlantic City were not built on winners. They were built
on dreamers. But is this to say there doesn't exist a select breed of
very talented individuals who *always* make money in casinos? Notice

I did not say "win" money in casinos. We already know that's impossible.

Yes, there are people who always make money in casinos. In fact, lots of money. These people are very few in number, and they all have one thing in common: they cheat. I know this firsthand because I am a professional casino cheater, have been all my adult life. And I'm very good at what I do. Or I should say "did," because now I'm retired. Not because I got busted and put out of business, then copped a plea and decided to write a book like so many convicted scam artists or criminals having nothing to do but tell all. In this sense I am unique. I retired in my prime, clean as a whistle, not the slightest blemish on my record, not forced to stop cheating casinos for any reason. So why did I stop? Simply because I could no longer resist telling you my story. It really is incredible, and I never would have believed that everything you're about to read happened to me.

In this book I will tell you how I so successfully cheated casinos for so long, as well as why I cheated them. I will reveal everything, all my secrets and methods that I'd guarded with my life for twenty-five years. I will give you all the splendid details. I will tell you about the magic involved, but even more impressive than that, the psychology and the manipulation of people's minds. I will show you how I controlled casino personnel like puppets on a string, and did so without the slightest bit of ego. I will show you how I used casinos' omnipresent surveillance cameras above as my number-one ally, how improvements in casino surveillance only aided and abetted me. I will develop all my cheating "moves" in your presence, and you'll surely appreciate their simplicity as well as their sophistication.

And then I'll take you on an exciting twenty-five-year journey through the world's casinos, cheating their pants off. From Vegas to Monte Carlo. From Atlantic City, island-hopping through the Caribbean, all the way to Sun City, South Africa. We'll even take a detour, stop off farther back in time where you'll meet the inventors of my clever little tricks. It was not I who opened the gates to casino cheating; I only improved on it. It was my mentor who introduced me to the founding fathers of casino cheating through colorful anecdotes he recounted to me over the years while he trained me. And without corrupting any I will relate them all to you.

Along the way we'll meet other groups of organized casino cheaters, contemporary ones, from all over the world, each with its little bag of tricks, some nickel-and-diming it on a rough road, others nearly as crafty as my own teams, but certainly none better. You'll see how we divided up the international casino turf when necessary; there was always enough to go around, no need to be greedy. And we'll also take a peek into the future, at the next direction of the ongoing wars between casino cheaters and casino surveillance personnel. There will be no winner, just never-ending battles and many more stories for someone else to tell you after I'm gone.

But remember one thing: I'm not telling you all this so that you go out and become a casino cheater. I'm simply recounting my story to entertain you, just as I've done so many times with captivated audiences gathered around me at parties, in bars, someone always saying with an appreciative smile and glistening eyes, "Richard, you've really lived an unbelievable life. You ought to write a book about all your casino experiences."

Well, here it is, and I hope you enjoy reading about my experiences as much as I did writing them. So climb aboard my ace-of-spades carpet and let's go for a little ride. I promise when we get back you'll never think the same about casinos, and if you've never before been inside one, don't worry, you'll be just as amused and entertained as any seasoned gambler.

Savannah

WHEN IT FIRST HIT ME THAT I HAD PROBABLY DISCOVERED THE BEST cheating move in the history of casino gambling, one that appeared absolutely flawless, with minimal risk—even when getting caught red-handed—I experienced a feeling of euphoria that would have been complete had it not been for the sliver of doubt that naturally crept into my brain. During two decades of cheating the world's legally operating casinos at their own games, using a variety of sleight-of-hand moves, some rank, others good, still others *really* good, that so-called dream move had eluded me until that hot August night in 1995.

I was sitting at the bottom of a shabby roulette table inside the dingy Silver Spur at the intersection of Main and Fremont in downtown Las Vegas. Diagonally across the worn, coffee-stained layout sat my partner in crime, Pat, who'd been working the casinos with me for the past sixteen months. We were both casual in jeans and cotton shirts. Also at the table was the usual downtown assortment of multiracial degenerates, some wagering with two-dollar-gets-you-three-dollar paper coupons that dripped beer—or God knows what else—others with the remnants of their social security checks, which by the looks of what they were wearing could have certainly been put to better use. The occasional tourist dropping a bet on that table didn't even hang around for a second spin when it won. If it wasn't the bowling-alley smell or clanging slot-machine noise that chased them out, it was the horrific click-clack cocktail-waitress call emanating from the device being squeezed in one of the oily-looking pit boss's hands. I would have been chased out of there myself, had it not been true that the Silver Spur was probably the only casino left in Vegas where I wouldn't run into anyone I knew or, better yet, run into someone who knew me.

Pat and I often went downtown to test new cheating moves before going for the real money on the Las Vegas Strip. The trick here was to place a red five-dollar chip atop a green twenty-five-dollar chip on the roulette layout in such a way that the dealer would not see the bottom chip's greenness and therefore assume both chips were red. Knowing that dealers in the bust-out joints downtown were required to announce green chips on the layout, we'd know right away if the little Korean girl named Sun saw the one I was trying to hide underneath the red. We hoped she didn't, but as I delicately placed the two round chips in the first of the three 2-to-1 column boxes at the bottom of the layout, carefully measuring the angle and distance that I let the top red chip protrude off the green, I had serious doubts about the whole damned scheme. I even thought about saying good night to Pat so that I could rush home to catch a rerun of *Law & Order*.

But Sun never called out, "Green action on the layout," and I was absolutely sure she'd looked at my bet—at least three times. Seeing it from the back, the green chip stuck out like a sore thumb.

Pat and I shot each other surprised looks. I furrowed my brows at him as if to say, "Maybe she actually didn't see it." But I was thinking she *had* to see it, that perhaps she was just too lazy to call it out to the supervising floorman, or she had indeed called it out but had one of those ultra-soft Oriental voices that didn't carry well amid the din in the casino. As an ex-casino dealer myself, I knew a lot of dealers didn't give a shit and wouldn't bother straining their voices to alert superiors about the presence of a lousy green chip.

Sun spun the ball and we waited. If the bet lost, we'd place it again; if it won, we'd have our answer. Would she correctly pay me twice the $30 in chips sitting in the betting box, or mistakenly pay $20—2 to 1 for the two red chips we hoped she *thought* were there?

The ball dropped into the black number-10 slot on the spinning wheel, a first-column number that made my bet a winner. I tensed and watched the dealer. Both her hands swept piles of losing chips off the layout, then one reached for a stack of five-dollar reds in her multicolored chip well along the base of the wooden wheel. She cut swiftly into my two chips twice, paying me only $20 instead of the $60 she should have paid.

Which meant she hadn't seen the green chip underneath. She'd taken it for a red. She had made the mistake we'd wanted her to make.

I looked down on the layout at the perfect linear formation of three sets of two chips, specially admiring the set containing the green. I didn't bother to claim the $40 Sun still owed me. That would have been one of the claims from the old days. Instead, I glanced over at Pat and met his large smile with one of my own. We both knew at that instant we were on to something big: we were going to be rich.

A week earlier, we had been relaxing in Pat's apartment, our habitual Las Vegas meeting place, having just returned from a casino-cheating road trip to Reno and Lake Tahoe. Vegas had been a bit "steamy" that summer; in addition to the searing desert heat outside, the heat *inside* the casinos was getting to us. We'd been doing a bunch of the old blackjack moves, getting paid big chunks of money a little too often to suit the pit bosses. The town's surveillance network had put out the word on us. So we had to cool it in Vegas, hit the road for a while. We'd picked up six grand on the weekend trip, not bad for the "biggest little town in America."

Pat popped open a beer, stretched out on the sofa. I was installed in the recliner, munching from the bag of Doritos I'd just ripped open. On the TV, Harry Caray was going through his seventh-inning-stretch routine while the Cubs were getting soundly beaten at Wrigley. The Pizza Hut delivery guy showed up with our two large pizzas with extra cheese. We were all set.

"You know what, Johnny," Pat said (we called each other Johnny, I guess out of some sort of mock affection), "I've been going over something in my head. Did you ever think about putting the big-valued chip under the red *before* the dealer deals the cards . . . and then do a switch when the bet loses?"

I knew exactly what he was thinking. At the time, all our cheating moves were based on switching chips only *after* winning bets. We'd bet five-dollar reds and switch in chips of much higher denominations once we knew the winning outcome. The casino term for that move was *pastposting*. Bookmakers in the Roaring Twenties used it to refer to sharpies who called in winning horse bets from the track just after the race was over. The principle was the same in the casino: Press up your bet the moment you knew it had won.

What Pat was visualizing was doing just the opposite: Make the big bet up front legitimately, then pull it off once you knew it had lost. The casino term for that was *pinching* (or *dragging*). Sure, I'd thought of it. It would be nice to bet a couple of grand and leave it there if it won, rake it off when it lost. But the only way such a maneuver was feasible was to somehow hide the fact you were betting big at the outset, which was very difficult to do, and then to rake off your big bet when it lost, leaving the casino in the dark. Casino personnel were thoroughly trained to combat such scams, but there had always been crafty cheaters who attacked their weaknesses. I'd once read in an old casino surveillance manual how a guy back in the fifties came up with a clever pinching move. He'd approach a roulette table just as the spinning ball was about to drop and the dealer was announcing, "No more bets," and place a thin folded-in-half packet of dollar bills on red. As it appeared to be a small bet of only a couple of bucks, the dealer usually let it play. If black came in, the guy would scoop up his packet and put down in its place another that appeared identical. If the dealer challenged him, he'd just make up a dumb excuse like he was drunk, and since all the dealer ever saw was dollar bills the guy never got much heat. The shocker was that when the ball landed on a red number and the guy won, the dealer, opening up the packet to see how many dollar bills were inside, would find that the rest of the bills folded up were not ones but hundreds. The guy ended up beating Vegas for tens of thousands (big potatoes back in the fifties) before the casinos finally got wise to what was hitting them. To put him—and any other potential copycats—out of business, the casinos implemented a simple policy that still stands today: The dealer had to announce, "Money plays!" as soon as cash appeared on the layout. Then he had to count and spread the bills for the cameras above *before* spinning the ball, dealing the cards, or allowing the shooter to throw the dice on a craps table. Ever since, most pinching moves were either badly conceptualized or just plain acts of desperation by people not wanting to lose their last dollar.

Getting back to Pat, I said, "You want to bet a five-*thousand*-dollar chip underneath a five-dollar red and yank it off when it loses?" I whistled at such audacity.

At the time, in certain casinos, we'd already been working with five-thousand-dollar chips, provided they were the same size as the smaller denomination chips, which was the case in about a third of Vegas's casinos. Since we'd been working mostly on blackjack tables, I envisioned his pinching scenario on a blackjack layout. There were seven betting spots on it, never more than seven bets. American blackjack tables were not like the ones in Europe or on some of the islands, where one gambler was permitted to place his bet behind another's inside the betting circle. But even if multiple betting were permitted in American casinos, I could never imagine a dealer, even the most inattentive one, failing to see a big-valued chip underneath, no matter how many bets were jammed up on a blackjack table. The dealer was just too close to the chips, practically right on top of them.

I told Pat my thoughts and he let the idea go, nodding his agreement that I was probably right. We settled in to watch the rest of the Cub game, then a cop flick on cable. During the movie my mind churned, and before the first dead body turned up on the screen, I grabbed the remote at the foot of my chair and zapped off the TV.

Pat glanced over, not the slightest bit aggravated that I had shut off the film. "What's rolling around in that head of yours, Johnny?" he asked, anticipating correctly that I had an afterthought about pinching the big chips.

"You know something, Johnny," I said. "Your idea has possibilities. But not blackjack . . . roulette."

Pat wasn't as sharp as I when it came to creating and designing casino moves. His real talent was taking off the money, playing the part. He would've been a great actor. With his stout body and pleasant features he had the presence of a Jackie Gleason. What I had was twenty years in the ripping-off-casinos business. So I explained the thought that he'd actually put in my head.

"That trick—hiding a five-thousand-dollar chip underneath a red—just might work on a roulette table, at the bottom. With all the action on a crowded roulette layout, a dealer never has the time to really case all the bets. And if we built camouflage bets around it, it's possible the dealer won't see it, especially in casinos where the lighting creates good shadows." Dim casino lighting would naturally help us hide that chip.

Pat caught on instantly, so we got to work designing the prospective move. All our casino material was kept in Pat's spare bedroom. We had table layouts, cards, dealing shoes, chips, dice, even a regulation blackjack table that I'd inherited from my old casino mentor. A roulette wheel and table would have been welcome but were just too big to fit.

I brought out a green-felt roulette layout and spread it snugly over the dining room table. Lying on the coffee table facing the sofa were two stacks of red chips from Caesars Palace and the Mirage we hadn't bothered cashing out the last time we were inside those casinos. I grabbed both and sat them on the bottom edge of the layout, then told Pat to get into his little hiding place and extract a big chip. We never practiced with fake or minimum-value chips. When we worked with purples ($500 chips), we practiced with purples. The same went for yellows ($1,000 chips) and chocolates ($5,000 chips).

Pat sprang off the couch, scurried into the kitchen, and opened a box of Kellogg's Special K. From underneath the half-empty paper bag of cereal, he pulled out a creamy chocolate gaming chip from Caesars Palace. He smiled as he let it drop into my hand. I couldn't think of anything so small and round and so valuable other than diamonds and rare coins.

"That could turn out to be a very expensive hiding place," I said, pointing to the Special K box.

"You're right, Johnny, but I've only had to run down to the dumpster once. Got there just before the garbage truck did."

I didn't ask him why he hadn't changed his hiding spot; he might not have done so even if the garbage truck had beaten him to the dumpster. You never knew with Pat; sometimes he was a crazy Irishman.

I placed the chocolate chip in the first-column box on the layout, then capped it with three reds, cracking them slightly off the chocolate toward the imaginary dealer. I moved up to the dealer's spot to determine whether I could see the chocolate beneath the reds. I saw it easily. Discouraged, I reached back down the layout and adjusted the chips, trying to find the precise angle at which the obtruding wedge formed by the three reds hid the chocolate. I was not seeking to defy the chocolate chip's being there, only prevent its color from being seen from where I stood. Of course, the dealer would know the bottom chip was there but not its denomination. The crucial idea was to make him assume it was also a red. Roulette dealers seldom peeled chips off a bet to peek at the bottom one. I had only seen that happen when casinos were particularly steamy after having been attacked by bands of cheaters, but in normal circumstances dealers trusted their eyes.

Pat took my position at the top of the layout while I tinkered with the bet at the bottom.

"There!" he cried out suddenly. "I can't see the chocolate."

I broke out laughing. "You shittin' me?" I wasn't sure I really wanted to believe him. I didn't want to be a victim of false hope.

"Johnny," he said deliberately, tilting his big head playfully as he always did when he was making a point or mocking me or himself. "I just told you I don't see that chocolate chip." He bent down, craning his neck from side to side, examining the stack of chips from different angles. "Johnny, I still don't see that chocolate chip."

I was delirious with pleasure and excitement. I went over to him, gently shoved him out of the way, and looked down at the bet. What I *didn't* see amazed me. Not only was the chocolate completely out of view, I had to strain to determine that four chips, not three, were there. The chocolate chip seemed to vanish, to sink into the felt below. To see it I had to meander around the layout and put myself where the dealer would never be. I went back to the dealer's position and admired the little stack in the first-column box for several seconds. Then I peeled off one of the red chips, which didn't change anything. I peeled off another, and still the chocolate underneath remained hidden. I could barely tell there was a chip under there at all. It was impossible to hide the slight difference in elevation between one and two chips, but that was not our objective.

Now we knew that a single chip, when angled correctly atop another, would conceal the bottom chip's denomination. It was also evident that the first-column box, the farthest betting point on the layout from the dealer, was ideal for hiding chips.

"Johnny, I don't fucking believe it," I said, looking up at the bright chandelier above the dining room table. "Look at this. We're standing under this bright light. Can you imagine what this'd be like inside a casino with all those shadows?"

We stood silent for a few moments, each contemplating what this little discovery could mean for our cheating-the-casinos business. If not a hell of a lot more money, at least a hell of a lot more adventures. We broke out a bottle of champagne, toasted the new findings optimistically, polished off the bottle, then got to serious work on the layout.

Six hours later, at dawn, the move in its basic form was designed. One of us would place three slightly protruding red chips atop a chocolate in the first-column box at the bottom of the layout. The other would stand by the spinning roulette wheel to signal the outcome of the bet. As in any other business, legitimate or not, things kept simple were the most efficient. The idea we came up with to communicate this information was deliciously simple. If the ball fell into a losing number, the person watching it, whom we called the *caller*, would yell loudly, "Damn it!" at the earliest possible instant, in some cases even before the dealer could read the number. That would signal the person at the bottom, whom we called the *raker*, that he had to immediately rake off the chips, stick the chocolate safely into his pocket, and replace four red chips in the first-column box, apologizing to the dealer for not having realized that the ball dropped when caught. Since people got excited and cursed all the time in casinos as their bets won and lost, the caller's shout would be nothing out of the ordinary.

When the bet won, all the caller had to do was remain silent. The raker would simply leave the winning bet there on the layout and just claim it, saying excitedly something like, "By golly, I hit a big one!" and then collect the payoff as one expected to do when winning a bet in a casino.

It was that simple. The most ingenious casino cheating move in history entailed nothing more than making a big bet that you raked off the layout when it lost and collected the money when it won.

Two days after our successful Silver Spur experiment we flew back to Reno to test the move with a purple five-hundred-dollar chip. Before venturing chocolates on the Vegas Strip the kinks had to be ironed out. I would be the caller and Pat the raker, mainly because he was better at interacting with pit bosses in difficult situations. Pat had a tremendous gift for ingratiating himself with people. He knew how to take the edge off tense situations, which this new move certainly risked provoking. Grabbing a losing bet off a gaming table before the dealer could sweep it was as flagrant as you could get. Dealers might freak out and scream. We had to be prepared for anything.

The third week of August is always the busiest time of year in Reno. It's when the Hot August Nights Festival comes to town, a four day bash that brings to Reno thousands of vintage automobiles mostly from the fifties and sixties. During the day the precious cars parade down Virginia Street, and at night the parties from the street spill over into the casinos, mobbing them up real good for us. We preferred working inside crowded casinos where we meshed with everyone else. And we dressed that way, too. On the day shift we were casual in shorts, T-shirts, and ball caps. At night we'd put on jeans and neat polo shirts, sometimes sports jackets if it wasn't too hot outside, but never leather because that was too slick and stood out. Nobody ever took special note of us, and we took precautions to hide the fact we were together.

The first afternoon, in between the motorcar parades, we went out and picked up a couple of grand pastposting blackjack tables. We wanted to be assured of making our money for the trip before venturing into the unknown with the new roulette move, which we christened *Savannah*, because before going back out to work on the evening swing shift, we'd taken a little detour into a "titty bar," where one of the nude dancers who successfully hustled us for a lap dance went by the obvious fake name Savannah.

We chose the Eldorado for the first Savannah-move experiment. We'd always been lucky there, and its tables were usually jammed up with action. By the time we got inside around midnight, the place was really hopping and filled with a chorus of slot machine tunes. You could barely walk behind the tables, let alone find one with a vacant spot to get down a bet. We waited forty minutes before Pat was able to squeeze through the noisy crowd and stand at the bottom of a roulette table with a cute blond dealer. I managed to twist my body forward enough near the spinning wheel so I could follow the ball's revolutions with my eyes. From where I stood there was a little revolving blind spot on the inner disk, which would delay my call by a fraction of a second if the ball dropped into a number slot passing momentarily out of view. But that small risk we were willing to take.

Pat cautiously placed his four chips in the first-column box as early as possible, the moment the dealer removed her marker from the previous winning number. Like everything else intrinsic to the move, the timing of his bet placement was crucial. When doing something underhanded like this, you want to avoid eye contact with the dealer. You want to pass unnoticed. It was second nature for dealers to glance at a player's face when seeing him place chips on the layout, and that glance lengthened when a player put his bet down late. By placing his bet early, while the dealer was busy restacking the chips swept from the previous spin, Pat avoided spooking her. When she finished stacking and cased the layout for the upcoming spin, Pat's bet was one of a hundred already out there. It blended in perfectly, the three reds jutting off the purple. There was no need to camouflage it with stacks of chips as we'd discussed in the planning stages. Several other players at the table did that for us. They couldn't help but become our unwitting accomplices.

Pat looked at me and grazed his chin subtly with his thumb and index finger. This was our signal that everything was a go.

I returned Pat's "chin" to let him know I was ready.

The cute blonde spun the ball, then began recasing the bets on the layout, her eyes washing over the chips. She still did not notice Pat's purple chip hidden underneath the reds.

I concentrated deeply as the ball whizzed around the wheel several times, each revolution a little slower than the last. When it finally fell into number 16 in the first column, I let out a sigh of relief. But then it bounced out, ricocheted around the bowl and dribbled along a few more numbers before dropping dead in the black number-8 slot—a loser. I hesitated a half second to be sure the ball didn't bounce out again before yelling, "Damn it!" maybe a bit too loud. I was all pent up and equally pissed off that the ball had jumped out of a winner.

By the time I got my eyes off the wheel and down to the first-column box, there were no chips in it. Pat had scooped them up, and there hadn't been the slightest peep from the dealer. She'd seen absolutely nothing. There was no need even to replace the chips.

Pat flashed his eyes at me. He was clearly impressed by what he'd seen. So was I. Neither of us had expected the rake-off to go unnoticed.

He gave me a soft nod, then eased away from the table toward the darkened lounge off the casino floor. I stayed behind for fifteen minutes to see if any steam came down afterward. Though that purple chip had been invisible to the dealer, it could have been seen by any number of gamblers or spectators around the table—who might decide to rat, for whatever reason. Though most people didn't alert casinos when they witnessed cheating, probably because they tired of seeing the house win, we always had to be prepared for those who did.

When I joined Pat at the packed bar and ordered a Coke, he was already hopping in step with the jazz combo and on his second beer.

"Johnny, that dealer was dead standing!" he said in a flourish, without breaking stride from the music. "If they're all like her, we'll never have to give these casinos back a chip."

We clinked glasses, then I said, "All we need to know now is how dealers react when they catch you raking the chips, and how the pit handles our winners."

"We'll find out soon enough," Pat said, and gulped down the rest of his beer.

Anytime you had a large-denomination winning chip showing up on a casino layout without being announced beforehand by the dealer, you had steam. Even in the classiest casinos in Vegas. Dealers everywhere were required to announce "black action" once a black chip was spotted on the layout, or "purple action" if a player laid down a purple. Approval had to come from the floorman before the dealer spun the ball or dealt the cards. Only at craps was this practice forgone, simply because there was always a minimum of four employees on the game, with a floorman or pit boss behind in the pit. The first thing casino employees often thought upon learning of the presence of an unannounced large winning chip was that it had probably been pastposted and the casino was getting taken for the wager. The beauty of our little gig was that if there was any question as to whether our roulette bet was legitimate, and not a pastpost or late bet, all the casino had to do was call up their surveillance "eye in the sky" and have the operator on duty run back the tape. By the late 1980s, just about all the casinos in America—in the world, for that matter—had twenty-four-hour video surveillance on all their tables. So, in theory, we were actually protected by the casino's own security system, the very fact that so juiced us up about this new move. In the past, the cameras had been a constant threat to our operation because we'd always slipped in the big bets late. When pit bosses had threatened to review tapes in challenging the legitimacy of our bets, we had to back off claims and get the hell out of Dodge. But now we actually wanted their surveillance systems in perfect working order.

At three o'clock in the morning we were back in position at another Eldorado roulette table as the ball spun around the shallow bowl. The casino was still crowded, but this time we didn't have to wait to get our bet down. Pat was readying himself to either pick up the chips or claim; I was up at the front by the wheel, getting ready to signal the outcome. The ball landed on a losing number, I yelled, "Damn it!" and Pat raked off the four chips.

He got caught red-handed.

"Hey!" another little Oriental female dealer screamed. And this one's voice *did* carry amid the casino din. "What are you doing, sir! Put those chips back down! Your bet lost!"

Pat went into his drunken routine. "Oh, I'm so sorry," he blurted out, as he swayed unsteadily with an empty glass in his hand. "I guess the ball already landed. I didn't realize it." He reached down with calculated clumsiness and placed three red chips on the layout. I noticed right away he didn't put down four, the number of chips that had originally been there.

So did the dealer. This little girl was sharp. "Sir, you had *four* red chips out there, twenty dollars!" she said just as sharply.

Upon hearing that I smiled inwardly. She had never seen the purple chip underneath.

"Oh. I had four of them red . . . red . . . redbirds out there," Pat said, slurring his words perfectly, the consummate actor.

"Put the fourth one back down!" she barked, like a little oriental dictator.

Pat did as he was told.

The floorman, who'd noticed the ruckus, came up to the table from behind the dealer. "What's the matter?" he asked her.

"No big deal," she said, toning it down. She indicated Pat with a slight head movement. "The gentleman didn't realize the ball dropped, so he tried to pick up his bet."

Pat kept playing the part, knowing it wasn't curtains down until the situation was totally defused. He offered the floorman his wavering handshake. "Yeah, she's right," he said with a slur. "I tried to pick up my bet like a real slob."

The floorman laughed easily and said, "No big deal, sir. Enjoy yourself at the Eldorado." Then he walked back into the pit and forgot about it. I said to myself, If you only knew how big a deal this was eventually going to be!

Pat hung around five minutes, made a few foolhardy five-dollar bets before leaving the table for our predetermined meeting place outside the casino. We had chosen the keno pit at the Circus Circus casino down the road. Whenever there was steam, even if the situation was smoothed out as Pat had done at that table, we met outside the casino. You never knew what could happen afterward—the rats, or the dealer could get steamed up again on her own, suddenly remembering something that could alert her to the reality of what had happened.

I stayed at the table ten minutes, concluded everything was clean, then went off to join my partner at Circus Circus.

"Johnny, this is big!" I said with a grin.

"They already forgot about it?"

"Nobody said another word."

A half hour later we were in position at a roulette table inside Harrah's Casino. We'd decided to leave the Eldorado alone. We'd been in there long enough and picked up a little steam with that second dealer. Though this was only our third attempt at the new Savannah move, we were already quite coordinated with its mechanics. We'd experienced two losers without any communication problems; my two damn-its had been heard by Pat, and he'd managed to get the purple chip off the layout both times without incident. The dealer's catching him the second time was of no concern. The key was that she had never seen his purple chip. We had worried about the possibility that the chip would become visible as the dealer's eyes were drawn to the action of the rake-off, but now that appeared like another obstacle we could put to bed. The farther we progressed into the experiment, the more potential obstacles dropped like dominos. I was becoming more and more convinced that our new dream move was turning into reality—even before seeing a payoff. It had already dawned upon me how easy it was. Its simplicity was astounding.

The dealer on the game, a tall Nevadan named Randy, had a seemingly carefree attitude. The table was full, the atmosphere seductive. Half the people seated and standing around the table were clad in their Hot August Nights T-shirts and ball caps; almost everybody had a drink or cigarette in hand. The casino was still humming with noise.

Pat laid down the bet, again paying special attention to crack the three red chips slightly off the purple to create a perfectly angled wedge. The girl next to him did a double-take at his chips. She probably saw the purple underneath, but I had no intention of calling off the move because she was a potential snitch. In ripping off casinos you lived with that possibility.

Randy took a cursory glance at the layout and spun the ball. In synch with his size, his spin was powerful. The ball made several revolutions before the hissing sound of its speed cadenced into a plunk-plunk rattle as it began careening back and forth, landing in one slot, popping out, then landing again. The ball's course tested my patience. When finally all the sounds from the ball were gone, and there was just the steady hum of the revolving wheel, a sudden burst emanated from the bottom of the table.

Pat exploded. He'd seen the ball land and stay put in the red number-1 slot as soon as I had.

We had a winner!

"That's me!" Pat cried, clapping his hands loudly, pointing to his winning chips, clenching his fist as he jerked his arm outward and pulled it back, a gesture reminiscent of a hockey player's reaction after scoring a goal. Had Pat had his stick, I'm sure he would've raised it above his head, too. "That's my five hundred bucks in the first-column box!" He pointed again at the chips. "That's my purple chip sitting under there."

The exact words of Pat's claim were also rehearsed. Following the script was essential. Knowing that the dealer hadn't seen the purple chip before spinning the ball, we knew as well he didn't see it now, either. It was of the utmost importance to make him see that purple chip as soon as possible, because now it was a winner. Had Pat started claiming a winner without actually saying he had bet a purple chip, the dealer would not have realized its presence, so well was it hidden underneath the three reds. He most certainly would have figured Pat was just gassed up about winning a twenty-dollar bet. We knew we couldn't allow such a scenario to take place. The more time that elapsed before the dealer realized the purple chip was there, the more dangerous the situation became. If too much time passed, the dealer, and then the floorman or pit boss arriving on the scene later, might have the audacity to think the bet was late or even pastposted and hold up the payoff to check with the eye in the sky. Of course, the legitimacy of our bet would be protected by the camera, but we wanted a quick payoff without steam, so Pat kept repeating, "Five-hundred dollars on the column, five-hundred dollars on the column," as he pointed at his chips, not letting up until he was certain the dealer saw the purple.

Randy at first looked down confusedly at the smaller Pat. I interpreted his bizarre facial expression as the unspoken words, What is this ranting and raving lunatic at the bottom of my table talking about?

But Randy's facial muscles contorted quickly when he picked up Pat's bet and the purple chip on the bottom jumped up at him. He knew he was going to catch flak for not having called out the purple to his supervisor.

I backed off the wheel to watch from the background as the scene developed. The people around the table began laughing and cheering for Pat as if he'd brought everyone luck. It never hurt to have the support of other gamblers around the table. It was a heck of a lot better than the rats. In negative situations people at the table often helped us unintentionally. Sometimes a suspicious pit boss, wanting to hold up and delay a game because of a questionable bet, refrained from doing so because he didn't want to aggravate the players and give the impression that the casino was fretting over having to pay a big bet. Also, a table going good with lots of action was highly profitable for the house, another reason for a pit boss not to stop a well-run game in progress.

Randy immediately called over the floorman, who'd been leaning against an adjacent blackjack table to flirt with a pretty girl playing the end seat. The floorman would've preferred that Randy find someone else to bother, but duty called.

"The man standing at the bottom bet a purple on the column," Randy told him, with a demeanor not at all as calm and carefree as it had been before he got bit by Pat's purple chip. "It won."

The floorman shrugged. "Why didn't you call it out before you spun the ball?"

"I never saw it."

The floorman got a little interested. "Was it there before you spun it?"

Casino people can be really stupid sometimes. The dealer had just told the floorman he never saw the purple chip, and now the guy turns around and asks him if it was there before he spun the ball. You'd be amazed at the thousands of incredibly dumb questions and comments I've heard from otherwise intelligent casino personnel over the years.

The only thing Randy could tell the floorman was that he was sure there were four chips in the first-column box before he spun the ball. That was his subconscious memory talking—an element we always counted on when our bets won.

The floorman pressed him on it. "You're certain?"

"I always case my bets," Randy answered quickly, to let the floorman know he never missed a chip on his layout.

"Then pay him," the floorman instructed, returning to the blackjack table to resume his conversation with the pretty girl on the end seat.

Randy plucked two purple chips from the purple stack in his chip well, grabbed a stack of reds with his other hand, dropped the two purples next to Pat's purple, which he'd removed from the bottom of the bet to show the floorman, and cut into Pat's three red chips with his own red stack twice.

Well, there it was! We had our first payoff on the new Savannah move—$1,030. The two bets we lost cost us a total of twenty bucks. Had Pat replaced the chips both times, we would have lost forty. In any case, who wouldn't like those odds?

We met up at the Circus Circus keno pit. Pat gave me all the chips. I went back to Harrah's to cash out. Before doing so, I took a final evaluative look at the wheel where we'd just taken off the money. Randy was still dealing, and the floorman was still flirting with the girl. Everything was spotless.

It was past four o'clock in the morning and we were both feeling pretty beat, so we called it a night. Before going back to our hotel room we stopped back at the titty bar. To our surprise, Savannah was still there wagging her butt. Pat was really in a jolly mood, so he splurged for back-to-back titty dances. After the lovely Savannah finished her little number of waving her tits and ass in our faces, Pat laid a hundred-dollar bill on her. Usually he gave the dancers twenties, but his high spirits warranted the hundred. All expenses incurred on road trips, including entertainment tabs, came off the top of our bankroll.

"That's a big number you gave her," I said, after Savannah flashed us her pretty, phony smile and was gone.

Pat reached across the table and rubbed my shoulder, almost condescendingly. "Don't worry, Johnny," he said merrily, "Savannah made that little dance well worth it. And I'm not talking about the girl." He paused for effect. "Did you get that, Johnny?"

I got it.

Later, back in the room, we were in our respective beds as the first light of dawn penetrated the curtains, streaking the walls in linear patterns. Neither of us thought about getting up to draw the curtains tighter; we were too pumped up by the day's and night's activities for sleep. Instead, we talked incessantly about the move. Besides the simple ingenuity of its design, the risk factor—even when we got caught—was extremely low. After all, how could we ever be prosecuted if one day the casinos got wise to us? Let's say, for example, the worst-case scenario occurred. For me, that meant getting caught raking the losing bet and having the purple chip exposed. If that ever happened, we'd have to assume the casino would put the whole thing together, comprehend we were basically taking free shots at them. That would surely get them pissed off. But what could they do about it? The old stories you hear or see in the movies where cheaters and card counters get their hands broken or taken out to the desert to get whacked were no longer anything but that—just stories. Nowadays casinos had to take cheaters to court just like department stores did with professional shoplifters. They needed evidence that would stand up, mainly surveillance video from the eye in the sky.

In our case, what would the casino and later the prosecutor claim? That the defendant bet four chips, three reds on top of a purple, which he premeditatedly concealed, with the intent of switching out the purple and replacing it with another red if the outcome of the bet was not favorable to him? Sure, that makes a pretty good argument, and any jury would understand it. But one key piece of evidence would be missing. How could the casino prove there had ever been a purple chip under the three reds in the first place? The answer was that they couldn't.

All the fantastic things you hear about casino surveillance systems, such as that famous cliché about surveillance cameras reading the date off a dime, are only partially true. Yes, they can read the date off a dime, but only if the lens is zoomed in for that particular purpose. Casino cameras are only zoomed in when surveillance personnel are already suspicious of certain activities and are trying to get a closer look at a suspected cheating move and film close-ups of faces and fingers to use later as evidence in court. But against us, that was zero. We were hit-and-run cheaters. We never got involved in prolonged operations that gave the casino time to set us up. We hit, and then we were gone. One spin and out. Their cameras never had the chance to zoom in on us. Furthermore, even if by some miraculous chance a camera above a roulette wheel was zoomed in on our bet, it could never see that bottom chip well enough to positively identify it. *Never.* That is because zoomed images are grainy.

I had a friend, Donnie, working in the surveillance room at a major casino on the Strip. I greased him up periodically, and he gave me the lowdown on casino surveillance and kept me posted on intercasino communication about what cheaters were doing. He also passed me copies of my mug shots, which were passed frequently around the casinos. Seeing them helped me choose hairstyles or disguises to avoid detection while I worked the tables. If a recent mug shot showed me with long hair and whiskers, I'd run to the barber for a snip and a shave.

Often Donnie'd bring copies of his casino's surveillance tapes to my apartment. We'd watch them together. On the screen I saw everything their cameras were capable of. I learned all the details and became a sort of surveillance expert myself. Donnie taught me about the camera movements—pan and tilt, angle shots, zoom-ins, every minute detail of surveillance procedures. I noticed on the tapes that the close-ups were always fuzzy, often blurry. On still shots taken with the lens in normal position, the images were clear. But those were taken from overhead cameras that had no minds of their own. They couldn't get close enough without human help to really see anything. The flagrant cheating moves were caught by fixed cameras, but that was it.

Another thing I learned from Donnie was that the surveillance inspectors themselves were quite ineffective. In the old days Vegas used casino cheaters who'd gone straight to spy on their ex-partners from above. These guys in the eye knew something. They were capable of recognizing something going down in the casino. But today everyone working surveillance, including my friend Donnie, was a legitimate person who had taken a six-week training course before getting his job. Imagine the level of incompetence existing when comparing today's book-smart casino sleuths with yesterday's sharpies who could read the date off a dime *without* the help of cameras. Asking someone fresh out of surveillance school to spot a slick move going down in a casino was tantamount to putting a cabdriver in the cockpit of a 747.

Aside from the cameras, what other tangibles could the casino have on us? I painted a scenario for Pat: "Say I get caught picking up the bet, and they search me—or better yet, while snatching up the chips, I drop the purple and it rolls right to the dealer, and she grabs it and puts it in her chip well, insisting that I had bet it and lost and was then trying to grab it off the layout before she could sweep it. That's about the worst-case scenario, right?"

Pat nodded his agreement.

"Okay, what do I say? I don't say anything. I just keep my mouth shut and wait till my attorney gets there. But what I'm thinking is that even if they could prove the purple chip was in my possession, that doesn't prove I'd bet it. Because if I'd actually bet it, then why didn't the dealer call it out to the pit, in accordance with casino dealing policy? See what I'm saying? The casino's own policy protects us. Any black, purple, thousand-dollar, or five-thousand-dollar chip on the layout must be announced to the floorman before the dealer spins the ball. If not, then technically it's not there. No bet with a big chip has ever been made. So how can a prosecutor say, 'The defendant bet a purple chip under three reds,' if casino policy itself dictates that no purple chip had been bet? And not only is that the policy in all the casinos, it's also one of the Nevada Gaming Control Board's regulations."

"Johnny, the more you talk, the more I like it," Pat said, grinning.

I continued: "And even if they got lucky and had two different tapes of me—one showing me getting paid, another showing me grabbing up losing chips on a different table, they couldn't use the tape from the payoff to support the tape from the rake-off because no crime was committed by simply getting paid, nor could they use the tape of the rake-off to say I *would have* swiped off the chips on the tape where I got paid if *that* bet had lost. It's like double jeopardy. Just because I was presumably committing a crime on one tape doesn't prove I was conspiring to commit the same crime on the other tape. I know all that sounds a little confusing. Shit, I'm even confusing myself. But imagine what a prosecutor would have to do to untangle all that tape and get a conviction."

"Johnny, I think what you're trying to say is that they can't use evidence from one crime as evidence for another."

I laughed. "You're right. I think that's what I was trying to say. And I'm glad to see you're learning something from watching every second of the O. J. trial every day."

"Don't forget about *Geraldo Live* and *Court TV*."

"You know what, Johnny," I said after a moment's reflection, "I think we got the *nuts* with this move."

In all, it had been quite a night. I was completely drained. Not only was there all that excitement with the new move, but also the emotional swings that came with the anticipation and doubt. I got a few hours of agitated sleep. In the morning it was breakfast and then right out to work. Reno may have gotten a taste of Savannah that night, but for the rest of the weekend they were going to get the full dose.

During the next three days and nights Pat laid $515 dollars down in the first-column box on thirty-three different roulette tables in all the major casinos in Reno. Our luck ran pretty good. The bet won fourteen times, better than one in three. Of the nineteen times it lost, Pat got the purple chip off smoothly eighteen of them, more than half the time without the dealer even noticing. Each time he got caught, he went into the drunken "I didn't know the ball had dropped" routine, successfully avoiding major confrontations with irritated dealers.

The one time Pat didn't get the purple off the layout was nobody's fault. The rolling ball hit the little blind spot just as it fell into a number slot and my call was too late, so the dealer swept away Pat's chips, including the purple, and stacked them in his chip well. The dealer had actually stacked the purple chip with all the reds, never noticing it had been on the layout, not even when he had it in his hand. Losing the purple chip was no big deal, just a little expense incurred during the learning process.

Of the fourteen winning bets that weekend, twelve passed without incident and Pat got paid quickly by the floormen. Every time, of course, the dealer went through the initial shock of seeing the purple chip buried underneath, but none questioned the legitimacy of the bet.

At the Reno Hilton, after a floorman instructed his dealer to pay Pat the $1,030, he went deep into the pit to tell the pit boss what had happened. The pit boss approached the wheel to see who their purple-chip player was. By the time he was at the table, Pat was already gone and heading to our meeting place outside the casino. His sudden disappearance bugged the pit boss, who immediately scanned the casino with one of those patented pit-boss eye-tours in search of Pat, which was funny because he had no idea who he was looking for or what he looked like. Shaking his head, he went back to the podium and picked up the phone, probably to call the eye in the sky, or maybe alert the shift boss about the incident.

As always, I stayed behind to gauge the casino's reaction. When there was steam, I stayed as long as necessary, determining to what degree it might affect future moves. Usually I could tell by certain actions what a pit boss was saying without hearing his voice. In a noisy casino you couldn't depend on your ears. You made judgments based on nuances and experience, as well as the gestures of casino personnel, who never behaved subtly or tried to hide their actions when their suspicions were aroused. With all the knowledge I'd nurtured over the years, I had no need to lean into a pit in order to hear the conversation among casino personnel, because doing so risked bringing steam onto myself.

When that Reno Hilton pit boss hung up the phone and swiftly strode out of the pit, his fashion told me that wherever he was going had something to do with Pat's bet. I followed him across the casino. He went into the main craps pit, where an older, obviously higher-ranking pit boss—maybe even the shift boss or casino manager—was standing behind a busy craps table with a lot of heavy black-chip action. The big casino bosses usually hung out in the main craps pit.

They conversed a minute or so, but the big boss didn't seem too concerned about hearing that somebody had won a grand off a purple chip nobody had seen on a roulette game before the dealer spun the ball. By chance, a big player with a rack full of purple chips was betting off two grand with each roll of the dice. The big boss was more intent on watching him than listening to the pit boss's report. Situations like that, legitimate high rollers in casinos, often helped take heat off us. Had the casino been dead, that big boss might have investigated the incident further. But he just shook it off, and the roulette pit boss returned to his pit.

Pat had aroused that pit boss's suspicions because he'd left the table after only one very unusual spin. It might seem to someone not privy to the business that a better course of action would have been to have Pat stay and play awhile at the table, to sort of "unsteam" the casino. But doing that would have subjected him to exposure, giving surveillance enough time to zoom in their cameras and snap close-ups, which could then be attached to alert bulletins and faxed around to the other casinos in town. In the long run, it was better to get out early, even if that risked bringing the steam.

We ran into another sticky situation at the Silver Legacy, Reno's newest and now largest gaming establishment. It boasted a giant mining rig in the middle of the casino that every so often swung into action and created the movements and sounds of digging up silver deposits. We'd put in many hours there, as the opportunities were endless. Pat had already picked up losers and gotten paid four times when we found ourselves on what turned out to be the last wheel of the trip.

The dealer called for the floorman as soon as Pat made him aware of the winning purple chip. I could tell immediately that the floorman was a wiseass type and was going to be a problem. He had an annoying strut with a chip on his shoulder. As in all walks of life, casinos had their share of assholes.

The guy visually measured Pat, who was dressed casually in jeans and a light designer windbreaker, and for whatever reason decided to challenge him. Pointing disdainfully at Pat's bet, he said derisively, "You know something, I've been in this business twenty years, and I've never seen anyone make a bet like that."

This punk of a floorman didn't know who he was up against. Pat took his time sizing up the guy. Then he said, "You know something, I've also been in this business twenty years . . . and I don't give a fuck."

Wasn't much room for a riposte there.

It was never our intention to get fresh with casino personnel. We were always a class act, but sometimes assholes provoke you and you have to hold your ground. That floorman had come off as both obnoxious and strong. In effect, he was telling Pat his bet was suspect and at the same time saying he was just another run-of-the-mill cheater. But he didn't know who he was dealing with and made the wrong call. Pat may have been a cheater, but he was certainly not run-of-the-mill. He reacted to the insult instinctively, more from who he was than where he was, and his retort was a polite way of saying, "Take a walk, you fucking little scumbag."

Pat was incredibly quick under the gun. He always had an appropriate response in every situation, no matter how serious the problem. Earlier that same day, in the same casino, a floorman had asked Pat in a suspicious but not impolite tone why he'd put three red chips atop a purple. Though his bet structure was indeed a bit odd, because legitimate purple-chip players didn't normally mix purples with reds, it was none of the casino's damned business how Pat placed his chips. But since the floorman had asked courteously, Pat didn't need to come off rude. As always, he found the perfect response, one that even served to dissipate the steam. He said simply, "The three red chips I bet for the dealer." The floorman had smiled his acknowledgment and told Pat that players wanting to bet for the dealer usually placed those chips directly in front of their own bets, not on top, so the dealer would understand the bet was for him. Pat played dumb and laughed with the floorman at his ignorance. Before the incident was over, the floorman ended up giving Pat a comp for two in the hotel's best restaurant. Pat had lobster, I had steak.

The next morning, flooded with excitement by the weekend's results and the promising new Savannah move, we caught a flight back to Vegas. In our four-day trip we had cleared seventeen grand after expenses, including the hundred-dollar bill Pat laid on the lovely Savannah. We couldn't wait to get back to Vegas and try

Savannah with five-thousand-dollar chips in the big Strip casinos. For me, this anticipation was even greater because Pat and I had decided to switch roles. He would be calling "damn it" at the top of the table by the wheel while I got paid or raked off the huge bet at the bottom of the layout.

But before I tell you how we made out with Savannah in Vegas, let me tell you a little about myself and how I got involved in all this casino cheating.

Las Vegas

I NEVER GREW UP ASPIRING TO BE A CASINO CHEATER, BUT I COULD never write in my memoirs that ending up as one surprised me. From a very tender age I was hooked on gambling. It started with flipping baseball cards for keeps. At one time I had the biggest card collection in the neighborhood, and was awfully proud of it. But then I lost it "flipping colors" in the school cafeteria when I was supposed to be in class. It was there in elementary school that I actually first learned about cheating at gambling.

The fronts of baseball cards all had a colored banner screened into the photograph, and on it the player's name and his team logo were printed. Two teams shared one color. When flipping colors, each flipper held his pack of cards facedown, and each, in turn, turned the top card over. When the color of the card being turned over matched that of the previous card sitting faceup on top of the pile, that flipper won the pot. To make matters more exciting—and costly—five- and ten-"potters" were initiated, where little untidy mountains of base-ball cards formed and were not swept away until one of the flippers matched colors that many times.

I was horrified to see my twenty-shoebox card collection get distributed among my peers, and even more so later when I learned they had cheated me. I'd been the sole victim of a vicious sixth-grade scam. What my evil classmates had done was memorize all the teams and their colors. When they read the players' names off the backs of my top card and theirs, and saw that I would match colors and win the pot, they pulled seconds. They held their top card in place while sliding out the one underneath and turning it over, killing the winning match I would've made. The move was no different from a crooked blackjack dealer dealing seconds in a casino, and it knocked me out of the ranks of joyful baseball-card-collecting youngsters and into the cruel adult world of gambling.

Before I hit thirteen, I'd graduated from baseball cards to real money, and I learned quickly that a gambler needs a constant cash flow to support his habit and that, as an eighth-grader, I needed to be clever if not a bit dishonest to get a bankroll together.

The first moneymaking scam I put to use after going broke in a backwoods poker game was one I learned from a movie. I didn't remember which kid actor I'd seen walk inside a busy deli and buy a sixty-cent hot dog with a twenty-dollar bill and get the change. What I did remember was that his cohort, an innocent-looking not-yet-teenage girl, followed him inside and also bought a sixty-cent hot dog, but paid for it with a one-dollar bill. When the clerk gave her the forty cents change, she claimed indignantly that he had tried to rip her off because she had given him a twenty-dollar bill and got back only forty cents change. Of course, the clerk protested and refused, absolutely certain that little Miss Innocent had only given him a dollar. The girl replied that she could prove it, that she could even identify the same twenty-dollar bill she had given him because her grandfather had given it to her the night before and had drawn a heart on it. Once the heart on the twenty-dollar bill popped up at him from the top of the twenties pile in his cash register, I knew chances were good that any clerk in any busy deli could be had.

My best friend at the time, Paul, an Italian kid from a Mafia family, met me in front of the neighborhood candy store after school. The scenario was a bit different from the movie's, though the principle was identical. Paul, who'd been a bit hesitant at first, went into the busiest candy store in Hackensack, New Jersey, and bought a couple of packs of baseball cards, a Milky Way bar, and a sports magazine, paying with a twenty-dollar bill on which I'd drawn a tiny red heart next to Andrew Jackson's portrait. Three or four customers later, chancing that nobody in between paid for anything with a twenty that would have been placed on top of the bill Paul spent, I walked in to buy two newspapers for "my grandmother" and a bag of potato chips. Only I fucked the whole thing up because the total came to a dollar and one cent, and obviously I couldn't give the clerk just the dollar bill. Back out in the street, Paul called me a wimp and said I probably didn't have the balls to go through with it. I got all pissed off and convinced him to go into another candy store with another twenty on which I drew another tiny heart. When it was my turn again to go inside and get the money, I gave the clerk the dollar and the same line that the girl had given in the movie, except I told him it was my grandmother who'd drawn the heart on the twenty-dollar bill. The clerk ended up giving me an apology with the nineteen dollars and fifteen cents change.

We must have tried it a thousand times, all over Bergen County and New York. On Saturdays we'd bus into Manhattan, go up and down the avenues hitting the candy stores, delis, even the upper-end supermarkets. In all, we probably batted around .333, not bad for a couple of junior-high brats risking nothing more than a lecture from the police the few times merchants called them. The only real heat I got was from my parents, who couldn't understand why their thirteen-year-old kid was going into New York so often. I lied the best I could, but fooled nobody. I'd often overheard my father telling my mother that I was headed down a bad road, but the excitement of that easy money had the same effect as wearing blinders. I was not to be deterred.

Four years later, when Paul and I were spending most of our time cutting senior high school classes in favor of Aqueduct or Belmont Raceway, I came up with our next little gig all by myself. And it was a beauty. When I detailed it, Paul had a hard time believing that I didn't also see it in a movie, or at least read about it somewhere. It was the ultimate capitalization of human greed.

Paul drove his shiny GTO into a service station, had the attendant fill it up with gas, paid with a hundred-dollar bill which he peeled from a thick wad of cash, making sure the guy got a good peek at the wad before stuffing it back in his pocket. When the attendant went back into the office to fetch the change, Paul dropped to his hands and knees and began a frantic search of the blacktop. The attendant returned and naturally asked Paul what he was looking for.

"Shit!" Paul screamed, standing up and banging the hood of the GTO. "My father's gonna kill me."

"What for?" asked the attendant.

"Yesterday was my eighteenth birthday. My dad gave me a ring for the occasion. I think I fucking lost it. I know I had it on just five minutes ago."

"That's a bummer," the attendant said.

"That's life," Paul said nonchalantly. "The thing's probably worth two grand but it's really the sentimental value that counts." Then he got into his car and started the engine, but before pulling away, as a calculated afterthought, he craned his head out the window and added, "Hey, look. I doubt I lost the ring here but if by chance you happen to find it, I'll give you five hundred bucks for its return. I'll be over at McCann's watching the Giants game." He drove off, peeling rubber.

An hour later, I pulled into the same station in a beat-up Chevy. I told the attendant to give me five bucks worth of gas and paid him in an assortment of loose change. I purposely let a few of the coins fall to the ground, giving me an excuse to bend down and "find" Paul's missing ring. When I straightened back up, the only thing glistening more than the cubic zirconia in my hand was the spark in the attendant's eyes.

"Hey, look what I just found," I said invitingly to him. "You think it's worth anything?"

The attendant took the ring from my hand, examined it as if he were Harry Winston, and then played the hand they all played. "It's probably one of them cubic jobs," he said. "Ain't no way nobody's losing a real one in a fucking gas station."

"You're probably right," I agreed. "Ah, what the hell, I'll give it to a girl while I'm giving her a line. Maybe it'll get me laid one night."

The guy fell right in. "Look, if you need a little cash, I'll take it off your hands."

"Yeah? Whaddaya give me for it?"

The guy pursed his lips, shrugged, went into a whole damned routine. And I just loved it. This is where the word *sucker* came from.

"I'll give you twenty bucks," he said.

"Twenty bucks!" I cried with the same indignation I had displayed in that candy store. "Even the cheap cubics are going for more than that today."

"Well, whaddaya want for it?"

It was my turn to shrug. "Seeing there's at least a small possibility the thing is real—and it is pretty big—I gotta get two hundred for it."

"What, are you fucking nuts!" the attendant cried. And he genuinely thought I was nuts.

"Look, it's not a big deal. I'll just keep it, that's all."

Thinking *he* had me, the attendant played his trump card. "Wait here a second," he said. "Lemme go inside and call a buddy of mine. I'm a little short of cash right now. If he can spot me a few bucks, maybe we can make a deal."

In front of the TV watching the Giants game at McCann's, Paul heard the barman call out, "Is there a guy in here who lost a ring at the Texaco station down the road?"

Paul took the call on the phone at the edge of the bar.

"Hey, buddy," the attendant's raspy voice came over the line excitedly, "I found your ring. Do you want—?"

"I'll be right over."

The attendant came back outside, and I detected a trace of a smile on his lips. "I'll tell you what," he said, "I can go a hundred on it."

We settled on a hundred and fifty. He gave me the cash, and I met Paul on a roadside hill overlooking the Texaco station. We sat in his GTO and alternated watching the attendant through a pair of binoculars. After pacing around the lot looking at his watch for several minutes, he couldn't take it anymore. In spite of the three or four customers rolling into the station, the attendant jumped into his own car and headed for McCann's, probably thinking Paul was still there watching the game, perhaps delayed by overtime.

We couldn't resist, so we followed him in the GTO. When he came out of McCann's with that dejected look of a con man's victim, we roared by in the GTO and Paul yelled out, "Asshole!"

That gas station scam almost never failed, provided the intended victim had the money. And the kicker was that the $20 the attendant had originally offered me for the ring was exactly what we'd paid for the cubic.

I was ten days shy of my twenty-first birthday when I drove out to Vegas in my Mustang convertible in the summer of 1976. Both the car and the twenty grand burning a hole in the trunk came from a big score I'd made at Saratoga a week before. I couldn't wait to step inside one of those showy casinos I'd heard so much about. I'd already been a full-time gambler nearly a decade but had never seen the inside of a casino.

My first stop on the gaudy neon Strip was the Riviera Hotel, where like a real big shot I took a suite high above it and ensconced myself in the casino high-stakes baccarat pit. For a while I went on a roll. I turned my twenty grand into fifty, then a hundred, and was soon thinking a million. I was living like a king. The casino paid for my suite, wined and dined me in the hotel's fine restaurants, and filled up my ego along with my champagne glass at its private high-roller parties. Nobody bothered verifying my age. In Nevada you had to be twenty-one to gamble legally.

Naturally my big champagne bubble burst. I celebrated my twenty-first birthday by losing the whole hundred grand during a single nightmarish session at the baccarat table. The next day I sold the Mustang and blew the money from that, too. Suddenly I was penniless, staying in a suite that went for $800 a night if you weren't gambling lavishly in the casino. I stretched my stay as long as possible, but casinos catch on to deadbeats fast, and they have no pity. Three days after going broke, I found myself "pinned" out of the suite. I had to go to hotel security and have them enter my room to get my luggage, and that only after a lengthy discussion during which I'd been reduced to begging. The hotel had wanted $2,400 for the three nights I spent in the suite without gambling.

Roaming Vegas's streets in a hundred-and-ten-degree heat isn't much fun, especially when you're broke and have nothing left to sell or pawn. I called some gambling buddies back in New Jersey for a loan, but they just blew me off. I thought of calling my parents, but I hadn't spoken to them since high school and figured they'd blow me off, too. So to avoid burning up alive in the desert I called upon primitive instinct and began looking for shelter.

My second "suite" in Las Vegas was below an I-15 overpass. There I slept for ten nights among a band of winos and drug addicts, using my duffel bag as a pillow. Sleep was difficult to come by. The noise from the interstate and the stifling heat, coupled with the ranting and raving of the drunks who often stumbled over me, turned whatever sleep I got into a nightmare. In the mornings, I slipped into hotel pool areas and used the outdoor bathrooms to wash and shave with toiletries I was forced to steal. The only facet of life where I didn't suffer was in eating. Three times a day I ate in hotel coffee shops and rolled the check. When the waitress put it on the table, I would roll it up inside a newspaper and walk out. What bothered me about that was not being able to leave a tip.

As the heat began wearing me down, I realized I had to get some kind of job quick. The only element of life I was familiar with was gambling, so I asked around to find out how dealers got jobs in casinos. I learned that they started by going to dealing schools, and after a course of about six weeks they were ready to walk the casino beat looking for a job. If you didn't have the Vegas juice to get yourself hired right away in a decent casino, you had to make the rounds in all the shit joints downtown, asking casino bosses for auditions, where they would put you on a live game to see if you knew your way around a table. A lot of these guys were unsympathetic assholes who would tell you to come back tomorrow, and then tomorrow come back the next day, and so on, laughing at your back as you walked away dejectedly. You had to be lucky to fall upon an audition.

So I got familiar with how things worked in the casino dealer industry. Only I had a problem. The six-week course at the dealer school cost three hundred fifty bucks, which I neither had nor a means of getting. Since I'd been in and around gambling my whole life and knew how to handle cards, I brazenly decided I was going to seek a dealing audition without the schooling.

I got up one morning after a sweaty night of restless sleep under the overpass, put on the cleanest T-shirt I had with a pair of jeans, then went over to the Sahara pool bathroom to freshen up. I headed downtown and began making the rounds of the casinos along Fremont Street. At the Union Plaza a pit boss looked me over and laughed.

"Kid, you gotta come in here in black-and-whites if you want to audition."

It was really degrading getting mocked like that by some idiot working in a verifiable toilet, especially when just days before I had a hundred grand stashed at the classy Riviera.

After four days of pounding the pavement, I got my first audition at the Lady Luck casino, a little higher up on the toilet scale, though it still smelled like a bowling alley. I was wearing a white dress shirt and black trousers I'd lifted from Sears.

"What games can you deal?" the shift boss asked.

"Blackjack."

"That's all?"

I don't even know if I can deal that, I said to myself.

The shift boss gave me a jerk of his head which told me to follow him inside the pit. The first time actually going inside a casino pit, walking behind the dealers' backs, I had a surreal feeling of being out of place. The shift boss indicated a girl dealing blackjack and told me to "tap her out." I went up behind her and gently tapped her shoulder. She immediately spread the blue-backed deck of cards facedown on the green layout, then clapped her hands and opened her palms upward to show the camera above she wasn't stealing any chips, and left me to take over. Suddenly, I found myself standing behind a blackjack table looking at seven seated people who were looking up at me. They seemed impatient, as if they couldn't wait for the game to resume. Of course, it was my own imagination at work.

I forced a smile at no one in particular, picked up the cards, and began shuffling. Moisture began breaking through the pores on the skin of my hands, and I had difficulty getting the two split packs of cards to mesh together without letting the bottoms leave the surface of the table. I hesitated for the players to make their bets, then began pitching the cards with very little style. After the hand was played and I had to pay the winners, I began fumbling the chips like a real dope. I dropped a handful that swiveled on the layout, overpaid one player while shortchanging another. I dealt a total of three rounds before I felt a gentle tap on my shoulder. The girl who I'd tapped out was back to resume her game. I felt relieved but forgot to clap my hands and show my palms to the camera.

The shift boss got right on me. "Don't ever forget to show your hands," he said. "That's the cardinal rule." Then he gave me a condescending slap on the back as he walked me out of the pit. "Go back to the school and practice a little bit. Come back and see me in a few weeks."

But I didn't have a few weeks, nor a readily available place to practice. My life under the overpass was draining me. Not having a penny in my pocket, my only means of transportation was my feet, and in the midday desert heat, being Lawrence of Arabia in Vegas was neither fun nor heroic.

It became obvious that I'd never land a casino dealing job without sharpening my skills. I had to find a way to practice dealing without paying. I passed by the International Dealers School located in a commercial strip mall on Twain Avenue. When I peeked inside, I noticed there was only one instructor. Two dozen or so students were practicing dealing on blackjack, craps, and roulette tables scattered inside the school. I had nothing to lose, so I walked inside, unnoticed, and went directly to a blackjack table at the other end of the long room from the instructor. A young girl was dealing to three students from a card shoe that held six decks. I sat down and played a hand. Everybody said hello to me as if I belonged. The conversation around the table was about auditions and which casinos downtown were supposedly hiring. I listened intently and watched what the students were doing as they dealt. I understood they were all inexperienced people learning the trade, but I picked up on the mechanics of what they'd been obviously taught by the instructor.

When it was my turn to get behind the table, everybody had a helpful hint to give me. One of the guys showed me how to get the cards to slide easily out of the shoe. Another gave me a pointer on handling and "cutting" chips. The young girl, who had a lovely smile and a boyfriend, gave me a crash course on casino language.

I'd been dealing for twenty minutes, starting to get the hang of it, when the instructor suddenly sat down at a vacant spot at the end of the table. I was waiting for him to boot me out of the school, but he didn't say anything. He just put his chips in his betting circle like everyone else, so I dealt him a hand.

"That's better," he said as I swept the cards off the table and put them in the discard rack. I didn't know whether he was confusing me with someone else or whether that was just his stock line. He played several hands, giving me a few instructions along the way. Before he got up, he asked whether I had already auditioned. I told him no. Leaving the table, he said, "Go practice a little on roulette."

I did as I was told. I went over to one of the roulette tables in the front of the room near the entrance. A group of students was practicing sliding stacks of chips across the layout. I joined in and quickly learned that dealing roulette was more complicated than blackjack. You had to handle stacks of chips all the time. A full stack contained twenty chips, and sometimes a roulette payoff exceeded a half-dozen stacks, thus you had to be capable of sliding those stacks out to the players without having them collapse into messy heaps, not particularly evident for a novice. And as far as the payoffs were concerned, you had to be able to calculate them. With various bets offered on the layout, a good grasp of multiplication was essential to the job. I noticed right away at that dealers' school that a fair number of students simply did not know how to multiply. My strong grasp of mathematics might prove handy.

Spinning that little white ball was no easy task, either. You had to do it with just enough force so that it took to the groove without flying off the cylinder. I didn't know how much time I had before the instructor caught on to my trespassing, so I capitalized every moment there to learn and practice. Landing a job as a casino dealer really was a matter of life and death.

Two days later, dressed in my now very wrinkled white shirt and black trousers, I continued my job-seeking assault on the Fremont Street casinos. I started with the Las Vegas Club. A pit boss told me they didn't need anyone. At the Mint I was told they only auditioned on Mondays. At the Golden Nugget they said dealers without experience weren't hired. I was ready to pack the whole thing in, thinking maybe I'd try to hitchhike back to New Jersey, when I walked into the Four Queens casino as a last-ditch attempt.

"Can you deal roulette?" a rather surly shift boss asked.

"And blackjack," I answered, trying to sound confident.

Whatever confidence I had disappeared quickly when the shift boss put me on a jammed-up roulette game at the front of the pit near the entrance. I immediately proceeded to make an idiot of myself. My very first spin turned the ball into a bullet that might have indeed killed a passerby had it struck him in the head. The ball not only escaped the spinning wheel but also the entire casino. The Fremont Street casinos were all open to the outside, like arcades along beach boardwalks. The ball I'd just spun had no trouble exiting through this large opening and was now literally rolling down Fremont Street. The dealer who I'd tapped out took off after it. It had to be one of the most embarrassing incidents of what was becoming my very pathetic life.

The surly shift boss surprised me when he appeared from behind and told me to just relax a little in an incongruous soft voice. I settled down and got the game under control. He left me on the wheel for a half hour. I could sense he was impressed by my speedy calculations of the payoffs, even if my hands sliding the chips around the layout couldn't keep pace with my brain. When I was finished on roulette, he put me right on a handheld blackjack game. This time my palms sweated only a little when I lifted the edges of the cards gently off the layout to shuffle. I had finished dealing out the cards for the first hand and was peeking at my hole card when the shift boss leaned over and said so only I could hear, "That four of clubs you got in the hole, they can probably see it across the street at the Fremont."

The message was clear. I was making another rookie dealing error. When you dealt from a handheld deck, you were required to peek at your hole card whenever your up card represented a possible blackjack (there were no card readers built into the layout at the time). You were expected to do it subtly and in a manner that only you could see it. The casino worried that someone standing behind you could also see it and then signal its value to a player seated at your table who could use that information to obtain an edge against the house. The shift boss was telling me in an exaggerated fashion that I was flashing my hole card. During the next hand I cleaned up my act.

After ten minutes of dealing on the blackjack table I was tapped out by the regular dealer. I looked for the shift boss in hopeful anticipation, but he had gone further down the pit and was talking to a floorwoman. I wondered if he had completely forgotten about me. I walked back through the pit, purposely slowing down as I passed the shift boss. He stopped me just before I was out of the pit.

"You start tomorrow as a shill," he said.

"A shill?" I had no idea what he was talking about, though I was fighting to hold back my smile of relief.

"Go to personnel and fill out an application. They'll explain it to you."

Walking back up the Strip toward my overpass in the heat, I yanked off my shirt and thanked God that soon I'd be able to eat without running out of coffee shops. I almost promised Him I'd never gamble again. Whatever fate had in store for me, at least now I had a job and would soon be able to get myself away from the winos and into a cheap apartment.

———

I learned that all dealers at the Four Queens started out as shills. Shills were necessary to the blackjack tables only in slack hours because gamblers shied away from dead tables. A shill's job was to sit at these empty blackjack tables and play with the casino's chips so that other players would be attracted like flies to the table. Also, the dealers wouldn't be standing around doing nothing, which was bad for the casino's image. You were given twenty one-dollar chips, and you always bet the table minimum, $2. When you ran out of chips, the dealer gave you twenty more. If ever you got ahead $20, you gave the dealer back twenty chips. While doing this, we shills wore white and black with red aprons just like the dealers. The aprons were worn to cover our pockets, making it harder to steal chips. I thought that the whole shilling business was stupid and did nothing to entice gamblers to dead tables. If anything, it chased them away. Prospective gamblers sitting down at the table would ask upon seeing my uniform, "Are you a shill?" More often than not, they got right back up and left upon learning that I was. Apparently, all the other casinos in Las Vegas agreed with me; the Four Queens was the only casino in town to employ uniformed shills. The others used shills undercover, but they still had to admit their function whenever questioned by gambling customers.

After a month of shilling, I was promoted to dealer. I was assigned to the graveyard shift, which started at midnight and ended at eight o'clock in the morning. It was common to put break-in dealers on the graveyard shift because that's the least busy time in the casino, and, congruently, the action is at a minimum. During the first week I was excited about the job, about having someplace to go every night, but by the second it began to grind me down, like the cards I dealt ground gamblers into desert dust. I began tiring of the robot-like monotony of dealing. I dealt the cards, I spun the ball. I took their chips, I paid out. Soon I was mentally comparing it to stuffing envelopes. The human contact was completely artificial, and I really got annoyed by the uncomfortable positions I was put in when the real bust-outs hit my table. Sometimes I felt sorry for these people because they reminded me of myself and of the very reason I was now imprisoned by this job, but the occasional bursts of compassion were smothered by the long periods of boredom. Before long I was dreading the very approach of players to my table. I preferred just standing behind dead games. Fortunately, shills were used less on the graveyard shift.

When you work as a casino dealer, you see a lot of people and listen to a variety of stories. In some ways the job is like that of a bartender. The vast majority of people who gamble regularly do so for reasons that have nothing to do with the enjoyment of gambling itself. Many casinogoers find gambling attractive because it fills some void in their lives. Others use it to escape reality altogether. For some, casinos are interior island getaways loaded with seductive artificial splendor where one can falsely elevate himself to a world that assigns identity by the colors of gaming chips. People feel cuddled in a casino's warmth, vitalized by the excitement that speeds up the blood in their veins, seduced by the temporary but total pampering, the phony respect bestowed upon them as long as they continued putting chips on the table. Once they ran out, everything turned cold and mean; the strangers who'd been sitting next to them and fast becoming their friends went back to being strangers again.

Back in the midseventies, Las Vegas was a relatively small town. Along the Strip there was no traffic congestion, and looking out your car window you didn't see any volcanoes, swashbuckling pirate shows, amusement parks, or giant manmade lakes. What you did see was pure gambling. At the time, gamblers coming out to Vegas left the spouses and kids at home. Today Vegas is considered a family vacation paradise; back then it was certainly R-rated.

The casinos themselves were much smaller than the monsters you see today. Inside them there was a certain intimacy, which now exists only in casinos outside the country. That intimacy was palpable around the gaming tables. It induced more talk. The players often told you their life stories when you dealt them their cards. I heard about the sons in medical school, the daughters who were now assis-

tant prosecutors, everything from cobalt treatments to mistresses in
Italy, who were often kept in neighboring hotels while the wives of
these storytellers were kept busy at slot machines.

And then there were the nuts, the raving lunatics. Bars had
drunks; casinos had degenerates. After being transferred to the swing
shift, which ran from six o'clock at night to two in the morning, I
became familiar with a pathological gambler of about fifty, who
looked at least seventy and went by the name of Whacky. Everybody on the swing shift knew him. He came into the Four Queens
every night at nine o'clock and had been doing so for years. One
night while I was standing on a dead mini-baccarat game, Whacky
told me an incredible story, which, to my amazement, turned out to
be true.

Whacky spent most of his adult life panhandling on Las Vegas's
streets to scrape up whatever money he could to booze and play slot
machines. He was also a roulette junkie. One rainy night the day
before Christmas Eve ten years before, he rolled into the casino a
little earlier than usual because of the rain. He was drunk as usual,
although the coins in his pocket weighed less because the streets
were deserted.

He quickly lost all his coins in the slot machines. When he approached his favorite roulette wheel in the middle of the sparsely
peopled casino, he had a solitary one-dollar bill left in his pocket. He
put it on his favorite number: 4. The dealer spun the ball and it
landed on number 4. Whacky won thirty-five dollars. Intoxicated,
but knowing instinctively what he was doing, Whacky put his lucky
dollar bill back in his pocket and let the thirty-five bucks he won
ride on number 4. It came in again. Now Whacky was ahead $1,225.
He wanted to let it ride again, but the casino limit on betting a
number straight up was $100. Whacky bitched at the pit bosses, but
they refused to raise the limit for him. Annoyed, and cursing loudly
for the whole casino to hear, Whacky bet the $100 on number 4, and
it won a third time. He was up $4,725. The casino manager was
called over to the wheel. He immediately yanked the dealer, put in
another one with a mean disposition. But that didn't cool off Whacky.
He not only won a fourth time but an amazing fifth in a row. Not
too unofficially, that was a Las Vegas record for consecutive times a

number came out on an honest roulette wheel. The Nevada Gaming Control Board examined Whacky's favorite wheel the next day and concluded it was both honest and free of defects.

Whacky took his nearly twelve grand in roulette profits and sat down at a blackjack table, where he placed a thousand-dollar chip on all seven betting squares. Being that a single deck was in use, the four blackjacks Whacky got that first round were the most possible. He went on a massive winning streak. The Four Queens kept changing the dealers in order to break the streak, but Whacky kept beating them all. He was ahead three hundred grand by the time he got to the craps table. And there he held the dice an amazing two hours. By the time it was over Whacky had the Four Queens beat for a cool million. At that point he passed out and fell *into* the craps table. The casino manager, in a panic, immediately coaxed Whacky into allowing the casino to lavish its most luxurious suite on him. Whacky agreed, let the Four Queens put his million bucks in the casino cage for safekeeping, but not the lucky dollar bill that had started it all. He took that up to the suite and went to bed with it, putting it safely underneath his pillow. When he awoke the next day realizing that he was a millionaire, and that he no longer had to go out begging on the streets, it was just too much. Having nothing else to do and perhaps following his destiny, Whacky went back into the casino. It took him a whole week to lose back the million bucks. Before they booted him out of the suite into the street, the casino manager offered Whacky $100 for the lucky one-dollar bill that had remained in his pocket. Whacky refused and went back outside, where eerily it was raining again in the desert. The very next night Whacky was arrested in the Four Queens Hotel gift shop for stealing a candy bar and pack of chewing gum that together cost one dollar.

After he had finished his story, I asked Whacky why he hadn't paid for the candy bar and chewing gum with his last dollar. I should have known the reason. All he had left in his life was his lucky dollar. The Four Queens, he said, was never going to get that.

As a dealer, you also got your fair share of propositions to turn against the house. There's always somebody with an ingenious idea for ripping off the casino who wants to make you his partner. The first flagrant one came from a Southern oddball with a drawl and a tux who wanted me to signal him the value of my hole card at blackjack. For that he offered me 10 percent of the take. When I told him deadpan that *he* would get the 10 percent, he called me a greedy Yankee bastard and gave me the finger. A more tempting divvy for the same hole-card help came from a good-looking local woman in a miniskirt with huge tits and long legs who happened to be the Four Queens's first lady of degenerate gambling and was always going down the drain at blackjack. She constantly let me know she was ready to match my time spent helping her on my table with her time spent helping me in her bed. Of course, I never involved myself in such rinky-dink scams, which at best got dealers fired. I figured I'd walk the straight and narrow until I could get another gambling bankroll together.

But one night in June 1977, a man sat down at my mini-baccarat table and not only changed my mind, but my life forever. It was late in the shift, and as usual my table was dead. He was a very handsome guy in his midforties with a full head of thick graying hair and sharp Grecian features. He was dressed casually, with taste, and spoke and acted with class. He bought in with a hundred-dollar bill, bet $10 a hand on Player but seemed more interested in conversation than the outcome of the hands.

"Where in Jersey are you from?" he asked.

I was immediately impressed that he distinguished a New Jersey accent from a New York one. When I told him Hackensack, he smiled broadly and said he was from New York.

"How did you end up dealing in the Four Queens?" Though he didn't imply it, I understood that he considered dealing in the Four Queens casino below me. I told him the simple truth, that I'd come out to Vegas the previous summer with twenty grand, blew it off, and had to get a job to avoid becoming desert cactus. He laughed. We began talking about places in Manhattan we both knew, the Yankees and Knicks, not much about gambling and Las Vegas. But for some reason I had the distinct impression he was totally about casinos and gambling. I also felt very comfortable with him. I couldn't remember ever having related to someone as quickly as I had to him, and I knew he wasn't gay or weird. He was sharp and had a radiant intelligence. His use of the English language was even extravagant, without being condescending.

Just before the graveyard dealer relieved me, he suggested we meet at the Horseshoe casino bar for a drink when I got off work. I had never before socialized with a customer; casino dealers rarely did that. But in this case, not accepting his invitation never entered my head. I sensed he was going to lay something on me, and I sensed just as well it wasn't going to be stupid.

Binion's Horseshoe is certainly one of the most, if not *the* most famous casino in the state of Nevada. Its colorful history centered on a Prohibition-era Texas bootlegger and gambler, Benny Binion. The Horseshoe was uniquely known for three reasons. The first and most recognizable to the public was its glass-encased display of one hundred authentic ten-thousand-dollar bills, a million bucks cold cash. Tourists from all over the world, millions of them, stopped to pose for a picture in front of the money. Second, the Horseshoe was the home of the annual World Series of Poker tournament. Poker legends and amateurs alike came to battle for the one-million-dollar first prize. And third, for the real gamblers, and for what was undoubtedly the pride of the constantly boasting Benny Binion himself, the Horseshoe casino accepted any bet. All other casinos had table limits. Not the Horseshoe. In Binion's casino you could bet whatever you wanted whenever you wanted. And gamblers did. It was not unheard of for a guy to walk into the casino, dump a suitcase loaded with a million bucks cash on a craps table, and let it all go with a roll of the dice. And no questions got asked. Ole Benny didn't give a shit where your million came from.

I spotted the guy with the thick gray hair at the center of the bar, thinking he had deliberately placed himself so that I'd see him easily. I laid back and observed him a minute before approaching. He was sipping his drink, not talking to anybody. If other people were with him, for the moment he kept them at a distance.

"My name is Joseph Classon," he said as we firmly shook hands.

"Call me Joe." He ordered me a drink; we toasted each other, then he led me down the length of the long bar to the corner, where it was quieter.

I learned from the very beginning that Joe Classon was not a bullshitter and didn't have the time or patience for anybody else's bullshit. He came directly to the point, without the slightest preamble, and it was exactly what I'd expected of him.

"I've been watching you deal baccarat for a week," he said matter-of-factly. "Neither the players nor the floormen at the Four Queens casino have the slightest idea what's going on with baccarat, yet you didn't steal a nickel during that whole time. Not from the table chip rack. Not from the players. You're the only baccarat dealer in the joint not reaching into the cookie jar. Why's that?"

I shrugged. "Nothing really worth stealing in there." He was right about the players and floormen not having a clue about baccarat. The game had just been installed in the casino, and half the personnel didn't even know the basic rules. I'd been chosen to deal it simply because I was one of the few dealers in the house who knew the rules, thanks to my high-rolling days playing baccarat at the Riviera. More players than not coming to my table thought they were playing blackjack, until they realized that their hand of an ace and a picture card was just one notch above zero in baccarat, and watched their chips get swept away. I could have surely dipped into the till by robbing these ignorant players of their wins and putting the excess in my pocket, but as I told Joe, "All these dealers who are risking their jobs to palm a dozen or so five-dollar chips every night are fools. They're blowing their future chances at good dealing jobs on the Strip."

Joe smiled as though he appreciated my familiarity with penny-wise and dollar-foolish people. He rattled the ice cubes in his drink and gave me a hard look. "Is that what you want to become? A Strip dealer?"

"They make real good money up there in the classy casinos," I told him. "And for the time being, I don't have many other possibilities in life." I said this very frankly and held his eyes with my own. I knew this man was very interested in me for some reason, and for some other reason I was not suspicious of him. I sensed right away that he was not trying to hustle me, and I sensed as well that he knew I knew this.

"Maybe you do have other possibilities in life," he said with a slight nod.

"How would you know that?" I asked.

"I'm a pretty good reader of people." He paused a second, then said, "In my business I have to be."

I did not ask him the obvious question, and wanted him to appreciate that. Whatever he had to tell me, or wanted to reveal, he certainly didn't appear to need a nudge. I was a pretty good reader of people too. He'd decided that since I was the only baccarat dealer at the Four Queens to resist such easy pickings, I was approachable.

"Those Strip dealing jobs are hard to get without the Vegas juice," he said pointedly.

"It sure helps to know key people in this town," I agreed.

"And for the moment you don't."

"Nope."

"What are you going to do if you can't get hired on the Strip? Surely you're not going to spend the rest of your life working in that shithole across the street."

I laughed ingenuously at his reference to my workplace. Then while I pondered a response, I rattled the cubes in my glass. After a while I said, "Maybe I'll just bide my time in Vegas and wait for something to come up."

"What? A score?"

I shrugged. "*Something.*" I didn't really know myself.

"Perhaps I can give you a little push in the right direction," he suggested as he searched my eyes. At that moment I felt that I was being read. I held his gaze and let him continue. "Before you quit dealing in the Four Queens casino, I think you should give it a little farewell party."

I smiled at him, undaunted by his straightforwardness. "What did you have in mind?"

Joe Classon pursed his lips as he shook his head. "No," he said quietly. "It's not what I have in mind. Rather it's what *you* have in mind."

I looked at him quizzically; he stared back silently, forcing me to think. And then I understood. He was presenting me with the challenge of introducing him to an inside casino scam coming from my own ingenuity, and naturally I wondered why. Why did this complete stranger come out of left field and so forthrightly propose a dangerous criminal partnership against the casino? Didn't he worry that I would run to my superiors and report this strange incident? Surely he must have known that dealers were often approached by scam artists looking to turn a fast buck, and that the vast majority of them avoided these contacts like the plague. So why then had he picked me? Especially after witnessing that I hadn't stolen a single chip while other dealers were stuffing their pockets? What had he seen in my behavior that made him so confident I would risk everything to enter his world, which at the moment I knew nothing about?

Asking him these questions was pointless, I knew, for I could never have faith in the responses of someone I did not yet know well enough to trust. I figured he must have just sensed by watching me, and by our little conversation at my baccarat table, that I was perfectly capable of stealing from the house but at the same time knew how to practice restraint. Whatever, I was indeed overcome with curiosity, so I decided to play along, of course telling myself that nothing would ever really materialize with this guy.

Joe Classon just sat there at the bar looking at me, a slight smile on his face. I think he knew exactly what thoughts were swimming around in my head. His whole being conveyed an easy confidence as well as a measured patience. He silently let me know that for the moment he wasn't hurried, his gestures soft and not invasive. He'd moved close enough to me on his stool so that our legs were touching, yet this did not bother me. Midway through our second drink together I found myself taking him seriously. Maybe this polished guy was indeed going to show me a new direction in life. Dealing at the Four Queens was getting old quick, and the classy casinos just a few miles away on the Strip seemed much farther in the distance.

I nodded to show him I understood, then said with a smile, "Yeah, you're a pretty good reader of people. Maybe I can come up with something that'll interest you."

I had often thought about what I could do to augment my income a little while dealing the cards. If I'd had a trustworthy friend, perhaps I would've had him—or her—come into the Four Queens every once in a while so I could dump out a little money to be split up later. There were several ways to do that where a dealer could remain relatively safe, provided the greed factor did not prevail. But that was minor-league bullshit and went against the iron rule of not working with cohorts where you exposed yourself to getting ratted out into a conspiracy charge. Such monkey business was not what Joe Classon wanted to hear.

He smiled his appreciation. I had the feeling he took pride in his judgment of people. I thought at that moment that if you were an idiot, Joe Classon would know it right away.

"Casinos are my business," he said with forceful candidness. "I do nothing else in this life but cheat them out of their money. And when I do my thing, I do it without inside help. Whatever it is that we're going to do on your account, that's fine. I won't be considering you as inside help. I'll be considering myself as outside assistance."

I noticed he didn't say, "Whatever it is that we *might* do." He was obviously quite confident that something concrete was going to come out of our conversation. What he did say was "I'm sure you can devise an adequate plan to beat the Four Queens casino for a couple of grand. If, when after it's all said and done, you want to become a part of my team and—," he paused and smiled warmly— "live the life of Reilly, you'll have the chance." He looked at his watch, not bothering to conceal that my time was up. Whatever he did to recruit people was done in my case.

Before leaving, he gave me a sheet of paper that he'd already prepared with his name and telephone number on it. He was staying at the Tropicana Hotel. He said he wasn't coming back inside the Four Queens casino, and that if he hadn't heard from me within a week, he'd assume that either I was not interested or couldn't come up with a decent plan to present to him. I hardly believed for a second that he thought I wouldn't be interested in joining his "team."

I spent an entire week thinking about Joe Classon and the ingenious plan I was knocking myself out to come up with for ripping off the Four Queens. I had never felt so challenged in my life. I was thinking that Joe was a capable manipulator who used psychology to get people to do what he wanted. Not only was I right, but the mini-baccarat scam I ended up proposing to him had to have come from my subconscious, so absolutely brilliant it was. I must have dreamt it. No way I could have thought it out myself (no false modesty here). When I explained it to Joe on the seventh day of that allotted week, he actually kissed me. In order to understand what I had conceptualized, one must first appreciate certain procedural differences from blackjack when dealing mini-baccarat, as well as its basic rules.

Baccarat is actually the simplest table game to play in casinos. There are no decisions. You bet either player or banker and await the outcome. The bank has a slight edge, therefore you pay a 5 percent commission on it when it wins. Two cards are dealt to each side, tens and picture cards count as zero. In certain situations there is a third-card draw for one or both sides, but this is mechanical and based on set rules like the dealer's hitting and standing at blackjack. Though this third-card rule complicates matters a bit for the dealer, it stays unthinking for the players at the table who just watch and hope for the best. The side finishing with a total closest to nine wins. Baccarat is known as the streakiest game in casino gambling, and some long high-rolling winning streaks have on many occasions whipped pit bosses into agonizing frenzies. One bad night at the baccarat table could wipe out the profit from all the other action in the casino that day.

Mini-baccarat at the Four Queens was dealt with six decks from a card shoe on a blackjack-size table, where only the dealer handled the cards. Procedure for shuffling differed greatly from blackjack. First, the cards were spread faceup and washed in swirls around the layout. Then they were gathered and stacked facedown into one tall pack, which was then divided into several small packs that were shuffled repeatedly until a new six-deck pack was formed. At that point the dealer "laced" the cards. Holding the long pack horizontally down on the table with one hand, he used his other to remove a one-deck clump of cards from the bottom which he spliced loosely into the top of the remaining five-deck pack. Then he ran the clump down the length of the pack in a slicing motion reminiscent of sawing through a block of wood, creating a fan of cards arching uniformly over the pack. The dealer's final touch was to gently push the fanned cards downward to complete their integration into the pack. Before beginning this lace, the dealer was required to announce it to the floorman, who would acknowledge it but not necessarily watch.

Another distinct difference in procedure from blackjack was that if the action stopped in the middle of a shoe, the cards were not spread atop the layout to await the next shuffle. Instead, the unplayed cards remained inside the shoe and the deal simply resumed as soon as new players placed their bets. The reason for that was because at baccarat players could bet with or against the house, so a baccarat shoe could never be set up in advance to bust them out. Since baccarat players knew that, casinos reasoned, why waste time and money shuffling?

This practice led me to discover the casino's vulnerability to an innovative mini-baccarat dealer looking to rake off. My first thought was that if I could set up the outcome of a few hands while washing the cards, I'd pass that knowledge on to my cohorts who could then bet the fixed hands. My next thought was to do that *without* my presence at the table when the money came off it. And that's were the real stroke of genius would come in.

I reasoned that with a lax floorman working my pit (I was counting on an ex-boxer from Milwaukee named Buster) I could probably set up four natural winning hands favoring the player. As there were seven betting positions on the layout, with a maximum bet of $500, $3,500 could be taken down with each hand. Four fixed hands at the maximum would yield fourteen grand, not a bad little scam for a onetime shot in a downtown shithouse casino.

By the time I called Joe at the Tropicana, I had the scam completely worked out. Inside his hotel room I met the rest of his team. It consisted of Duke and Jerry. Duke was a short balding guy in his early thirties with baby blue eyes and an innocent smile. Jerry, a few years younger, was a stout, good-looking, rugged type who could have walked off a Marlboro billboard. They were both living in Northern California but had midwestern origins. When I'd entered the room they were passing around a joint. I didn't smoke, so I declined and got down to explaining what we'd do to rip off the Four Queens.

"At the end of my shift," I was saying, "Joe plays my table until all the cards in the shoe run out, so I can reshuffle. Then while I'm washing the cards, I'll set up as many hands as I can. I'll protect that clump of cards while I'm shuffling and lacing. When I'm finished lacing and put the cards back in the shoe, Joe gets up and leaves. The cards stay fixed up in the shoe until you all return to the table on the graveyard shift and take off the money. I'll already be gone."

Even Joe, who I assumed had as much casino knowledge as any-one on the planet, had a confused look on his face, but it was Duke who verbalized it.

"We're gonna take the money off the graveyard shift *after* you're gone?" he asked, taking a hit off the joint.

I couldn't restrain my smile, and when I noticed that Joe was smiling, too, I realized that he had suddenly understood how I was going to make my escape.

I laid it out for Duke and Jerry. "Since the cards always stay in the shoe until played out, all we have to do is wait till the first graveyard dealer relieves me. Then you guys come in and bet the five-hundred-dollar max on the hands I set up for the graveyard dealer to deal you. This way, when the money comes off the table, I won't even be there. If the bosses get steamed up about it, they'll logically think it was the graveyard dealer who robbed them."

They were all quite impressed and now everybody was smiling as the joint passed amongst the three of them. I could tell Joe was proud of me, and I felt good about that. I was wondering what it was he'd eventually teach me when I solidified my position as a member of his team.

Jerry asked an integral question. "If you're not gonna be on the table when we hit it, how are we gonna know how many hands to play and which side to bet?"

"Simple," I said. "First of all, you don't have to worry about which side to bet. I'm going to fix up all the winners for the player. The only thing you'll have to know is how many consecutive hands are set up. That information I'll pass on to Joe myself before I leave the table. The graveyard shift starts at 2:00 A.M. The number of cards left in the shoe toward the end of the swing shift will determine the exact moment I signal Joe to come to the table and play them out. He stays at the table, betting black chips every hand until the shoe runs out. That will help set him up as a high roller. If my timing is accurate, the shoe should be finished just a few minutes before two o'clock. We want to minimize the possibility of another player coming to the table between the setup and the arrival of the graveyard dealer. Of course, if somebody else makes a bet after I set up the cards, our sequence gets fucked up and we'd have to try it again another night. But usually at that hour the mini-bac table stays dead.

"While I'm washing, shuffling, and lacing the cards for the new shoe, Joe watches my back to make sure the floorman isn't looking too close at what I'm doing. Then, as I'm putting the cards back into the shoe, I give him the information verbally. For example, I say to him 'two-four.' That means the graveyard dealer will turn over a deuce and burn two more cards before starting to deal out the hands. Then the player will win four consecutive times. If I say 'three-five,' that means the dealer will turn over a three and burn three more cards before starting the deal. Then the player will win five consecutive hands. Remember, I'm only going to fix the winning hands for the player side, never the banker. And also remember—extremely important—that the first card the dealer turns over determines the number of cards to be burned. For example, if a 5 is turned over, then five more cards will be burned in addition to the 5 that was turned over. So if I tell you 'two-four,' you *must* see the graveyard dealer turn over a deuce and then burn two cards with it. If the first card turned over is *not* a deuce, then you know that something got fucked up and everything is off." Obviously, I would try to find a deuce to put on top to minimize the number of cards burned, which in turn maximized the number of hands I could set up, but I'd be under the gun and couldn't guarantee it.

"If the dealer turns over the appropriate burn card and burns the correct number of cards with it, you know that everything's a go. Be careful there. You have to verify that the dealer doesn't make a mistake while burning the cards. If the burn card is a deuce, make sure you see the dealer burn two cards—not one, not three. Dealers make mistakes like that all the time. A little mistake like that and we're out thirty-five hundred."

We spent several hours discussing the fine points of the scam. To get the maximum money out of it, we had to cover all seven betting spots on the layout. Both Duke and Jerry had girlfriends coming to Vegas that weekend who could participate. I told Joe about a young Mexican couple living in my apartment complex with whom I'd become friendly. I didn't know if he wanted to involve any outsiders in the scam, but Raul and Rosa Garcia could be trusted and would accept less than a full share of the profits. Joe said that if I trusted these people, go for it. So we had our full table.

In any scam of this nature there are three precise phases. The first is the set-up phase where you prepare the casino for the coup. You can't just breeze inside a downtown casino that never sees big action on its mini-baccarat table and let the bombs fall. So, instead of having the participants immediately storm the mini-bac table, they'd enter the casino separately at ten-minute intervals beginning at 1:00 A.M. Each couple and Joe alone would enter the casino through different entrances and begin gambling on different craps and blackjack tables with green and black chips. We wanted the casino to notice them right away as high rollers *before* they got to the mini-baccarat table. We knew we would lose some money playing out this charade, but it was necessary to protect the cover of the operation. We had to give the casino a few jabs before knocking it out.

The second phase of the scam was the money coming off the table, the easy part. The three couples would all converge on the mini-bac table and join Joe, already in place. Once everybody was seated with their chips from the other craps and blackjack tables in front of them, the only thing left to do was bet the five-hundred-dollar maximum on each fixed hand. Once those hands were over and the money won, the second phase was complete.

The third phase of the scam was the most difficult and also the most important. In any criminal enterprise, whether it is an armed robbery or a Wall Street stock fraud, you have to manage an escape. Getting the money alone wasn't the end. You had to get the money and then take it with you to a safe place so that it would eventually serve you in a way that made stealing it worthwhile. Of course, in an armed holdup the escape undertaken by the robbers is dramatic, and subtlety is not going to be part of the plan. In our case, however, subtlety was not only necessary but intrinsic to the crime itself, to the point of hiding the fact that an escape was taking place at all. When pulling off a scam of this nature, you didn't rush out of the casino once you had the loot. Instead, you stayed as long as necessary to smooth everything out the best you could, reducing the steam to a minimum. The idea was to make the casino bosses never realize they'd been robbed.

The game of baccarat itself afforded us a method of doing just that. Since you could bet player or bank, we could keep everyone on the table gambling without losing much. By going into an offset procedure, three of our cohorts would bet player while the others bet roughly the same amount on bank. All we'd lose was the 5 percent commission paid to the bank, because our winning bets would approximately match our losers. In this fashion, they could all stay at the table for a long time, maintaining the appearance of gambling heavily while in fact the casino had absolutely no chance of recovering but a tiny fraction of the thousands it would be stuck for. And to make all that even better, each couple could leave individually while those who remained could adjust their bets in order to continue the offset. Finally, when only the last couple remained at the table, the man would bet $500 on player while his companion bet the same amount on bank.

We planned the big mini-baccarat scam for Saturday night. On Friday afternoon I went to the airport with Joe, Duke, and Jerry to pick up the two girlfriends flying in from San Francisco. Marla was with Duke, the prettier Sandy with Jerry. They both seemed friendly enough and willing to participate in the scam.

Duke and Jerry got their separate rooms at the "Trop," but we invariably met in Joe's room to shoot the shit. They almost always lit up a joint when we kicked back. At first I'd been concerned about their pot smoking, but it turned out to be no big deal because none of them did cocaine or any hard stuff—at least not in my presence. Joe seemingly liked his pot as much as the others. He tried to get me to try it once, but I declined, telling him kiddingly, "I'll get my high robbing casinos." He responded, "Don't worry. In that case, you're gonna be high all the time." I appreciated Joe's not pushing getting high on me.

In a very short time I grew to respect Joe immensely. The guy had an incredible talent for recognition of detail, no matter how minute. Even without knowing what it was that *he* did in the casinos, I knew he was a perfectionist down to the tiniest matter. He was also, I noticed, a stickler for respect. Although I had planned the entire Four Queens scam, there was no doubt that he was in command. Joe had a military bearing about him (it turned out he had served in Korea and even spoke a tad of Korean), and his mere presence did not go unnoticed. On the other hand, Duke and Jerry were both easygoing and seemingly less disciplined. I imagined that whatever talents they had in the business had been developed and controlled by Joe.

I'd also learned that Joe had once been a whiz kid on Wall Street affairs with his own consulting firm in California. When I asked him why he gave all that up to involve himself in ripping off the casinos, he smiled and said, "It's just what I like to do." I imagined that someday I'd entirely understand what he meant.

Joe had been reading the *New York Times* when we all converged on his hotel room Saturday morning after breakfast to go over the Four Queens scam taking place that night. He was almost always reading when not discussing casino business, hence his wealth of knowledge and mastery of English.

Duke had a bong in his sports sack, and he got the thing going as everybody found a comfortable spot in the room. Joe stayed propped up in one bed, the two girls on the other one, while the rest of us sat in chairs around the coffee table. It was obvious that Marla and Sandy had vast casino-cheating experience as they didn't ask any dumb questions while everything was being explained. They both had brought exquisite cocktail dresses with them. I thought that Sandy, being a real looker, would turn a lot of heads at the Four Queens. We didn't get too many hot-looking numbers going through there.

A few minutes later, Raul and Rosa Garcia showed up at the room and sat humbly on the floor. I had already run the scam by Raul. Since he clerked at 7-Eleven while Rosa took care of their six-month-old baby, they both appreciated the opportunity to earn whatever money they could on the side. The only problem was that Raul's English and Rosa's dress were not exactly up to par for the occasion. Joe quickly rectified that when he began explaining in fluent Spanish to Raul whatever he didn't exactly understand. He told Marla and Sandy to take Rosa over to Neiman Marcus immediately after the meeting to buy her an outfit. The guy was all class.

After the meeting, everyone confident with their roles in the scam, we went down to the Tropicana coffee shop for a bite to eat, then out to the pool. It was the first time I got a look at Joe's torso bare—and shit!—the guy was really barrel-chested. Didn't at all look like someone you wanted to fuck with, despite his age. He was ordering everybody fruit drinks, rambling with Raul and Rosa in Spanish, just having a good time. It appeared that Joe didn't have the slightest worry about the success of the operation going down that night.

I was also confident, albeit a little nervous. For me, that evening would mark the point of no return. Once embarked on a course of cheating the casino from the inside, there was no going back. I would never again work in a casino. That they could probably never prove I fixed the cards didn't mean I couldn't be blacklisted by the gaming industry. All they had to do was suspect a dealer of something and his casino career was over. But I didn't let any of that change my mind. More important than the success of my little operation, I thought, was going to be my future with Joe and his team. I totally

trusted his intentions despite the fact I'd known him just a little more
than a week. I had absolutely no doubts about him or the integrity
of whatever operation he directed. I only wondered why he had chosen me to join him. He'd said that he'd been watching me for a
week and had seen that I hadn't clipped the Four Queens for a
penny. Was it because of this alone that he arrived at a decision to
take me under his wing? Or was there something more he saw in my
character, something I was ignorant of, that bound me to Joe Classon?

That particular Saturday night the Four Queens Casino was busier
than usual. Shuffling the mini-baccarat cards during my first hour on
the game, I had the worrisome thought that the casino would remain
crowded into the graveyard shift and we wouldn't be able to secure
all the betting spots on the mini-bac layout. We had discussed that
eventuality and had agreed that if we could obtain at least five spots
we would give it the green light. If it turned out that the whole team
couldn't sit at the table, Raul and Rosa would stay on the bench but
be paid anyway.

The shift passed agonizingly slowly for me. In order not to torture
myself, I left my watch at home, and casinos don't have clocks. But
I couldn't stop looking at the customers' watches at my table. Each
time I estimated the time, someone's watch was fifteen minutes behind. Whenever you're impatiently awaiting something that's extremely nerve-racking, the clock does a number on your head.

During the breaks (fifteen minutes every hour) I couldn't eat
anything besides a piece of fruit. I didn't drink much either, but I
was pissing like crazy. When I finally saw Jerry and Sandy circling
around a craps table at what I assumed was one o'clock in the morning, I let out a big sigh of relief. Finally the show was about to begin,
and my table had emptied out.

Jerry and Sandy had already been shooting craps for fifteen
minutes when Duke and Marla entered the casino. The second couple chose the blackjack game adjacent to my mini-bac table and
bought black and green chips. I made eye contact with Duke. He

gave me a soft chin to let me know things were proceeding on schedule.

Next it was Raul and Rosa crossing the casino to a roulette wheel. Rosa's new dress was no *shmatte*, and Raul also looked sharp in his beige summer suit. Joe was the last to enter the casino, but he didn't approach a table. He went directly to the casino bar, ordered a drink and watched the action unfold from his stool. I had been expecting him to show action like the others, but obviously he deemed it unnecessary. I noticed he was the only one of the guys not wearing a suit. He favored a Ralph Lauren T-shirt and slacks. I would later learn that Joe's constant casual dress served a purpose.

Just as I was ready to signal Joe to my table, the floorman Buster drifted over to bullshit, and once there he was difficult to get rid of. Buster knew I followed boxing, and he always had a ring tale to recount or an obscure trivia question to ask. He started rambling about a fight he'd once had with Dick Tiger, a former middleweight champion. I kept looking at his watch as he spoke, and finally he asked me if I had a hot date or something. I used his wisecrack to get rid of him. Buster also liked to look at the broads, and that made me think of Sandy. I pointed her out at the craps table and said, "Not really, but I wouldn't mind a hot date with her." When Buster got a gander at Sandy in her practically see-through dress, he was knocked out enough to forget both Dick Tiger and me, and duly abandoned us to get a better angle on her.

I signaled Joe by running a hand through my hair, then washed my hands high in the air for the cameras. Anytime you touched a part of your body while behind a table you had to open your palms immediately to show you weren't stealing chips. Joe showed right up and put a black chip on player, establishing himself both as a high roller and player-bettor. We went through the shoe together, then Joe rubbed his chin to let me know it was safe to proceed: Buster was either still gawking at Sandy or daydreaming about a boxing title he might have won had things gone differently.

I began washing the cards, spreading them faceup on the layout, rotating them randomly while looking for that first deuce. Surprisingly, I was no longer the least bit nervous. My concentration was complete. I focused on the swerving cards. I found the deuce, picked it up with two other meaningless cards to be burned with it. Then I found two 8s and two 9s and loaded in the four natural winning hands for the player, two with natural 8 and two with natural 9. Realizing that I still had time to fix another hand and that a 7 and a 6 were next to each other in the pile, I set up a 7-over-6 fifth winning hand for the player. All the other cards used in the fix were 10s and face cards that had no value in baccarat. These combinations assured all the winning hands without the possibility of a third-card draw, maximum utilization of twenty-three cards: a deuce, two burn cards of whatever value, two 8s, two 9s, one 7, one 6, and fourteen 10s or face cards. When I had all those cards in order, I began the lengthy shuffling process, always guarding against an intrusion by the other unimportant cards as I broke down the big pack into smaller ones, shuffled, and then again formed the single large pack.

I was ready to lace the cards. I called out to Buster, "Lacing!"

He shot back his okay without as much as turning his head, so I began sawing through the pack, protecting the top clump. After the lace, Joe inserted the red plastic cut card into the rear of the pack, and I carefully placed the cards in the shoe.

The fix was in.

As Joe got up, I said clearly, "Five player hands."

"Five!" He wasn't expecting the fifth-hand bonus.

I nodded with a rogue smile and watched him walk off. Within minutes I'd be relieved by the graveyard dealer and on my way out of the casino. Before I hit the street, the scam would be underway.

But then the unbelievable happened.

A Filipino in a wrinkled sports jacket sat down at my table. He was pulling out his billfold ready to buy chips. Fucking shit! I said to myself. This guy's gonna blow the whole thing.

"How's the table been running?" he asked with the predictable accent.

"Cold as ice," I said discouragingly. "In fact, nobody's won here in a week."

"Has it been running for the player or bank?"

I gave him a sardonic laugh. "Sir, it's been real choppy. When you bet player it goes bank; when you bet bank it goes player. You'd probably be better off playing blackjack." I was trying my best to run this guy off my table, but it didn't seem to be working. When he put his hundred-dollar bill on the table, I tried one last trick to get rid of him. "Did you see the gimmick they're running on baccarat at the Horseshoe?" I asked him.

"I don't like playing at the Horseshoe."

"Do you usually bet on player or bank?"

"I always bet on the bank."

"Then you really should go play at the Horseshoe because their commission on the bank is only 4 percent." This was true. The Horseshoe was the only casino in Vegas that offered 4 percent commission on the bank, instead of the usual 5.

"Four percent commission?" That interested him.

"It can make a big difference during the course of an entire shoe."

He picked his hundred-dollar bill off the layout, stuffed it in his pocket without bothering to put it back in the billfold, and headed over to the Horseshoe. I breathed another sigh of relief, and then Joe was suddenly standing in front of me. I immediately sensed something was wrong. His index finger was rubbing the tip of his nose, telling me the scam was off. He made eye contact with me and then he was gone.

I looked over to the table where Duke and Marla had been playing blackjack; they were gone, too. My eyes shot to the craps table where Jerry and Sandy had been—disappeared. And Raul and Rosa were nowhere to be seen in the casino.

What the fuck could have happened? I asked myself, completely bewildered. Everything seemed to be going down perfectly. I'd set up five hands without the slightest problem. I was absolutely sure that I had committed no error. The burn card was a deuce and then there were five winning player hands ready to come off the top of the shoe. And while I'd been setting up the cards, Joe was seated at the table, constantly assuring me that everything was clean. The floorman was the only casino employee in the area, and he had never returned to my table after I'd sent him off to go gawk at Sandy. What could have happened?

At two o'clock sharp I got tapped out by Alan, the tall graveyard mini-bac dealer. As I walked back through the middle of the pit to dump my tokes (tips) in the toke box, I thought about how Alan would avoid the shock that awaited him in the card shoe lying on the mini-bac table. I clocked out of the casino and walked toward the downtown bus station to get a bus back to my apartment. Before I reached the end of the block, I heard a horn honking in my direction and turned to see Joe's rental car pulling up alongside me.

"Get in," Joe called from the driver's side window.

I got in the car and joined Jerry in the back seat. Duke was up front with Joe. The girlfriends and Raul and Rosa were not in the car. For a moment I got spooked. I wondered who these guys really were and what the hell was going on.

"What happened?" I asked Joe.

It was Duke who answered. "I recognized one of the floormen working the other end of your pit. I had a run-in with him a couple of years ago at the Stardust. Had he seen me on the mini-bac table while all that money was coming off, we could've had a problem."

I didn't question Duke's explanation. That he had seen a floorman who once worked at the Stardust casino made sense, because casino employees very often changed jobs and got shuffled between the Strip and downtown. Since I didn't yet know what they did in the casinos and what kind of heat they took doing it, questioning their judgment in calling off our gig at the Four Queens served no purpose. I only asked Joe if we would try it again the next night.

"Duke is out," he said crisply without turning his head, his eyes on the road. "I'll go into the casino with Marla. We'll play six spots instead of seven."

We drove to a McDonald's on Las Vegas Boulevard where Marla, Sandy, and the Garcias were seated in a booth. They had taken a cab there from the Four Queens on Joe's instructions. We had a late-night breakfast, then Duke, Marla, Jerry, and Sandy took a cab back to the Trop while Joe drove me and the Garcias back to our apartment complex. Just before he pulled away, Joe said, "Don't worry, we'll get it done tomorrow night."

That night I did nothing *but* worry. I lay awake wondering what I had gotten myself involved in. It struck me for the first time in my life that I was following somebody else's guidance in a criminal operation. Up to that point I hardly considered myself a real criminal, though I had committed my share of larcenous scams that never really hurt anybody. But now, even though I didn't consider ripping off a casino a serious crime, I was graduating into the major leagues by conspiring against one. I had seen all those movies and read the stories about people ending up buried in the desert, and although the image of Las Vegas had changed by the late seventies, when casinos began shedding their Mafioso skins in favor of corporate coating, I still wasn't too sure about what I was fucking with.

Then I was hammered by another terrifying thought. Suppose this whole scenario was coming at me from another angle. Maybe it wasn't the casino getting set up; maybe it was me. Perhaps Joe, Duke, and Jerry were all undercover gaming agents looking to snare dishonest dealers. That would make sense for a gambling town trying to remove the tarnish from its image. I had recently read a book about a major undercover investigation into corruption within the New York City Police Department and thought that the same sort of thing could be underway in Las Vegas. Weed out dishonest dealers like the Knapp Commission weeded out the dishonest cops.

Maybe I was being a little paranoid. When I got over the initial panic, I started to reason. If Joe and his team really were gaming agents wanting to bust me, why hadn't they done it already? My end of the crime had already been committed. I had set up the cards under a camera that would have been zooming in on me if surveillance had been tipped off. Furthermore, had this been a sting operation against me, Joe would have been wired up and my intent to enter into a conspiracy against a casino would have been clearly recorded on tape.

No, it wasn't that, I concluded. My initial judgment of Joe had to have been correct. My instinct would never betray me. The next night I would go right back in the Four Queens and fix up the cards again. Either I was going to enter a whole new universe or go out of this one with a bang.

Sunday night the Four Queens casino wasn't half as crowded as it had been the night before, but I didn't care. I just wanted the scam to go down that night. If not, we'd have to wait three more days, because Monday and Tuesday were my nights off. That afternoon the team had again met in Joe's hotel room at the Trop, had lunch and drinks by the pool, and gone for a swim. Joe had lost about $600 the night before financing the operation, but he didn't seem the slightest bit disturbed by it. Everybody's spirits were still high. I had gotten over the nightmarish jitters I'd had in bed.

At 1:00 A.M. I was dealing mini-baccarat to the same Filipino who had come in the night before. He said that the Horseshoe did indeed offer a 4 percent commission on the bank but his luck had gone terribly bad there and his bankroll for the night had been wiped out. There were no other players at my table, so the risk that our seats would be blocked when the graveyard shift started in another hour was small.

The three couples were again in position inside the casino. Joe and Marla were playing blackjack on the adjacent table. Jerry and Sandy were at craps; Raul and Rosa found their favorite roulette wheel. The only difference was that Buster had called in sick and had been replaced by another floorman named Harold, who just happened to be the floorman who'd had that altercation with Duke at the Stardust a few years earlier. It was a good thing we left Duke behind. I had given him the keys to my apartment, where he was to meet me at 2:45.

It didn't take me long to bust out the Filipino. Every time he bet player, the bank won and vice versa. I guess he should have taken my advice about not playing baccarat at the Four Queens. Upon leaving my table, he hissed at me, "I never win in this goddamned casino."

At 1:40 I ran my hand through my hair. This time it was Jerry who sat down at my table to play out the remaining hands in the shoe. When it was all played out, he gave me a chin as he watched Harold behind me. I began washing the cards, scooping up the ones I needed for the fix.

This time I went further. Thinking about the loss we would incur because of the vacant betting spot, I decided to make up for it on my end. After finding the deuce needed to burn only two additional cards, I set up seven player winning hands. Which meant that, based on the five hands we would have won the previous night with all seven spots filled, the two bonus hands would increase the overall win from the fix by $3,500, despite the loss of one seat. And I had the impression that the time it had taken me to set up the seven hands was less than it had been to set up the five the night before.

I glided through the false shuffling, then announced to Harold I was ready to lace the cards. He came over and leaned against the inside edge of my table as I began sawing through the pack, protecting the fixed clump of cards blatantly. I couldn't tell whether Harold was really watching me, though I felt his breath. I held back the impulse to turn my head and look at him, which might have alerted something in his brain. Even if he saw the unlaced clump, I reasoned optimistically, he'd probably just think I'd performed a lazy lace. When I finished, Harold pushed himself away from the table and went back to an adjacent blackjack game. If he'd noticed anything, he kept quiet. I passed Jerry the cut card, and he eased it into the bottom of the pack. Then I carefully loaded the cards into the shoe without disturbing a single one of them.

"Two-seven," I said.

"Seven?" Jerry was even more surprised than Joe had been the night before upon hearing "two-five."

"That's what I said. Two-seven." My voice was loaded with confidence.

Jerry went back to the craps table where Sandy was standing and being admired by two craps pit bosses and a few gentlemen shooters. Joe and Marla were playing blackjack at an adjacent table. I peeked at them through the corner of my eye. In the distance I could make out Raul and Rosa by their roulette wheel. I pictured them all sitting at my table, pushing their black chips into the betting circles and catching their winning streak.

At 2:00 A.M. I felt a very soft tap on my shoulder and knew instantly it wasn't Alan from the night before tapping me out. I clapped out, showed my hands to the camera, and turned around. A tiny Korean girl named Bang was standing there. I had never seen her before. I assumed she was new at the Four Queens.

"How was the action tonight?" she asked in a soft voice that went perfectly with her tiny frame.

"Real quiet night," I said.

"Oh, that's good," she said with relief. "It's my first night dealing mini-baccarat. I'd prefer a quiet night."

I didn't know what to say to her. She was going to receive a "bang" in a couple of minutes. I clocked out of the casino, caught the uptown bus at the station, and reflected, as I looked through the window at the glittering neon lights of the Strip, that the scam was in progress at that very moment. It was just such a shame I couldn't be there to witness the staging of my creative work. I amusedly compared myself to some great artist who never lived to see the reception of his masterpiece.

When I arrived at my apartment, Duke was already there, stretched out comfortably on my couch with a joint in his hand. He had the TV going. I noticed that one of my favorite movies was on the screen, *The Gambler*, with James Caan. In fact, I had arrived just in time to catch my favorite scene, where Caan (Axel Freed) hits the 18 at the blackjack table and catches the 3.

I sat down on the recliner across from Duke.

"How did it go?" he asked with an anticipatory smile.

"No problems up until the time I left. I managed to fix seven hands."

Duke whistled. "Seven hands!"

I saw that he was calculating in his head how much that meant. "Twenty-one thousand," I said, beating him to the figure.

"That's enough for a little celebration when everyone gets back," Duke said with one of his engaging laughs. I noticed that in his mind there was absolutely no chance that something could have gone wrong after I exited the casino. That I told him seven hands had been fixed in cleanly assured Duke that his partners were coming back with the money. All he needed to know was that Joe was there until the last detail of the scam played out. The fact that Duke had such absolute confidence in Joe boosted my own confidence in him as well. Joe's decision to sideline Duke, instead of delaying the operation until the floorman who had spooked him took a day off, sat perfectly well with Duke. If Joe had told Duke not to worry about that floorman, Duke would have been at the Four Queens playing his hand, whether he thought that such audacity was foolish or not.

We watched the rest of *The Gambler* while we waited for the others. At the end of the film, Axel takes the ultimate gamble, risking his life in a dingy Harlem hotel room over a fifty-dollar dispute with a hooker and her vicious pimp. He ends up getting slashed in the face by the pimp's blade. The brutal scene made me ponder my own life. What risk had I taken by involving myself in this scam against the Four Queens, and how would *I* be scarred by it?

My thoughts were interrupted by the loud tooting of an automobile horn. I did not make the connection that it was Joe and the gang returning in triumph and celebration.

Duke started laughing and said, "I hope that's them."

We got up and listened to the metallic chorus of car doors opening and shutting mixed with voices filled with laughter.

The first one rushing through my apartment door was Joe. He was slugging champagne from one of the open bottles he held in either hand. The rest of the gang spilled inside behind him, drinking their champagne from paper cups. The party had obviously begun in the car coming up the Strip.

"The troops are back," Joe declared ceremoniously, raising the champagne bottles by their necks, which signified our victory over the Four Queens casino. When he lowered them to his waist several seconds later, he let one bottle drop and roll around on the carpet while shaking up the other like a Formula One driver on the winners' podium, spraying me head to toe with machine gun–like bursts. I noticed that neither bottle of champagne was the dime-store variety. He was blasting me with a Taittingers while the Dom Pérignon parked on the floor leaked its bubbly contents.

"You're a genius," Joe kept saying as he worked me over with the bottle, Duke hunched over laughing behind him.

Jerry and Raul began dancing in the middle of the room, Jerry doing his best to keep up with Raul's version of *Féliz Navidad*. They whirled each other around and took turns throwing hundred-dollar bills into the air as they sang, Jerry turning it up a notch when they arrived at the English verse "I want to wish you a merry Christmas." Sandy and Marla unwrapped packets of Four Queens cash and began stuffing the hundred-dollar bills down the front of each other's dresses. Rosa got into the act too, catching the raining bills out of the air and tossing them back up again. Everybody was genuinely over-joyed at our little baccarat score.

"Knock it off, Joe," I said, trying to contain my laughter. "We didn't win the Super Bowl, you know." Joe ignored me and didn't stop spraying until the bottle was empty. Then he picked up the second bottle from the floor and spilled the remaining contents over my head. By the time he'd finished, I was really soaked good.

The celebrating lasted fifteen minutes. Joe seemed so happy that I doubted he even cared about the money. "Let me tell you what happened," he said when everyone had finally calmed down. "What a shame you both missed it. It was fabulous, and you, my little ge-nius"—he rubbed my head—"are really just that. We're gonna make a whole shitload of money together!"

Joe went on to recount the happenings at the Four Queens casino so thoroughly and animatedly that I actually felt like I *had* been there. As soon as I'd left the casino, they all converged on the mini-bac table. The dealer, Bang, immediately turned over a deuce and burned two more cards with it, just as I had explained was necessary to initiate the action. Then, to the astonishment of the pit personnel, they each put five black chips in their respective betting circles on player. Bang dealt the first hand and the player won with a natural nine. Six more times Bang dealt the player a natural winner, and six more times she paid each person at the table $500, just as I'd told

Jerry she would. The phones started buzzing in the pit, and the pit bosses were running around like disoriented monkeys in search of the graveyard shift boss, who had not yet entered the casino. It was the swing shift boss, who had not yet clocked out but was upstairs in the coffee shop in the middle of a peaceful early-morning breakfast, who finally appeared at the table to gauge his never-before-seen group of five-hundred-dollar-a-shot players. By then the Four Queens had already lost $21,000, and the offset procedure was underway. Joe said he had actually seen the shift boss's face crinkle up in annoyance at the exact moment he realized that the bets on the layout were equally distributed between player and bank, and that the casino was never going to recover more than the crumbs of the lost money before he clocked out at 2:30. That annoyance was verbalized when he snarled at a pit boss standing glumly next to him watching the fake action, "How the hell are we gonna get twenty grand back if they bet like this?" And to himself he said aloud, looking at his watch, "Why couldn't this have happened a half hour later?"

After five offset hands Raul and Rosa got up and left, cashed out gaily at the cage and walked over to the Fremont keno pit, the prearranged meeting place Joe had chosen in the car just before dropping me off around the block from the Four Queens employee entrance. Five hands later it was Jerry and Sandy making their way to the cashier and then over to the Fremont. Then Marla, and finally Joe, who complained to Bang that he hated playing alone. Before the panic-stricken little Korean dealer realized what had hit her, she was looking at an empty table and a chip rack almost as empty and listening to the shift boss and pit bosses bickering behind her. The entire action on the baccarat table had lasted less than thirty minutes.

Joe had decided to stick around the Four Queens a few more minutes to observe the scene, knowing that the bosses figured everyone from the high-rolling band was gone. Hidden behind a bank of slot machines, he watched a previously unseen casino employee wearing jeans enter the pit and go directly up to the shift boss, engaging him in conversation. Though he could not hear what they were saying, Joe was certain that the casually dressed newcomer was the on-duty surveillance inspector, and from his gestures determined that he was telling the shift boss that everything was kosher, that in running back the video tape from the mini-bac table he hadn't picked up on anything suspicious. After that final confirmation that all had gone according to plan, Joe rejoined the others at the Fremont and they picked up the car from the hotel's garage. From there they drove to an all-night liquor store, where Joe insisted on buying the best champagne.

When Joe finished praising the operation, we picked up all the bills from my champagne-soaked carpeting and stacked them on the coffee table. Joe counted them twice. He didn't let anyone else assist with the count. Not because of a question of trust, but simply because he knew his count was beyond scrutiny so far as accuracy was concerned. He determined that the net profit, after all the set-up and offsetting losses for the two nights, came to $18,500. From that figure he deducted the expenses for the champagne and meals. The net-net profit was $17,500.

Joe put the bills to cover expenses off to the side before cutting out seven packets of $2,500. "There are seven of us here," he said. "That comes to $2,500 apiece." He began handing out the packets to each of us. Raul and Rosa were absolutely flabbergasted to be each receiving a full share. They'd probably been expecting just a few hundred bucks. In a gesture of supreme class, Joe had decided beforehand that everyone involved was entitled to an equal cut and that neither he nor I deserved a bigger cut than the rest.

Of course, I realized that I was entitled to much more than that, probably half the profits. It was me risking my ass, my job, my future—my everything. But I had absolutely no qualms risking all that for a mere $2,500, because I was now a made member of the team, and like Joe, I was much more thrilled about what I'd accomplished than by the fruits my labor produced. I took to heart what Joe had said about making a whole shitload of money with him. I was thinking about the future.

We'd discussed the timetable for my quitting the job at the Four Queens. It wouldn't look good if I quit the next day I went in to work, so we decided I'd stay there two more weeks and then my dealing days in Nevada would be over.

The following Wednesday, after two days spent mostly on the golf course with Joe, Duke, and Jerry, I reported back to work on the Four Queens swing shift. Everything appeared normal as I entered the pit and headed for the mini-bac table at the end. Then, all of a sudden, something strange took place. Just as I passed the podium in the center of the pit where the shift boss was talking with one of the pit bosses, I felt a slight tap on my rear end. I turned around and the shift boss and pit boss were both looking at me. The shift boss had a droll smile on his face. This was odd, because in my ten months at the Four Queens the shift boss had never once acknowledged my presence in any way.

I planted myself behind the mini-bac table and stood over the dead game, thinking about what that little tap on my ass could have meant. My best interpretation of it was that the shift boss had put the scam together and *liked* it. Tacitly, he was saying, "Nice job, kid, you really put one over on us."

Apart from that, there were no other incidents during the shift. Despite my visions about being pulled off the table in handcuffs and grilled by gaming agents in the back room, I was in the clear. I stayed on the job two more weeks, then phoned the personnel office to notify them I was quitting.

My casino dealing career, however brief, was over. My new, adventurous life as a casino cheater was ready to begin.

Initiation

ANY CAREER CHANGE REQUIRES SOME SORT OF INTRODUCTORY TRAIN-
ing. As you're about to see, mine required not only a complete over-
haul of everything I thought I knew about casinos but also an
uninhibited willingness to believe the impossible.

Joe did not renege on his promise to teach me his business. During those last two weeks at the Four Queens, I spent most of my
free time with him at the new apartment he'd taken just a few blocks
from mine on the east side of town. He called it his cave. Duke and
Jerry had gone back to California with their girlfriends and were due
back that weekend when we'd go "out to work." It was to be my
initiation weekend. In the meantime, I got to know Joe a little better.
He talked about his life in New York, his tour of duty in Korea and,
of course, some of his experiences in the casinos.

"What would you say," Joe asked me one morning over his
kitchen table while we were munching away on our breakfast of
bagels and cereal, "if I told you I could bet fifteen dollars on a hand
of blackjack, or on a roll of the dice, and get paid a thousand bucks
if the bet wins and only lose the fifteen if it loses?"

"If it wasn't you telling me, I would say that's impossible."

Joe smiled at my vote of confidence. "It *is* impossible, but we do it all the time."

When we were finished eating, he invited me into his private study. I followed him into the room. It boasted ceiling-high mahogany bookshelves on three walls and had a handsomely carved blackjack table with surrounding oak chairs in the middle. Every inch of the bookshelves was packed solid with encyclopedias and atlases and literary works and trashy novels. No wonder the guy was well read.

Joe had me stand in the dealer's position behind the blackjack table while he sat down on the last seat to my right known as third base. From one of the tubes in the chip rack he grabbed a stack of reds he had kept from the Tropicana and placed three chips in each of the seven betting squares on the layout. The chips he didn't use he put back into the tube. A second tube was filled with Tropicana green chips; the rest of the tubes were empty.

"Deal out a hand to all seven spots," he instructed me.

The shoe on the table was loaded with six decks of cards. I pushed it into position and dealt the round. Joe played each blackjack hand accordingly—hitting, sticking, doubling down, and splitting pairs. Since I had a 5 showing—a bust card—Joe did not risk busting out (going over 21) any of his hands. He was, I noticed, a very capable blackjack player.

I ended up busting, and Joe said, "Pay all the hands exactly as you would in the casino."

I removed a stack of red chips from the rack and proceeded to pay the bets. I'd just finished cutting into the first three-chip set in front of Joe and was moving toward the second when I felt his hand slapping my wrist. Though his touch was soft, the effect was that of a thunderclap.

"Hey!" Joe roared, shocking the hell out of me. "You paid me wrong! I'm betting five-hundred-dollar chips here and you're paying me with reds! What is this crap!"

I couldn't believe my eyes. On the first betting square in front of him sat two pretty Tropicana purples with a red chip on top, placed perfectly next to the three reds I'd just paid him. Behind them, close to the cushioned edge of the table where players normally kept their chips not in action, sat a stack of seven or eight purple chips. I had not previously seen any purples, nor had I seen Joe sneak them onto the table. I was certain that he'd only bet three red chips in that first betting square. Looking now at the six others, each had three reds inside.

"Wow!" I exclaimed. "What the hell did you do?"

"What I did," Joe explained, "is the classic 'ten-o-five.' I bet $15, three reds, then, after the bet won and you paid me, I pulled a switch. I took out the three reds I'd bet and replaced them with two purple chips and a red *capper* on top. While doing that, I also exposed the eight purples hidden on the layout in front of me. Had my bet lost, I would have done none of that. Instead, I would have simply left the three reds I'd originally bet in the betting square and let you take them. Do you see what I'm getting at?"

It started to sink in. What Joe had just pulled on me and called the ten-o-five was, in fact, an extremely effective blackjack pastpost combining simple ingenuity and pragmatic psychology. Its name ten-o-five was derived from the value of the chips switched in, one thousand five dollars. Had he originally bet two red chips and switched in one purple and a red, the move would have been called a "five-o-five," designating five hundred and five dollars.

Naturally, I had a plethora of questions, starting with "How could a dealer miss a purple chip on the layout?" Before dealing a hand, dealers cased all the bets; they were trained to do so. A purple chip represented a major bet. It was difficult to imagine that a dealer could actually overlook it. Seeing the purples in the betting square now, I'd have to say it was impossible.

Joe had the answer. "Of course a dealer could never miss a purple chip on a blackjack layout. But that makes no difference. What matters is what they see when you're claiming that you've been paid wrong. When I touched your hand, you were a bit startled. Imagine a dealer being touched like that in a live casino by a player that he or she doesn't know. That's a real shock. And the player yelling that he'd been paid wrong intensifies it, and then when he points to his chips"—Joe pointed to the purples in the betting square—"and the dealer sees the purples, he's completely gone, knocked out. Whatever image of the original bet the dealer had stored in his brain is shattered and replaced by what he sees at the moment. In effect, he completely forgets what he had seen in the betting square before dealing the cards. And these purples here"—Joe indicated the eight purple chips stacked behind—"strengthen the claim. They're called backup chips. They're there to back up your claim. They give you credibility, make the casino believe you're a legitimate high roller playing purple chips. What would a player with thousands of dollars' worth of chips on the table be doing betting $15 on a hand? That makes no sense for them. With all this going for us— a good move, a strong claim, and appropriate backup—we get paid nine out of ten times. When we don't get paid, we follow certain procedures to get safely out of the casino

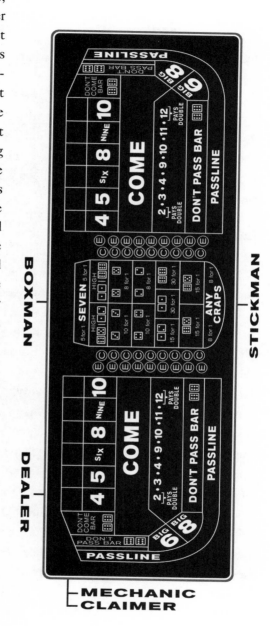

before they mobilize to grab up our claimers. We'll get into that later. For now, let's put this blackjack move aside. I'll teach you all its mechanics when you're ready. Let's talk about craps."

For the rest of that morning we sat at the blackjack table and Joe explained his craps move and what my role in the first one that weekend would be. Like blackjack, craps could be pastposted effectively. The premise was the same, but the procedure differed significantly. At craps Joe used a two-man mechanic-claimer operation. The claimer stood behind the mechanic on either end of a busy craps table. The mechanic bet $15, three red chips, on the pass line where players betting with the shooter placed their chips. If the shooter rolled a 7 or an 11 on his first roll he won. If he rolled a 2, 3, or 12, he lost. Any other number rolled was called a "point" and had to be rolled a second time before a 7 in order for a pass-line bet to win. If the 7 came out first, pass-line bets lost.

If our pass-line bet lost, the mechanic simply made the same bet for the next roll after the dealer removed his losing chips. When it won, the mechanic reached down to the layout as soon as the dealer paid his bet and made the switch, taking out the three original red chips and replacing them with two purples and a red—a ten-o-five. This was done by picking up the three reds with one hand while laying down the move-chips with the other, all in a split second. The move done, the mechanic yielded his place to the claimer, who put his stack of backup purple chips in the players' rack along the rail and began claiming that the dealer had paid his bet wrong, that he had bet purple chips and had only been paid with reds. The beauty of this procedure was that the dealer, stickman (croupier who announces each roll of the dice and pushes them back to the shooter with his stick), and boxman (supervisor seated between dealers at either end who verifies their payoffs and watches over all the action) never saw the claimer until he was already claiming. This was important, because if the same person betting $15 on the pass line for several losing rolls all of a sudden shows up a winner on a thousand-dollar bet nobody had seen him make, the pit would become much more suspicious than if it was evident that a *new* player's thousand-dollar bet was his *first* bet. It was with that philosophy that a good pastposting team distributed the roles of a craps pastpost among its members. Also, when dividing responsibilities, the pressure on each person was kept at a minimum. The mechanic was responsible only for the mechanics of the move. The claimer's responsibility was limited to claiming the money. The person on the outside, who was not directly involved in the laying or claiming of a move, was in charge of security and observation, the most important role. That would always be Joe's function, which made sense because he was the most experienced and senior member of the team, the commander in chief as he liked to refer to himself.

I would be the claimer, Jerry the mechanic. Duke would be strategically positioned next to Jerry, one spot farther away from the dealer. His identical fifteen-dollar bet on the pass line next to Jerry's facilitated the mechanics of the move by maintaining the fluidity of the dealer's motion as he paid the winning bets. Since both Jerry's and Duke's bets contained only red chips, the dealer would not have to retreat into his chip well (stacks of casino chips in front of dealer) for another color as he moved from Jerry's bet to Duke's. When doing a move, you always wanted the dealer moving forward and away from your bet, in essence forgetting about you.

While all this was transpiring, Joe would be somewhere in my view around the craps table to guide me with an assortment of visual signals he'd already taught me.

"You stand behind Jerry to the inside," Joe was saying, "on his side closest to the dealer. You relax and you wait, always keeping your eye on me until the last instant before Jerry does the move. At any time I might call off the move for one reason or another, even *after* Jerry puts it in. You've got to be alert at all times. We cannot afford the slightest mistake; this is serious business here." Joe's tone had now taken a turn I'd never heard before. He was talking in staccato bursts like a drill sergeant pepping up his troops for an obstacle course. "As soon as Jerry puts in the move and I'm giving you the chin, you rush the table, slap the dealer's hand"—he slapped my hand, slightly startling me—"and claim that he paid you wrong. Be aggressive. Be a tiger. Repeat after me: 'Hey! You paid me wrong!

I'm betting purples and you paid me five-dollar chips. What is this crap!' "

I repeated it word for word with the same intensity, and Joe made me repeat it three more times.

"And be careful with the language you use," he went on. "Don't use terms like 'nickels' for five-dollar chips. That's too slick. You don't want to come off like a wiseass. You only want to sound like a legitimate high roller insulted by the dealer. And most important of all, do *not* hesitate. Jump in there immediately. If you're a fraction of a second late, the whole thing is blown. Make sure that your purple backup chips are correctly placed in your rack as you're claiming. You put them there as soon as you hit the table. While you're claiming, you keep looking at me. I'll be where you can easily spot me. As long as I'm chinning you, you continue claiming. If during the claim I put my finger to my nose, you abandon the claim, pick the move off the layout, take the backup chips out of the rack, and get out of there. When you leave, you leave aggressively, not like a wimp. You want to give them the impression that you're coming back, not running out of the casino. While you're walking away from the table, you maintain a steady pace. You walk rapidly but you don't run. I'll be following you. If the situation deteriorates and I want you to quicken the pace, you'll hear me shout 'Chester.' That's just a name we use to indicate serious steam in the casino and you really have to get out of there fast. If you hear me shout 'Gallo,' you *run* out of the casino, and I mean as fast as you can, because you're now in their sights and they're coming after you. Once you get out of the casino, you go to the emergency meeting place, which will never be in a casino. If ever grabbed up, you say nothing, not one word— *absolutely* nothing. You don't try to talk your way out of it; you don't lie. You just keep your mouth *shut*. If they call Gaming and have you arrested, then you're arrested. Opening your mouth can only make the situation worse." Joe paused for a split second to let all that sink in. Then he said significantly, "I think you know all that already."

He really wore me out, but I knew it was necessary. There was no room for fuckups, and I knew that my first claim would be the most difficult. I would have to be a tiger, like Joe said, and at the same time be calm when necessary. I respected the way Joe drilled me on details. The precision involved was like a military operation. There was no such thing as an inconsequential mistake.

Joe wanted to cover one last phase of the craps move: the "bet-back."

"After you get paid," he said, "you bet back $205, two black chips with a red on top. Win or lose, you leave the table and head for the meeting place outside the casino. That bet-back will make them digest easier what has just happened. They'll think it weird that you'd bet a red chip on top of two purples, but doing it a second time on top of two blacks will make them think you're just the kind of high roller who likes to cap his big bets with a red chip, like a superstitious quirk. If I'm giving you a nose after you get paid, you don't bet back at all. You just say, 'Thank you very much,' and you leave. Sometimes steam comes down *after* they pay."

When he was finished going over the move, Joe asked if I had any questions.

"Just one," I said. "Why me?"

"Because Duke and Jerry are both burned out as claimers," Joe answered matter-of-factly. "I needed someone else, so I chose you."

I accepted Joe's answer warily. Time would tell.

Friday night Duke and Jerry were back in town without the girl-friends. Just before midnight, after a rapid meeting in Joe's apartment, the four of us went into the MGM Grand, where I'd claim my first pastpost on a craps table. I wore a nice-looking light gray suit I'd bought with some of the profits from the baccarat score. Joe wanted me to wear his diamond-studded gold watch and one of his diamond rings to enhance my appearance as a high roller. I felt funny doing so but, of course, complied. Everyone else dressed with casual Strip elegance.

I waited in the keno lounge while Joe, Duke, and Jerry went to get the purple chips. That was another operation in itself. If the acquisition of the purple chips was not done correctly, you could pick up steam that, in effect, blew the move. Not many players in the casino handled purple chips, and the casino bosses followed them closely around the casino. If they noticed that a player who didn't show enough action to warrant the purples was trying to obtain them, they would become suspicious. You couldn't just go buy the purples at a table unless you were a legitimate high roller putting them in action with every hand or roll of the dice. We would only use them on a one-shot deal, and couldn't let the casino know that beforehand.

Duke and Jerry sat down at a mini-baccarat table at the other end of the large casino from the craps pit. Duke bought in for $2,000 cash, obtaining 15 blacks and $500 in greens. He could not ask for purples on the buy-in. That would draw attention. Jerry already had a handful of green chips he'd bought off a blackjack table. Joe didn't want them both buying in for significant amounts of cash on the same table. Everything was done to prevent pit bosses from thinking that Duke and Jerry were together and implementing an offset. Casino bosses were wary about offsets all the time because people often utilized them to make the pit think they were high rollers deserving to be comped for restaurants and into hotel rooms. That was commonly seen on craps tables. One player would bet the pass line while his partner would offset the same amount on the don't pass line, where players betting against the shooter placed their chips. One bet won, the other lost. They would show a few hours of action, then ask for comps on both ends. Pit bosses found the practice annoying, and many of these would-be high rollers often found themselves embarrassed when comped for nothing more than a hot dog at the snack bar.

At baccarat, the offset was better camouflaged because there generally was an equal distribution of bets between player and bank, whereas in craps the "don't pass" players were relatively rare. Duke was betting two green chips on player while Jerry offset the fifty bucks on bank. They played a half hour, then Duke pushed his chips to the center of the layout toward the dealer and said, "Color me out, please."

The dealer broke down and restacked the chips for the camera before announcing to the floorman how much was there. It turned out to be $1,800, so the dealer slid Duke three purple chips and three blacks. Duke took his chips and headed for the keno lounge. The floorman came over to the table after Duke was gone to visually count the purple chips in the dealer's rack, marking the number on his pad. Jerry stayed at the table a few minutes longer, reducing his bets because the offset was no longer in effect. Not having them both leave the table together was also by design, to conceal their collusion.

For this particular move, Joe decided that one purple chip and five blacks would suffice as backup. For bigger moves we used more backup chips, which entailed longer and more complicated buy-in procedures. But for a simple ten-o-five, Joe had explained, one purple and five blacks did the trick.

The craps pit was hopping. Because of the heavy action on both sides of all the tables, there were two boxmen seated next to each other at most of them. Sometimes you had to go up against this situation, but you always tried to find a good table with a single box. The advantage was that the lone boxman had to constantly turn his head from side to side to watch all the payoffs. With double-box, where each boxman watched only the action on his side of the table, neither one had to turn his head. The ideal situation at craps was a table that had only one boxman and heavy action at only one end of the table. That left the other end of the table more or less unsupervised. In such conditions the dealer was in effect isolated to face the claimer. The boxman couldn't back him up and say that our past-posted bet wasn't there before it won, simply because he hadn't been watching that side of the table.

The table Joe selected for my first experience had only one boxman with good action on either side—heavy green-chip betting with a few blacks scattered along the perimeter. There were also plenty of red-chip bets along the layout with which Duke's and Jerry's would blend in perfectly. We waited until the dice "sevened out," then took our positions around the table. Jerry squeezed in first, with me behind him, then Duke next to him on the outside. Joe stood directly across from us on the other side. Duke and Jerry each put three red chips on the pass line. The dealer, a macho Italian type with black hair oiled to perfection and slicked back, didn't seem to acknowledge their presence. The new dice shooter was two players away from Duke, around the horn of the table. He was wearing a

Yankee baseball cap that made me think of Mickey Mantle, probably because I was hoping he'd roll a seven (Mantle's jersey number) on his first roll. He jiggled the dice in his hand and let them go. And just like that my casino-cheating career was born.

I hardly had time to think before the glittering red dice skittered toward the other end of the whale-shaped table, crashed into the wall, and tumbled to a halt near the center of the green felt layout and flashed their white dots. Peering out over Jerry's shoulder, I saw the two dice the instant they landed. One came up 6, the other 1—a pass-line winner 7. I looked across the layout, spotted Joe chinning. The stickman from the middle of the table across the boxman called out, "Winner—seven!" As I watched the dealer begin paying the pass-line bets, Jerry's body jerked forward to make the switch. The move was lightning quick. Then Jerry turned and was gone.

Instinctively, I bolted forward and grabbed the Italian dealer's arm with a force strong enough to knock the stack of red chips he had in his hand all over the layout. I realized that I was much too violent, that I had practically attacked the guy, but my bottled-up energy had come gushing out like agitated seltzer. Now I only had to think about getting the money.

"Hey!" I barked, loud enough that the eyes of the stickman and boxman jumped on me. "I just bet $1,000 here and you're paying me with five-dollar chips. What is this crap?"

The dealer was shocked by the sight of the two purple chips sitting underneath the red, just as Joe said he'd be. He turned to look at the boxman, who just shrugged, then picked the three red chips he had paid me off the layout, grabbed his stack of black hundred-dollar chips, cut out ten of them, and placed them with a lone red chip on the pass line next to the chips Jerry had switched in. There was not a single word said between the dealer and boxman. The dealer then proceeded to pay the rest of the winning bets on the pass line while I looked across the table at Joe. He was chinning constantly, and he had a slight appreciative smile on his lips. At that moment I picked up the chips the dealer had paid me along with Jerry's move-chips and put them in the table rack, realizing at the same time that I'd forgotten to put my backup chips there before claiming. I scolded myself for the error, wondering whether Joe had noticed.

Following Joe's instructions, I placed two black chips on the pass line with a red on top, $205. The shooter shook up the dice and rolled a 6. For my bet-back to win he needed to roll another 6 before the fatal 7. The guy turned out to be very lucky and held the dice twenty minutes before rolling the 7, great for players around the table buying all the numbers. But he never rolled that second 6, and for me that could have been dangerous, because I'd been obliged to stay at the table, literally stuck there, until the shooter either made his point or sevened out. Had steam come down off the move on the previous winner, prodding a nose from Joe, I would've had to abandon the $205 on the layout before its fate was determined.

Fortunately, the move was clean, so when the shooter finally did seven out, I walked away from the table casually, through the casino to the exit on the far side and across the street to the Barbary Coast, where I found Jerry in the keno pit.

We were both smiling when I said to him, "Nice move."

"You liked it?"

"You were like a cat. They paid instantly, no questions asked."

"That's how it's supposed to be," Jerry said proudly. He had a lot of pride in his skill as a mechanic. Joe had already told me that Jerry was the best blackjack mechanic he'd ever seen. Duke's specialty was roulette. But the list of all-time pastposting greats would change as I gained experience.

"There's one thing I fucked up," I admitted. "I forgot to put the backup chips in the rack."

Jerry laughed. "Don't worry about it. We all make rookie mistakes. The important thing is that you had the balls to get in there and claim."

"Do you think Joe will have noticed that I forgot those chips?"

Jerry's eyes widened. "*Noticed?* Are you kidding? That's the first thing he'll say when he gets here. Even before he congratulates you."

"How much do you want to bet?" I ventured.

"Well, Joe doesn't permit gambling between team members, but if you don't tell him, I won't either. Fifty bucks?"

"You're on," I said, and we "slapped five."

The next person inside the Barbary Coast keno pit was Duke. "Looks pretty clean to me," he said with his blue-eyed grin. We all shook hands, got a drink at the bar, and waited for Joe. When Duke heard about the bet I'd made with Jerry, he immediately wanted a piece of it, too—on Jerry's side. Now I had a hundred riding that Joe would congratulate me before bringing up my negligence with the backup chips.

Ten minutes later, Joe stepped up to the bar with an accomplished smile on his face, persuading me that I was about to win a hundred bucks. But before even shaking hands, he said, "Kid, you forgot to put your backup chips in the rack."

Duke and Jerry cracked up, and it was contagious; I started laughing, too. And when Joe learned that we'd bet on his reaction, he joined in with us.

"Listen, kid," he said, "you were really good over there. You got right in their face like a tiger. But next time, try not to assault the dealer like that. You scared the living daylights out of him. And one more thing: don't look around the pit so much after you get paid. You don't want to make eye contact with anyone."

Was there anything this guy ever missed? I asked myself. I didn't realize I had been looking into the pit while on the craps table.

We hung out at the Barbary Coast another half hour, then Joe got back to business. "You guys ready for another move?" It wasn't really a question.

Joe collected everybody's chips and went back to the MGM to cash out. We had cleared $700 and change on the move, including the losses on the buy-in and bet-back. An hour later we were on a craps table at the Dunes. Everything was the same except for one thing: this time, if the shooter didn't hit a 7 or 11 winner on the come-out roll of the dice, Jerry would do a double-decker move. He would not only switch the chips on the pass line but the odds chips behind them as well. At craps, after a point was established you had the option of taking odds for an amount equaling your original pass-line bet. Naturally, the odds proposition was very favorable to us, giving us the opportunity to more than double our profit on any craps move.

When I learned that Joe's team had that capability as well, I was quite impressed. And to think they also had a portfolio of numerous roulette moves in addition to the blackjack move, which I had not yet witnessed but begun to visualize after seeing what was being done at craps. The only thing Joe didn't do in a casino was fuck with the slot machines.

"Leave the slots to the slot guys," he had said. "The penalties are much too severe. Us—we're just little pastposters."

Our craps table at the Dunes was also a single-box situation. This time we were on the other side of the table but in the same positions. The dealer was a guy in his forties, with a bit more experience than the Italian from the MGM, but that was of no concern to Joe or his boys. "They're all beatable," Joe had said, speaking one night about casino dealers. "The sharpest dealers in Vegas are no match for the power of the move."

The table had been cold awhile, shooters rolling a lot of craps dice (2, 3, or 12), then sevening out quickly after establishing points. We found ourselves in a situation where we couldn't move because there wasn't enough action on the table. When craps tables go cold, they empty fast. When that happened we had to be patient and wait for the table to regain its momentum. During a lull such as this, Jerry and Duke stayed at the table, protecting their positions, while I waited off to the side watching for Joe's signal—a tug on his ear-lobe—to return and stand behind Jerry. I couldn't just stand behind him when the table was dead. That would arouse curiosity as to what I was doing there. They might take me for a pickpocket or some-thing.

When the table warmed up, I curled in behind Jerry and readied myself for another claim. The stickman pushed the dice toward Jerry, who declined with a brushing-off movement of his hand, not making eye contact with anyone. Whoever was "mechanicing" the move never rolled the dice. Doing that brought attention to him and could later cause a problem for the claimer while claiming from the mechanic's vacated position.

Duke, however, could roll the dice because he was not involved in the move or the claim, so he picked up two of the five white-dotted red cubes offered by the stickman, shook them up in his hand like any other dice shooter would, and tossed them against the mirrored wall at the other end of the table. They came up 4, so he'd need to roll another 4 before a 7 to win. Jerry placed three red chips behind the three he'd originally bet on the pass line, paying special attention to their placement so that the dealer would not have to touch them. Odds chips placed too close or too far behind the pass line risked readjustment by the dealer.

Duke did not make the 4, so the dice passed along to the player on his right. We all prepared again for a winner and a move; if the shooter won on the come-out roll with 7 or 11, Jerry would make the switch. We'd have to wait for another occasion to do the big odds move. Joe's philosophy was always to move when you had the chance, that old cliché.

The new shooter crapped out snake eyes (two 1s), then established 8 as the point on the following roll. Jerry meticulously placed the three red odds chips. Duke did as well. Duke's taking odds was also strategic. Since his bet was next to Jerry's, which would later become mine, the dealer would most likely be in the process of paying Duke when I touched his arm and went into my claim. By taking odds, Duke was forcing the dealer to spend more time paying off his bets. The idea was to keep the dealer's hands as close as possible to my chips so that when I claimed he would not have passed me by too far. If the dealer had already paid two or three people after me by the time I claimed, there was that much more room for suspicion on the casino's part, because even though the time lapse would have been the same, the dealer's hands would have been farther away from my chips, perhaps pushing the thought into his head that someone had had enough time to slip in a late bet. Again, it was all psychological.

The shooter rolled three different numbers, and then—boom!—a pair of 4s for a winner 8, the hard way.

Jerry needed just an instant longer to do the double switch. He had already cut the move-chips in his right hand into two layers which facilitated laying them in. He had the three chips (ten-o-five) for the pass-line move angled off the three chips (another ten-o-five) for the odds move. What the dealer would see when I claimed was two sets of two purple chips underneath a red, two separate bets of $1,005.

The dealer's chip-filled hands passed in front of Jerry's waiting hands and dropped off three red chips to pay Jerry's pass-line bet, then three red chips behind to pay the even-money portion of his odds bet. Since the odds on the 8 paid 6 to 5, the dealer capped the odds payoff with three blue one-dollar chips, bringing the total amount of the odds payoff to $18 for the $15 bet. In effect, the dealer had "bridged" that odds payoff, placing the three blue chips evenly across the top of Jerry's set of three red chips and the identical set he had just dropped off next to it, forming the bottom of the bridge. That bridge complicated the move for Jerry, but he was well prepared for it; experience had taught him that many craps dealers paid in that fashion. What he had to do was gingerly slide the bridge to the left by pushing it with the move-chips in his right hand until those chips had taken the position vacated by the right side of the bridge, which was the three original red chips Jerry had placed as the odds bet. Then with his left hand he had to pick up the left side of the original bridge, which was the three red chips the dealer had paid, while his right hand slid the three blue chips back toward the right until they were evenly across the top of the newly formed bridge. The final result was that Jerry's original three-red-chip odds bet was now the left side of the new bridge and the two-purple-chip-one-red-chip move the right. The three blue chips, still evenly on top, locked it all perfectly in place. Seeing the new concoction, the dealer was made to believe that he never saw the two purple chips now "buried" underneath the bridge. The effect of that construction, compounded by the two purples also sitting at the bottom of the pass-line bet in front and the claimer's back-up purples in the table chip rack, was staggering.

Click . . . click . . . clack, and Jerry got the move in cleanly. I claimed as soon as possible, remembering this time to put the backup chips in the rack, but the dealer was real quick and had already paid and gotten past Duke. That was no cause for alarm, because there were still four more bets left on the layout to be paid. It would have been a disaster if the dealer had finished paying off everyone before I claimed. Then the claim would have been glaringly late.

"Hey! Hey! Hey!" I hollered. "What is this crap! I'm betting thousands here and you gave me red chips!"

When the dealer saw the double whammy and lifted the blue chips off the top of the odds payoff to see the purples underneath, it blew his mind. Mine was blown as well. The two ten-o-five sets were laid in perfectly, the changed odds-set locked in under the bridge made by the three blue chips. As I claimed, I was thinking that the dealer and boxman had to be reasoning that it was impossible for someone to make a move like that—if that thought had occurred to them at all. In fact, Joe told us later at the meeting place inside the Aladdin that the dealer had said to the boxman, "Impossible that it was a move; it was too fast." I got a big kick out of that statement. What the dealer was saying, at least subconsciously, was that it *had* to be a move, but so fast they had to pay it. In any event, at the table there were absolutely no doubts, and I got paid $1,005 for the line bet and $1,206 for the odds, $2,211 in all.

Afterward, we were kicking back at the Denny's restaurant next to the Dunes, eating a late-night breakfast.

"How do you feel about your first night claiming?" Joe asked me.

I picked up my glass of orange juice and offered it as a toast. Joe, Duke, and Jerry picked up theirs, and with an assortment of juices and milk we toasted my first night as a made member of their casino-cheating team.

"I can't think of anything else I'd rather be doing with my life," I said honestly.

"In that case, long life to our rookie teammate," Joe saluted, and we clinked the glasses again.

I really felt good. For the first time in my life, I felt like I belonged to something. It wasn't only the money that appealed to me. The camaraderie of "being on the road" with the guys filled a giant void in my life. I was growing extremely close to Joe. I was drawn in by his strength. For me, he represented the ideal being, in spite of the illegality of what he did. He had courage and integrity, wit and personality. I looked at him as my leader, my friend, and in some ways even as a father figure. I never had much of a relationship with my own father. I never got from him the encouragement and discipline I was getting from Joe.

The next night we went to Caesars Palace. That in the future this wonderful casino would become my sweetheart—and treasure chest—did not become evident during my first cheating experience there.

We were in position on a craps table in the main pit. The shooter rolled an 11 on the come-out roll and Jerry popped in the move, a lone ten-o-five on the pass line. I made a good claim, but the dealer wasn't going for it.

"That wasn't there!" the bitchy little redhead with glasses said.

"What do you mean, it wasn't there?" I retorted with false indignation.

"There were just three red chips. If there had been purples, I would have seen them."

I looked at the boxman. "What *is* this crap?" I said, then looked at Joe, who was chinning me from the other end of the table, telling me to fight.

The boxman said arrogantly, "The dealer said that the purples weren't there."

That really got me pissed off. "I know what the dealer said." Then I took a shot, maybe a bit below the belt, and added, "That's why she wears glasses. She can't *see* what was there."

Naturally, the dealer got all offended and started bitching at me. The argument became heated, and I was defending my turf as if I had actually made that bet and the casino was trying to cheat *me*. I didn't lose my cool, though. I glanced intermittently at Joe, who was still chinning. I imagined that the nose would come soon.

The boxman told me he wasn't paying my bet, and as far as he was concerned, that was the end of it. I continued battling, but he ignored me and told the stickman to pass the dice back to the shooter.

The dealer crudely knocked my purple chips off the pass line and told me to pick them up. I refused and kept arguing. Finally, the pit boss arrived on the scene, and the dealer jumped all over my case. After the pit boss heard the story and saw my two fallen purple chips lying behind the pass line, he came outside the pit and right up to me. Hunched over, he said so only I could hear, "If I were you, I'd pick up those two purples and get out of this casino as soon as I could . . . before you'll be needing them for bail money." His voice was quietly formal.

I got the message. Without looking back at Joe, I picked up the purples and left the table and the casino. I walked over to the Barbary Coast and found Jerry. The first thing Joe said to me upon his arrival was "Don't ever again insult a dealer like that. All that does is infuriate them and further aggravate the situation."

He was right. After that night, I never again attacked a dealer or any other casino employee personally.

Joe was not upset that we didn't get paid at Caesars Palace. Over chicken chow mein in the Barbary Coast's famous Chinese restaurant, he discussed the positive aspect of my first "miss." "It's good that you experienced a miss early in your career," he was saying. "Now you know what that's about. They're not just going to hand us the money every time. If they did"—Joe paused and smiled—"it wouldn't be any fun." I thought that Joe Classon really did prefer to have a miss every once in a while. Getting paid every time wiped out the challenge of having to develop new moves and imaginative claims.

He went on talking about security procedure in negative situations, the importance of protecting our asses. Before going into a casino, three meeting places were designated. There was the internal meeting place inside a casino, always off the main casino floor, where we gathered to discuss strategy or wait for other team members in the casino performing various tasks, such as getting chips or casing tables we'd later be working. Then there was the primary meeting place outside the casino, practically always in another casino—usually in a bar or in the sports book, or in the keno pit—where the mechanic went immediately after putting in a move, followed by the claimer, who headed directly there—whether or not he'd been paid—as soon as he left the table on which he'd been claiming. The last person arriving at the outside meeting place was always Joe. He remained inside the casinos where the moves went down, observing pit personnel, watching the steam—in short, gathering all the useful information concerning how and where we'd proceed for the next move. Often, when a move had gone down clean enough, we could go right back inside the same casino and do another. That, too, was always Joe's decision.

The third meeting place was called the emergency meeting place and was only used in case of serious problems. It was never located in a casino or gambling entity. It was usually a restaurant or a local pub. In Vegas it was always the Gingermill Lounge, just south of the Riviera on the Strip. A mechanic caught red-handed switching chips might find himself running through a casino to avoid capture, jumping into a cab to escape the casino's property. A claimer in the same difficulty—having a steamy miss or a rat after getting paid—could also be making a dash through the casino. These were the kinds of scenarios—which didn't happen often—that led to reunions at the Gingermill and other emergency meeting places around the world.

After the Chinese food at the Barbary we took a cab to the Sahara. Jerry popped in a ten-o-five for me on the craps table that got paid but took steam. The dealer and boxman wouldn't stop whispering to each other while I was still at the table. After Joe gave me the nose, I quickly left the casino and then decided to go to the Gingermill, just in case security followed me. I knew that going there cost us valuable time, but I knew as well it was better to be safe than sorry. Joe never got on anyone's case for unnecessarily going to emergency meeting places.

I was quite surprised upon entering the Gingermill. The place was one of those extremely cozy and velvety joints with waterfalls surrounding a Polynesian rain forest. I'd been expecting a typical saloon with pool tables and maybe some cowboys. But the Gingermill catered to a well-dressed clientele that invariably had something to do with sex, paid for in one way or another. Most of it had to do with extramarital affairs, the rest high-class hookers. When my partners arrived, we'd surely be the only people inside the seductive lounge discussing business that had nothing to do with the pleasures of flesh.

"This place is perfect for us," Joe explained to me as my three partners sank into the plush circular sofa I'd found at the edge of the rain forest. "There're never any rowdy people in here and we can talk."

When I saw the prices of the Polynesian drinks we ordered, I couldn't help but comment.

"Don't worry about that," Joe said with a smile. "We work hard, and when we have an emergency and meet at the emergency meeting place, we enjoy ourselves and drink well." He patted Duke's and Jerry's shoulders. "Right, boys?"

They both raised their glasses and laughed. I sure didn't argue.

Joe went back to the Sahara to cash out the chips. I asked him before he left why it was necessary to cash out chips all the time. Why couldn't we keep the purples to be used again in the same casino, thus avoiding repetitive buy-ins that cost time and money? Joe appreciated my pragmatic thinking and explained that when the team bankroll was flush, they did just that. But at the moment we didn't have enough working capital to keep reserves of our favorite casinos' five-hundred-dollar chips. Farther down the road, I would have a safe-deposit box where I kept casinos' five-*thousand*-dollar chips on reserve.

My first Saturday night pastposting ended on a sour note. We went to the Maxim, a small, classy casino on Flamingo Road that Joe seemed to have a particularly hard nut for. I found out why when, in the middle of claiming another one of Jerry's craps moves, the pit boss came over to me and said dryly, "Take it down the road, jerkoff."

All in all, despite the two misses, it was another positive experience. I continued learning my new business and now knew the flip side of the coin. I never deluded myself with thoughts that everything would always go according to plan.

Sunday afternoon we didn't work. We hung around Joe's apartment pool, barbecued, and watched baseball on TV. After dinner

Duke and Jerry caught the last plane for San Francisco to spend some time with their girlfriends. I went back to my apartment and crashed. I needed a good night's sleep because I had to be back at Joe's apartment at 9:00 A.M. Monday to begin roulette class. Craps may have made a believer out of me, but with the introduction of roulette I'd truly learn the incredible diversity of casino cheating.

The Wheel

When I knocked on Joe's door at nine o'clock sharp Monday morning, the kitchen table was already set with hot muffins, croissants, cereal, fruit, and freshly brewed coffee. Joe was in his bathrobe and looked completely refreshed. He had obviously gotten a good night's sleep but had risen early enough to prepare that breakfast fit for a king. Joe treated me royally without being condescending. He felt we were entitled to the best treatment, given the class of the operation and the fact that we were out there constantly risking our asses.

After an hour at the kitchen table, we stepped into the study and Joe began his dissertation on roulette. If pastposting craps tables was bang-bang and out, the transition to roulette, I learned, was a true, prolonged form of art.

The casino game of roulette is a pastposter's paradise. The reason is it offers a wide variety of betting propositions and is the only game in the casino where players are always frantically placing their bets, spreading them wildly in what is, more often than not, a race against the clock. On a busy roulette table, by the time the dealer calls out,

"No more bets," you can barely see the numbers on the layout, so completely covered are they by the multicolored roulette and casino chips. That continuous activity leaves little time for the dealer to rest, and it prevents his clearly seeing *every* chip on the layout. With this knowledge the skilled pastposter has numerous opportunities.

Roulette pastposting was much more complicated than what I had seen in craps and blackjack. The objective was the same, to get the money, but the procedure was entirely different. In craps the moves were boom-boom, and the claims were accusations that the dealers were making mistakes with their payoffs. In roulette the moves were extremely creative, almost artistic. They were designed step by step to force the dealer to make certain movements that enabled the pastposter to lay them in at a precise split second. On craps tables you moved right under the dealer's nose. At roulette you moved behind the dealer's back. But you couldn't just move blatantly, as Jerry did on craps tables. You had to create perfect conditions; you had to take control of the dealer's movements.

To achieve these ends Joe used a process called check-betting ("checks" is casino jargon for chips), which comprised numerous betting schemes where your "check-bettors" made predetermined bets with predetermined numbers and colors of chips corresponding to what you wanted the dealer to do—how you wanted him to

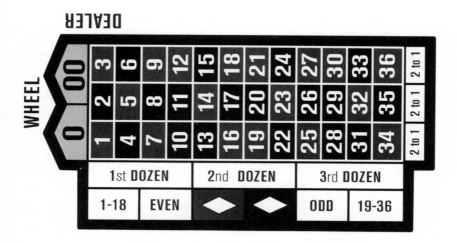

physically move his body, primarily his head. By doing that you created a vulnerability in the dealer's built-in pastpost-protection mech-
anism that gave your mechanic just enough time to perform the
move. The casinos also knew that roulette was a pastposter's Garden
of Eden, so in order to get the money you had to be good—*real* good.

Joe had already covered the blackjack table in his study with a
roulette layout he'd bought in a casino supply store. Several stacks
of multicolored roulette chips sat neatly in the middle. The clear
plastic marker that dealers placed on the winning number stood
squarely on double zero. I wondered if Joe had a reason for placing
it there. The only thing missing was the roulette wheel itself.

The first move he taught me was fabulous in design. "This move
here is called a third-section-straight-up," Joe said as he indicated the
bottom third of the roulette layout containing the numbers 25 through
36, and the rectangular third-dozen box that bordered the left side
of these numbers. "It's important that you know every detail of the
roulette layout like a map. Study it. The fact that it's perfectly sym-
metrical as far as its betting propositions are concerned aids us immensely. Notice that each dozen numbers—1 through 12, 13 through
24, and 25 through 36—have a corresponding 'dozen box' bordering
them where you can bet on all the numbers in the dozen at odds of
2 to 1. When working in the third section we concern ourselves *only*
with the numbers 25 through 36 and the corresponding third-dozen
box . . ."

I listened intently to every detail as my eyes followed Joe's hands
placing four dark blue chips on all the third-section numbers, and a
stack of twenty orange ones in the third-dozen box. I wanted to
understand exactly why each facet of the move was necessary, what
purpose every one of our chips served on the layout. Ideally, as Joe
explained it in depth, you needed two check-bettors to complement
the mechanic and claimer when you attempted a third-section-
straight-up. Only the mechanic and the check-bettors needed seats
at the table. Inside the casino, we'd have to wait patiently for those
seats to become available and take them in the order they did so.
The check-bettors could sit in any chair; the mechanic had to be

seated in one of the two chairs at the bottom of the table, because that's where the move was taking place.

Once in position, the check-bettors bought in for roulette chips, those redeemable only at the roulette table. These chips had no intrinsic value. Each player assigned the value to his own chips, in accordance with how much he wanted to risk and casino minimums. Our check-bettors always played with minimum-valued chips, anywhere from a quarter to a dollar, depending on the casino. This cut losses so as to increase the overall profit of the move.

Each check-bettor had to play specific chips and make specific bets. The first check-bettor had to play chips that were stacked in the *rear* of the dealer's chip well, behind the dealer, regardless of their color. The position of those chips in the well controlled the dealer's body and eye movements by forcing him to turn for them each time he had to pay them out. The second check-bettor had to play a specific color, the *darkest*, regardless of where those chips were positioned in the well. This was solely to camouflage the black hundred-dollar chip being pastposted *underneath* his dark roulette chips.

The first check-bettor playing the chips corresponding to the stacks at the rear of the chip well bet a stack of twenty chips in the outside 2-to-1 third-dozen box. On a winner, the dealer was forced into the rear of his well to fetch *two* twenty-chip stacks needed to pay that bet, which required the use of both his hands. Doing this made him turn his body and take his eyes off the layout, at least for a split second, at which time the mechanic would pop in the move. The second check-bettor with the dark color simply bet four chips straight up on all the numbers in that third section, 25 thru 36. The pastposted black chip would show up camouflaged on the one which won.

The mechanic needed three of the second check-bettor's dark chips to do the move. He obtained them by pinching them off the layout. Since it would be sloppy and unprofessional—and risk detection of the conspiracy—to have the check-bettor overtly pass the three roulette chips to the mechanic, the transfer was made while the check-bettor was spreading his chips on the numbers. The check-bettor would *one time only* place three of his dark chips on a number in the second section, just above the bottom third of the layout, so that the mechanic could go out and snatch them up as he put his own bet in the second-dozen box. With all the outstretched arms and hands placing bets all over a congested layout, nobody ever noticed this organized theft of chips. The mechanic never bought in for roulette chips. He used red five-dollar casino chips and only bet the second-dozen box, ensuring that his bet lost every time a number in the third section won. In that fashion, he could make his third-section move and then be free to leave the table without having to wait for any of his own winning bets to be paid. By operating in this manner, the mechanic avoided all contact with the dealer.

The move itself, pastposting a black hundred-dollar casino chip straight up on any of those third-section numbers covered by the check-bettor's dark roulette chips, paid $3,500. When the check-bettors and the mechanic were in position and had all their chips, the claimer then approached the table on Joe's signal and *legitimately* bet a black chip in full view straight up on a third-section number. This was the setup. Dealers always announced the presence of black chips on the inside numbers to their floormen, who came directly to the table and looked over the hundred-dollar-a-spin roulette player. The floorman would stay there, watch the dealer spin the ball, and supervise the big payoff if the number won. Win or lose, the claimer then left the table and disappeared from both the dealer's and the floorman's sight, but stayed close enough to the table where he could see Joe and receive the signal to come back to the table when it was time to claim. The key was that the dealer and floorman would both remember the claimer had bet that hundred-dollar chip, the floorman even more so, because by the time the move actually went down, there might be another dealer on the table who had no prior knowledge of the claimer's setup bet. But floormen usually had only one break during a shift, thus we could count on the duration of their presence in the pit.

The setup completed, we went into the move sequence. Before the claimer's initial appearance at the table, it was not necessary that the two check-bettors make their strategic bets. Since no move could yet be done, they could just spread a few chips anywhere on the layout. It was only when entering into the move phase that the check-bettors began betting four dark chips on the third-section numbers and the stack of twenty in the third-dozen box every spin. If there were other players on the table interfering with our bets by betting straight up on third-section numbers, we didn't move when one of those particular numbers came in. In the past, Joe had okayed moves involving other people's chips, but found that with having to steal other players' chips (to be used in the move) and having these people unwittingly involved in his moves, the dangers outweighed the benefits—mainly increasing the potential for a rat, who might blurt out that his chips had been manipulated by another player.

The first roulette move I claimed was to be at Joe's favorite haunt, the Tropicana. Duke, the roulette specialist, would lay in a black chip straight up on a number for me while Joe and Jerry did the check-betting. It was a Saturday afternoon and the casino was busy but not as packed as Saturday nights, the vast majority of gamblers attired in swimwear or shorts. I wore a designer tennis outfit with Joe's diamond-studded gold watch on my wrist, the glitz, as always, enhancing my credibility as a high roller. I had been waiting across the pit for over an hour before Joe finally tugged on his earlobe to signal me over to the table and make the setup bet. I approached the table at the top by the wheel, leaned over, and bet my black chip on number 33. All the other players at the table not involved with us looked up at me after they spotted the black chip on the layout. I suddenly felt like a star.

The lady dealer, Betty, who'd been mucking chips (picking them up and restacking them), took a few moments to recognize the black chip, but as soon as she did, she called out, "Black on the inside."

The floorman came right up to the table, and I made it my business to greet him. Betty spun the ball and it dropped into number 4. I shrugged as if my lost hundred bucks was no matter and sauntered away from the wheel, posting myself behind a blackjack table farther down the pit out of view. I kept my eye on Joe. From where I was standing I could only see the back of his head. He couldn't see me at all, but he knew I was there. The next tug on his ear would mean that one of our numbers had come in.

Now it was just a matter of waiting. At roulette that wait could be interminable. Since we were only working the third section, our chances for a winning number were slightly less than one in three on each spin. At craps or blackjack, they were slightly less than one in two. At roulette, when a dealer kept hitting the first two sections, you could get the impression that the bottom twelve numbers didn't even exist, or if they did had been banished to hell. Cold streaks seemed exponential. You had to have an abundance of patience in this business, I thought, hearing the tick-tick of the little white ball bouncing into a number slot—yet another loser in one of the first two sections.

Another element of roulette that exacerbated the wait was that it often took the dealer a few minutes to get all the winners at the table paid off. At a busy roulette table you might not have more than fifteen spins in an hour. Betty failed to hit a third-section number during her hour at the wheel, and now a tall, lanky guy named Willie relieved her—and hit number 33 on his first spin.

Joe gave me the ear and I walked slowly to the table. There was no need to rush. I knew a few seconds would elapse before Willie swept off the losers and turned his back, giving Duke the opportunity to do the move. Again, I positioned myself at the top of the table, as far as possible from the move and directly in front of the dealer. My position was strategic for two reasons. First, by being far away from the black chip that Duke was going to pastpost, it would become readily evident that *I* could not have pastposted it. Second, when I went into my claim right in the dealer's face, his attention would be drawn directly to me so he wouldn't even notice Duke leaving.

Now planted up top by the wheel, I watched the coordinated beauty of a roulette pastpost. Willie had already placed the marker on top of the four dark blue chips Jerry had bet on number 33 and was now sweeping piles of losing chips off the layout with both hands. He then paid a few red-casino-chip bets on the outside to one of the other players in the middle of the table. Next, he looked at the stack of Joe's twenty orange chips, strategically placed in the third-dozen box. Since this bet paid 2 to 1, Willie had to pay Joe forty chips. The way a dealer executed that payoff was to take two stacks of the corresponding orange roulette chips in his chip well (there were twenty chips in a stack) and cut into Joe's stack from both sides. Because Joe had expressly chosen the orange chips at the extreme rear of the dealer's well, Willie had no choice but to turn his back a split second to grab two orange stacks. Dealers were taught never to completely turn their backs on roulette layouts while paying off, but almost all of them did a little, and no two dealers turned exactly alike. Mechanics had to have a feel for dealers' turns, had to know when to push themselves forward in unison with a dealer beginning his turn, and at the same time avoid falling for a false turn. Dealers sometimes made false turns by starting their turn and then jerking back without warning to the layout. Whether it was because of some subconscious protective device or just a quirk certain dealers had, it was extremely dangerous—somewhat like a baseball pitcher with a tricky pick-off move to first base. From a mechanic's point of view some dealers turned better than others. A seasoned mechanic like Duke could get the move in against most of them, but even *he* had to grudgingly admit that certain roulette dealers were unbeatable, especially those who backed up to the chips in the rear of the well with their noses pointing like a hawk's at the layout, giving Duke no turn at all. He referred to those paranoid-type dealers as "backers."

Willie's turn at the Trop was not long, so Duke needed to get his hands out there as soon as possible, allowing himself enough time to switch the chips and get his hands back off the layout—and out of Willie's peripheral view as the dealer turned back toward him. Mechanics were often caught at the very last instant, after having put in the move cleanly but having failed to get their hands completely off the layout. A barely perceptible flash of hand movement was enough to alert the dealer to the pastpost and nullify any chance the claimer might have had of getting paid.

The move that Duke put in before my eyes was a skillful combination of timing, agility, and soft touch. With Willie's back turned a fraction of a second, Duke lunged forward with his two hands surging toward the marker. With the move-chips gripped by the fingers of his right hand, he gently nudged Jerry's four blue chips to the left, the marker sliding along on top of them. Then he laid down the move, a black hundred-dollar chip with three of Jerry's dark blue roulette chips on top, exactly where Jerry's four original dark blues had been. His left hand then picked those originals up while his right slid the dealer's marker back on top of the four chips he switched in. I noticed that the mechanics for this move were similar to the odds move with the bridge at craps, but the danger of the marker falling rendered it more difficult. The result was that now the marker was placed atop the four move-chips, giving the effect that someone had bet one black chip, and that Jerry had bet three of his dark blue roulette chips on top of it. Looking at the new set of chips underneath the marker, you had to strain to see the black chip on the bottom. It was beautiful.

"I hit the big one!" I screamed, after visually confirming that Duke had not been caught switching the chips. "I had a hunch and bet a bunch! One hundred dollars straight up on my favorite number 33." The last sentence of my claim was to make sure the dealer realized right away that I had bet a black chip. The sooner he saw it the better.

Willie's eyes went right to the chips lying underneath the marker on number 33. "Oh shit!" he said. He shook his head in annoyance and called out to the floorman, "Charlie!" gesturing him to the table. Then he looked up at me and said candidly, "I didn't see that black chip."

All the other players on the table were looking up at me, too, including the portly woman sitting in the chair at the bottom of the table, next to the chair formerly occupied by Duke, who was now gone and on his way to the Marina casino keno pit across Tropicana Avenue. I was sure she had seen the move, but she remained silent as Willie told Charlie what had happened. What she had witnessed will one day make a good story for her grandchildren, I thought.

Charley did not immediately authorize Willie to pay me. Instead, he told him to wait while he went in search of the pit boss. Oh no, I said to myself, dreading another incident like the one that had occurred at that Caesars Palace craps table with that bitchy bespectacled dealer. My first roulette claim wasn't going to be a "collection."

Joe and Jerry did the best they could to help me out on the table. They were congratulating me loudly, bantering about how lucky I was to hit a number head-on like that. They encouraged me to let the $100 ride on number 33, saying anything that came into their heads. Jerry was yakking away about 33 being Kareem Abdul-Jabbar's jersey number while Joe carried on about gambling legend which held that double-digit numbers liked to repeat. It was all a bunch of hot air to keep the atmosphere jolly. "I feel a repeater in the air," Joe kept saying with feigned enthusiasm.

It was extremely important to keep spirits high on the table while the claimer waited to get paid. The last thing we wanted a pit boss to run into when arriving at the table was a wall of silence. Silence was negative; noise was jovial.

When Charley returned with the pit boss, the decibel level was still strong and I was still claiming. A few of the other players had joined in, following Joe's lead. It was like an orchestra, I was thinking. Joe was actually *conducting* people's behavior on the table. Even the woman who'd been sitting next to Duke, and who I feared would rat us out, was now smiling broadly and talking to Jerry about how nice it was to see somebody win for a change. Where did Joe's talent end?

The pit boss asked Willie if the bet had been there. Willie replied that it absolutely had been; he just hadn't seen the black chip underneath. The second question asked by the pit boss was a bit more worrisome. "Did you see him [me] bet at all?" Willie replied that he hadn't, but it was the floorman Charley who saved the day. *He* told the pit boss that he'd seen me bet a black chip straight up an hour before. That seemed to remove the suspicion from the pit boss's brain, and after a few more moments of conversation he told Willie to pay me. The importance of the setup, I saw firsthand, could never be overstated.

I let the black move-chip ride on number 33. It lost, then I headed for the door and the meeting place at the Marina across the street, delighted to have that first roulette claim under my belt.

Duke was smoking while he marked his keno ticket inside the Marina. We shook hands, then I emptied my shorts pockets and heaped all the black chips from the Trop onto the small table affixed to his seat.

"Not bad, Duke," I said with an exaggerated nod. "You're a fucking monster under pressure."

"*Pressure?*" There's no pressure. I love this game!" He reached into his pocket and pulled out the four dark blue roulette chips he'd removed from the layout while putting in the move. "Here," he said, "keep these."

"What for?"

"A souvenir. The chips from your first successful roulette claim. You should see all the chips I have in my collection from roulette moves. I must have at least a thousand, and when I look at any chip I can remember the move that it came from, who the claimer was, how much they got paid—everything."

"Do you keep the chips from moves that don't get paid?"

"Of course. A miss is just as much an experience as a payoff."

I had a final thought on the subject before Jerry arrived. "Don't the casinos notice that those chips are missing at the end?" I was thinking that perhaps later on in the shift, they might connect the missing chips with the move, actually figure out the whole thing.

Duke just laughed. "Are you kidding? People keep roulette chips all the time. Others use them to tip cocktail waitresses, who sometimes bring them to the wrong table for redemption. Even though roulette chips are marked so they can only be played on one particular table, they're always getting misplaced or lost in the casino." Duke laughed again when he told me the team was probably out over a grand because of all the roulette chips he had never redeemed over the years. "Just a road expense," he said, shrugging with a devilish smile.

Jerry congratulated me, then Duke, and sat down on the other side of Duke. They began talking about some marijuana deal they had going in Northern California. Evidently, they had been doing some growing, and things were beginning to prosper.

Joe was all chins when he came into the keno pit a half hour after Jerry. "Clean as a whistle," he said, shaking our hands in turn. "The pit boss was a little buggy at first, but the ole setup bet won him over." Joe collected everybody's chips and returned to the Tropicana to cash out. Tired from the long wait at the wheel, we took the rest of the afternoon off.

Normally, when breaking between shifts, Joe and I hung out at Joe's apartment while Duke and Jerry stayed at their hotel. I noticed that Joe had an intensely private side, and he didn't let anyone, including me, penetrate the shell protecting it. Sometimes he would go into his bedroom to read or listen to classical music while I watched a ball game in the living room or went outside to soak up some rays. Though he never locked the bedroom door, I avoided Joe when I sensed he wanted to be left alone.

Duke and Jerry showed up at the apartment at 9:30. Duke was wearing a T-shirt, jeans, and a ball cap. Jerry had on a dress shirt and slacks. Their respective functions as mechanic and check-bettor made no particular demands on their wardrobe, so each attired himself to his own taste. I, however, had to put on the suit, despite the heat that didn't let up much summer nights in the desert. Joe had gone through my bedroom closet and decided that the lone suit hanging there wasn't suited to my role, so he bought me two new ones with money from the team bankroll. Everybody's clothes came off the top; nobody got chintzy if one guy got a suit while another only a shirt or a pair of pants. Joe tolerated no unclassy acts in his operation.

Our goal for the night was two paid roulette moves, to try and pick up $7,000. The first target was the Sands, another classy Strip casino used to the big action. Jerry got on the table first and bought in for their dark brown chips. They went best with the black. Joe followed a few minutes later and bought the off-whites from the stacks at the rear of the dealer's chip well. They both sat at the table making minimum bets, waiting for one of the chairs at the bottom of the table to become vacant. Duke stood nearby, waiting to pounce on it; he didn't want to lose it to yet another player who might end up staying there a long time, further delaying our move.

Again, it took over an hour for the team to get properly in position—Joe, Duke, and Jerry on the table, me observing from behind another wheel across the pit. Joe signaled, and I walked up to the table and made the setup bet, again on 33. The dealer alerted the floorman, who came over and watched her spin the ball. I lost the bet and retreated back to my position across the pit.

Four spins later, the dealer hit number 31, and Joe eared me back to the table. In the same basic fashion as at the Tropicana that afternoon, the dealer swept the losing chips off the layout, then turned to get the two off-white stacks he needed to pay Joe's winning bet on the third-dozen box. This particular female dealer's turn was more pronounced than Willie's had been at the Trop. Duke went right out and popped in the move, casually leaving the table. While claiming, I noticed that two of the dark brown chips now underneath the marker were a little beveled, one slanted slightly off the other, and that all four of them, including the black, were slightly off center. Duke's speed had been good, but his placement was just a little off. I feared the inaccuracy of the move might cause me a problem but didn't let it stop me from claiming. I had discussed that exact situation with Joe. He'd said that if I ever noticed something amiss during a move, I had the final say regarding the claim and could cancel or abandon it at any time. The chins he gave only concerned conditions inside the casino and at the table. They represented a positive evaluation of casino personnel, determining that the atmosphere was right for a move. It was also Joe's responsibility as head of our security to observe the other players wherever the move went down. Had he seen somebody that bothered him—a potential rat or undercover gaming agent—he would obviously nose off the move.

Nobody in the pit seemed to notice the imperfection of Duke's move, and I was quickly paid the $3,500. I let the black chip ride on number 31. After it lost, I left the casino and walked across the boulevard to the bar in the Castaways casino.

The second $3,500 payoff came off a roulette table at the Barbary Coast, a casino we didn't work much because of its proximity to the Four Corners, the intersection of the Strip and Flamingo Road where Caesars Palace, the Dunes, the MGM Grand, and the Flamingo Hilton all stood. Since those four casinos were all majors, and very important to us, we found ourselves very often using the Barbary as the primary meeting place after a move. It was for this reason Joe wasn't too crazy about working it. If we had a problem there, we'd have to abandon it as a meeting place and find another. Joe and Duke had discussed that before we went inside. Joe's final decision was "Let's go in there and get the money. If we have a problem, we'll deal with it later."

There was no problem at all on the move. In fact, it was so clean Joe decided to go back there Sunday afternoon and do another one. Which we did. And the result was the same: a $3,500 payoff and comp for four at our favorite Chinese restaurant, as well as a "Thank you very much, sir" from the dealer when I toked him two green chips before leaving. That second move at the Barbary Coast was also the first time I'd ever claimed against a dealer-helper formation. A few spins after we'd been set up at the table, the dealer was joined by a "helper" who stood behind him in the well. His function was mainly to muck and restack chips and prepare chips to be paid out. He was an assistant dealer of sorts. Helpers were supposed to case bets on the layout, but since they were a bit farther away, and knew that dealers primarily cased the layout, they often neglected that part of the job. Casinos employed helpers on wheels when the action proliferated and dealers needed help in order to maintain the speed of the game. Speed saved time, which saved money.

Joe had never mentioned the double-dealer situation during my roulette classes, thus I'd figured he was going to call off the move when he got up from the table and eared me to the internal meeting place. But instead he'd said, "Don't worry about the helper. He has no effect on the move. In fact, he makes it easier for Duke." Watching Duke put in the move, I understood. What the helper's presence actually did was widen the dealer's turn, giving Duke an opportunity to move earlier, at the end of the sweep. When the dealer swept the last batch of losing chips to clear the layout (busy wheels required two, sometimes three sweeps), his turn toward the helper as he pushed the chips to him was exaggerated to the point of an about-face. After the move, Joe explained that all dealers naturally changed their mechanics when supported by a helper. They often let their guard down because they felt secure with the helper there. That last sweep was always exaggerated, as if the dealer were saying to the helper, "Here's your last batch of chips to muck," as he served them up on a silver platter. When I voiced my concern about the possibility of the helper having seen the move, Joe responded, "That never happens. The dealer's body effectively blocks out the helper, cancels him out."

After the second shot at the Barbary, we crossed Flamingo Road and went to work at the MGM. We found a table with perfect conditions: an older dealer with a big turn, relaxed pit personnel, and plenty of action on the table. The only problem was that by the time we got everybody on the table, the dealer had been replaced by a woman whose turn was abbreviated, very tough to beat. Furthermore, the helper who had been on the game when the layout was jammed up with chips was sent off to an adjacent wheel. That wiped out the chance that the dealer might give Duke one of those silver-platter turns on the final sweep. When Duke saw the lady dealer's flash-turn a second time, he signaled Joe that he wanted to discuss the situation at the internal meeting place, which was downstairs below the casino in the MGM arcade. When I saw them leave the table, first Duke, then a few minutes later Joe (I knew they weren't going to the bathroom—once in position, that was only done in case of urgent need), I went downstairs to join them. Jerry, who knew that the problem didn't concern his check-betting role, stayed put at the table.

"She's going to be tough to beat," Duke was telling Joe.

"It's your call, Duke," Joe said. "You're the mechanic. If you're not comfortable, call it off."

Duke loved the challenge. Calling it off never entered his head, but he was obligated to report to Joe the potential for danger. And Joe, knowing that Duke was capable of making a foolhardy decision out of pride and daredevilry, still let him make it anyway—knowing also that Duke would not proceed if the odds were *too* stacked against him. This mid-move meeting was born out of mutual respect for each other. They'd shared a lot of time together in the trenches.

Duke decided to have a go at it. His reasoning was that if he couldn't go on that dealer, we could just wait out the return of the first dealer, or any other dealer who might eventually work the table.

As it turned out, a third-section number came in only once during the forty-five minutes the tough lady dealer dealt the game. Duke had steeled himself to make the move, but when she made her slight turn to reach for the chips needed to pay Joe on the third dozen, he froze up like a snowman. He grimaced, bit his lip in annoyance, lit up a cigarette, and ordered a drink from the cocktail waitress. Then he gave a chin, letting everyone know that he was okay and would be ready to move at the next opportunity. A third dealer arrived at the game, but the wheel went cold and our numbers refused to come in. Finally, more than three hours after we'd taken our positions at the table, the original dealer Duke had staked out returned and mercifully spun a 36 right off the bat, making us $3,500 richer.

We went back to Joe's apartment and divvied up the money. After deducting all expenses, including the cost of Duke and Jerry's hotel room and my suits, we cleared $16,000 for the weekend. Joe distributed to each member of the team and himself $3,000. The remaining $4,000 was put into the team's operating bankroll. Joe kept accurate books on all transactions. Each member owned a certain percentage of the team bankroll. Joe tried to keep that ownership balanced among the four of us, but that wasn't always possible because Duke and Jerry constantly needed cash for their personal enterprises in the Northern California mountains. With my $3,000 I paid my bills and started putting money aside for the purchase of a car. Joe had offered to lend me money if I wanted to buy the car right away, but I declined, fully appreciating his gesture.

A funny thing was happening to me as I got deeper and deeper into the pastposting business. I was losing interest in gambling. As I saw considerable sums of money come off the tables with a flick of the wrist, I began to see legitimate gambling in an entirely new light. Whereas, before, I was capable of losing tens of thousands of dollars on a single shoe of baccarat, the thought now of risking a quarter aboveboard in a casino seemed ludicrous. Stealing casino money just to give it back gambling was as absurd as drug dealing just to stay high. I wanted to avoid that revolving-door kind of life lived by so many compulsive people, hastened by the sudden appearance of quick cash. For once in my life I was determined to keep the casinos' goddamned money.

The following week Joe continued schooling me on pastposting wheels. Learning that art, he said, was not just about doing the moves. At roulette you had to appreciate the nuances. The atmosphere and tempo surrounding a roulette game changed constantly. It was not at all like a blackjack table where you had the continuous drone of the cards sliding out of the shoe with unvarying speed, and where the dealer's movements were 100 percent predictable and repetitive every hand, limiting you to a single move. At roulette there were several moves that could be done at different junctures, and there were so many different scenarios that the planned series of events often had to be rewritten between spins, then communicated to everyone involved in the move. Communication between team members around a roulette table was indispensable. Since so much time was needed to set up and carry out roulette moves, any lapse in communication could completely nullify what we'd spent all that time setting up.

Straight-up moves were just one facet of the roulette portfolio. There were also "split" moves. Instead of betting straight up, the check-bettor put his dark chips on the dividing line between two numbers, either of which paid off at 17 to 1. Then there were "corner" moves, where the check-bettor placed his chips on the point of two intersecting lines touching four numbers. That paid 8 to 1. Another one was the three-number "street" move, which paid 11 to 1. There the check-bettor put his chips on one of twelve points along the vertical line at the left side of the layout that bordered all the first-column numbers. Each point along this line represented a row of three numbers. Street moves were usually done up top in the first section, which lent roulette pastposts more credibility, in view of the fact that casinos were aware that most roulette pastposts occurred at the bottom of the layout.

All these moves were identical in theory but differed in procedure, and they had to be interchangeable once the team was set up at the table to do any one of them. If, for instance, we were positioned to do a third-section-straight-up and changing conditions rendered that move impossible (other players betting too many of our numbers, or a spooked dealer refusing to turn), we had to conform to those conditions and do another move. That was the strength of a good roulette team—not to be limited to just one move in one area of the layout. In order to retool for any changeover while on the table, we had to silently communicate exactly what we wanted to do, and each team member had to know what would happen next and how his role would change, which in the case of the mechanic and check-bettors was drastic, because they often switched roles in mid-move and had to pass off and rebuy chips.

The scenario Joe depicted was a mid-move changeover from the third-section-straight-up to a first-section street. In that instance, the mechanic and one of the check-bettors did switch roles. Since Duke would have been sitting at the bottom of the layout to mechanic a third-section-straight-up, he could not perform a move in the first section, simply because he would be too far away from the chips he had to switch. He had to pass the move-chips to Joe, who could perform the move from his chair across the top of the layout. Duke then bought roulette chips which he used to check-bet in Joe's place. For the street move, the color of the chips Duke acquired as well as their position in the dealer's chip well had no importance, for two reasons: one, the black move-chip still went underneath Jerry's dark roulette chips, now being placed on each of the first-section streets; and two, it was no longer necessary to turn the dealer because the street move went in as the dealer reached down the layout to pay a stack of twenty chips Duke had strategically placed on one of the column boxes at the bottom. Finally, Joe had to cash out his roulette chips so that he'd be free to leave the table after putting in the move.

As claimer, my role didn't change except I had to naturally make the setup bet on one of the streets. That way, when I came back to the table claiming, the floorman would remember me as the guy who'd already bet a black chip on a street.

Another element which sometimes changed along with the move

was the value of the move-chip itself. We always had to pay strict attention to the table limits posted at the top of the layout. The limit was different for each particular bet. For example, some casinos that had a hundred-dollar limit on a straight-up bet let you bet $200 on a street, which meant we could switch in two black chips. The higher-end casinos sometimes had two-hundred-dollar limits straight-up and five-hundred-dollar limits on the street. In that case, we could lay in a purple chip on the street and pick up a juicy $5,500.

We also had to be careful not to accidentally exceed the limit, which was a very dangerous mistake. You never knew how a casino would handle it, and that in itself created steam. If a hundred-dollar unannounced chip showed up on a straight-up winner in a casino with a maximum payout of $3,000, what would the pit bosses do—pay you the $3,000, the $3,500 the bet was worth, or rule the bet null and void because you had exceeded the limit? Best to avoid the confusion.

Whenever we changed course on a roulette wheel where Joe became the mechanic, Jerry took over his function as security and last man out of the casino. I would then be forced to trust Jerry's judgment and evaluation of postoperative steam. I was not totally comfortable with that, but if it was good enough for Joe it would have to be good enough for me.

During that week of furthering my knowledge about the intricacies of roulette, I had been bugging Joe to teach me that sacred blackjack move. I sensed it was the ultimate casino move and therefore wanted to be part of it. Since that impressive demonstration he'd given on the blackjack table in his study, Joe hadn't talked about it again, and I was growing rather curious why. It was the first thing he had shown me about his business. Then as soon as Duke and Jerry came into the picture it was forgotten. I began wondering whether they had something to do with Joe's hesitation about teaching it to me. Perhaps Jerry, whom Joe had already told me was the greatest blackjack mechanic alive, didn't want me to be privy to that particular art. Perhaps he felt that if I was, his value to the team would be reduced. But if such was the case, I wasn't hearing any of it. That was bullshit. Either I was a full member of the team or I walked.

I had been taking a swim in Joe's apartment pool when I decided to confront him about it. I toweled myself off and went inside the apartment. Joe was in his bedroom with the door closed. I knocked, and he called out for me to enter.

He was lying on the bed, chipping away at a *New York Times* crossword puzzle.

"Did you ever finish one of them?" I asked.

"Four times," he recounted. "It's very good exercise for my brain. Now, what can I do for you?"

He seemed just a tad annoyed at my interruption. "I would like to learn the blackjack move," I said straight out. "It's been a month already that we're together."

"You're not ready yet to learn the blackjack move," he said rather sternly. "That will be the last phase of your training."

"Then why did you show it to me in the study before anything else?"

"Because it was the most effective way to make you see what pastposting was all about from the start. Since you *were* a blackjack dealer when we met, I knew you'd appreciate the move when it was actually done on you. In fact, I was going to do a real two-o-five on you at your mini-bac table at the Four Queens—and then tell you what I did before you got the floorman involved."

"That would have been a little risky."

"Exactly. I could have alienated you right from the get-go. Had I done that, you wouldn't be here right now, would you?"

He was 100 percent right, and that was starting to bother me. He always had the answers. However, I took a final shot and tried to convince him to give up the move to me then. "Are you sure that this reluctance on your part has nothing to do with Jerry? Maybe he wants to be the lone star at blackjack."

"That's ridiculous," Joe said, making me feel just that. "Nobody else involved here has any say in the matter. Your time will come for the blackjack move, but not now." Joe got a little literary in closing the discussion. "Any further talk on the subject will fall upon an unreceptive recipient."

So I'd just have to be patient, I thought as I closed his door and went back out to the pool.

During September 1977, Las Vegas's roulette layouts were stealthily bombed by camouflaged black chips. Every weekend, Duke and Jerry would arrive and we'd go out to work. Usually we worked Friday and Saturday, day and night, and sometimes Sunday afternoon, depending upon the profits and steam already realized. If the town had become too steamy, we couldn't press it, even if the weekend's earnings were not up to par. We basically did the straight-up moves. In a few of the classier joints that handled the action, we slipped in purple chips on streets, relishing the $5,500 payoffs. Those moves were by design and put in by Duke, who sat alongside the table at the top. Joe took Duke's third-section seat at the bottom and check-bet, in addition to providing security. Our communication skills were impeccable, and when we were forced to change the move in "mid-air," there were never any procedural problems. Chips got passed smoothly around the table; check-betting and mechanic roles alternated between Duke, Joe, and Jerry, but it was always Duke doing the straight-ups, which required putting the moves underneath the marker.

The payoff rate for roulette moves was about 85 percent during the first three weeks of the month. We'd had a few steamy misses, but each time I managed to get out of the casino. Misses at roulette were the steamiest because casinos were most aware of pastposting at that particular game. At craps the misses had been generally blown off by the bosses; nobody went into the sort of panic they did in the roulette pit.

My teammates had identified a lot of the plainclothes security agents in the various casinos. Whenever they spotted one, they had me follow them to where the guy was in the casino, and I would steal a furtive look. This paid dividends right away, because one Saturday night at the end of the month, while Joe, Duke, and Jerry were positioned on a roulette table at the Las Vegas Hilton, I saw one of these plainclothes guys speaking secretively with the roulette pit boss at the podium in the middle of the pit. I approached them as close as possible, craned my neck to pick up what I could of their conversation. What I heard was shocking. The security guy was telling the pit boss, "Be on the lookout—there's a roulette team in town pastposting black chips." Which is exactly what we were there at that very moment to do.

I circled back to the table where my team was seated and called out, "Chester," as if I were addressing someone else across the pit. Everyone quickly scrambled out of the casino and headed to the primary meeting place outside.

"What happened?" Joe asked as soon as we were all gathered at the Landmark keno lounge. I told him what I had heard. He evaluated the situation and decided we would test the steam in another casino—to what degree had word spread? I remembered that I had claimed a hundred-dollar straight-up move at the Hilton on another shift that had been paid cleanly. Joe's ledger attested to that. He kept records detailing every move, and before going out to work each shift he consulted his ledger.

We went into the Riviera later the same night. This time we didn't bother setting up for a move. Joe just told me to go up to any roulette wheel and make a hundred-dollar bet on a third-section number with a black chip while he watched. I did what I was told, and we had our answer.

They flipped out. The dealer yelled out, "Black on the inside," as if he were warning of a Russian nuclear attack. The wide-eyed floorman couldn't contain himself, and his walk toward the podium at the center of the pit evolved quickly into a trot. He telephoned somebody, probably the shift boss, then hurried back to the wheel as if the future of the casino depended on his arrival. The dealer had deliberately stalled, not spinning the ball until the floorman returned. Then they were joined by a rather homely woman pit boss who had an unpleasant frown chiseled onto her face. Her glance at me was as far away from flirtatious as you could get. All eyes in the pit were pasted on me. This was the most I had ever felt the heat, despite the fact that no move had been—or was going to be—done.

Then, when the dealer unbelievably hit the number I'd bet, the heat got even more intense. The shift boss—or maybe he was the casino manager—arrived just in time to see the dealer pushing two stacks containing thirty-five black chips across the layout toward me. His first words to the floorman were, "Did you *see* him make that bet?" The floorman turned crimson as though his job were on the line, and to tell the truth, under all that heat, I would rather have lost the damn bet. I took the chips, hastily put them in my pockets, and jumped into a cab for the Gingermill. My three teammates, who had not been near the roulette table at the Riviera, were able to stay in the casino and watch and evaluate the situation.

Inside the Gingermill, Duke couldn't stop laughing. He couldn't get over the fact that we were all sitting inside the *emergency* meeting place after winning a legitimate bet. "What's this world coming to?" he cracked.

As was customary at the Gingermill, we ordered expensive fruit drinks and lounged around a bit. Joe was saying we'd picked up major steam in Vegas with black chips at roulette. I thought he would then say we had to return to craps moves, but instead he said to Duke and Jerry, "Go back to California and take care of whatever business you got there. Next week we're going on a road trip—a long one." Then he looked at me and said, "Pack a bag. You and I are leaving tomorrow."

On the Road

MY FIRST ROAD TRIP LASTED ONE YEAR. IT WAS FILLED WITH ADVEN-ture, hilarity, fear, invention, uncertainty, stupidity, and downright fun. When you're on the road with three guys for a long period of time, and the only women involved are those you pass in the night, you are *really* on the road. We started in Reno and Lake Tahoe, arriving there in early October, a beautiful time around the lake. Joe and I arrived in Reno a week before Duke and Jerry, so we spent a few days in a cabin on the North Shore of Lake Tahoe and did a little fishing. I noticed that Joe was a skilled fisherman and outdoors-man. What a contrast to his life in the casinos!

The week waiting for the guys was not totally spent away from business. We cruised all the major casinos in Reno and Tahoe during the day and swing shifts. Joe charted roulette dealers that he deemed beatable. When I asked him why he wasn't doing the same for craps dealers, he explained that it wasn't necessary. *All* craps and blackjack dealers were beatable. Again, I was longing to be trained for that blackjack move. I figured that sometime during this road trip I'd get my wish.

We picked up Duke and Jerry at the airport in our rented car and drove back to the Quick Inn Lodge just a mile or so away. Joe liked to stay at hotels near the airport when on the road. You never knew when you had to get out of town quick. When Duke saw the name of the hotel, he kidded, "I hope we don't have to get out of the Quick Inn quickly."

The atmosphere in Reno, Nevada's second largest gambling town, is considerably different from Las Vegas's. Apart from not being in the desert, it attracts a different crowd. You don't see the hordes of foreigners that converge on Vegas. You don't see nearly as many high rollers, and the casinos are smaller. The only huge Vegas-like casino was the MGM Reno, situated away from the downtown casinos near our motel by the airport.

Another perceptible difference between the two gambling towns is that the dealers behind the tables in Reno seemed friendlier. As did the floormen and pit bosses. Perhaps here, I thought, nobody would tell me to "take it down the road, jerkoff."

We went right to work on the wheels. Most of the casinos had lower limits than their Vegas counterparts, so we couldn't put black chips straight up on a number, except at Harrah's, the most popular casino in town. In the others we did a lot of black-chip corner moves that paid $800. That was the ideal move for Reno's roulette wheels, given that a lot of the casinos had a thousand-dollar maximum payout. That first week in Reno we did fourteen moves without a single miss. Whatever steam was circulating around Las Vegas had not blown northward to the High Sierras. Joe had explained that even though surveillance inspectors from Las Vegas communicated with their counterparts in Reno, steam from one town did not generally travel to the next, unless it was superserious. Slot teams looking to crack million-dollar jackpots generated that kind of steam.

Up at pretty Lake Tahoe the next week, I learned two things: One, we were not the only roulette pastposting team in business. Two, never mix business with pleasure.

We were in position at a roulette table at Harrah's Lake Tahoe on Saturday afternoon. We had already been paid three times at the Harrah's down in Reno, so we figured that would be a good place to start. The limits at Lake Tahoe were higher than in Reno; they accepted black chips straight up on a number. Number 25 had just come in and I was subsequently eared to the table for the claim. Everything was a go, and I waited for Duke to make the switch. The dealer turned her back and Duke pushed forward. As his hands arrived at the marker placed atop Jerry's winning chips, there was a crash. The marker got knocked over and the move-chips in Duke's hand went flying off the layout onto the floor.

The incredible had happened.

That crash was the result of a collision between Duke's hands and the hands belonging to a swarthy European-looking guy sitting between Joe and Jerry along the table. Duke and this other guy looked at each other wide-eyed, both in shock, then they both pulled back their hands. What had occurred was that the other guy, also a roulette mechanic, was looking to do his move the instant Duke was doing ours.

The middle-aged woman dealer's head snapped back toward the layout in horror, bulging eyes fixed on her marker lying incongruously between numbers 0 and 00, all the way at the top of the layout. I saw the expression on her face and thought she was going to drop dead.

Then I saw Joe do the most amazing thing I would ever see him do. In the split second between the collision of the two pastposters' hands and the dealer's recognition of what had happened, Joe spilt a full glass of tonic water onto the layout, soaking it thoroughly. He then stood up and went into an act I could not believe.

"Oh, I'm *so* terribly sorry," he began his profuse apology. "I cannot believe that I am such a klutz. Look what I did to the layout. I knocked over your marker, Barbara. Please forgive me. I really didn't mean to do that . . ." He went on and on.

When the floorman came over, Barbara was already soothing Joe, just as profusely accepting his apology. "Oh, that's alright, sir," she was saying. "These kinds of accidents happen all the time on my table. Don't worry about it."

The floorman instructed Barbara to pay off the winning bets, and after she did, he went to the mid-pit podium, returning with several rags to dry up the layout. He then called the cocktail waitress over to bring Joe, who was still apologizing, another glass of tonic water. A few minutes later the game resumed.

When the fracas was over, the guy who'd collided with Duke cashed out his roulette chips and left the table. Then one by one the three remaining male players who were not with us did the same. It was quite obvious that all four of them were together, which meant that Barbara's roulette table at Harrah's Lake Tahoe that Saturday afternoon was completely filled with pastposters from two different teams and two different countries, probably the only time in the history of casino gambling that such a strange event took place.

Later, back in our motel room on the California side of the lake (we always stayed on the California side for security reasons in case we needed an escape), Joe awoke from a nap with a start. "They didn't have any winning bets on that spin," he said starkly. I didn't have the slightest idea what he was talking about. "The guy who bumped into Duke," Joe continued, "did not have any winning bets on the number 25. The only winners on the layout were Jerry's chips straight up on the number and my stack in the third-dozen box. Whose chips was the guy planning on switching? Or was he just going to lay in a naked capper?" (In a naked capper move a pastposter slips in a big denomination chip on the winning number, underneath a roulette chip stolen from another player.)

Joe had noticed that three of the other four guys who'd been at that table were playing roulette chips and betting large stacks of about twenty chips on the inside numbers. The fourth guy had been constantly betting on even, so it was easy for Joe to recall that none of them had a winner that particular spin. As far as he could remember, each of the three betting the inside numbers had made two bets, covering a total of six numbers. The more he reflected upon what he was recalling from their betting sequence, the more curious he became. They were much too organized, he decided, to just be laying in naked cappers.

Joe picked up the phone and called Duke and Jerry.

"Come over here," he told them. "Sorry to disturb your nap but we have to discuss something."

Ten minutes later we were all in our room. Joe explained what he had seen and, more important, what he *hadn't* seen. "I want to know what those guys were doing," he said. "Tonight, we're going to suspend operations and find them in the casinos. When we spot them, we lay back and observe. I'm pretty sure I've seen these guys somewhere before. It must have been several years ago, which means they've been around a long time and are extremely good."

Suddenly, I felt as though I had jumped over to the other side of the fence. Now *we* were looking to conduct a surveillance on another team. It was all kind of ironic—a pastposting team going under cover to spy on another pastposting team. Since there were only four major casinos on the South Shore of Lake Tahoe, we didn't separate while conducting our search. We entered each casino and spread out around its perimeter, not getting too close to the wheels.

We eventually spotted them, all casually dressed in jeans with sweaters or lightweight jackets, on a wheel inside Harvey's Wagonwheel casino, across the road from Harrah's. Jerry saw them first and immediately signaled the rest of us into the Harvey's keno lounge, where we discussed strategy. It appeared they hadn't seen us.

Joe told Duke and Jerry to observe them from behind a blackjack table down the pit from their roulette wheel. He told me to go right up and buy in at their table and watch everything they did. He was confident I'd catch their move. I was surprised at that blatant approach.

"They probably don't know you," Joe said. "You weren't on the wheel with them at Harrah's like we were. You only appeared when our number came in. If they see one of us, they'll remember. But not you. You're our best chance to pick up on their move."

I took the only vacant chair on their table and bought chips, avoiding eye contact as I watched them bet. Three of the four were betting stacks of twenty roulette chips on the numbers inside, two numbers each, like Joe had said. I noticed they each bet two numbers in a different section, covering a total of six numbers in the three sections. Besides that, there were no discernible patterns. They changed the numbers after every spin, but each stayed in his own section. The fourth guy, the mechanic, was only betting the even-money propositions on the outside. When one of their inside stacks on a number won, they got paid. When their stacks lost, they got swept. There was nothing happening out of the ordinary. After forty-five minutes on the table, I got up and met Joe in the keno lounge.

"Nothing's happening," I said. "There is no move."

"There *has* to be a move," Joe said emphatically. "That guy's hand was not out there to shake Duke's. Go back and stay there until they move."

I went back to the table, observed their unchanging betting patterns for another half hour, and still nothing happened. Then they began cashing out, one after the other, leaving me alone at the table. When I finally got up, I went first to the keno pit, then located my partners in the casino lounge where a band was playing rock music.

"They must have picked up on you," Joe said over the music, putting his drink down on the bar against which we were all leaning. "That's why they didn't move."

"They bet stacks of roulette chips on the numbers, all straight-ups," I said. "Whatever they do, I can't imagine them switching in *whole* stacks."

"No, it's not that," Joe said. "They're doing something else."

"You guys shouldn't be following us around." The voice was definitely foreign-accented. It belonged to the other team's mechanic, the guy who had bumped hands with Duke. He took us completely by surprise. "You don't think we're going to put on a show for your amusement, do you?" He was speaking to Joe, not doubting for a second that he was our leader.

Despite the accent his English was perfect, and the guy had class. He invited us all over to a table at the rear of the lounge and bought us drinks. His partners were not with him. "Obviously, you and we are in the same business," he said with a preening smile after sending off the waitress with a hundred-dollar bill. "However, I think the casinos in this pretty little town are big enough for everyone to work without getting in each other's way—"

"The Lido in Lake Como!" Joe cried suddenly. "That's where I know you from. You're Italian."

"Precisely," the now identified Italian said. "If my memory

serves me well, you were with a gentleman who looked just like you, but a bit taller—your brother perhaps—and also a pretty woman with auburn hair."

Joe mimicked the Italian's "precisely."

We had a few drinks with the Italian, who was joined fifteen minutes later by his partners. They didn't speak English nearly as well as their boss, but we all shared a big laugh about what had happened at Harrah's that afternoon. One of them was giving a demonstration of the collision between the two mechanics' hands on the roulette layout, going "Boom!" as he threw his arms up in the air to simulate an explosion. It was really funny, and the first of my downright-fun adventures on the road. After the drinks were finished, Joe and the Italian agreed to divide up the casinos. Since there were four workable casinos on the South Shore—all about the same caliber—we would take two, they'd take the other two. We all agreed not to step on the other guy's turf for the remainder of that and the following weekend. We took Caesars Tahoe and the High Sierra; they'd stay in Harrah's and Harvey's. After they left, Joe shook his head and said, "They have a fifth guy. He's the one that picked up on us following them. I made a mistake. Now they know all of us, but there's one of them we don't know. Don't think for a minute they're not going to spy on us to see what *we're* doing. We can't do anything but roulette for the rest of the time up here. I don't want them knowing we also work craps and blackjack."

Joe was really bugged about not finding out what the Italians' move was. He knew it was big. Unlike us, the Italian team only worked the wheels, and had been doing so for years. For a team to make a living off the casinos with just one move, it had to be really powerful.

Several times over the coming years we would run into them in different casinos all over the world. Always an agreement was made not to encroach on the other's turf, and sometimes we dined and drank together—but we never identified their fifth partner. However, one balmy night in the Bahamas when I was leading my own pastposting team on an island road trip some fifteen years later, I walked into Merv Griffin's Paradise Island Resorts Casino and caught the same group of Italians—with a new member or two—doing their move. As Joe had suspected, it was a beauty. What they did must have taken years and generations of Italian casino cheaters to master. They bet their six stacks of roulette chips on six numbers, two in each section. When one of their numbers won—they just left well enough alone. When their numbers all lost, they *fabricated* a winner. The mechanic, the same guy who had approached us in the lounge at Harvey's, simply slid their stack of chips which was closest to the winning number right on it. If, for example, the winning number was 5 and one of their stacks was on 4, he would slide that stack of chips onto number 5 with a movement so deft and swift it defied belief. They used a split-second distraction of the dealer that involved one of them who was away from the sliding stack asking the dealer for change at the crucial movement. This move was *unbelievable,* and the real killer was that they could stay on the same table and repeat it several times, as long as they didn't pick up steam. Their roulette chips were worth either $1 or $5, depending on the casino limit. Which meant that in a casino with a hundred-dollar straight-up limit, they were bopping them for $3,500 a shot. After witnessing their move three times, I shook my head in disbelief and then pushed it out of my mind—for I knew I could never even dream of duplicating their craft—not with Joe, not with anybody—not with ten, twenty, or even a hundred years of experience. It was only the grand Savannah that would one day prove to be even better than the Italians.

The following Saturday I got my lesson in eating and shitting in the same place. We took the afternoon off and went picnicking on the shore of the lake. Jerry and I met two women in their twenties doing the same, and we struck up a conversation. The one I was talking to was named Veronica. She was really hot. I hadn't gotten laid in a while and had a hard-on during half the picnic and was dying to take her right in the lake, in spite of the fact it was already October and the water might have frozen my dick. She said they were both secretaries with the same electronics firm in Sacramento, a couple of hours from Lake Tahoe. Since instant gratification seemed out of the question, I figured that I'd get Veronica in bed later that night after we finished working. She was so hot I couldn't let her out of my sight. After the picnic we all returned to Stateline. There was a Tom Jones concert that night at Caesars Tahoe. Jerry and I invited Veronica and Julie; Joe and Duke decided to kick back at the motel. We set 11:30 as the rendezvous time in the Caesars keno pit to go to work.

Jerry gave the maître d' a twenty-dollar bill as we entered the showroom, and he escorted us down to the very first table against the stage. Tom was right over us as he wailed away on "What's New Pussycat?" He was so close you could touch his cuffs. They served a prime rib dinner and we ordered a bottle of champagne. The girls seemed thrilled, and Veronica was getting a bit tipsy and brushing up against me, giving my penis one wake-up call after another. I wanted to have Jerry inform Joe and Duke that I couldn't work tonight, that I had my own moves to perform all over this woman's luscious body. But of course I couldn't do that. I would just have to wait till the wee hours. It had been awhile since I lusted for a woman like that. Back in Vegas I'd slept with a few cocktail waitresses working the casinos where I'd dealt or gambled, but since I got into this thing with Joe, I hadn't had that much time to think about women.

After the show we told the women to wait for us in the casino, but not approach us near gaming tables. They didn't ask any questions, nor did they seem interested in what we were doing, though it had to be obvious we were doing *something.*

Reunited with Joe and Duke in the keno pit, we chatted briefly and decided to put a black chip straight up on a number. Caesars, as it was in Vegas, was the class of Lake Tahoe and let you bet $100 on the numbers inside. The casino traffic had been light enough during the show for Joe and Duke to set themselves up on a wheel just before it let out. They returned to their seats as Jerry quickly pounced on the last available chair around the table, so we were ready to go. I was thinking that I wanted this to end quickly so I could pounce on Veronica. As I approached the table after getting signaled in by Joe to make the setup bet, I noticed Veronica and

Julie playing blackjack at a nearby table. Seeing them made me realize something: I had left my sports jacket in the showroom. I cursed myself, thinking I'd have to go recover it after the move.

Standing at the wheel with my hundred-dollar set-up bet on the layout and the ball spinning, I noticed something else: in the dealer's chip well there were no black or purple chips. The highest denomination chips were twenty-five-dollar greens. This posed a problem, because a payoff of $3,500 in green chips would mean I would have to take seven stacks off the table. Without my jacket I had no place to put them. And in the event of steam, if I had to get out of the casino quickly, I didn't want to risk getting bumped and leaving a trail of green chips rolling through the pits. I decided the best thing to do was delay the move until I could go retrieve my jacket from the showroom.

I caught Duke's eye from where I was standing and tapped the back of my left hand subtly with the fingers from my right. The signal was to lay low but stay in position; the move was being delayed. I then tugged at my shirt and opened my palms to communicate that I needed my jacket. I also indicated the dealer's chip well with a slight movement of my index finger. If he recognized the lack of black and purple chips, he'd probably understand what the problem was.

My setup bet lost. I tried to get Joe's attention but couldn't, and I had to retreat because the setup was done and I didn't want the floorman fixing in on me. Walking away from the table, I assured myself that Duke would pass the information to Joe, and there wouldn't be any fuckups due to this unusual occurrence.

I went back to the showroom, recovered my jacket, and slipped it on. I headed directly back to the casino. Once I had our table in sight, a strange thing happened: Somebody was tugging at my arm, saying, "Sir, you can't leave the table like that."

I turned sideways to find a guy wearing a suit and a mustache with a Caesars nameplate affixed to his breast. "What?" I said, taken completely by surprise.

"You have to wait to be paid before leaving the table. The dealer cannot pay out $3,500 if she doesn't know *who* she's paying it to."

I still didn't get what the guy was talking about.

"It *was* you who made that bet on number 35 at the roulette table, wasn't it?" He pointed at the table where Joe and Jerry were still sitting.

Then it hit me. Duke, who had already vanished, had gone ahead and put in the move while I was away retrieving the jacket. Evidently, there had been a miscommunication between us and he hadn't understood that I wanted to hold up the move. He must have thought I was in position ready to claim; his concentration completely on mechanics, he wouldn't have noticed I wasn't there. Then, after the move was in, there was no subsequent claim. Confusion had to have reigned when the dealer tried to identify whose winning black chip was lying underneath the marker. Finally, as I found out later, it was Joe, who alertly told the dealer and floorman that the same guy who'd bet a black chip straight up a few spins earlier also bet the mysterious chip then in question. "He must not have realized that his bet won," Joe had told the floorman, "and walked away thinking he had a loser." Then the floorman described me to the pit boss who'd come over to the table, and it was that pit boss now escorting me back to the table to collect my $3,500.

Everybody around the table was laughing, including Veronica and Julie, who had both given up playing blackjack to see what the fuss was about. I looked down at the chips underneath the marker, and there was the black Duke had slipped in. I was paid off as anticipated in seven stacks of green chips. I put them all in my sports jacket pockets, two on the outside and one inside. I was bulging chips all over. Then something else happened that had never happened before: I won the bet back! Number 35 repeated. The pit boss rushed frantically to the phone at the podium to call the cage for a black and purple chip refill. Meanwhile, the dealer paid me another $3,500—again in green chips, seven more stacks. I had now completely wiped out the table's green chips. I stuffed the chips everywhere. Fortunately, the jacket pockets were very deep, and I wasn't wearing tight jeans. I managed to get three or four stacks of chips in the pockets of my trousers. I was completely overflowing with chips. Because of that, I decided on my own to go directly to the cashier and cash out. I was sure Joe would understand that deviation from procedure, that I didn't want to lug all those chips over to the meeting place. As I left the table, the pit boss called out, offering metal racks to carry the chips, but I didn't turn around. I just wanted to get the chips cashed out and me out of the casino.

At the cage I began stacking the chips on the counter in front of the teller. As she began counting and restacking them, I turned around for no apparent reason to face the casino. What I saw sent shivers up my spine.

The same pit boss with the mustache who'd escorted me back to the roulette table was now heading toward me at a very brisk pace, huffing and puffing. On either side of him was a uniformed security guard. They were coming to get me! There I was, standing at the casino cashier with all these twenty-chip stacks of greens sitting on the counter between me and the teller, and they were coming to get me. I didn't have much time to think. Instinctively, I started grabbing back the stacks of chips like a madman, stuffing my pockets, but having the warped presence of mind not to let any of them go rolling on the floor. The startled teller gasped, "Sir!" and then shrieked as I peeled away. Instead of finding an exit that led to safety, I ended up in front of a bank of elevators. I pressed the call button, desperately hoping one of the elevators was on the ground floor and would open immediately. I didn't know which button I would press once I was inside, but didn't really contemplate what difference it made.

Unfortunately, none of the four elevators opened quick enough for me to make a clean getaway. I stepped into the one that finally did open and hurriedly pressed the button for the fifth floor and then the close button. The doors began an agonizingly slow movement to join together. I watched helplessly, willing them to shut faster. They were a split second away from being completely closed when a large, beefy hand cut into the shrinking space between them, knocking them open. I knew at that moment I was about to face my first real test. How it turned out would determine whether my cheating experiences in the casinos were to be cut short or would sustain my entire life.

The Back Room

THE FIRST FACE I SAW OUTSIDE THE DOORS I RECOGNIZED BY THE mustache. It was the pit boss, and he had that we-got-you look on his face. The large, beefy hand that had interrupted my passage fittingly belonged to a large, beefy security guard. He motioned me out of the elevator with a crooked finger while his partner said, "You'll have to come with us, sir." They led me back through the casino to the security office, which was down a narrow corridor at the side of the casino cage.

Inside the chilly, naked room were two metal desks on opposite ends of a colorless linoleum floor. There was a bank of steel-gray file cabinets behind one of them, on top of which sat a crackling radio broadcasting security transmissions throughout the hotel. A large bulletin board on the wall displayed those ugliness-enhancing photos and sketches of various people wanted for questioning or arrest.

I was told to empty my pockets and put the contents on the desk nearest the door. I removed all the green chips and stacked them on the desk. That took a few humiliating minutes. I also had the black chip from the move, my driver's license, and the hundred-dollar bill

I always kept on me for emergencies when working the casinos. Then I was told to sit down in the chair adjacent to the desk. The big security guard who had led me into that back room said, "You know that the Nevada Gaming Control Board gives us the right to detain you a reasonable amount of time in order to notify a peace officer if we have probable cause that you've committed a crime on our property."

I didn't respond. I had seen the same warning engraved on plaques affixed to casino entranceway walls a thousand times.

The pit boss left the room briefly, then returned with two chip racks and put all my chips in them. He picked up the racks, exchanged a few hushed words with the two security guards, then walked back out of the room, closing the door behind him. I was thinking that the $7,100 in chips were gone forever.

I was left alone in the back room with the two guards who stood by the door. Aside from their occasional small talk and the intermittent crackling of the radio, I sat there in silence for twenty minutes. I was very uncomfortable but tried my best not to let them know it. I had known since the day I'd claimed that first craps move at the MGM in Las Vegas that this confrontation was inevitable, but still, sitting there in that barren security room, I felt vulnerable and very alone.

Finally, a brutish character with a pockmarked face dressed in plainclothes entered the room. He was carrying a folder that he laid on the desktop adjacent to my chair. Then he sat behind the desk while the two guards remained standing by the door. He gave me a disdainful look, then began tapping the desk with his fingers as he continued looking me over. His whole being was unnerving.

"That was a cute little act you pulled there on the wheel," he said at last sarcastically, nodding his big head. "Did you know that cheating in a Nevada casino is a felony?"

I remembered how Joe had drilled me about how to handle myself in this very situation. He had said to keep my mouth shut, not to come off like a wiseass, and not to lie or deny anything. Nothing you can say can help you, he had stressed. Whatever they had, they had. If it was enough to arrest and charge you, they would. If not, they had to cut you loose. Remembering all that, I sat there and kept my mouth shut.

"You can be sentenced by a judge to ten years in state prison for a trick like that. Did you know *that?*"

I remained silent. Whatever trouble I was in, I knew I wasn't going to prison for ten years. It was about a simple pastpost in a casino. I wasn't caught crossing Stateline with ten kilos of heroin in the trunk of my car.

Joe had briefed me well about casino security tactics in the back room. He'd said that the very first thing they'd do was try to intimidate me. I figured the big brute in front of me was probably thinking he could just scare the living shit out of me by his presence alone. I was only twenty-two years old and looked even younger.

"You got any ID on you?" he asked.

I gave him my Nevada driver's license.

He looked it over and laid it on the desk. "I wouldn't have even thought you old enough to legally enter the casino," he said with that same trace of sarcasm. "I'm sure all the convicts up there in Ely will just love getting a piece of your ass." Ely was Nevada's harshest state prison. I knew he was pressing the intimidation tactics.

He got up and went to the bank of file cabinets. From the top sliding drawer he pulled out a voluminous book that I later learned was called the *Hanson Mug Book*, a compilation of known casino cheaters distributed to the casinos by the Hanson Detective Agency, based in Las Vegas and headed by an ex-Vegas cop named Clint Hanson. He had gotten the brilliant idea of exclusively servicing casinos and so had an immediate client base. Instead of tailing unfaithful spouses like most of the other private dicks in town, Hanson and his half-dozen associates chased slot, card, and dice cheaters, thieves and pickpockets, and various other organized and unorganized casino scammers.

The brute laid the book on the desk and sat back down. He opened it to the page where my name and photo would have been alphabetically, then nodded as he closed the heavy book with a resounding thump. He put my driver's license inside the folder lying on his desk.

"You're not in the book," he said with a smirk. "Well, you are now, my friend." He leaned back in his chair. "My name is Garrison. I'm the head of security and surveillance for Caesars casino here at Lake Tahoe. If you come clean now, I'll see what I can do for you with Gaming Control. It's up to them how far they want to press the matter in front of a judge."

"I have nothing to say to you," I said flatly.

The radio on top of the file cabinet crackled, and Garrison paused to take in the transmission. I garnered that they were searching for a guy with long blond hair who was loose on one of the upper floors with a stolen master room key. At least I wasn't their only concern, I thought.

Garrison turned his attention back to me. "You know, all you have to do is tell us who your buddy is that pastposted that bet for you, and you'll probably end up getting a walk on this."

"I'm here alone," I said. Despite everything Joe had told me, I knew there were certain things I *could* say under interrogation. Telling Garrison I was alone was not something that could eventually be used against me in court, even if it was a lie.

Garrison laughed sardonically. "You want to be alone? It's gonna be you who does the time *alone*." He reached over and picked up the phone at the edge of the desk. He said into it as his eyes fixed on me, "Bring them in."

I didn't know who he was having brought in but assumed that it must have been some of the players from the table. Somebody had probably ratted out the move just after I left with the chips. That would explain why they came after me so fast.

My theory proved to be correct, but in a million years I never would have guessed who their rats were. The door swung open and the pit boss came in first, followed by the two rats and the floorman who'd been working the roulette table. When I saw Veronica and Julie come into the room, I nearly died. My disbelief turned quickly into anger. Not at them but at myself. I had let myself go down on the count of a broad. I had let my dick take the place of my head. And beyond all the threats menacing me now, I was thinking about how Joe was going to react to this. He had told me never—*never*—

let a woman into my confidence when I was involved in a criminal enterprise, not even my mother. How could I have been so stupid?

The two women took a few steps inside the office and stood next to the floorman. They were both looking at me. Julie's face was a mask of contempt. The expression on Veronica's was void, as if she were seeing me for the first time.

Garrison sensed my shock and played on it. "Would you be kind enough to tell me what you saw?" he asked Veronica in a smooth, almost caressing voice.

"I saw the balding guy with the cap [Duke] at the table switch the chips, then I saw him"—she pointed at me as though I were part of a police lineup—"come to the table and get paid a lot of money."

Garrison asked Julie to recount what she had seen. "I saw the same thing," she answered. "His friend did something with the thing the dealer put on the winning number. Like Veronica said, he switched the chips. I saw him"—pointing at me—"talking to the guy wearing the cap in the keno pit before they were playing roulette. Also, the two of them were together at the lake this afternoon."

Garrison thanked them both and had one of the guards escort them to another security room to sign their statements. Then he said to me, "You still don't have anything to say?"

"No."

"Alright. We'll let Gaming handle it." He got up, took the folder from the desk, and passed it to the lone security guard in the room. He said, "Keep an eye on him," before going back out into the casino.

They let me sweat it out for two hours before a Nevada Gaming agent stepped inside the office carrying a briefcase. He was about thirty years old. He dressed in a jacket and tie and wore glasses. He did not have the physical presence Garrison had. He removed his jacket and sat down behind the desk. The guard brought him the folder that Garrison had given him before leaving. The gaming agent looked briefly inside it and put it down. Then he opened his briefcase and took out a writing pad, unclipping a pen from his shirt pocket.

"My name is William Brown," he began amicably, "I'm an enforcement agent with the Nevada Gaming Control Board. It's my job to investigate casino crimes in the state of Nevada. Before I continue, I must notify you that you do not have to talk to me if you don't want to."

I could see that Brown's approach was entirely different from Garrison's. There wasn't going to be any of that getting-fucked-in-the-asshole-by-convicts crap.

"I really don't have anything to say," I said politely but short.

"You don't want to give me your version of what happened? I already have theirs."

At that moment a thought came to me, and I acted on it. I visualized exactly what had happened on that roulette wheel, remembering that it was not I who had claimed the bet, but the pit boss who had brought me back to the wheel to get paid. Perhaps there was an opening through which I could maneuver my way out of the predicament. Joe had said to keep my mouth shut, which is always the smart thing to do, but this situation was unique because I had never actually *claimed* that bet. What I was thinking was worth the shot.

"I'll tell you exactly what happened," I told Brown, who readied himself to take notes as I spoke. "I went up to that roulette table and bet a black chip and lost. I usually don't bet that much money, but I'd been drinking the whole night and started gambling recklessly. I was making bets all over the casino. I don't even remember on which tables. After I made that roulette bet, I went to the showroom to retrieve my jacket, which I had left there after the show. I was drinking champagne all during the show . . . probably the reason why I left the jacket there in the first place. I was just too drunk to remember to put it back on. Then when I came back into the casino, the pit boss from that roulette table walked up to me and told me I had a winning bet that couldn't be paid if I wasn't at the table. To tell you the truth, I don't remember making a second bet at that table. I *was* drunk, but even so, I should have remembered that. Well, I didn't argue. I mean, after all, if a pit boss came up to *you* and told you that your bet had just won $3,500, would *you* argue? So I figured that I must have made that winning bet if he was telling me that I did. I went back to the roulette table with him and they paid me the money. Then I let the bet ride and won again. I thought it was going to be my lucky night. The next thing I know, I'm sitting here being accused of a crime." I had recounted all that as fast as it came into my head.

Brown finished jotting something on the pad, then asked, "Why did you try to run away when you were at the casino cage?"

"Try and run away?" I feigned confusion. "What are you talking about?" Regardless of the fact that Brown knew I was full of shit, I must have sounded convincing.

"The pit boss and security guards all stated that you ran away from them as they approached you at the cage."

"I wasn't running away from anyone," I retorted, my mind moving as rapidly as possible. "I was at the cage cashing out all those green chips they paid me at the roulette table. The woman counting my chips on the counter was taking forever, and then I remembered that I had a date with this girl Veronica whom I'd met at the lake. You should see her." I was thinking that he'd already interviewed her. "Then you'd understand why I didn't want to be late."

Brown removed a photograph from the folder on the desk and passed it to me. It was a color still of Duke wearing the cap, taken by the overhead camera at the roulette table. "Do you know this man?" he asked, without implying that I did.

"No," I said, giving him back Duke's photo.

He replaced that photo and took out another. It was Joe's, taken by the same camera. "And him?"

"I never saw him before in my life." I knew that the two girls had squealed everything, including the day spent at the lake with all of us, but I also knew that none of that could be proven. Perhaps they had proof I'd been with Jerry inside the showroom, but he wasn't the guy who'd switched the chips, so that wouldn't matter much.

"You weren't aware that these two guys were playing roulette on that table?" Brown asked.

"I don't bother looking at other players when I'm gambling. The only thing that concerns me is whether I win or lose."

I expected him to show me Jerry's picture then, but he either didn't have it or deemed it no longer necessary, given my uncooperativeness. He put the notepad back inside the briefcase and left the room, leaving the briefcase on the desk.

I knew he would be back shortly and was starting to get confident. I knew they didn't have much on me. The story I gave the gaming agent was as feasible as it was a lie. The photos he'd shown me were all still shots. Back in the late seventies, it was rare that casinos ran twenty-four-hour videotape on all their tables. If the Caesars Tahoe camera above that roulette wheel had not caught the actual move, I was walking out of there, no matter what anyone said they'd seen.

Agent Brown returned ten minutes later and took his seat behind the desk. From the briefcase he removed a form document and filled in the blanks, starting with my name on top. "I'm not arresting you," he said. "Consider yourself lucky that surveillance has no taped evidence against you." Then he looked up at me with a serious frown. "Be careful about the people you're involved with. They can get you in a lot of trouble. Remember, gambling crimes are felonies in Nevada. You get time." He pushed the document to me. "If you'll just sign this, we can be finished here."

"I'm not signing anything," I said, thinking how lucky I was that they hadn't caught the move on tape.

"It's just a release form saying you were advised of your right to remain silent."

"I don't care what it is. I'm not signing it."

Brown nodded his acquiescence, gave me back my driver's license, closed the briefcase, and left. A minute later Garrison came back into the room. "It looks like I gotta cut you loose," he said grudgingly. Then he read me the riot act that effectively eighty-sixed (barred) me forever from Caesars Tahoe. He wanted me to sign a document to that effect, but again I refused. He told me I'd be guilty of a criminal trespass if ever again caught on the property, or on any other properties owned by Caesars World, including Caesars Palace in Las Vegas. That was no big deal. Joe had told me that he had difficulty remembering the casinos that he *wasn't* already eighty-sixed from.

"And remember one other thing," Garrison said tersely, just be-

fore motioning me out the door. "Now we know who you are. Every
casino—not only in Nevada, but in the rest of the world—will also
know you. Hanson is gonna distribute your picture to all the surveillance rooms in the state. Your career is going to be very short-lived."

He took me back through the casino but not immediately to the
exit. I was surprised when we stopped at the casino cage. In front of
one of the tellers, he said something to a boss deeper inside the cage.
The man nodded, then disappeared from my view an instant before
returning with two racks of green chips that he placed on the counter.
When I saw the lone black chip sitting on top of one of the racks, I
realized that the chips were mine. I had completely forgotten about
them in the anxiety of spending four hours in the back room. Then
when the teller began counting them down in front of us, it hit me
that I was being paid. They actually gave me the cash, $7,100! After
we left the cage, Garrison led me to the main entrance where we
exited the casino. He walked me to the edge of the property by the
road. His last words to me were "It was a pleasure meeting you."

It was nearly six o'clock in the morning, and I was beat. But the
ordeal was not yet over. I was sure that Garrison was having me
followed. I had to be extremely careful not to lead Caesars security
or gaming agents to our hideaway on the California side. If we were
all caught together, that might lead to a conspiracy charge.

The South Shore of Lake Tahoe was not very large, and all four
casinos were located on the same road running into California and
our motel. In order to shake a tail, I had to meander through the
woods and go where vehicles were impeded. I wasn't more than two
hundred yards from Caesars, on a narrow, loosely paved parallel-
running road behind Harrah's, at the other end of the casino run,
when I noticed a light green van parked anything but innocently
behind a thick tree with spread-out dipping branches that nearly concealed it. I couldn't see a driver behind the wheel, but assumed one
had probably ducked just before I passed by, and it was quite possible
I was at that moment being watched from one-way windows at the
back of the van. My suspicions were confirmed a minute later when
the same van appeared at a clearing on the far side of a patch of
woods. I cut back into the woods and made several long maneuvers

around the perimeter of trees and bushes, finally managing to lose the van at a pond it couldn't cross. At that point I ran full speed for about five hundred yards, found another densely wooded patch, and emerged undetected on the California side. Before going near the motel, I took one final precaution and mounted a rocky hill, then descended it in a roundabout fashion. When I got to the room, it was 7:00 A.M. I had spent over an hour covering the half mile between Caesars and the motel.

Joe was absolutely livid. I had never before seen a human being so furious, not even in the movies. "What the fuck were you thinking!" he roared. "You jeopardized our entire operation for a broad! Do you think I've spent all this time training you to be a fuckup? I put my heart and soul into making a warrior out of you, and you pull a motherfucking stunt like this on me!"

There was nothing I could say or do to calm him down. I just had to weather the storm—and it was violent. I never felt so shitty before in my life. I had let down my teammates, had exposed them to a tremendous amount of risk just because I was lusting after Veronica. Even Jerry, who'd also been horny, had been reluctant to take the two women to a show in the same hotel we'd later be working. Given the deal we had made with the Italians, we were limited to just two casinos. I should have had the bitches wait in the other one.

I was proud of the story I had fabricated for the gaming agent, which may have ultimately been the reason why I walked, but bragging about that now to Joe would only have infuriated him more.

"How long do you think those two broads waited to start ratting after you left the table?" Joe asked, still enraged. I didn't say anything. I didn't dare interrupt the cadence of his outburst. "They *didn't* wait. As soon as you turned your back, they started right in. And it was the one *you* were with that opened her fucking mouth first."

That made me feel like an even bigger idiot.

Duke and Jerry's knocking on the door saved me from the rest of Joe's tirade. He finally calmed down a little, and then I recounted everything that had happened in the back room, not skipping a single detail. When I was through and tossed the seventy-one hundred-dollar bills on the bed, the tension lightened up a bit. Duke laughed at the fact they'd cashed me out. A little of the anger on Joe's face had been wiped off, but I still had trouble looking him in the eye.

"We're finished for a while up here on the wheels," Joe said after I was done recounting my trip through the woods. "We'll go back to Reno and do some blackjack moves."

Then Jerry joked to me, "You'll do anything to force us to teach you that blackjack move."

Duke and Jerry laughed. Joe and I managed a faint smile.

The Blackjack Move

I<small>F THE ROULETTE PASTPOST WAS THE MOST INTRICATE AND CREATIVE</small> move in the business, the blackjack pastpost was certainly the fastest and most efficient. I would soon learn it was the real bread-and-butter move that would undoubtedly remain productive as long as gambling casinos offered the game of blackjack. The first time I had seen it done in a live casino was at the Reno Hilton, just a few days after the Lake Tahoe disaster. Jerry walked up to a blackjack table as the dealer was sweeping up the cards after paying the last winning bet from the previous hand. He put three red chips on the first betting circle to the dealer's right, the position we called third base. As he sat down, he placed five black chips on the layout in front of him, covering them with his right hand in the same motion so that they remained hidden from everyone else in the casino. Tucked in the fleshy crevice of that same hand, between the thumb and index finger, were the move chips. With his left hand he played the cards, scratching the green felt with them when he wanted to hit, tucking them underneath the three red chips in the betting circle when he wanted to stand. At third base, Jerry was the last to play his hand but the first to receive the dealer's attention after the round was finished and all the cards played. This meant that Jerry would be the first paid on winners, the first to have his chips swept on losers. The importance of the third-base position was the angle it formed between its betting circle and the dealer's head while the dealer performed the mechanics of paying bets on the layout. The blackjack move could also be done from the other positions, but third base was optimal. Each spot to the right of it made the move that much tougher.

The first hand, Jerry was dealt two 8s by the dealer, Ralph, a tall fair-skinned blond with Nordic features who had an imposing presence and a fluid dealing motion. Ralph had a 6 up card. Normally, the skilled blackjack player splits the two 8s into separate hands because that strategy increases the percentage of winnings. However, in the pastposting business you never split or doubled-down hands because you didn't want a situation where your original bet had to be matched, giving the dealer another glance at your chips.

Jerry stood on the 16 and tucked the cards under the three red chips, hoping Ralph would bust. Ralph made a hand and swept away Jerry's $15. While Ralph was sweeping away the cards remaining on the table, Jerry again placed three red chips in the betting circle,

never lifting his right hand off the black backup chips hidden on the layout in front of him. Jerry worked everything with his left hand. He had a full reserve of two-dozen reds in his left jacket pocket. He used his left hand to reach into the pocket for the chips and place them perfectly centered in the betting circle. By exacting perfect placement, you never had to worry about the dealer touching or doing a double-take on your chips.

Jerry lost the second hand, then placed his third three-red-chip bet. This time he was dealt two kings against Ralph's 7 up card. He quickly tucked his cards, waited for the other players to play theirs. When the last player at his right busted, Jerry's body stiffened in preparation for the move. He had to be ready fast because his cards were the first turned over. I noticed from where I stood behind a blackjack table across the pit that Joe, standing opposite Jerry at first base, was gripping his chin firmly. Then Ralph turned over his hole card; it was a queen, giving him 17. He immediately flipped over Jerry's cards, reached into his rack, grabbed a stack of red chips and cut evenly into Jerry's bet, resulting in a chop that left three red chips lying snugly against Jerry's. As he proceeded to turn over the next player's cards, Jerry's left hand eased out onto the betting circle and scooped up the original three red chips he'd bet, while his right hand laid in two black chips with a red-chip capper *exactly* where the three original chips had been. All in the same motion, the left hand dumped the three reds removed from the layout in his left jacket pocket, while the right hand chased down the dealer's hand and tapped it. As Jerry went into his claim, both his hands were completely empty and exposed palms up. And now his stack of black backup chips was in plain view. Ralph was shocked by Jerry's soft touch. No matter how soft, it was reverberating because a player never touched a dealer's hand.

"Hey!" Jerry said harshly, "you paid me wrong! I bet $200 here. You paid me $15. What is this nonsense!" Then with a little flick of his index finger, he kicked the three red chips that Ralph had paid out of the betting circle. This was done to subconsciously push the dealer to put those chips back in his rack, so when the floorman arrived he'd only see Jerry's $205 bet and black backup chips on the layout. Ralph instantly apologized. "I didn't see that, sir." He put the three reds back in the rack, then paid Jerry two blacks and a red. He called to the floorman, "Black out." The floorman walked up behind Ralph, took a cursory look at Jerry and watched his next bet.

For a two-o-five, standard bet-back procedure called for a fifty-five-dollar bet, two green chips and a red capper. Jerry purposely broke down a black chip, asking the dealer for four greens, to show more black action to the floorman. There were dozens of little subtleties like that which enhanced the overall power of the move. All blackjack moves had built-in bet-backs unless there was steam after the payoff and the mechanic had to leave quickly.

Jerry won his first bet-back, then lost. After he left the table, the floorman went back to his business in the pit, not giving Jerry a second thought. With the two fifteen-dollar losing hands before the move and the break-even on the bet-backs, we cleared $175.

After getting paid on the blackjack move, the mechanic did not go to the primary meeting place outside the casino. Instead, he either went to the internal meeting place inside the casino being worked or just strolled down the pit a few tables away, out of the beaten dealer's and floorman's sight. There he waited for Joe, who hung back as long as necessary to evaluate steam, to pass him by. If Joe gave the chin, they'd go right back into the cruise, looking for another table to move on. When he gave a nose, the mechanic retreated to the internal meeting place to await further instructions. The few times Joe made a brushing-his-teeth motion, rubbing his clenched teeth with his index finger, the mechanic immediately left the casino for the external meeting place outside it, because that particular signal meant steam.

The blackjack move was bang-bang. After a payoff, Joe usually stayed at the table for just a minute or two. If nobody ratted, there was rarely a problem. And the rats were rare because the move was so quick. Its inherent beauty was that it was done when your hands were *supposed* to be out there. It was normal for a player to go right out and collect the chips the dealer had just paid him. For that reason,

the mechanic could go right out and move under the dealer's nose
without being seen switching the chips. It wasn't like roulette, where
your hands being seen by the dealer meant you were caught. Rarely,
if almost ever, did a dealer say to a blackjack mechanic, "I saw you
switch those chips." And if he did say that, he didn't really see anything; he just *figured* a switch had been made because he was convinced that the chips being claimed weren't there before he made
the payoff.

The blackjack move was the most psychological of all our moves.
Since on a blackjack table there was a maximum of only seven bets,
the dealer got a cleaner look at chips on the layout than dealers did
at the other games, and was also closest to the players. But these
negative aspects were blown right out of the water by the psychology
of the move, what Joe liked to call the "shock factor."

"Nothing matters," he explained to me in the car as we drove
down the mountain to Reno. "Not what the dealers see, not what
color the chips are . . . *nothing.* The move is too powerful. You bet
three red chips; the dealer can look at it ten times. Then when you
go out there and slap his hand while you're claiming, with your
backup chips sitting on the table, you knock the dealer senseless.
The backup chips," Joe stressed. "They're your protection. They
fucking brainwash the dealer—and then the floorman and pit boss.
The dealer calls them to the table after a move goes down, and they
see nothing but blacks on the layout—or purples if we're moving
purples. How can they think the guy sitting behind those chips, always dressed to perfection, was only betting $15? They'd have to be
morons to think that. So with all that working, you think this move
is good?" Joe didn't wait for my response. "I'll tell you how good it
is. The first hundred and fifty blackjack moves were done by Jerry—
zero misses. That's how good it is. We've been doing it for eight
years. After the first miss, the payoff rate has leveled off at 90 percent."

That hundred and fifty in a row without a miss was impressive.
And Joe went on to say that 40 percent of those moves had been

done with purple chips, mostly ten-o-fives. He also explained the subtleties of the move. Gently pushing the three red chips the dealer initially paid you out of the betting circle was one of them. Avoiding eye contact with the dealer when you approached the table was another. To do that naturally, you could strike up a little friendly conversation with the player seated next to you as you sat down, saying something mundane, like "How's the table running?" You always placed your bet when the dealer was sweeping the cards. If you came to the table while the dealer was shuffling, you waited till the end of the shuffle to place your bet. If you smoked, as did Duke and Jerry, you kept your cigarettes and lighter in your right jacket pocket, which was not needed for chip storage during the move. And, of course, no smoking during blackjack moves.

Certain situations occurred where you didn't move. If at the end of the hand yours was the only winning bet on the table, you didn't move. That was because, after paying you, the dealer had nobody else left to pay, and his hands would either be going back to his rack to replace chips—if he had taken excess chips from it to pay you— or right to your cards to sweep them up. If you moved and the dealer was in the process of sweeping the cards while you claimed, you were late and could have a very dangerous situation. If that occurred, the dealer would have to stop in mid-sweep, a very awkward position. Dealers tended to pass on their discomfort to the players causing it. So, to put it simply, you do not put the dealer in an awkward position.

We also didn't move when we were dealt blackjacks. A natural 21 on the deal paid 3 to 2. Dealers almost always paid those winning bets with bridges, placing that 50 percent supplement evenly on top, as they did with certain odds bets at craps. Doing a move inside that structure took too much time, so we let it go and settled for winning the hand with the little blackjack bonus.

There were also situations where we created possibilities to move on otherwise unworkable tables. If a table was dead, we filled it with the whole team to create the action needed for a move. That scenario was even better than a table full of unknown players, because when playing blackjack we never busted our hands; when the dealer did bust, he would have at least three more hands to pay after paying the mechanic, assuring him that he wouldn't find himself claiming while the dealer was sweeping the cards. Other players might have played their hands differently and busted, leaving the mechanic's winning hand alone on the layout, prohibiting a move. And, of course, with only us at the table there was no chance of a rat.

Back inside the Reno Hilton, Jerry did three more moves without a miss. Then we went over to Harrah's and Harold's Club, where Jerry did a half dozen in each—no misses. It was all very quick. Getting black chips, the moves, bet-backs, and cash-outs—no more than an hour in each casino. On the night shifts (swing and graveyard) we went back into the same casinos and most of the others in town. It was a veritable massacre. Jerry just kept pounding the blackjack tables. At $200 the moves were not big by pastposting standards, but the volume of Jerry's attack fattened up the team bankroll at a very healthy rate. The first three days and nights in Reno, Jerry did a hundred moves with just three misses. He even ventured at the end of his onslaught to do a couple of three-o-fives (four-chip switches with 3 blacks and a red capper) that got paid. I couldn't wait to see the big blackjack moves with purple chips. Joe had told me that in Reno it was difficult to get the purple chips, which is why he favored doing roulette moves with blacks. There was, however, one casino that sometimes had their purple chips in the dealers' racks: the MGM Reno. We would go there before leaving town so that Jerry could pop in a few.

Brainstorm

RELIGIOUSLY, IN THE MORNING, WHEREVER I WAS, I WENT OUT FOR A five-mile run just after waking up. I ate a banana and sometimes a little piece of chocolate and took off. While on course I often killed the time thinking, since I'd never been able to run comfortably wearing headphones or carrying a radio in my hand. It was on a clear, crisp morning in Reno during the second mile of my run that I had my first pastposting brainstorm. I speeded up my pace to hurry back to the room and tell Joe.

He was seated at the round table next to the window, drinking coffee as he studied the pieces on the chessboard he had laid on the table.

"Joe," I said excitedly as I breezed into the room, "I think I came up with something!"

"A chess strategy?"

I was not absolutely sure he was kidding. "Listen, it has to do with roulette. Remember when you said that once the black-chip setup bet starts taking steam, we have to abandon the move until it cools down?"

Joe nodded and mumbled the name of a chess gambit as he moved a white pawn forward to be sacrificed.

He wasn't listening to me. At times the guy could be really frustrating. "I think I figured out another way to claim the blacks on the wheel," I pressed. "The steam from the current move won't affect it."

He continued rapidly moving pieces across the board in both directions, then finally said, "Check," as he moved the white queen to threaten the black king.

"Joe, are you going to listen to me or not?" That was the loudest I had ever raised my voice to him.

"We'll talk about it after our *petite partie d'échecs*." He really annoyed me when he spoke French; it sounded condescending.

I had no choice, so I sat down and took white. We had already played a half-dozen times. Though I was not a bad chess player, I had managed only one stalemate against Joe in six *parties*. After he checkmated me, he finally listened to what I had to say.

"Instead of having the claimer come to the table and set the casino up," I began, "we have the claimer buy in for a dark color, taking a seat at the top of the table away from the third section. As soon as he receives his stacks of chips, he mixes three or four black chips into one of the stacks and puts that stack in the rear, out of the dealer's sight. The rest of his stacks will keep that 'mix-up' stack hidden. Then he makes his own bets with his own chips on the third-section numbers. The other check-bettor still bets his stack in the third-dozen box to assure the dealer's turn so Duke can do the move. Then, once the move is in, the claimer quickly places his mix-up stack in front of all his other stacks—in plain view of the dealer—and begins claiming that he *accidentally* got one of his black chips mixed up with his roulette chips and it won. He can say something like, 'Oh, my God, I got one of my black chips mixed up and it won!' When the dealer sees the mix-up stack that the claimer just put out front in his view, he'll understand immediately what we want him to think happened. In effect, the black chips mixed up with the roulette chips in that front stack serve as the setup bet, but only *after* the move goes in." I paused a second to let it all sink into Joe's brain, then said, "What do you think of that for *checkmate?*"

Joe Classon's eyes widened as the genius of my mix-up claim dawned on him. It was the first time since he had been taught the pastposting business that somebody else working with him invented a new claim, and given that I'd only been involved in the operation a few months, it was even more spectacular. It didn't take him more than a few seconds to grasp exactly what the enormous strength of that claim was. The fact that the claimer was claiming that he had made an "honest" mistake, that he never had the intention of betting the hundred-dollar chip, removed the inherent steam that went along with unseen black winning chips on roulette layouts. Hearing this claim would make the bosses think that the claimer was just a lucky idiot whose own stupidity had paid off big. And then seeing that mix-up stack in front, the black chips deliberately misplaced in a stack of roulette chips. That was the real clincher. How could they not go for it?

"We'll do it when we get to the islands," Joe said, not expressing the enthusiasm that I had. He didn't want it to go to my head, but I knew he loved it. I saw in his eyes the same reaction he'd had when I first laid the idea for the mini-baccarat scam at the Four Queens on him.

We had lunch together at a Jo-Jo's restaurant near the motel. There was no talk about the new roulette claim. Joe was more interested in discussing the upcoming itinerary for the road trip. After Reno, we'd take a break until after Thanksgiving. Joe said that he wanted to fly down to Miami to spend the holiday with his mother. Knowing that I had no contact with my own family, he invited me to go along. Duke and Jerry would go back to California and tend to their girlfriends and marijuana plants. At the end of November we'd all reconvene in Puerto Rico to begin our Caribbean tour. Joe estimated that we'd stay in the islands around four months, but would return to Las Vegas for the big New Year's Eve weekend. New Year's Eve was to the pastposting business what the Friday after Thanksgiving was to retailing. Everybody agreed with the plans. We finished our desserts, then went back to the rooms and prepared to work the day shift.

The inside of the MGM Reno casino was chillingly identical to its Las Vegas counterpart. If you had been blindfolded and dropped from an airplane into one of the two MGM casinos, you wouldn't know which one you were inside unless you had an intimate familiarity with them both. Outside, however, they were completely different. Whereas the MGM Vegas was one of the centerpieces sentineling the Las Vegas Strip, the MGM Reno was totally isolated from the other casinos, the lone concrete tower that loomed up at you just off the runway when you landed at the Reno airport. Surrounding the behemoth building were its roadways and parking lots. There were no other commercial buildings around. No restaurants or bars, either. This posed a problem, because we had nowhere to establish a meeting place outside the casino. In the event of steam, the person taking it would have to jump in a cab outside and go to the emergency meeting place, which in this particular case was our motel.

Jerry was to do blackjack ten-o-fives with purple chips. While he waited in the keno pit with Duke, Joe and I went to the craps pit to get Jerry the purples he needed. Strangely, there were no purple chips on any of the craps tables. Standing at one of them was a big curly-haired guy who the craps crew was calling "Mr. M." He was on a big winning streak and had racks full of black chips. Everyone around the table was cheering him. He was betting three or four hundred every roll, taking odds and buying numbers, but the table handled his action with only blacks. We cruised the rest of the casino and couldn't find purples in any table rack—not even in the main baccarat pit.

Back in the keno pit, we discussed the situation. Joe was saying that it was sometimes difficult to get the purples in that casino, but he recalled never having seen it completely devoid of them. Yet Joe did not want to leave Reno without at least getting a few ten-o-fives paid on the blackjack table. "Here's what I want you to do," he said to me. "Go up to the cage and tell the teller that you want to buy two purple chips. Normally, they don't sell chips at the cage, but you're going to give them a story. Say that your wife just loves this hotel and wants the chips to put on the necklace she just bought at the MGM jewelry shop. You're gonna take a little steam, but maybe they'll sell you the chips. We've got nothing to lose."

I wasn't too crazy about Joe's idea. "What happens if Jerry takes steam on the moves?" I asked. "How will we get rid of the chips?" The questions I posed were well founded. Since we'd have the only two "walking" purples in the casino, we'd have a problem cashing them out if we took steam. If Jerry had a miss, or got ratted out after a payoff, all the pit boss had to do was notify the cashier cage to be on the lookout for anyone trying to cash out purple chips. All the other pits inside the casino could be alerted likewise, and then we'd be stuck with the purples and might *really* have to consider putting them on somebody's wife's necklace.

Joe was all too aware of that possibility, but once again his confidence in the move won out. He sent me to the cage with $1,000 in hundred-dollar bills. I chose the teller with the friendliest disposition, gave her my story. She smiled, but said I'd have to buy the chips at one of the gambling tables. The cage did not sell chips.

"But ma'am," I protested beseechingly, "there aren't any purple chips in the casino. And my wife will never settle for blacks. I *have* to do this for her."

The teller laughed. "I wish my husband thought like you once in a while."

"Can you ask your supervisor permission to sell me the chips?"

"Yes, sir, I can do that. But you do know that if you put holes in the chips they'll no longer be redeemable, and also that every three years or so the casino replaces its chips and you have a hundred and twenty days to redeem the old ones. After that, they're worthless."

"All that's my wife's problem. She just told me to buy her the purple chips, and I don't want to upset her. That would ruin my whole vacation, if you know what I mean."

She laughed again and went to talk to her supervisor. She reappeared a few minutes later with a broad smile. "Tell your wife to wear the necklace with a lot of good luck," she said kindly as she placed the two purples on the counter.

So Jerry had the purples for the ten-o-fives. He would have to use black chips for the backups.

The casino wasn't very crowded; there were a lot of dealers standing on dead blackjack tables. On one of those dead games stood a tall, gawky dealer named Skip, whose nameplate said he was from Redding, California. My teammates sat down at his table to create the action Jerry needed to do the move. I stayed in the background, knowing that my presence at the table might bring unwanted attention, given I had just bought the purples at the cage. I could easily be seen across the practically deserted casino floor by any pit boss who had been buzzed during the time I was at the cage. While I watched the blackjack table, I heard intermittent cheers coming from the craps pit where Mr. M. was playing. He must still be on a roll, I thought.

While Skip shuffled the six decks of cards he would use, Duke made small talk with him about Redding. Duke knew the area well, having undoubtedly conducted business matters there that concerned smoke rather than steam.

Skip clacked the large pack of cards against the side of the shoe to even them out, then placed them neatly inside it. He dealt the round and Jerry had a winner right off the bat. Duke and Joe had played two hands each to spread out the action. Skip busted, so all five hands on the layout were winners. An ideal situation for a move.

Skip grabbed a stack of red chips to pay off the hands. He cut first into Jerry's three red chips. Jerry moved on him like a cat and was already claiming before Skip had paid off Duke's first hand. Joe was at the other end of the table chinning.

"Hey, Skip!" Jerry shouted, revealing the stack of black backup chips in front of him. "You paid me wrong. I'm betting a thousand dollars here."

Skip's head wobbled back to Jerry. He looked down at the two purple chips underneath the red. For a moment, he didn't say anything. He just stood there with his mouth slightly agape. He looked like a big dope.

But then he screamed. I mean *screamed*. Like someone hit a

nerve switch connected to his brain. He started yelling at Jerry. "I saw you switch that bet! When I turned my head, you switched the chips. I saw you. You're a cheater."

This was one of those rare times that psychology worked against us. There was no way that Skip had seen Jerry switch the chips. In fact, it had taken him more than a second—relatively a long time—to realize what it was that Jerry was talking about. Suddenly, something had triggered a reaction in his brain that made him accuse Jerry of switching the chips. He may have known subconsciously that the purple chips underneath weren't there, but he could not have known that Jerry switched them in, even though he now really believed that he had seen Jerry do the switch. Nothing was perfect, I mused afterward. Nothing could work all the time in your favor.

Jerry did not have to wait for Joe to say "Gallo" to know he had to get out of there. With Skip still carrying on like a lunatic, Jerry snatched up his chips—which caused Skip to scream again—and darted across the casino at what seemed like the speed of light. As he headed toward the exit, a security guard carrying a chip-refill box to one of the tables crossed directly in front of him. The guard heard Skip screaming and realized immediately that Jerry was the culprit, but he could not put down or abandon the refill box when it contained chips for any reason. It was an unwritten law, like cops not giving up their weapons in any circumstances. The guard stopped and broadcast Jerry's escape over his radio. And that's exactly what it was. In broad daylight.

Jerry had a half-dozen security guards chasing him by the time he was out the door. He didn't have time to jump into a cab as planned in emergencies. The pursuing guards would have noticed and just as quickly radioed the Reno police department, who shared a common frequency with casino security. Jerry would have been trapped in the cab even before it got off the MGM property, and that's if the cabbie driving didn't just stop altogether when he realized he was participating in a getaway.

The closest building to the MGM was a First Interstate Bank of Nevada branch a mile away. Jerry was in excellent physical shape despite the cigarettes. He would need to cover that mile in perhaps world-class time to avoid capture.

Back at Skip's table inside the MGM there was total chaos. The floorman, pit boss, and two security guards were hovering around Skip, waiting for him to calm down. "What happened?" everybody kept asking him. "What did that guy do on your table?" Skip was panting as if *he* had just run a mile in record time. He couldn't find his voice to respond. Joe and Duke continued sitting at the table and witnessed the whole thing close up. It never occurred to anybody that they were involved. I went out another exit, then circled back to the front entrance to get a cab back to the motel. I had to get out of there quickly because I could be connected to Jerry's purple chips.

Skip finally caught his breath and told everyone what had happened. Unfortunately for us, his description was painfully accurate. "That guy bet three red chips on third base," he said to the pit boss, who was all ears. "Then after I paid him the $15, he switched in two purple chips underneath and accused me of paying him wrong. When I caught him, he got up and ran." When Skip had finished his recounting, he actually asked Joe in front of the pit boss if he had seen Jerry "sneak in the purples." Joe responded that he didn't generally mind other players' business.

Regardless of the fact that Skip had pretty fairly described what had happened, the proof that he didn't actually see the switch made was contained in his words. He told the pit boss that Jerry had switched in two purple chips after he had been paid. Though that was basically what it amounted to, it was not *exactly* what Jerry had done. Jerry had pulled out the three chips originally bet, switching back in two purples and one red—*three* chips. But for us, the damage was done. No more purple-chip pastposts in Reno that trip.

A half hour later, I was lying on my bed at the motel, nervous as hell. When someone knocked on the door, I jumped with a start. My first thought was that it was the police or gaming agents. Maybe Jerry had gotten grabbed up and had a pack of matches on him with our motel's name on it. We were all trained never to carry motel items on us when working (hotel keys were always removed from

their key rings), but it was possible that Jerry had forgotten and inadvertently left something identifying the Quick Inn in his pocket.

I was superrelieved when I looked through the peephole and saw
Jerry's distorted image at the door.

"Shit," he said, stepping inside. "That was a close shave."

"How'd you get back here?" I asked, closing the door quickly
behind him.

"I ran a fucking mile to that bank on the edge of the MGM
property. There were no cabs around and the dicks were coming after
me. I thought I was done. Then I saw a guy sitting in a convertible
at the drive-in window. I flashed two twenties in his face and told
him to step on it. He took the money and said, 'Hop in.' "

Jerry tossed the two purple chips on the bed. "I guess we're stuck
with them awhile."

Twenty minutes later Joe and Duke were back in the room. We
were all laughing about Skip's hysterical reaction.

"Too bad we're stuck with those purples," Duke said.

"Maybe not," I said.

Joe's eyes raised from the *Wall Street Journal* he'd been reading
on the bed. "How's that?"

"Did you notice that high roller on the craps table with all those
blacks, Mr. M.?"

"Yeah, why?"

"Maybe I can sell him the purples. He had at least ten grand in
blacks when I passed him by on the way out the door. I'll put on a
ball cap and zeros"—glasses whose lenses have no ocular power—
"so nobody recognizes me from the cage. Then I'll go right up to
Mr. M. on the craps table and wait for the right moment to propose
a chip exchange."

Joe liked the idea right away. "Let's go," he said. "Just be careful
not to let anyone in the pit see what's going on." We discussed the
strategy in the car on the way back to the MGM. Even this minor
operation to cash out $1,000 had to be planned efficiently. There
was the danger that Mr. M. would find it insulting that I approached
him on the craps table to sell him chips. If he became upset, he

might alert the pit, and then I could all of a sudden be grabbed up and detained as a coconspirator to the move.

When I entered the casino and approached the craps table, Joe followed at a distance, prepared to hustle back to the car and scoop me up if a problem developed. Mr. M. was still playing, his racks still filled with black chips, though their numbers had dwindled a bit. The length of each row was about the same, but the chips were fitted in just a little looser, tilted ever so slightly on their sides. Mr. M. was one of those gamblers who constantly rearranged his chips to psychologically soften the blows of the casino axe chopping away at them. But he still had several thousand bucks' worth in his racks. I just hoped he wasn't superstitious against purple chips.

I squeezed in next to him as he took the dice from the stickman but stayed a little bit behind to avoid being overly noticed by the dealer and boxman on the table. I couldn't interrupt Mr. M. while he was shooting, so I waited until he sevened out, which he did after making a couple of points. I edged up to him and spoke as though we knew each other. "Mr. M., how they [the dice] treating you today?"

Mr. M. had certainly downed a few that afternoon at the craps table. When he turned around to face me, I got a nice whiff of the alcohol. However, his inebriety served my purpose. When he said, "Not too bad, partner," I had the impression he really thought he did know me.

I didn't waste any time on him. "Mr. M.," I said casually as I boldly dropped the two purples in the corner of his chip rack, "you wouldn't mind giving me ten of your lucky blacks, would you? I gotta get some of my money back from this damn casino."

Mr. M. laughed, slugging a mouthful of his scotch. "I know what you mean, partner." He picked up the purples and stuck them in his jacket pocket, the best thing he could have done from my perspective. He was placing them immediately out of view, which avoided any chance of casino personnel seeing them and sounding the alarm before I got out the door. He then gave me the blacks and wished me luck.

When I placed the black chips Mr. M. had given me in front of the cashier I got a pleasant surprise. There were eleven of them.

Watching the local evening news in the room, everybody enjoyed a laugh when we saw poor Mr. M. being led away from the MGM casino cage in handcuffs, undoubtedly accused of possessing two purple chips used in a pastpost.

The Reno-Lake Tahoe leg of my first road trip was over. We had a big dinner at a well-known Reno steakhouse, then went back to the room to split up the money. For the three-week trip we cleared about $30,000. Duke and Jerry were each given $5,000 cash. The other $2,500 they each earned was left in the team bank. Joe and I left all our money in the bank. While on the road, I surely didn't need much cash. But I was thinking that when the road trip was over and we got back to Vegas, I would get myself a really nice apartment and a new sports car. With all this hard work and risking of my ass, I deserved both.

Joe Classon and the Pioneers

It was over Thanksgiving dinner at Marlene Classon's condominium apartment in Miami Beach that I learned the colorful history of pastposting casinos. Joe's mother, a rather stylish woman in her seventies, actually referred to her son as "my son the casino pastposter." Listening to Joe's narration while we ate and drank, I was enthralled, so much so that I must pass his story down to you. Of course, I did not witness any of these events firsthand, but the way I will recount it to you is exactly how he told it to me.

To appreciate the history of pastposting and all its legendary characters, you have to first start with the Classon family. Joe was the second son born to Marlene and Herman Classon in 1933, on New York's predominantly Jewish Lower East Side. Herman was a bread, eggs, and milk deliveryman who managed to make a decent living thanks to various well-thought-out fudging methods that allowed him to steal half the loaves and cartons from his own van and sell them along his own private route when he was finished with his assigned one. Joe's eight-years-older brother Henry was forced to quit school while still in his teens after Herman was unfortunately killed by a

wooden board that had fallen on his head from the roof of Yankee
Stadium. It was never determined whether or not someone had
thrown the board, nor was it determined what Herman was doing
outside Yankee Stadium on a midsummer Sunday afternoon when
the Yankees were in Chicago.

Henry got work in a little East Side grocery that had been on
his father's legal route. He stocked the shelves, took inventory, and
made deliveries on foot. But he wasn't much for that kind of work,
and it wasn't long before he was running numbers for the neighborhood's Jewish bookmaker. One of the bookmaker's customers was
Stanley Berron, Marlene Classon's brother. Both Henry and his little
brother Joe loved and admired their uncle Stanley. When Stanley
wasn't gambling, he was usually doing something creative, which
wasn't much of the time. One of the things he *did* do was write a
book about how the Great Depression affected the Jewish immigrants
in New York. A few years later, tapped out after blowing his royalties
from the book, Stanley was arrested in a New York bookstore for
stealing his own book. He'd needed it as proof to win a bet with an
Italian bookmaker who refused to believe that Henry had ever written anything more than an IOU or bad check. When the clerk caught
him stuffing the book into his trousers, Stanley protested, "I'm not
stealing it; it's *my* book." The clerk took him for a nut and called
the cops. When the cops found out that Stanley had actually written
the book they had arrested him for stealing, they had a station-house
war story that would be passed along to generations of Irish, Italian,
and even Jewish cops in the squad room.

Stanley taught his two nephews how to play poker, eight years
apart, and they both developed into skilled players. But there were
a lot of skilled players on the Lower East Side, so Henry, no longer
wanting to leave the outcome of the neighborhood poker games to
chance, began cheating. He learned how to operate with both shaved
and marked cards. Then he got into crooked dice. He even learned
how to manipulate legitimate dice, control their tumble as they were
thrown. When Joe was fifteen, Henry began teaching him everything
he himself had learned. They became partners and started working
the Fourteenth and Twenty-third Street card and dice games to-

gether, ripping off the neighborhood's tailors, grocers, and shoemakers.

Joe stayed in high school and managed to get his diploma despite a few suspensions for gambling in the cafeteria. His best friend was a chubby Italian kid named Chester Gallo. Chester was famous in the neighborhood for probably being the only person in the history of the world to get hit in the head by two baseballs off two bats from two different ball games at the same instant. Unfortunately, at the time, there were no portable camcorders to catch the hilarious moment when Chester Gallo was playing right field for his little league team and lost one high pop in the sun while another from the neighboring baseball diamond arced at him from the rear. The ball dropping out of the sun hit Chester smack in between the eyes just as the one from behind clanked off the back of his head. Both balls ended up home runs. Amazingly, Chester wasn't injured. He even got his picture in the paper. The caption said the occurrence was as odd as getting hit by lighting. In remembrance of Chester Gallo, Henry and Joe Classon would later use his name for communicating trouble in casinos. It was like a "Hey, watch out!" that evolved into a "Run for it!" which is probably what Chester should have done that unforgettable day on Manhattan's Lower East Side the moment he heard the cracks of both bats.

In 1951 Stanley Berron died of a heart attack, causing Joe to plunge into depression. His uncle had been like a father to him. Now that he was gone, Joe lost interest in the poker games and began wandering the streets aimlessly, sometimes panhandling when he needed money. A few months after they put Stanley in the ground, Joe went off and joined the army, and soon found himself in Korea.

Henry stayed in New York, working the craps and poker games by himself. He had also developed an affinity for horse betting. Most of the money he made nights at the East Side house games he blew off during the day at Aqueduct or Belmont, depending on the season. One cold winter afternoon at Aqueduct, Henry noticed a gaunt older man bent over in the throes of a nasty coughing fit by the snack bar on the lower level. He had just come in from the freezing air, watching another one of his horses get nosed out at the finish line.

"You want a glass of water?" Henry asked the man, tenderly hovering over him.

"Yeah, thanks," the man said in that hoarse, throaty whisper that rang of throat cancer.

Henry got a cup of water from the snack bar, cursing the attendant who demanded money before he let it go.

The man gulped down the water, let the cup fall to the floor, and straightened up. "Thirty-five years in a fucking grimy pocketbook factory in West New York," he rasped between coughs. "Now I got cancer in my throat. Must've been breathin' poison eight hours a day all them years."

Henry helped him over to a row of hard metal chairs by the men's room. He stayed with him long enough to miss betting the upcoming race.

"My doctor tells me I oughta go down to Florida for the winter, be better for this son-of-a-bitching cough I got. I ain't never been lucky at Hialeah, though, or any of them other goddamn Florida tracks for that matter. I don't know, I got a sister in Puerto Rico. She's a nurse. Maybe I oughta go there. They got the flats there too, you know. Come on, let's go up to the clubhouse."

Henry saw the man again at Aqueduct a few days later. This time he told him his name.

"Call me Mumbles," he said.

"Mumbles?"

"Yeah, *Mumbles*, like it sounds. My buddies think it's funny." Mumbles sensed that Henry wanted to know if he got that nickname before or after the big C, so he told him. "Yeah, I picked up the name when my voice box started goin'."

Henry began hanging out regularly with mumbles at Aqueduct. Each afternoon they'd meet on the ground level, then Mumbles would take Henry up to the clubhouse, where a friend of his working the turnstile let them in for nothing. Mumbles was coughing all the time and even had an occasional cigarette despite Henry's objections. Every so often Mumbles gave Henry a tip on a horse, and it usually won. At the end of the meet, Mumbles told Henry he was going to take his doctor's advice and spend the rest of the winter in a warm climate. He refused to go to Florida, so he decided to try his luck at the San Juan racetrack while he stayed with his sister, who was a registered nurse and could watch over him. Henry and Mumbles said their goodbyes at the end of the ninth race on the last day of the winter meet. Henry wondered if he'd ever see Mumbles again.

The next time he saw him was two years later. Mumbles hadn't been to Aqueduct since he'd last seen Henry, and had gone there specifically to find him. He had an incredible tale to tell his young friend, who was more surprised that Mumbles was still alive than he was by his reappearing at the finish line.

Mumbles had found the tropical climate of Puerto Rico very agreeable with his health. The cough had substantially subsided, and his new Puerto Rican doctor promised a few more years of life. He had decided to make the best of whatever time he had left. Every morning before his sister went to work at the hospital, she drove Mumbles to a coffee shop near the San Juan racetrack. There he read the racing forms and after lunch walked over to the track. Mumbles soon discovered that Florida was not the only tropical place whose racetracks treated him shitty. After quickly burying himself under losing horses, Mumbles took what was left from his pension and social security checks and tried his luck at San Juan's craps tables. He didn't fare very well in the casinos either, but one day stumbled onto something that was to drastically change what was left of his life.

Mumbles had been gambling at a craps table at the Americana. He was betting red five-dollar chips on the pass line next to another player who had just increased his previous ten-dollar bet of two red chips to a thirty-dollar bet of one green and one red chip. The shooter threw a seven on the come-out roll and the dealer paid the pass-line bets. A funny thing happened: the dealer shortchanged the guy betting next to Mumbles. He hadn't seen the green chip underneath the red. He'd thought the guy's bet was just two red chips and therefore only paid him $10. The guy hollered at the dealer, claiming he got gypped. The dealer slid the top red chip off his bet, stunned to see the green underneath. He quickly apologized and correctly paid the guy $30.

Mumbles was recounting the incident to his sister that night at the kitchen table. "Imagine that," he said indignantly, "even when you win in these damned casinos you gotta watch out that you don't get robbed."

"I'm sure that the dealer made an honest mistake," his sister said, defending the casino and mankind. "They couldn't stay in business by doing things like that on purpose."

Mumbles dismissed what he considered his sister's ignorance and went into the parlor to watch television. He couldn't stop thinking about the incident. He was watching the *Honeymooners* in Spanish when the thought that would eventually lead him to invent modern pastposting entered his head. It was the word *honest* that was gnawing at him. His sister had said that the dealer at the Americana had made an honest mistake. Then why, Mumbles asked himself, couldn't casino dealers make more honest mistakes like that? How could they be prodded to make that mistake? It was in the answers to those questions that casino pastposting was born.

Mumbles had kept the image of what he'd seen at that craps table in his head. The dealer had paid him, then paid the guy next to him errantly, then paid three or four more players along the table before the guy realized the dealer had shortchanged him. Although he knew it wasn't the case, Mumbles reasoned that the guy would have had enough time to slip that green chip under his bet while the dealer was occupied paying the other people at the table. And he also realized there was nothing sneaky about having your hands out there after you've been paid because it was quite natural for players to pick up their chips immediately. So, concluded Mumbles, if a player with a larcenous heart pulled a little chip-switch after the dealer made his payoff, he should be able to coerce that dealer into thinking he had made an *honest* mistake and underpaid the bet. That the dealer at the Americana never questioned the legitimacy of the green chip's presence, despite having never seen it, was what really stirred Mumbles up.

The next morning at breakfast his sister asked if he wanted to be dropped off at the coffee shop by the track. Mumbles told her he wasn't betting on horses anymore. "I'll take the bus to the casino," he said.

"*The casino?* I thought you didn't trust the casinos."

"I don't, but I'm going there anyway."

Less than an hour later Mumbles was hunched over a craps table at the Americana, in the corner, right next to the dealer. He figured being so close was advantageous. The angle was good, and he could switch the chips underneath the dealer's outstretched arms which gave him shade (cover). He put two red chips on the pass line. The shooter threw craps dice and Mumbles watched his chips get swept off the layout. He put down two more and watched the dice seven out. Mumbles cursed, coughed, and lit a cigarette as the stickman passed him the dice. Then he did something he had never before done in his life: he declined the dice. At that very early stage of conceiving the pastpost, Mumbles had instinctively realized it was not a good idea to shoot the dice while thinking about cheating the casino at craps. It was kind of like mixing booze and medicine.

The dice passed to the man on Mumbles's left, who established a point, then a winner. The dealer paid Mumbles, then proceeded along the pass line paying the other players. Mumbles bent over and carefully switched the $30 for the $10. He was not very fast, he knew, but the chip placement was perfect. Mumbles gave his work a final look-see before opening his mouth. He took a deep breath, was delayed by a cough, finally getting his hoarse whisper out to the dealer. "Hey, I bet $30!"

The dealer heard nothing. Mumbles's vocal cords, eaten away by the cancer, were not strong enough to deliver the claim.

Mumbles picked up the chips and went back to the drawing board. He knew he had a serious problem. In casinos with all that noise all the time, especially the clanking slot machines, how the hell was a dealer going to hear him? He thought about employing some-body else to do the move. There was Roberto from the track, an elderly Puerto Rican gentleman with whom Mumbles had shared opinions on horses while sipping coffee and reading the racing form. But Mumbles quickly disqualified that option. He knew he was onto something with vast potential; he couldn't trust anyone with his knowledge. Oh sure, he could trust his sister, but no Florence Nightingale was going to get behind a craps table and start switching chips.

The decision Mumbles came to was that he had to physically confront the dealer. Grab his arm, make him aware that he'd bet a green chip underneath. It was a little blatant, but they'd have to understand that a guy who couldn't speak had no other alternative for getting the dealer's attention.

Mumbles went back to the Americana. He made the ten-dollar bet on the pass line, and when it won switched the chips and grabbed the dealer's arm—and got paid.

Mumbles was in business. Every day he went to the casinos in San Juan. Between the craps tables at the Americana, El San Juan, and Condado Beach casinos he was popping in ten thirty-dollar moves a day. Minus the losing bets, bus fare, and whatever he ate and drank, Mumbles was making $150 a day. His sister nearly collapsed from shock when Mumbles announced he was taking her out for dinner in the El San Juan's gourmet restaurant.

Another casino game soon intrigued Mumbles: roulette. He mused, as he watched the little ivory ball spinning around the cylinder with all those different colored chips on the layout, that there had to be some good opportunities to cheat the casino. He noticed right off that dealers worked like robots. They spun the ball, announced and pointed to the winning number on the layout (the roulette marking piece was not yet in use), swept the losing chips, and paid the winners. The first thing striking Mumbles as opportune was that dealers often turned their backs to the layout when sweeping off losing chips.

If I could only take advantage of that and slip in a bet after the dealer indicated the winning number, he thought.

He knew he couldn't do it with a bare five-dollar casino chip. Casino chips weren't often bet at roulette and stuck out conspicuously on the layout. One suddenly found on top of a winning number would be too obvious; the dealer would know it hadn't been there before his back was turned. But in order to make pastposting roulette worthwhile, casino chips *had* to be used. The problem was how to pastpost five-dollar chips in a more subtle or camouflaged way. The solution was what Mumbles would later call the "naked capper." By stealing a roulette chip off the layout and then waiting for that particular player to win on one of the numbers inside, Mumbles could capitalize by pastposting two additional chips on top of the winning chips already placed while the dealer's back was turned—his red five-dollar chip covered by the stolen roulette chip. And stealing other players' chips proved easier than he had imagined. People scattered their chips over roulette layouts by the fistful and in such a hurry that a few could be scooped up by quick fingers without anyone noticing. Harried roulette players hardly ever kept track of all their chips on the layout. There simply wasn't time.

Mumbles went into the Condado Beach casino and stole an American tourist's sky-blue roulette chip. He waited until that tourist hit a number straight up at the bottom of the layout. When the dealer turned his back while sweeping off the losers, Mumbles laid his five-dollar chip, covered by the roulette chip stolen from the tourist, on top of the tourist's chips already on the number. He got paid $175! The tourist got paid a bonus, too, and smiled along with Mumbles.

Mumbles estimated that 25 percent of roulette dealers accorded him a sufficient turn for pastposting while sweeping chips. But that was not enough, he decided. He needed to find another chink in their armor through which he could do more moves. He envisioned using a "block" with an obstacle formed to hinder the dealer's line of sight. Perhaps he could engage an unwitting coconspirator to play roulette on the same table. He would have this person stand on the inside of the table, as close to the dealer as was permitted, placing bets on red and black at the other side of the layout. In those days casinos let you begin placing bets for the upcoming spin before the dealer finished paying off the previous spin's winners. When a third-section number won, this check-bettor could lunge across the layout and bet any outside proposition that had just lost, momentarily obscuring the dealer's vision of the bottom of the layout. By the time the check-bettor was again upright, the move would already be in.

Mumbles worked on his sister a week, trying to get her interested in playing roulette, but she refused, saying she had caught a cold the

last time she'd entered "that freezing casino." He was forced to turn
to his friend Roberto from the track, but without compromising the
move. He told Roberto that he wanted to test a red-black betting
system, and that since he had to keep track of the outcomes in his
head, he didn't have time to place the bets himself. He offered Roberto ten bucks an hour to make the bets, plus a bonus if he won.
Roberto agreed and they went out to work. If he was suspicious that
Mumbles was bullshitting him, he didn't care at ten bucks an hour.

Roberto's being short was advantageous because he really did
have to lunge to reach the red and black boxes on the outside. Mumbles had him wear a sports jacket that was several sizes too big and
hung loosely, so that when Roberto leaned over the table making
the bets, his jacket tails blossomed, widening the dealer's blind spot,
and that gave Mumbles plenty of time to lay in the five-dollar naked
cappers while keeping Roberto in the dark. They worked together
in that fashion for several months, Mumbles telling Roberto that once
in a while he felt lucky and made five-dollar bets straight up on the
number.

Beatable dealers had risen to 60 percent. The problem that eventually developed with the block was that a lot of dealers felt uncomfortable with a player so close to them, and some began complaining
to the pit bosses. Soon the casinos began installing wooden rods that
protruded from the inside of the table between the dealer and the
bottom of the layout. Players had to remain on their side of the barrier, so the effectiveness of the block was greatly reduced. With the
advent of the rod Roberto was given his walking papers.

Mumbles next turned to designing betting schemes which made
dealers turn as often as possible. He accomplished this by putting into
play the stacks of chips deepest in the dealer's well. But he couldn't
create the ideal scenarios himself; he needed help. If somebody else
made the bets, he could pop in his naked cappers a lot more often.
Reluctantly, Mumbles finally decided it was time to get someone
else *knowingly* involved.

He didn't trust Roberto or any of the other Puerto Ricans he
knew—they talked too much over rum—so he telephoned a ruddy-
faced Irishman he'd met in the trenches in France during World War

I. The Irishman's name was Rusty, but after he took a shard of shrapnel in the spine at Verdun, Mumbles (who was not yet Mumbles) and his platoon buddies nicknamed him Wheels because Rusty was about the fastest thing around in a wheelchair. Mumbles had hung out with Wheels in the Irish bars in Manhattan. They'd often gone to the track together, but Wheels favored the watering holes. The dominant memory Mumbles had about Wheels gambling was that the Irishman, drunk or sober, hated to lose. With that in mind, Mumbles tracked down his buddy at a Blarney Stone bar on Forty-eighth Street in Manhattan.

"Wheels, it's me," Mumbles said. A formal identification was never necessary, given the state of Mumbles's voice.

"Mumbles, what's up, good buddy?"

"I got a gambling proposition for you."

"You know I don't like to lose, Mumbles."

"You won't, Wheels."

"I'll drink to that."

Mumbles and his sister picked up Wheels at the San Juan airport. Mumbles had rented a van with special equipment for Wheels. They drove back to the sister's apartment where she made them Irish stew. Then when the sister went to bed early in order to get up for work the next morning, Mumbles got the chips he'd hidden in the cookie jar and began demonstrating his tricks to Wheels on the kitchen table.

The next day they were at a roulette table at the El San Juan. Mumbles had Wheels roll up to the table and buy the roulette chips stacked at the back of the dealer's chip well. "All you do is bet a stack of chips in the third-dozen box," he had told him. "That's the box that covers all the numbers from 25 through 36. You got that?" And so the implementation of the check-bettor was complete.

Wheels caught on quickly. He bet his stack in the third-dozen box while Mumbles laid his naked capper on top of another player's winning chips, and claimed. Their first collusion worked beautifully; Mumbles got paid $175, clapping loudly, pointing at his bet to make the dealer aware of the five-dollar chip. After ten moves they really had it down. After twenty, Mumbles began making structural changes. He realized they could do the moves without any players on the table. If Wheels bet the third-dozen stack *and* all the third-section numbers straight up, they'd have twelve numbers covered every spin. All Mumbles would have to do is pop in the capper with one of Wheels's chips and claim. In fact, Wheels became so good that Mumbles got the clever idea of having *him* pop in the cappers. Mumbles no longer had to sit down at the tables. Wheels bought his chips, made the bets, and popped in the five-dollar chips for Mumbles under his own roulette chips. Mumbles then arrived at the tables to claim the win. At the time, you could play roulette with ten-cent chips, so the spread to $5 was quite significant. Those $175 payoffs in the early fifties were big.

Thus the two-man "lay and claim" was born. Wheels became a proficient mechanic; Mumbles mumbled away the best he could with the claims. He would have liked Wheels to do some of the claiming, but he came to his senses when he realized that his buddy might have a little difficulty if he had to *really* hurry out of a casino.

Mumbles recognized the value of the lay-and-claim method at craps. At first, he believed it impossible that Wheels could mechanic craps tables. How could a guy in a wheelchair get up to a craps table and then reach way down on the layout to switch the chips? Well, Wheels's paralysis affected his body only *below* the waist, and coincidentally, he had unusually long arms. When Mumbles had related his doubts to Wheels over a beer in the only Irish pub in San Juan, the Irishman raised his glass triumphantly and laughed. "You must be joking, old buddy. You think that after being in the trenches in France and getting my ass shot off, a little bloody craps table in Puerto Rico's gonna frighten me off?"

Despite the courage and determination Wheels showed on the craps tables, he was better on the roulette wheels. Besides, Mumbles enjoyed the legerdemain at roulette much more. He appreciated the simple complexity of designing roulette moves. It was clockwork. You made certain bets, the dealers made certain movements, and you moved. Mumbles loved the feeling of control he had over roulette dealers. By betting his patterns he controlled them like puppets on a string. And with his buddy Wheels at his side, it really was reminiscent of a military operation. But on the green felt battlefields in the casino, there wasn't the risk of flying bullets and shrapnel.

Mumbles had heard a lot of stories about the fifties gambling boom in Las Vegas from the old cronies at Aqueduct. Now in his sixties—and dying of throat cancer—he decided to have one final thrill in life before going up to the giant casino in the sky. He tossed around the idea of going to Cuba but opted rather for an adventure in the world's gambling capital, Las Vegas, Nevada. He had given his sister a shoebox before they left for the airport. "Put this in your closet," he had instructed her. "It might come in handy for you." His sister put it on the top shelf of her closet, underneath the shoeboxes she already had there. She didn't open it but guessed ominously that it contained money. However, she would have been bowled over that there was $15,000 inside.

Neither Mumbles nor Wheels had ever been out west. The exhilaration of heading there made the two old men feel young again, like two pastposting pioneers. And that's what they were. Instead of the picks and axes taken out west by the gold rushers a century before, Mumbles and Wheels went with the only tools they had— their wits and their balls. If there had ever been a casino pastposting hall of fame, or a museum, Mumbles and Wheels would have undeniably had their shrines there. They were the true founding fathers of modern pastposting.

In the 1950s there were only five (small by today's standards) casinos on the Las Vegas Strip: the Flamingo, Desert Inn, Sands, El Rancho, and Thunderbird. There were also the gambling halls downtown. Mumbles and Wheels decided to start downtown because its arcadelike casinos were all lined up one next to the other, and it was much easier for them to get in and out and around than it would have been on the Strip. They checked into a room at Binion's Horseshoe, already the downtown centerpiece in the fifties. Before they got up to the room on the second floor, Mumbles left Wheels at the clerk's desk and ran into the casino to pop in a thirty-dollar craps move. He told Wheels upstairs that he wanted to break the ice before they went to bed after the tiring journey.

Mumbles was fascinated by the difference in atmosphere between the Vegas and Puerto Rican gambling worlds. The Caribbean casinos in the hotels didn't have the garish neon lights. In Vegas, the hotels were *in* the casinos. How cheap everything was! For a quarter you could have breakfast, and lunch and dinner for ninety-nine cents. And the weather—how gorgeous! (It was early May, before the arrival of the searing desert heat.) Mumbles was thinking he would telephone his sister to tell her he was staying out in the desert forever; he'd found a new retirement home.

So, to solidify that retirement plan, Mumbles and Wheels went out to work. They hit the roulette tables on both sides of Fremont Street—day and night. Wheels rolled up to the tables, bought the roulette chips, check-bet the layouts, and popped in the moves, switching out stacks of chips, laying in the stacks containing Mumbles's five-dollar chips. Mumbles mumbled his claims in one joint after the other. Nobody questioned them. Nobody grew suspicious of the two old-timers, one in the wheelchair, the other gasping for breath as he collected the payoffs.

Those payoffs mounted. The first four days in Vegas they averaged ten a day, $1,750. On the fifth day, they began to experience fatigue and only got seven moves paid. At the end of the sixth night, they were exhausted and went to bed with just $450 in profits.

On the morning of the seventh day, Wheels died. He complained of nausea when Mumbles helped him out of bed into his wheelchair. Then, once in the chair, Wheels gasped, his eyes rolled, and he slumped over. Mumbles knew right away his old Irish war buddy was dead. But at least, Mumbles reflected as he watched the ambulance with his friend's body inside disappear into the morning sun, Wheels could not have asked for a better trench to die in.

And such was the tale Mumbles recounted to Henry Classon in the clubhouse at Aqueduct after not having seen him for two years.

Henry was utterly fascinated. Already educated in the art of cheating at gambling, he had no problem comprehending what Mumbles explained to him. He had always avoided New York's backroom gambling joints offering casino table games. The first lesson he'd learned from Uncle Stanley was never gamble away from your own backyard.

But cheating legitimate casinos without equipment was the ultimate! Henry knew enough about the dangers of plying the tools of the trade. He knew about craps sharpies switching in loaded dice, about "stringers" working slot machines with wire coils. All that, Henry knew, led to jail, or worse for stringers, who were occasionally unearthed in the desert, their own coils snaked around their necks.

Henry flew down to San Juan with Mumbles a week later. Though the tourist season was ending, there was still enough action in the casinos for Mumbles to teach him the moves. They started out on craps, Mumbles mechanicking, Henry claiming. After two weeks of that, Henry took his first shot as mechanic. Judging by his stellar performance as a claimer, Mumbles expected nothing but the best from Henry as mechanic. He was not disappointed; his junior partner began popping in craps moves all over San Juan. A particular talent, Mumbles noticed with proud satisfaction, was Henry's uncanny ability to squeeze into jammed-up craps tables without disturbing the players he brushed aside. He penetrated the human barrier against the rail just as the action peaked, seemingly melting inside it as he laid in the move.

Henry learned roulette, but he preferred craps. His appreciation of roulette's artsyness was less than Mumbles's. He liked the bang-bang at the craps table. Put the pass-line bet down, winner-seven and pow!—switch the chips. He loved the feel of clay chips, loved touching them and rubbing them up like a pitcher did a baseball. A casino chip's magical touch was something that could be passed down through generations, he reflected.

Young Henry Classon had a few ideas of his own. He recognized that Mumbles, being from the old school, wasn't thinking big enough. Those five-dollar nickels on the roulette numbers were chump change, Henry thought. Why not pop in quarters? Well, Mumbles had already thought of that but estimated it too big. The green chips on the inside, Mumbles protested, would bring the heat. The little nickels at $175 a shot were "swallowable" for the casinos. Henry didn't argue—he'd wait and see what conditions were like in Vegas.

Another of Henry's ideas blew Mumbles away: doing craps moves with the odds bet in addition to the pass-line bet.

"How the hell you gonna switch all them chips?" Mumbles had hoarsely whispered in astonishment on the balcony of his new beach-front high-rise apartment in San Juan's Condado Beach District. His sister had gone to bed in her private bedroom. Henry and Mumbles had been discussing business as they watched the scattered small boats drifting aimlessly on the moonlit sea. Henry urged Mumbles back inside the apartment to answer his reasonable question. He picked up the stack of chips sitting on the coffee table. "Like this." He showed Mumbles how to cut the move-chips into layers and how the double move took barely an instant longer than the single.

Mumbles didn't need much convincing. They did their first craps move with odds at the Americana casino. Coincidentally, the dealer they beat, Mumbles recognized, was the same dealer who had made the honest mistake on the $30 pass-line bet that had launched his whole casino operation. Mumbles had given him a little smile of appreciation just before Henry laid in the move. It was his own thanks to that dealer for his unwitting contribution to pastposting.

Henry and Mumbles arrived in Las Vegas in the summer of 1954. What they did there virtually changed the procedure for dealing rou-lette all over the world. Mumbles had been right about pastposting green chips straight up on the layout. The $875 payoffs for $25 bets were not digested as easily by the casinos as the $175 for nickels had been. Henry's philosophy differed from the old man's. He was ada-mant that it was better to go for the throat, to get the max every time. In the fifties, most of the wheels in Las Vegas were not yet taking black chips straight up on numbers, thus greens were big time. Henry reasoned that heat would eventually come from the nickels also—albeit slower—but not *five times* slower. He didn't like the idea of having to do five moves to obtain what they could in one. Like any craggy old-timer, Mumbles was tough—but he bent. When at the crossroads, Mumbles always thought about mortality. What a shame it would be to die without seeing the pastpost reach its next level of development, its next plateau. And he loved Henry's spirit.

So they swept through the downtown casinos and onto the Strip, moving quarters on the wheels. The heat came as Mumbles had predicted, but there wasn't much the casinos could do to protect themselves. In those days casinos didn't have the surveillance systems they do today. Instead of the ubiquitous cameras in the sky, surveillance depended on the old catwalks above the casino floor. They were similar to narrow prison tiers and crisscrossed the entire casino. Surveillance inspectors walked along them with binoculars, spying the action below through one-way-mirrors. Wise guys used to joke that casino catwalks were modeled after the sewers of Paris, which traversed the depths of the City of Light like a subway system.

After nearly two months in Vegas, word about Henry and Mumbles was spreading around to casino surveillance offices. They become known as roulette pastposters and their photos taken from above (not very good quality) accompanied the warnings casinos sent each other. But no casino had managed to set up the two-man team and film the actual move.

Henry and Mumbles were no dummies. They didn't press their luck. Feeling the steam rise in the casino air above roulette wheels, they snuck over to the craps tables and continued plying their trade. The money wasn't as big as in roulette, but Henry was popping in moves as fast as the dice could flash seven. Mumbles had his craps claim down pat. Taking the strain off his degenerating vocal cords, he was grabbing dealers' arms, then mumbling unintelligibly as he pointed to his bet. The shock his touch generated was very effective and more than made up for the lack of sound. In fact, *grâce à* Mumbles's vocal handicap, all craps moves, and later all blackjack moves, were to be claimed by physically touching the dealer as soon as the chips were switched. That interruption magnified the words coming with it.

In their hotel room one night at the Horseshoe, Henry wanted to bring up the subject of moving black chips on craps tables. Before he got the chance, Mumbles began coughing and gagging uncontrollably. Henry immediately called casino security and they rushed Mumbles off to the hospital. The next morning Henry went to visit him. His face was ashen and his voice practically gone. They had him all doped up, so at least he wasn't in pain.

Mumbles motioned Henry over to the bed. Henry bent down and put his ear to Mumbles' mouth. The foul odor of his dying breath was disgusting, but Henry braved it to hear Mumbles's final words. The father of modern pastposting mustered everything he had left to manage a whisper to his young protégé. His final words were: "It's your war now. It's your war against the casinos . . . casino wars . . ."

Henry removed a red five-dollar chip from his trousers pocket and placed it inside Mumbles's hospital gown, on his heart. Then with tears in his eyes, he said, "Mumbles, you get to join your old partner Wheels again. Good luck to both of you."

The Classon Pastposting Team

JUST A FEW MONTHS BEFORE MUMBLES DIED, JOE CLASSON RETURNED from Korea and was honorably discharged from the United States Army. Though his time spent abroad had not been as lucrative as Henry's in the casinos, Joe had not starved. Not daring to cheat his army buddies at poker underneath the Pyongyang bridge, Joe consistently beat them honestly. When he arrived back in Manhattan, however, Joe had other things on his mind besides gambling. He had become interested in Wall Street, thinking that stocks could present him with interesting challenges, a kind of honorable gambling. He decided to learn everything he could about the market. He read the *Wall Street Journal* daily, became familiar with trader terms. Then he got himself hired as a "squat" on the NYSE. Had his brother Henry never met Mumbles that day at Aqueduct, Joe Classon probably would've had a dynamic career in Manhattan's financial district. But when he listened to his brother recount all the adventures in Puerto Rico and Las Vegas, Joe Classon—at least temporarily—forgot the very existence of Wall Street.

He kissed his mother goodbye and joined Henry in Vegas. The

elder brother had already very comfortably installed himself in a brand-new house overlooking the Desert Inn golf course. He didn't yet own it, he explained to Joe, but was working on it.

Joe put his duffel bag in the second bedroom and took a short nap before the training program began. The fact that he had just gotten out of the army was a plus as far as Henry was concerned. Joe was quick to learn and able to follow instructions. In Henry's eyes, the war against the casinos that Mumbles had wanted him to continue needed to be conducted like a military operation. Procedure had to be adhered to. Joe soon realized that his older brother was as strict as any drill sergeant he'd had in boot camp.

The first time Joe claimed one of Henry's craps moves was at the Golden Nugget casino downtown, two months after Mumbles's death. He came off aggressively, as Henry had told him, but had a miss. The dealer said there was no green chip on the pass line and the casino refused to pay. Joe argued like a monster, but the pit boss refused to budge, telling Joe if he didn't like the casino's decision he could take it up with the Gaming Control Board. Joe told the guy to fuck off. Then he and Henry went right into another casino and did the same move and Joe got paid.

They continued doing craps moves. Henry was itching to put his younger brother on the wheels but figured it was still too dangerous, given all the recent steam he had taken at roulette with Mumbles. In order to increase profitability without using black chips, Henry began doing three-chip switches, two greens and a red replacing three reds. Along the way Joe had occasional misses, but the brothers kept plowing forward. After fifty payoffs on the craps tables they agreed it was time to do the first move with a black chip. It was at that juncture they came up with the bet-back procedure. It would look too suspicious to hit the casinos with a hundred-dollar bet and run, they reasoned. So each time Joe got paid $105 for a one-o-five, he bet back $30. When they opted for the three-chip two-o-five with two blacks and a red, Joe bet back $55, two greens and a red, conforming to the three-chip format of the move.

While working the craps tables, the newly recruited Joe Classon visualized another potential moneymaking operation that he deemed worthy enough to mention to Henry. On craps tables running hot with a lot of action, Joe told his brother, there were usually several players gathered around them with chips swelling in their racks. These players were always bending down to place their bets and pick up their chips from the layout. Their movements were in unison. When a shooter rolled a winner, the players bent down as one to collect their winnings. On a loser they did the same, replacing the swept-away chips on the layout. What Joe had noticed was that during these movements many of the players left their racks exposed. He figured that their chips could be picked away at. In Korea, one of the soldiers in his squadron had done something similar at campsite poker games. While other soldiers next to him on the ground leaned over to rake in winning pots, the crooked corporal deftly reached underneath them and pecked away at their chips. Had it not been for a curious and sore-losing captain, who one day after a long march decided to spy on him from behind with binoculars, the squadron chip-thief might have gone undetected for the rest of the war. Joe, who had lost who-knew-how-many chips to the corporal, had been quite impressed by the captain's demonstration of the corporal's art.

Henry and Joe Classon began closely observing other players around the tables. Henry soon came to the conclusion that his younger brother had been right. Many of the players made themselves susceptible targets for an agile chip-thief with quick hands along the rail of a craps table. Players drinking heavily as they gambled made the best targets. Another aspect of stealing other players' chips that delighted Henry was that you were no longer ripping off the casinos, so you couldn't take casino steam. Your principal danger was getting caught by the victim himself. True, there was the chance of being seen by a surveillance man walking the catwalks above, but that risk was minimal, because the catwalkers mainly looked for thieves and cheaters victimizing the casino, not its players.

Cruising the El Rancho one night in search of a mark, Joe came across a tall wobbling craps player underneath a Stetson hat who seemed to never put his whiskey in the glass-holder built into the rail. He constantly held it in his left hand, handling his chips with his right. His chip rack on the rail was filled with green chips.

Joe had wanted to be the first "railbird" (the art later became known as "railing") and pass whatever chips he could pick off to his brother standing behind him, but Henry vetoed that idea and told Joe to stand behind *him*.

Henry squeezed in between the mark and another player while Joe stood behind. He already had a fistful of red chips when he approached the table, again avoiding the contact with the dealer and boxman that would have been necessary had he bought chips at the table. He had learned from Mumbles that early chip preparation was essential, no matter what move was to be done.

The first nuance of railing was to make your mark feel comfortable with your presence. If he became nervous or fidgety, his natural move was to excessively protect his chips. More important than talking to your mark was ingratiating yourself by your movements. The key was to follow him, keep the same rhythm. When he bent over to make his bet, you made yours. When he bent over to pick up his chips, you did likewise. A little chitchat didn't hurt but wasn't mandatory. Not all gambling drunkards were open to conversation. You had to feel your mark's vibes.

Henry bet two red chips next to the mark's green chips. He had to be careful about the placement of his chips because if the mark wasn't comfortable with them, the occasion could be blown. In the same manner that you didn't want to crowd the mark with your presence, you didn't want to crowd him with your chips, either. If you bet your chips too close to his, he might *feel* the encroachment. If you bet too far away, he might also be disturbed for one reason or another, though too close was definitely worse than too far.

A final precondition the railbird needed to victimize his mark was a table that stayed hot. When a table went cold, it was the casino getting all his chips. Soon there was nothing left in his rack for you to peck away at. A table could go from hot to cold extremely fast.

Henry got into the guy's rhythm after just a couple of rolls. They exchanged a little small talk about how the table was running good. The guy laughed, even patted Henry on the back. He would be a perfect mark.

When the mark reached down to pick up the chips the dealer

had just paid him, Henry reached down with him to pick up his. While they were both bent over the rail, Henry's left hand picked his own chips off the layout while his right hand slid underneath his outstretched left arm into his neighbor's chip rack. Then with a pinching movement of his thumb, index, and middle finger, he plucked three green chips from the end of the lined-up chips closest to him, and in the same motion passed them subtly behind his back to Joe, who put them in his jacket pocket. This chip pass-off was necessary to protect Henry in the event the mark caught him in the act or accused him afterward. If that happened, Joe would instantly leave the table. Since Henry had been betting only red chips, he could defend against any accusations by asserting that he didn't have a single green chip on him. How could he be guilty of stealing this man's green chips? If casino security searched him, they'd find no green chips at all, not in his pockets, not on his person. The pass-off to Joe was their cover and had to be done in the "dark."

Henry picked away at the mark for the hour that the table ran good. It was important not to be greedy. You chose your moments for picking. If you took too much at once, the mark was bound to notice. If the table was choppy, you held back. The old saying about getting your fingers caught in the cookie jar was every bit as applicable to railing craps tables.

When the table finally went cold and busted out the mark, Henry and Joe met outside the casino to count up their profits. Joe emptied out his jacket pocket. There were fourteen green chips inside, $350. They then proceeded to change twelve of the green chips into three blacks and did a two-o-five on the same craps table they had railed the tall guy for the three-fifty. They cleared more than $500 for the night.

The partnership between the Classon brothers worked nicely. They began railing regularly when they had heat on the pastposting. And when there were no swelling racks of chips along craps tables, they found other ways to make a few bucks in the casinos. Another new risk-free earn they inadvertently ran into on craps tables was picking up "sleepers." As craps was by far the most complicated game in the casino, due to its perplexing betting possibilities, players often lost track of their own bets. Some identical bets in craps were named differently when made at different times, confusing novice players. For example, the come bet was identical to the pass-line bet, except it was made *after* the come-out roll when a point had already been established. With such inherent confusion, it wasn't difficult to understand why players sometimes lost track and left their winning chips on the table, not realizing that a seven-out paid come bets made on that last roll of the dice. "Seven-out" had such a negative connotation—the most dreaded call made by croupiers in American casinos—that upon hearing it many inexperienced players just *assumed* they'd lost all their chips in play. It was these winning chips left on the table by players that were known as sleepers and could be snatched off the layout by anyone with a sharp eye. Casino personnel didn't watch or mediate what went on between players and their chips, and a lot of those chips ended up in Henry's and Joe's pockets.

The Classons had sufficiently fattened up their bankrolls by the time Thanksgiving arrived that fall of 1954. They flew back to New York to spend the holidays with their mom, planning to return to their house in Vegas after Christmas. They looked forward to working their first New Year's Eve together in the casinos. Henry was sure that it would be their most profitable night to date.

But they received a shock upon entering the Sands casino New Year's Eve. They approached a roulette table, and their eyes nearly popped out of their sockets when they saw the new tool the dealer was equipped with. They watched the ball fall into the slot for the winning number, hearing the dealer call it out as dealers had always done before. But this time the dealer had done something never *seen* before. He placed a little plastic marker the size of a saltshaker on top of the chips on the winning number. Henry and Joe stood frozen in disbelief and watched several spins of the ball, as if trying to convince themselves what they'd just seen was only occurring in a dream. But it was all too real. Each time the ball dropped into the slot for the winning number, the dealer called it out as he placed the marker over the straight-up winning chips on the layout. When there were no straight-up winning chips, the dealer simply placed the marker over the naked number in the center of the box. This was the casino industry's first coordinated counterattack aimed at roulette pastposters. Invented by an ex-cheater working in surveillance for the Sands, its purpose was to deny pastposters access to the winning chips underneath, as well as prevent the laying down of naked cappers.

They left the Sands and hurried over to the Flamingo to see if that casino had also employed the roulette marker. It did. All the casinos in Las Vegas were suddenly using the saltshaker-like anti-pastposting device. Within a few months every American or English roulette table in the world would be using it. The big French roulette tables didn't need it with their three croupiers working them, one on each side, one in the back.

Henry and Joe considered forgoing roulette in favor of craps moves, but Henry came up with a different idea. "We can work the splits," he said. "The marker doesn't touch the split bets between two numbers. That still pays 17 to 1. I'll check-bet the splits and lay in the move. You claim it. Everything works the same."

Joe agreed, and they went back to a roulette table inside the Flamingo. Henry bought the roulette chips and check-bet exactly as he had done in the past, except that instead of betting four roulette chips on each of the twelve third-section numbers straight up, he bet four chips on each of the nine third-section splits between two numbers. When the ball landed on number 32, he did the switch with a green chip on the 32–35 split. Joe claimed and was paid $425. They returned to the Sands, where Henry popped in two more quarters on two different roulette tables, picked up $850. At the Desert Inn they railed a high-rolling Middle Easterner at the craps table for $500 more. There was even time to pick up an occasional sleeper. By the time the sun came up for the first time that new year, Henry and Joe had earned nearly $3,000.

In 1956 they found a new gold mine for their wares: Cuba. Batista's Havana casinos were also using the roulette markers by the time Joe had perfected his claims in Spanish. To his surprise, Henry found the El Cid casino and the others along the Cuban coastline to be more to his liking than those in Puerto Rico. The island was a paradise. The Cuban bosses were eager to pay and apologize for the dealers' mistakes in the craps pit. At the roulette tables, the dealers were all smiles when they discovered the hidden green chips in the winning roulette stacks.

It was during their second trip to Cuba, a year later, that Henry Classon attempted—and failed—the first roulette straight-up pastpost with the obstacle posed by the marker. He had practiced in their hotel room for hours using a stick of lip balm as a marker. But the first live attempt was awe-inspiring. Sitting at the bottom of the table in the Hacienda Casino, Henry was thinking what Mumbles would have thought had his ex-mentor seen what he was about to do. Surely, the old man would've been amazed. And he probably would've liked Cuba, too.

When the dealer placed the marker on top of his winning chips on number 30, Henry was just a little bit too anxious. Joe's stack of chips in the third-dozen box made the dealer turn just enough, and Henry's timing was on, but when his hands shot out on the layout he knocked over the marker and it made a sickening thud. The green chip dropped out of his hand and was momentarily seen by the dealer before Henry swiped it back up.

"*¡Qué pasó!*" the dealer said directly to Henry, catching him red-handed as he tried to get his hands back off the layout. "*¡Qué quiere hacer con eso!* What are you trying to do?"

This dealer was not smiling, and Henry's face flushed red. His Spanish was not nearly as good as his brother's and he was terribly lost for words. He finally managed a "*Lo siento*" (I'm sorry) before he got up and left—in a hurry. The dealer cursed his back in Spanish, then called over a pit boss to explain what the *Americano* had done.

Joe listened to their conversation and got most of it. The dealer told the pit boss that Henry had tried to slip in a quarter chip under the marker when he had his back turned. The pit boss laughed because what he understood was that Joe had tried to pastpost a twenty-five-cent roulette chip, not the twenty-five-dollar green chip the dealer had described. Seeing that his pit boss was not too upset, the dealer decided not to be too upset, either, and they shared a good laugh together. But it was Joe who had the last laugh when he cashed out his chips and left the table. He knew they'd be back.

Henry got caught again on his second straight-up attempt against the piece at the El Cid Casino two hours later. This time he got the move in cleanly under the marker but was too deliberate and took too long and the dealer saw a flash of hand movement as his eyes came back to the layout. He instantly made the connection between the flashing hand and Henry's torso. But Henry was better prepared that second time for a bungling, and he alertly reached back on the layout and pulled off the chips he'd switched in, preventing the dealer from seeing the green chip on the bottom. The dealer and pit boss at the El Cid reacted similarly to their counterparts at the Hacienda. They exchanged a joke about Americans and forgot about the incident.

Henry succeeded on his third try, which was highly commendable when considering the task *literally* at hand. It was at the Havana Paradise, and the dealer had an unbelievable turn. When he put his back to Henry while reaching in the back of his well to get the stacks of chips to pay Joe in the third-dozen box, it was like he went out for coffee. A sexy American blonde was strolling across the casino behind the dealer and seemed to catch his attention. By the time he finally turned back to the layout, Joe was claiming, "By golly, I hit," and the twenty-five-dollar green chip was sitting under three roulette chips, all underneath the marker. It was a majestic sight.

Henry and Joe enjoyed a grand success in Cuba's casinos. They made a half-dozen trips there in the late fifties. They seemed unstoppable, but their island paradise came suddenly crumbling down just a few weeks after their final visit.

Fidel Castro had jerked their green felt carpet from under them.

By the mid 1960s, the Classon brothers had become notorious. After ravaging the casinos in Las Vegas, Reno, and Puerto Rico for a decade, and landing in the back room dozens of times, they were known in every casino surveillance room in North America. In fact, many casinos hung life-sized photographs of them both in the dealers' break rooms. Casino officials had become increasingly frustrated by the Classons. Their efforts at harassing them—dragging them repeatedly into back rooms on sight, even if they hadn't done anything more serious than pass through—only succeeded in slowing them down, or chasing them into other gambling towns where they'd work until the heat died down. Despite all the intercasino communicating between surveillance personnel, all the photographs and alerts passed from one casino to the others whenever the Classons were spotted, nobody managed to get the cuffs on them. Each time surveillance picked up on the Classons entering a casino and tried to set them up and film their move in order to bust them, either Henry or Joe sensed the setup and called off the move. The mistake surveillance crews constantly made was to alert casino personnel on the floor to keep track of the Classons. Floorman and pit boss alike could not behave naturally when they knew the infamous Classons were loose in their casino. By trying to play it too cool, as if they were completely relaxed and uninterested in the action they were supposed to be watching, they tipped off the Classons, who knew better.

The repetitive failures of their surveillance staffs to nail the Classons regularly angered the casino bosses—except one of them. Benny Binion, the fabled owner of the Horseshoe, was a hustler himself. He secretly admired what the Classons were doing to the casinos. Being one of the last of the old-time pioneering casino owners that never sold out to the big corporations taking over Vegas as a result of the widespread Mafia skimming scandals, Binion did things his own way. He dealt with cheaters his own way. Which in the Classon case had nothing to do with taking them out to the desert. Binion hated the slot cheats and the dice switchers who came into his casino armed to the teeth with their devices and gadgets. But the Classons, he noted, worked with nothing but their wits and their fingers. They switched the chips, and they were clever.

One Saturday night Binion was called into his office by his chief of security. The Classon brothers had been found inside the casino and were now being detained by security in the back room. Binion told his security man to hold them there and he'd be right down.

The first thing Benny Binion did to Henry and Joe Classon was apologize for the rude welcome given them by his casino. Then he bought them dinner in his steakhouse. Over generous plates of prime Iowa beef and potatoes, as well as a bottle of his best wine, Binion made the Classons an offer they couldn't refuse.

"Anytime you guys get broke," he said, "you present yourselves at the casino cage. You ask to see the boss working whatever shift it is and you tell him your problem. He will give you a thousand bucks each. In return, I just ask you to leave my casino alone." With that, Binion told Henry and Joe to enjoy the rest of their meal and got up and left.

The other casino owners downtown had neither the smarts nor the class of the uneducated Benny Binion. They did the opposite. They continued their harassment of the Classons as if these two little pastposters actually threatened the existence of their casinos.

Finally, Henry Classon got annoyed. He knocked on Joe's bedroom door one night when the younger brother believed it was a night off. "Let's go," Henry said. "I have a little business to take care of. I need you to be my eyes."

Joe was completely surprised by the intrusion and knew right away it was something serious. There was to be no discussion.

Downtown, outside the Fremont Casino, Henry gave Joe his orders. "I want you to follow me as I walk along the banks of slot machines. Stay twenty feet behind and watch everything and everyone *but* me. If you pick up on anyone else following me or watching me too closely, you give me a Chester and we meet at the Silver Spur shrimp bar. If anything goes wrong and I get busted, you call an attorney in the morning and get me out. You got that?"

Joe got it. He followed his brother inside the Fremont, only looking intermittently at him. But that was all he needed to realize what Henry was doing. As he walked along a particular bank of slot machines where he was well hidden, Henry stopped briefly in front of each one and made a motion with his fingers as though he were slipping a coin into the slot. But what was coming out of his hand was not at all metal; it was glue from the little tube he held inside it. Henry Classon was gumming up their slot machines, the equivalent of destroying a car's gas tank with sugar. He worked with robotlike efficiency. Stop—squirt—continue—stop—squirt. It was devastating. After the Fremont, Henry led Joe into the other casinos downtown and did the same thing, systematically gumming up the slot machines. He got all the casinos but one, and the one he missed was by design:

Benny Binion's Horseshoe. The total damage done in terms of repairs and, much more important, lost revenues, climbed into the hundred thousands.

The next day Henry entered the Horseshoe alone and went directly to the cage and asked for the cage manager. The manager knew who he was right away and appeared with two packets of $1,000 and placed them on the counter for Henry to take. Henry left the packets lying there and asked if Benny Binion would come down and see him. A few moments later, Binion was standing in front of Henry outside the cage. They shook hands.

"What can I do for you?" Binion asked.

"Nothing," Henry replied. "Nothing at all. I just wanted to stop by in person and thank you for the gesture you made to me and my brother the other night." Then he turned and left, leaving Binion's $2,000 on the counter.

Henry Classon never stepped foot inside Binion's casino again. Joe would enter the Horseshoe only a few more times, the first of which was years later when I met him at the casino bar the night he recruited me. But he never participated in another move inside the Horseshoe casino. He, too, had enormous respect for Benny Binion. And as of today, Benny Binion's offer to the Classons still stands. Before dying, he told his sons who took over his duties at the Horseshoe that as long as the Binion name was associated with that casino, *any* Classon could stop by the casino cage and pick up a thousand bucks when he got broke.

Ever since that famous "gum job," Henry Classon had become real mean. He seemed always on edge and attacked others at the slightest provocation. If someone looked at him wrong, Henry would punch him out. Naturally, some of his angry behavior was flung at Joe, who could not tolerate it. Joe got his own apartment in Vegas, hoping that no longer being with Henry all the time would ease some of his brother's tension. He had also found a dancer working the Lido show at the Stardust for whom he flipped. Her name was Ruthie and she was from Wisconsin. After accompanying the Classons on a Caribbean road trip that mixed pleasure with business, Ruthie accepted

Joe's hand in marriage. They got married in one of the little wedding chapels downtown.

It wasn't long before Ruthie was "dancing" around Vegas's roulette tables. An energetic, sexy redhead, she found the Classon number on the roulette wheels as entertaining as any show she'd ever done, on or offstage. She quickly took over Joe's role as roulette claimer. Joe became the check-bettor, and Henry continued popping in the moves. The new three-man (two-man, one-woman) operation was even more effective. With this diversification of roles, Henry was able to leave the table after he did the move, then circle around the pit and serve as team security. He observed Ruthie claiming from afar. From a distance he could better protect her. He could see the steam when it developed behind her.

When Caesars Palace opened in 1966, they did their first black-chip roulette move in the heralded new casino. And as Henry had by then mastered the straight-up move underneath the marker, they went right for the $3,500 payoff. They added a little twist. Knowing that the $3,500 was a big number, they decided to strengthen their chances of success with the implementation of a setup. With Henry and Joe in position at the table—Henry already having swiped three of Joe's roulette chips under which he would slip in the black—the sexily clad Ruthie, in her cocktail dress bought in the Caesars dress shop, sauntered up to the table and bet a black chip straight up on number 28. Leaving the table, she had to take a tour of practically the whole casino to escape the line of sight between her and the gawking floorman and pit boss, who had zoomed through the pit to the roulette wheel at her arrival. The next time they saw the curvaceous woman, she was claiming the hundred-dollar bet she had just won on number 34. They couldn't pay her fast enough.

The advent of the sexy woman claimer was fabulous. It added a whole new dimension to the operation. Not only were the brothers armed with a highly efficient portfolio of flexible casino moves, they now had an adaptable psychological weapon. Up against a beautiful woman claiming a bet, the casino bosses had no chance. In the heat of battle, Ruthie flirted endlessly with the floormen and pit bosses as she sizzled up and down pits. She played their ids, their egos—in some cases even their cocks. In the middle of a claim, she always gave the floorman and pit boss the impression she was available. When they asked the obvious questions "Where's the good gentleman tonight?" or "Does your husband always let you bet *that* much at roulette?"—Ruthie had the answers that charmed them, titillated them. She would say, "When I find *that* gentleman, I'll let you know." And then, "Now you know why I'm *not* married." It was not beyond Ruthie to go right into a pit while her bet was still unpaid and rub up against the ranking pit boss, whose decision it was to pay her or not. Even Joe could not be sure what she was whispering into that pit boss's ear. And while doing all that, the pit bosses knew she wasn't a whore. Even Las Vegas's finest did not bet black chips at roulette *alone*.

Ruthie was the ultimate performer. She had always wanted to be an actress. Before coming to Vegas to dance, she had tried a stint in Hollywood but couldn't land anything besides a few minor roles in sitcoms. Claiming in the Classon "road show" was ideally suited to her. She really took to it. And at craps she was a tigress. Male dealers being attacked by this fiery feline claimer on the felt dropped their chips in surrender. Once she was challenged by a boxman suspecting her of switching in a craps move herself and hiding the chips switched out in her handbag. Ruthie promptly turned her handbag upside down and let its contents spill out on the layout, stunning both the boxman and the dealer—as well as Joe and Henry. Just after the last vial of lipstick rolled toward the boxman, Ruthie asked him provocatively, "Is there anywhere else you'd like to look?"

Now that the Classons had Ruthie, they were able to work the casinos in Vegas without showing their faces. Henry and Joe took much less exposure because neither one claimed anymore. On the tables they began disguising themselves, without being obvious. Henry dyed his hair gray to appear older. Joe opted for the crewcut he'd had in Korea. He also had himself fitted for zeros at a trendy optometrist's office. Together they now appeared to be an experienced businessman and a young airline pilot. The effect of the makeover was such that much of that dense steam in Vegas began to dissipate. And with that, Henry began to calm down a bit. The brothers were getting along better, and there was no jealousy about Ruthie.

During 1967 and 1968, they worked consistently, dividing their time between Vegas and the road. When in Vegas they weren't always inside the casinos. Joe and Ruthie had built a charming house with a pool on the west side of town, which was just beginning to develop. In the mornings, Joe liked to take a swim, then dry off in a lounge chair while reading his books and newspapers. In the late afternoon he enjoyed barbecuing around the pool. Sometimes the neighbors came around and shot the shit over hamburgers and hot dogs. Joe would invite Henry, but he never came. He preferred staying out of their personal life.

Ruthie was a bit less enthusiastic about life's daily routine in the desert when they weren't inside casinos. She really missed them. When not working the tables she felt like an actress without a role. The glittering neon lights bathing the Strip had become her stage. Around the house there were no footlights to follow.

For Joe, the casinos had become a business. He did appreciate the skill and ingenuity put into their enterprise, but for him there was no glamour in it. The bright neon lights Ruthie bathed in at times blinded Joe.

Joe sensed that Ruthie constantly needed the limelight. The evenings not spent in casinos he took her to shows around town. Her favorite was Elvis at the International. Nothing could replace her own show in the roulette and craps pits, but at least when they were out on the town she had the chance to wear her sexy outfits and attract the small private audiences she needed.

One late night after a Vic Damone concert and drinks inside a casino cabaret, Joe touched a subject they'd never before discussed as they began making love on the living room sofa. He wanted to have a baby. Ruthie told him she wasn't yet ready for that, and Joe understood. He was thirty-five; she was only twenty-six. There was still time.

Henry, meanwhile, still had his house on the golf course. To go with it he had bought a small boat that he docked at Lake Mead.

He spent as many free afternoons as possible on the boat, sometimes alone, sometimes with a female companion.

Henry's outlook on women was different than Joe's. He considered them valuable for serving one basic purpose. Now into his early forties, all thoughts of marriage and family—which had never been omnipresent in his head—were gone. But he still needed women's company and, more so, the sex. He picked up single or adulterous women frequently, took them out to dinner, dancing, out on the boat, really knew how to entertain them. But when it was time to cut the bullshit and get down to bed, if they didn't come across they were gone. Some of the relationships Henry had with women lasted a few months, others were over with the rising sun. He often parted ways with women because they wanted to go along on one of his "business trips." That was one rule Henry Classon never broke: Don't work and fuck in the same place. If a woman was not an integral part of the operation, there was no place for her as a spectator. Henry appreciated the dangers that women posed to a criminal enterprise. Of all the guys he'd known back on the Lower East Side who'd done time in prison, 90 percent got their ticket there from a woman. For Henry, it was not only *Hell hath no fury like a woman scorned;* it was also *When they were scorned, they turned into rats faster than they could remove their makeup.*

On New Year's Eve, 1968, Henry and Joe Classon, in full disguise, were sitting at a roulette table in the Stardust Casino. Unbeknownst to them, and also to Ruthie, who had just walked away from a gallery of staring eyes after losing her hundred-dollar setup bet, a powerful Hollywood producer was sitting next to Henry at the bottom of the layout. When their number came in, Henry switched the chips and Ruthie returned to claim the $3,500. The Stardust was not Caesars, and the bosses there had a little tougher time coughing up the prize. When Ruthie realized she was going to have to *work* for the payoff, she was equal to the task. She spun into a Marilyn Monroe number, swirled her dress as she danced into the pit, smooched up to the pit boss, and must have had that mesmerized producer thinking that the name of that famous film should have been *Gentlemen Prefer Redheads.* Not only did she get paid the $3,500, she got the producer's business card before leaving the table. He had furtively slipped it into her hand, whispering that she should call him Monday morning at his Hollywood office.

Ruthie never claimed another bet in a casino. She called the producer Monday morning and was in Beverly Hills having lunch with him at one o'clock in the afternoon. It turned out that the producer had witnessed their entire New Year's Eve act at the Stardust. He saw Henry put the move in underneath the marker. Being an inveterate gambler, the producer understood everything. He even told Ruthie that he knew Joe was in on the caper because the move had gone in under *his* chips. He also told Ruthie that her playacting was the best he had ever seen. Where had she been all these years? When Ruthie told him she had spent nearly three years in Tinseltown and couldn't amass anything better than bit parts, he was hard-pressed to believe her. Nevertheless, three weeks later, Ruthie started shooting her first role in a major film. Her marriage to Joe she had quickly annulled. Though she never married the already married producer, she did have a long affair with him, and during the 1970s and 1980s she became a considerable movie star, under a different name, of course.

When Joe first heard about the producer it was by telephone from Hollywood that Monday afternoon. Ruthie was calling to tell him she wouldn't be home for the barbecue by the pool. Joe's first comment, in light of the producer's powers of observation, was that maybe he wanted to join the pastposting team. Or at least make a movie about what he'd seen. Joe knew that his relationship with Ruthie had always been precarious, sort of hanging by a thread that could be cut at any moment. He accepted the demise of his marriage without brooding an instant. At the end, he was thankful that he'd never managed to convince her to have children. In hindsight, he realized that his wanting to have a baby with her was a desperate attempt to hold onto their marriage. Ruthie was great, he surmised. Her sex was good, her claims even better. But the party was over, and he had to move on without her.

Henry, on the other hand, took the dissolution of his brother's marriage much worse than Joe did. He went flying into a rage when

Joe came to his house to deliver the news. With a frosty-eyed face coated with anger, Henry shouted, "How the fuck did you let her get away like that!" He picked up a crystal glass and sent it crashing into his living room wall, shattered fragments everywhere. "She was our meal ticket, baby! You and I got too much heat to work this town with one of us claiming. What the hell do you suggest we do now?"

Joe was more upset for his brother than he was for himself. The operation had been progressing beautifully. Ruthie was the link that made it perfect. The Classons' talents mixed with her beauty and sense of theater created the ultimate casino grifting team, never again to be duplicated. Getting another woman with looks, brains, balls, and charisma to willfully cheat gambling casinos would be difficult if not impossible. Though Joe had been more interested in Ruthie's charms as a woman and not as a thief, at the moment he was heartsick for his brother Henry, who seemed to have lost most by her departure. As Henry chewed him out, he felt humiliated.

Joe's voice trembled a little bit with emotion when he said to his brother, "I'm sorry about losing her, Henry. But I never thought she'd stay forever."

Joe and Henry both needed time alone to get over the disappointment and heal the wounds from Ruthie's disappearance. A month after she abandoned the Classons, a moving van showed up at Joe's house to take her belongings out to Hollywood. The same day a registered letter came from Ruthie in which she apologized for leaving and told Joe he could keep the house, and that she wouldn't cause him any problems. She wished him happiness for the remainder of his life.

There was no immediate need to pastpost; both Joe and Henry had copious little nest eggs hidden on their properties. But their mother had been talking about finally quitting her job in the garment center and abandoning New York completely for the sunny weather in Miami Beach. It was left unsaid that she was depending on her two boys to buy her a condominium on the water. In order to finance that, they both realized, they'd have to return to work soon.

After three months of inactivity in the casinos, Joe and Henry flew to San Juan to get the motor running again. They got a half-dozen moves paid before things began turning sour. Henry again turned into the mean character he'd become while gumming up the slot machines in downtown Las Vegas. He began snapping at Joe for the most minute things. Furthermore, a lot of the moves he was putting in on both the roulette and craps tables were sloppy, putting Joe at risk when he claimed them. That Joe was a little rusty as a claimer had nothing to do with the string of misses they began experiencing in Puerto Rico. Three quarters in a row missed straight up on roulette wheels. That was unheard of. Before, the only way you blew a straight-up move without knocking over the marker was getting caught red-handed by the dealer. But of late, the markers atop the stack of chips containing the quarter were landing way off center, sometimes even touching the borderline of another number. Joe claimed the bad moves gallantly, knowing that a claimer's cardinal sin was to leave a move unclaimed on a layout, but couldn't convince San Juan's sharpest dealers that it was *they* who were errantly placing the markers. At craps, Henry was fucking up just as blatantly. On his two-o-fives, Joe noticed that the blacks on the bottom were barely covered by the red on top. They were sticking out glaringly, propelling dealers into negative reactions which quickly spread to their superiors in the pit. Negativity in casinos traveled like wildfire and then turned into steam and disaster.

Joe couldn't help but think Henry was putting his ass on the line deliberately. Henry was a far too experienced mechanic to be putting in a rank amateur's moves. Maybe he had not yet gotten over what he considered as Ruthie's defection. Whatever his psychological problems, Joe reasoned, he couldn't let it go on much longer.

On a Saturday morning that followed a bad roulette miss the night before, Joe and Henry were having breakfast at the Americana coffee shop. Joe proposed that they trade roles. "I think we need to change the rhythm," he said. "I'm sure I won't have a hard time doing the straight-ups."

Henry was not the least bit favorable to Joe's suggestion. "What're you trying to say? That *I'm* the one having the hard time? Look, little brother, that'll be the day when I need *you* to replace *me*."

"I'm not talking about replacing you," Joe said, becoming increasingly annoyed at his brother's belligerence. "You know damn well that you've been putting in schlock moves all over San Juan. I don't want to end up rotting in a Puerto Rican prison because you can't distinguish between two different numbers on a roulette layout."

"Who the hell do you think you're talking to?"

The atmosphere was becoming more and more tense, and both Classons were getting aggressive. People began looking over from the other tables. A waiter came over to see if they wanted to order anything else and Henry rushed him off with a stiff bark. Joe began to realize that trying to get Henry to admit the truth was no lighter task than drilling through a brick wall. Henry Classon was bent on destroying either Joe or himself—or both of them.

"Look," Joe said after a minute of silence, the tension still thick in the air. "I don't know what the fuck it is that's eating you, but I'm not going to let it trash everything we've worked for all these years. If it's still Ruthie you're blaming me for, then fuck you. I was the one married to her. What did you want me to do? *Know* that some Hollywood bigwig was going to come into the Stardust that night and snatch her up off the table? You're the one who always said never trust a broad. Now *you* trusted one, and you're the one that's fucked."

Joe got up to leave.

"Sit down!" Henry barked. "We're going right back to work on the day shift this afternoon."

"Not with you putting in the moves, we're not." Joe did not sit back down. "If you change your mind and are willing to switch roles, let me know. I'll be sitting out by the pool." He turned to leave, but Henry hooked his arm, stopping his progress flat.

"Hey!" Henry snapped. "I told you to sit down!"

"And I'm telling you to fuck off!"

Joe started off, but Henry jumped up and struck him with a closed fist. Joe stumbled backward a few steps before regaining his composure. He looked wide-eyed at his brother, his mouth agape. It was the first time either brother had struck the other. Not once during their entire childhood on Manhattan's Lower East Side had Henry raised a glove to his kid brother. Not once in adulthood, either. But now, Henry Classon, forty-four years old, struck his thirty-six-year-old baby brother in the face.

Joe went up to the room, packed his bag, and hailed a cab for the airport.

He never spoke to his brother again.

In the summer of 1969, Joe emptied out his house in Vegas and dumped it at below market value and moved to Northern California. He took most of the cash he had hidden in a floor safe, strapped it to his waist with electrical tape, and flew it to his mother in New York so that she'd be able to buy that condominium in Florida. If the funds he was bringing her were not enough, he told her, she could obtain the difference from Henry.

In Redding, California, Joe opened a financial consulting firm. Within six months he had two dozen clients to whom he meted out stock market tips. And the majority of them proved profitable. He enjoyed the challenge of picking winners based on in-depth analysis. By that time, Joe's thirst for raw gambling had long since dried up. He now played his stock market hunches with other people's money. In his first year of business he earned $20,000. Though only a fraction of what he was earning cheating casinos, he didn't mind so much. Being alone in a small cabin-style house in the mountains, Joe didn't need a lot of money to live. The money he earned aboveboard covered his nut. And whenever he did need a little extra cash, he knew he could always fly to Vegas and pick it up on the tables.

Joe Classon might have retired permanently from the casinos before 1970 had he not hired the particular secretary that he did. Marla Donaldson went to work for Joe in the fall of 1969. She invited him to a cookout in the mountains and there introduced him to her boyfriend, Duke. Joe and Duke hit it off immediately. About the only thing they had in common was a cultured taste for hashish and marijuana, but Joe admired Duke's easygoing personality, a hundred-and-eighty-degree turn from that of his brother.

One night as they passed around the bong at Duke's rented cabin nearby, Joe told Duke all about the casinos after Marla had fallen asleep. Duke laughed and laughed repeatedly at the stories he was hearing, never doubting for a second their validity, which Joe had noticed with an appreciative eye. He knew that most people could never believe casinos being ripped off like that. People had certain impenetrable images of casinos: that you could never cheat them and get away with it because of all the cameras in the sky; that if you tried anything they would cut off your hands—or worse. Duke never mentioned that; he only wanted to hear more stories.

When Joe, Duke, and Marla went to not-so-far-off Reno to celebrate the New Year's Eve bringing the world into the seventies, it was hardly surprising that they ended up on a wheel at Virginia Street's Fitzgerald's Club. Going into the casino, Duke had asked Joe if he ever heard the tale about the two gay Irish cousins, John Fitzgerald and Gerald Fitzjohn. Duke was always cracking one-liners like that, which had a relaxing effect on Joe.

Joe had taught Marla how to check-bet, and she did just that as they set up to pop in a quarter on a split. Joe chose to do the split instead of the straight-up because he was a little rusty in the casinos and didn't want to chance blowing their first move together. He had also chosen Reno instead of Las Vegas for a purpose. Assuming that Henry was still working the casinos in Vegas alone or with a new partner, Reno figured to be less exposed to the moves. And he had no desire to run into Henry. Who knew how he'd react to seeing Joe taking other people into the casinos?

Joe made things as uncomplicated as possible for his new partners on their first move together. There was no need for a setup bet. Joe had told Marla to bet four roulette chips on the third-section splits. He had told Duke to stand near the top of the wheel and wait for his signal to approach and start claiming. When the move went down, Duke was cool. With a cigarette in one hand, a beer in the other, he came out with a flurry that was a combined claim and laugh. He got paid the $425 and a new partnership was born.

They crossed the street into Harold's Club, and Joe put in a straight-up. Toasting that $875 payoff at a bar in a small unworkable casino, Duke said, "That looks like fun. Let me try that." Of course, Joe said no and persisted in saying no. But over the coming months Joe realized that he was not the iron wheel-mechanic that his brother Henry was. He had blown too many straight-ups, knocking over the markers. Perhaps it was time to give Duke a chance. And Marla volunteered to claim her boyfriend's first wheel move.

The easygoing Duke was a natural on the wheels. With nerves as solid as the bottles he drank from, Duke maneuvered the roulette markers like a skilled pinball player did the flippers. No question that by the end of his first month doing straight-ups, Duke was already better than Henry. Joe knew immediately that his new team would dominate roulette pastposting. But still, he had to keep an eye out for his brother, not to cross his path.

Duke told Joe that his best friend, Jerry, was returning from military reserve duty the weekend they were planning to go to Vegas. He also told him that Jerry and his girlfriend Sandy would most definitely love to be involved in their gig. Joe was a little hesitant. He thought that maybe a five-man team was too big. But after hashing it around in his mind, he decided that it could probably be worked out, and besides, he saw that Duke and Marla really wanted to get them involved.

What a remarkable decision that turned out to be, for it was to be Jerry who would further revolutionize the pastposting business. Jerry Palmer was no stranger to either gambling or cheating at gambling. After serving four years in the army, where he spent more time on his butt playing poker than upright performing military duties, he'd seen his share of scams among the boys. But that had been nothing but small-time shit. When Duke told him what they were doing in the casinos, Jerry's reaction was for that much money and such little risk he *had* to get involved. "Shit," he said, "guys are robbing convenience stores for twenty bucks and getting twenty years."

Jerry quickly claimed and got paid on a half-dozen craps moves in Las Vegas. One night in the Aladdin keno pit, as Joe was readying the chips for still another craps move, Jerry asked him why the same move couldn't be done on blackjack tables.

"You're too close to the dealer," Joe explained. "And there's not enough action on blackjack tables."

"Shit," Jerry said with a cocky attitude. "Give me them chips." He took the chips from Joe and marched right up to a blackjack table with its third-base seat vacant. He put three red chips in the betting square. When he won the bet, he switched in two black chips with a red capper, the first blackjack move ever done. He claimed it as though he had years of experience. The dealer apologized for his mistake and paid Jerry the $205. Jerry didn't bother betting back. He walked three tables down the pit, sat down at another vacant third-base seat. He moved again on his first winning hand and got paid. The third table he sat down at had only one spot open: shortstop (next to third base). This did not bother Jerry in the least. Neither did center field or any other position on the table.

When Jerry Palmer finished his little demonstration, not only had he done a dozen blackjack moves, he had disproved a theory that Joe had believed since Henry first introduced him to pastposting: that a blackjack table couldn't be beat. Suddenly it was evident that its crescent-shaped perimeter created the perfect angle at third-base between pastposter and dealer. But what really revolutionized casino pastposting with Jerry's discovery of the blackjack move was simply the number of blackjack tables in casinos: more than all the other games combined. Profitability increased exponentially.

For the next twenty-five years, until my discovery of the Savannah roulette move in the midnineties, roulette as well as craps would take a backseat to the blackjack move. Each time the team went to work, it began by scouting and then pouncing on blackjack tables. Jerry was always the lead mechanic, but Joe and Duke had also become proficient at the move. When Jerry sat down at a blackjack table, he allowed himself three hands to move. If he lost all three, or didn't move for some other reason, he would cede his spot to the number-two mechanic, Duke, who followed the same rules as Jerry. If Duke experienced the same difficulties, Joe would replace him and take three more cracks at it. In effect, each time third base was vacant on a blackjack table, the team had nine different hands to do a move, which meant its productivity level was nearly a hundred percent—and that before taking into account the other positions on the table.

They functioned like a well-oiled military machine, marching up and down the Strip, popping in two-o-fives on blackjack tables all over Vegas. Joe's biggest worry was that Henry would one day stumble upon them in a casino and discover their blackjack move. Joe wanted it protected like a government's most important nuclear secret. Whenever they were in a casino and Joe spotted someone he recognized from another casino, he broke off their operation and led the team elsewhere. His theory was that anyone seen in a lot of different casinos was probably scamming something. Legitimate people usually remained loyal to the casino they gambled in. And his theory was even more applicable to persons Joe recognized from *other* gambling areas.

"If you see a guy here in Reno," he had told Duke and Jerry one night after calling off their blackjack patrol in Harrah's, "and then you see him a month later in a casino on one of the Caribbean islands, you know he's working."

In February 1970, they took their first Caribbean trip together. It was a big success, so they began returning annually and then bi-annually. They'd start in Puerto Rico, then island-skip to the Bahamas and Aruba among others. Islander hospitality in and out of casinos was greatly appreciated. And so was the opportunity to unwind at the beach.

The Classon team remained pretty much intact into the mid-seventies. Joe, Duke and Jerry, who had abandoned the U.S. military, were full time. The girlfriends were part-timers who preferred only going along on the Caribbean trips and the occasional trip to Europe. The blackjack move continued to be the strongest weapon in the arsenal and had been upgraded to purple chips. Craps and roulette moves still played an important role but were relegated to being done only when blackjack moves weren't possible.

By the summer of 1976, Joe, Duke, and Jerry all had a lot of heat in Nevada's casinos. They then decided, after working together for more than six years, that it was time to recruit another partner. That same bicentennial summer I drove my shiny Mustang convertible out to Las Vegas.

The Mix-Up

ON THE FRIDAY AFTER THANKSGIVING JOE TOOK HIS MOTHER SHOP-
ping along Collins Avenue while I hung around the condominium
pool, reflecting on the pastposting stories I'd heard at the Classon
Thanksgiving table. Mumbles had really stumbled onto a gold mine
when that craps dealer made his honest mistake at the Americana in
Puerto Rico, and Wheels had surely found a way to avoid losing in
casinos. I wondered what they both would have thought of the roulette mix-up claim I had envisioned back in Reno. And I was very
curious about Joe's brother Henry, too. Joe had never before talked
about him. I had the impression that he'd suffered a gaping wound
in his heart that might never heal, that night Henry struck him in
Puerto Rico.

We arrived in San Juan the first week of December. Joe kept
his word about experimenting with the mix-up claim. We were on a
roulette table with a pretty dealer and a prettier name (Wilamena)
at the Condado Beach casino. In this new scenario, I served as check-
bettor and claimer and sat along the side of the table. Jerry was the
second check-bettor, seated next to me, and Duke, the mechanic as

usual, sat at the bottom. Joe stood at the top of the table by the wheel, chinning us to proceed.

I bought in with $120 for six stacks of dark brown roulette chips valued at $1. When the dealer pushed the stacks across to me, I positioned them strategically to prepare for my eventual claim. I set them up in a bowling-pin formation, a triangular 3–2–1 configuration with the nose stack pointing at the dealer, the rear three stacks closest to me. I palmed four brown chips off the middle stack in the back row then mixed in four black hundred-dollar chips near the top. That stack would not be touched until the claim, when I would rotate it to the front where it would become the new nose stack in plain view of the dealer. I had to always protect that stack from the dealer's view until that moment of truth. In the event that my stacks dwindled from repetitive losing bets, I would rebuy new stacks immediately to rebuild the camouflage.

Jerry bought the pink roulette chips that were in the rear of the dealer's chip well. His duty was to bet the stack of twenty chips in the third-dozen box to force the dealer to turn when reaching for the two stacks she needed to pay that bet when it won. Duke needed only to bet a lone five-dollar chip in the second-dozen box, assuring himself of a loser when it came time to do the move.

With my bowling-pin formation in place, I looked up to the top of the table where Joe was still chinning. I bet four of my brown roulette chips on all the numbers straight up in the third-section. I also placed three chips on a number in the second-section that Duke quickly swiped off the layout for the move.

Wilamena hit our number (29) on her fourth spin. She placed the marker on top of my winning chips and swept the losers off the layout. Then she turned and reached for the stacks of chips needed to pay Jerry. I picked up the mix-up stack in the back of my chip formation and waited for Duke's move before putting it in front for Wilamena to see. Duke laid it right in smoothly; I put the mix-up stack in front, detached from my other stacks, then swung into action. I let out a scream and went into a false panic.

"I'm missing one of my black chips!" I cried, jumping up out of my chair to add to the histrionics. "I'm missing one of my black chips!" I had to be very careful there because I didn't want to give the impression that I was accusing either the dealer or one of the other players of stealing it. "I *lost* one of my black chips!"

Wilamena first looked at me like I was a complete goner. I got down on my hands and knees, playacted a search of the floor. I stood back up and went through my pockets, turning them inside out like a frenzied tailor. When I saw that Wilamena had seen the black chips in my mix-up stack, I suddenly "found" my missing black chip.

"Oh, my God!" I cried, changing the tune from panic to joy. "There it is! On number 29! I bet it! I bet my black chip by accident, and it won! I just won $3,500 . . . by accident!" I began making an assortment of oohing and aahing sounds, offering my hand to Jerry and the other players, who all shook it in a congratulatory manner. Duke would tell me afterward that he'd heard me carrying on from all the way on the opposite side of the casino when he was nearly out the door. And Joe would say, "That, my dear Watson, is the mark of a great claimer."

Wilamena's facial expression upon seeing those black chips mixed into my front stack like that, as well as the "missing" black, mixed one chip from the bottom into the four-chip winning bet on the layout, nearly defied description. It was an awkward split face, from top to bottom, not down the middle. Her pretty half-smile seemed compressed by the total disbelief which worked her brows into a frown and froze her half-parted lips before they could stretch into a full-blown smile. She looked like one of those computerized images of a person that taught you how different the two sides of your face actually were and how horrible you'd look if they weren't. The bottom of her face was certainly happy for me but the top of it was deeply concerned about the repercussions that would come from the pit.

When I read into Wilamena's thoughts, I instantly knew how powerful this new claim would be. All suspicion about the sudden appearance of an unseen black chip on the layout was removed by the claimer saying that it was *he* who had made the mistake.

The floorman was drawn quickly over to the table by my hysterics. He immediately understood what had happened. Wilamena even pointed out my mix-up stack to him, which made him laugh. He said to me, "Must be your lucky day in Puerto Rico. I wish *I* could make a mistake like that."

Wilamena paid me the $3,500, then suggested I remove the black chips mixed into my mix-up stack and put them with the black chips she just paid me, so I wouldn't make the same mistake again. Oh, how I love casinos!

With this new claim the bet-back was no longer necessary. There was no need to play the part of a high roller. In contrast to the old claim, where I had to set them up to convince them I was a legitimate black-chip roulette player, here I was only making them believe that I was just a lucky dummy who had stupidly mixed up his black hundred-dollar casino chips with his dark brown one-dollar roulette chips. There was no reason to give them back a black chip on the bet-back, so I just cashed in the remaining roulette chips, threw Wilamena a twenty-five-dollar toke, and left the table, finding Duke and his big grin at the meeting place.

The roulette mix-up became our primary roulette move. Its payoff rate was higher than the old moves done with the setup. Of course, as with all moves, there were occasional misses. But the strength of the mix-up claim was evident even when it missed. The moves that didn't get paid took less steam. Sometimes a rank pit boss would come over and tell me that he wasn't paying because I hadn't intended to make that bet. He would rule the hundred-dollar chip null and void and pick it up off the layout and toss it back at me.

The first time that happened, I retorted angrily, "What do you mean you're not paying it! You would have taken it had it lost!" Which was true. If, by chance, a player had really unintentionally bet a black chip on a roulette table and it went unnoticed and then lost, and the dealer swept it away, what chance would that player have to recuperate that chip by claiming he hadn't meant to bet it? No casino anywhere would return that chip in a million years, and rightly so, because anybody could claim that he hadn't meant to bet a black chip when it lost. So, inversely, the casino was obligated to pay that inadvertent chip when it won. Gaming Control regulations were simple concerning what bets casinos were expected to pay:

mainly any and all bets legitimately placed on table layouts. I knew that when having a miss for this reason, I could take the case to the applicable governing authority, but, of course, I would never initiate such a challenge from my position as a known casino thief. There would be forms to fill out, statements to make, video reviews of the table in question—all kinds of exposure that had to be avoided when we did what we do.

Our road trip continued through the islands. The second stop was the Bahamas. In Nassau and Paradise Island the limits and conditions at roulette were not as ideal as they had been in Puerto Rico, so we favored the blackjack move. Jerry did a spate of ten-o-fives with purple chips without a miss. In Freeport, I did my first blackjack move, a five-o-five with one purple chip. I was a bit late on the claim but still got paid. Jerry worked with me on improving my mechanics, and before leaving the Bahamas I got three more five-o-fives paid with one miss. He said I'd be ready for ten-o-fives once we were back in Vegas.

In Aruba our attack was equally deployed with everything in our arsenal. The best thing about the "friendly little island" was that each time we had a miss, none of the bosses became upset. So we just kept going back inside those casinos that refused our payoffs until they obliged. Joe and Duke decided that the atmosphere in Aruba was right for me to attempt my first roulette move as the mechanic. What a disaster that almost turned out to be!

We chose the Sonesta casino. I sat at the bottom of the table with Duke right next to me and Joe standing in front by the wheel, giving me the chin. The dealer had turned his back and Duke whispered, "Now!" I was so tensed-up with anticipation that I sprang forward as if I had been shot out of a cannon. My body collided hard against the edge of the table, which caused an aftershock that sent the dealer's marker spinning a few numbers up the layout and made winners of a few losing chips and vice-versa. The dealer saw the green chip I was trying to pastpost on the straight-up and yelled for the floorman as I "Galloed" out of the casino.

My second straight-up attempt at the Holiday Inn was even worse.

The dealer, whose back had been turned as he reached into his well for chips, turned back suddenly toward the layout as my extended hand was gripping the marker. Panicking, I pulled my hand off the layout but forgot to release the marker. I had actually swiped the dealer's marker off the table. And somehow the dealer hadn't seen me.

Duke, who again was sitting next to me, instructing, whispered sharply, "Wait! He'll turn back around." He kept his cool and didn't want me getting caught trying to replace the marker.

As I sat there shivering, the dealer paid outside bets on the layout, completely unaware of the marker's disappearance. I knew that I had to put it back before he turned his attention to the inside bets, when he'd look directly at the chips surrounding the winning number, which peculiarly had no marker placed on top of it. But I had to wait and be patient. Of course, I would have preferred just getting up and flying right out of the casino, then jumping into the ocean. I might have done just that had Duke not been there to guide me safely back down to the layout.

Incredibly, the dealer did turn his back again without noticing the anomaly, and when Duke nudged me with his elbow, I managed to get the marker back on the winning number without further disrupting the layout. Later on, before exploding into laughter, Joe and Duke chided me about not being cool enough to have also slipped in the pastpost when the dealer gave me that second chance. In hindsight, I most definitely could have.

A few tries later, I finally succeeded pastposting a green chip straight up. From time to time over the years, Joe let me mechanic wheel moves, though I never became half the mechanic that Duke was.

Before heading back to Las Vegas for New Year's Eve, we stopped off in Curaçao, Saint Martin, and the Dominican Republic. None of these islands was as good as Puerto Rico and Aruba, but we always made enough money to cover expenses, which were outrageous when you checked into hotels without reservations during peak season and took two rooms. With meals, poolside drinks, and recreational activities, our nut always exceeded $500 a day, and that didn't take into account plane tickets and other transportation expenses incurred when island-hopping. At least the casino bosses comped us for the shows.

Recreational activities were high on our list. At times, having fun even supplanted moneymaking as our goal while in the islands. In spite of the profitability of our business, and the fact that all of us enjoyed and respected what we did, there was a considerable amount of pressure on each of us inside the casinos. In certain casino areas there wasn't much else to do besides gamble—or cheat the casinos. In Reno, you had absolutely nothing to distract you in the winter; in Lake Tahoe you could ski, but that could be too tiring and time-consuming for a team putting in double shifts in the casinos. It was only in the islands where we could really enjoy ourselves. We had a whale of a time during the day while working at night. We all water-skied, jet-skied, and lounged around the pool. Jerry was into scuba diving and went off on a few excursions. I got a big kick out of going parasailing in Saint Martin in the same parachute with Duke, who was a little flabby. The guy running the concession and piloting the boat told us that it was a little too windy to put us both in the same chute, but I gave him an extra twenty and told him not to worry about it because Duke and I were a couple of real daredevils. The guy looked at us and laughed his island laugh. We had such a good time that none of us wanted to rush back to Vegas for New Year's Eve.

We were glad we did, because our first New Year's Eve working together in Las Vegas was even a bigger blast. When the clock struck midnight inside Caesars Palace, I was chanting "By golly, I hit!" to the tune of the revelers' "Happy New Year!" just after Duke had switched in the two black chips for what was at the time the biggest roulette pastpost ever. The move paid a whopping $7,000! I sang and danced with all the revelers, collected my chips, and headed over to the Barbary Coast to find Duke. Las Vegas Boulevard was so jammed up with throngs of people it took me nearly fifteen minutes to negotiate my way across the street.

Before the giant wheel move at Caesars, Jerry had set another record at the blackjack table in the same casino. He had done the first fifteen-o-five, a four-chip switch with three purples and a red. Not only was that a record in terms of money, it was the first time anyone put three large denomination chips (purple, yellow, or choc- olate) under the capper. Jerry had immediately wanted to do another fifteen-o-five but the casino was too crowded, and we couldn't find another blackjack table with an open seat.

After Caesars, we went to the MGM where I claimed another $3,500 mix-up off a wheel, and then to the Tropicana where Jerry went through the blackjack pit doing ten-o-fives. We had just enough time to stop off at the Dunes before the sun came up, and Joe let me attempt my first blackjack ten-o-five, and I was delighted to get paid, becoming a member of the revered "Ten-o-Five Club." The night was a smashing success. We cleared $20,000! Not bad for a hard day's night.

New Year's Day we watched the bowl games in the living room of Joe's apartment. During halftime of the Rose Bowl Joe made an announcement. Raising a glass of champagne, he said, "I want to wish you guys a very happy New Year. I know we didn't get a real chance to celebrate New Year's Eve because we were out there busting our asses, but anyhow, I want to take this moment to thank all of you for being a part of my team, and making this thing we do extremely worthwhile for me." We all clinked glasses and drank, and I'm not certain that I was the only one in the room with tears in his eyes. Joe went on to say that "1977 was the best year of my life and I'm looking forward to an even better one in 1978."

The second week of January we flew back to Reno. The town was much less crowded than it had been three months earlier, but we still managed to find spots ripe for wheel moves. After we'd done as many as the town could handle, Duke and Jerry met their girl- friends at Lake Tahoe and went skiing, while Joe and I stayed be- hind in Reno to work on my blackjack move. He had me going into all the joints doing little one-o-fives. He wanted me to be perfect, as good as Jerry, he said. I must have done a hundred of them before Joe finally said, "You're making progress." He didn't even give a shit about the $5,000 I earned while learning. He just threw the money into the team bankroll. Again, nothing but class.

We returned to the Islands and stayed until the end of April. We even took a cruise on one of the Carnival ships. The casino on board was hopping, but for Joe, working the cruise ships was out because of the inherent difficulties in escaping. I joked that Duke was a good swimmer and by all accounts could make his way to Florida if he had to jump. Everybody laughed, though I was certain Duke and Jerry *were* ready to work the cruise ships, such was the confidence they had in themselves and the operation. My feeling was that I'd go along with Joe's decision. Years later, when riverboats began cropping up all over the southern United States, I was faced with the same decision. I ended up taking my team on board.

On the Boardwalk

IN LATE MAY 1978, WE RECEIVED A SPECIAL TREAT: ATLANTIC CITY. After decades of haggling with other political groups, the politicians supporting legalized gambling in the decaying seaside resort finally won at the polls, and Resorts International opened the first casino on the heralded Boardwalk. The opening-up of Atlantic City was not only a major event in my life, it was, ironically, the determining economic happening in my father's, albeit at the other end of a completely different spectrum. It made him a multimillionaire. A struggling real estate developer, he had bought a strip of property on the already sinking Atlantic City Boardwalk in the late 1950s. Never having the money to develop it, he had let it sit vacant for twenty years. He had tried on several occasions to dump it but found no takers. Well, in 1978, he found his taker: Bally's Park Place Hotel Casino. I didn't know it then, but perhaps if I had followed my father's wishes and walked a straight and narrow path in my life, I would have become a millionaire *grâce aux* casinos in a slightly *different* way.

The very first time we entered an Atlantic City casino, we had to wait in line for three hours. The line stretched completely around the new Resorts International casino up onto the Boardwalk. Inside, the casino was giant—like a football field. It dwarfed all the Vegas casinos with the exception of the MGM. At that time we could only imagine what the town would be like in a few years with the whole Boardwalk lined with giant casinos.

What made Atlantic City such a treat for us was the incompetence of its casino personnel. Other than the small percentage of the casino elite who had come from Las Vegas and Puerto Rico, the overwhelming majority of the casino employees—and nearly all of the dealers—came from the Atlantic City area, and just a few months before they had absolutely *no* idea whatever about the mechanics of card-dealing, dice-throwing, or the inner workings of the casino floor. Every schoolteacher, prison guard, and convenience-store clerk with any desire to improve his lot in life ended up in Atlantic City casinos dealing cards or working the craps games. Surveillance positions were filled by young people whose closest experience to watching a card sharp or slot thief was *maybe* seeing a dishonest employee stealing a roll of quarters from the cash register. Overall, the situation was reminiscent of Hitler's sending teenage boys off to war in hope of averting the fall of the Reich. How could you expect anything but disaster? But, then again, Atlantic City's gambling was not World War II, and its casino owners knew that with a little time and experience their casinos would soon be all grown up and running as efficiently as those in Nevada.

But—boy!—did we take advantage of that interim period, which lasted a good three years.

To start, all casinos in Atlantic City would be uniform, meaning that their limits were the same, dealing procedures the same, and chip structure the same. The New Jersey State Gaming Commission wanted to keep the new gambling infrastructure as clean and as orderly as possible. Fearing the use of Mafia-employed handheld card mechanics once used in Nevada's casinos, the Commission ruled that only special card shoes, oblong wooden boxes, could be used to deal the cards. They also forbade casino employees to gamble in any of the casinos out of fear that a "hooked" dealer needing money could be bought off and made to cheat the casino. A final regulation—one that they probably didn't know would greatly reduce our earnings—was that all denomination gambling chips that exceeded $500 had to be slightly bigger than the rest of the chips, and that thousand-dollar chips had to be bright orange and five-thousand-dollar chips steel gray. I don't know for certain why the commission curtailed creativity as far as the chips were concerned, but later on, when we began working with thousand-dollar chips and then five-thousand-dollar chips, we couldn't use them in Atlantic City because of their difference in size. Our *whole* premise, our total pastposting operation, was based on being able to completely hide one chip underneath another, or at least create the appearance that one chip was completely hidden underneath another.

This setback did not stop us from *destroying* Atlantic City. Well-known blackjack card-counter Ken Uston talks about destroying Atlantic City in his book *Million Dollar Blackjack*. I don't know if we ever made as much money as his team, but what we did in those first few days in Resorts was an accurate indicator of what we would do in the Boardwalk casinos in the next three years, before profitability finally leveled off.

Naively, Atlantic City started off by letting you bet purple chips *inside* the roulette layout. Not on straight-ups, but they accepted $500 on the three-number street bets that paid $5,500. The dealers were so incompetent that Duke was putting moves in almost as an afterthought. We got four of those roulette monsters paid the first three days, and would have gotten more had the casino not been so wall-to-wall peopled-up. On one of the moves, another player had gotten in Duke's way as he was moving forward to switch the chips, forcing him to pull back. Disgusted by that inexperienced gambler's intrusion, Duke popped in the move so late that the novice dealer had already removed his marker from the layout and begun mucking chips. I wasn't going to claim it, but the dealer did it for me. He looked up and noticed the five-hundred-dollar chip sitting on the 1–2–3 street and thought that he'd made the mistake of overlooking that bet. He glanced at the players around the table as he pointed at the purple chip and asked, "Whose bet is this?"

I said, "It's mine," as if I were claiming a valueless object at a lost-and-found. The floorwoman happened by the table at that moment and just watched like a mannequin as the dealer paid me eleven purple chips. I nearly shit in my pants as I watched this. It became obvious as we kept getting paid and paid again that pit personnel were overly cautious about dealers making mistakes, completely ignoring the other side of that coin, where dishonest players were helping them along.

On the craps tables we also kept setting new pastposting records. The recent four-chip switch Jerry did on that blackjack table at Caesars Palace New Year's Eve—forget it! On one Resorts craps table, with me standing behind him, Jerry did a fifteen-o-five–fifteen-o-five. He had bet four red five-dollar chips on the pass line. When the shooter rolled a 10, Jerry took the odds and put four more red chips behind. A few rolls later, when the shooter made the 10 and won the bet, Jerry switched in the double four-chip bomber—three purples with a red capper in the front and three purples with a red capper in the back. The payoff was $1,505 for the pass-line move and $3,010 for the odds move—a $4,515 monster. Our only problem ended up being the confusion in the pit among all the casino rookies. It took them twenty minutes to sort it all out and get me paid. And again, there was never any question about the *fact* that the dealer had made an honest mistake. You can imagine the chaos we caused in Atlantic City's infantile craps pits.

But too bad for them. What counted was we got the money— more than $40,000 the first three days. When we weren't dropping those big bombs on the roulette and craps layouts, we blackjacked them to death. Jerry was let loose to run rampant through the pits; I followed in his footsteps, did my fair share of the moves. Between us, they got hit from every position on the layout, and on one table we *both* moved, claimed, and got paid, causing the poor dealer to rub the cobwebs from his eyes.

We rented a team house in Brigantine, figuring that we'd be there for a while, and be returning often once gone. The house had five bedrooms, one each for Joe, Duke and Marla, Jerry and Sandy, and myself. The extra bedroom was only used when either Duke or

Jerry had an occasional fight with his respective girlfriend. One rule strictly observed about the house by everyone was that there would never be any guests. Besides the occasional visit from the plumber or the electrician, we weren't entertaining.

Caesars Boardwalk Regency and the Brighton were operating before the end of the summer, and with their arrival the lines waiting to get into casinos disappeared. With the three of them now propped up along the Boardwalk like sitting ducks for us, Joe decided that our planned trip to the European casinos could wait awhile. The pickings were just too good, and more Atlantic City casinos were on the way.

When we weren't working, Joe sometimes conducted his private "Henry patrol." He would leave the house at any hour and patrol the casinos looking for his brother, knowing that he, too, must have been wetting his lips inside such candy stores. Just in picking up sleepers alone, Joe mused, you could make $500 a day, for the vast majority of players were as inexperienced in the casinos as the dealers. But Joe's primary concern about finding Henry in a casino before Henry found him was his fear that Henry would learn the blackjack move. His protection of the blackjack move had become excessive. I often had the worrisome thought that Joe would neglect his security duties while Jerry and I were on the tables doing the blackjacks. His preoccupation with Henry might lead him to be looking around the casino for his brother when he was supposed to be watching us at the tables. I once mentioned that concern to Joe; he told me not to worry, so I didn't bring it up again.

Sometimes the ignorance inside Atlantic City's casinos really ticked me off. One Sunday afternoon I was shooting craps at Caesars newly opened Boardwalk Regency. I'd arrived at the table with over $1,500 in black and green chips. I'd show a little action, then color out to the purple chips Jerry needed for blackjack moves. For my first bet I put a green chip on the don't pass bar. Chips lying on the don't pass bar stick out because the overwhelming majority of crapshooters bet the pass line, going with the shooter against the house. At that particular table, I happened to be crunched between two meaty tough guys at the horn, each with $2,000 bets on the pass line.

One had the dice, the other a thick wad of hundreds he let dangle over the rail above the felt, and with my measly $25 bet going against their four grand I felt a little uneasy. The guy with the dice rolled snake eyes, crapped out. When the inexperienced dealer swept away their $4,000, he also wrongly swept my green chip off the winning don't pass bar. I immediately protested, stopping the action as I would when claiming.

"Hey!" I cried. "You swept my quarter off the don't pass bar! What is this crap?"

The dealer looked at me blankly, not having the slightest clue.

"Your bet was on the pass line, sir." It was the boxman who spoke. He was one of those gym-rat types with big shoulders, thick chest, and oily slicked-back hair, and the attitude that went with it. Looking at that idiot immediately enraged me. A raw dealer's honest mistake was one thing, but for a boxman—just as raw—to back up something like that, which he obviously could not have seen, was another.

"My bet was on the *don't* pass line," I argued.

"I'm sorry, sir," retorted the boxman, "but your bet was on the pass line."

Now I was furious. I found myself in a situation where I was actually claiming a *legitimate* dealer mistake—probably for the first time in my life. And I couldn't win out, couldn't get paid the lousy $25. The thought that this was some kind of ironic payback from above for all the illegitimate claiming I had done flashed through my mind.

"He had his bet on the don't pass bar," the guy who'd just rolled the dice and lost $2,000 said. "I saw his bet going against mine."

I was quite surprised that the guy was backing me up. Seldom did a big craps player have any pity for a little green-chip pauper going against him.

"No, he didn't," the boxman said with arrogant defiance to the high-rolling shooter. "His bet was on the pass line next to yours."

I felt the veins popping out in my neck. I didn't appreciate the way that boxman said *his*. Weight-lifting dummy or not, I wanted a piece of the guy. I was really getting worked up. Then the other high roller—also a two-thousand-dollar loser on the roll—got involved.

"What are you, a *schmuck?*" he said to the boxman. "My buddy Jimmy here's telling you that the kid bet his quarter on the don't pass line, and you sez no. Whaddaya calling him, a liar?"

"The bet was on the pass line, sir," the boxman said to the second tough guy in the same tone. I couldn't believe he was going to the wall on this. I was beside myself. Here are two typical tough guys from Philly who just lost four grand on a single roll of the dice backing me up for $25 and the boxman doesn't want to believe them. What could he be thinking? That they were both working a scam with me, and that the three of us would cut up the twenty-five bucks in the john?

I couldn't take it anymore. My head was pounding from the anger. Despite the arrival of the floorman, who I figured would probably back up the boxman, I lunged forward and was climbing into the craps table to get at the boxman, who had stood up and steeled himself for my charge. Had one of the two tough guys not grabbed me around the waist and held me back, I might have killed that idiot with the big pecs and written this book from a New Jersey state prison. When it was all over, the pit boss (after the floorman's indecision) finally reversed the boxman's call and had the dealer put my quarter back on the don't pass line and pay it. During the ruckus the dealer had remained silent. I could see that he was fearful, and I felt bad for him. So instead of picking up the two green chips on the don't pass bar, I left them there and said to the dealer, "That's for you."

Who said that pastposters don't have a heart?

I thanked the two guys from Philadelphia for backing me up and went outside on the boardwalk to cool down a little.

"What're you, nuts?" Joe said, handing me a soda he'd bought in one of the pizza joints squeezed between two souvenir shops on the boardwalk. I had been leaning against the railing lining the beach, letting my head fall back as I watched and listened to the seagulls overhead.

"Probably," I said. "I just snapped. Two guys betting two grand a pop stick up for me and that idiot boxman doesn't believe them."

"Take it easy," Joe said, tapping me gently on the back. "You're not in Vegas. This is Atlantic City. You have to give these people a chance to learn."

From 1978 until 1984, we spent more time in Atlantic City than we did in Las Vegas. By 1984, there were eight casinos on the boardwalk and two at the Atlantic City Marina. We consistently hammered all of them during that six-year period. We had earned well over $2 million in the Atlantic City casinos before we decided to abandon our house in Brigantine. By the mid-1980s, the town's casinos finally began to mature and the dealers and pit personnel got a little wiser. Nonetheless, we continued visiting the East Coast casinos three times a year. New Jersey's fabled town by the boardwalk would remain our second most important destination after Las Vegas—until the gambling explosion in Mississippi in the early 1990s.

When we got back to Vegas after that first prolonged road trip in the fall of 1978, Joe and I rented a spacious three-bedroom house with a swimming pool in a quiet neighborhood with artificial palm trees. He christened it the "Castle," and promised that the next up-grade would be called the "Palace." We put a big-screen TV in the living room and a pool table in the rec room. Joe used the spare bedroom as his study, where he put the blackjack table and all his books. Every time I went in there I thought back to the first time he showed me the blackjack move. Once in a while I took a handful of the Tropicana chips still in the rack and nostalgically practiced. I made Joe promise he'd leave me that table and chips in the event he ever died or retired. He said that in the event of his death the table and chips were going with him. However, in retirement he would consider it.

I had been gleaning the automobile section in the classifieds, looking for a second-hand Jaguar convertible. I had always loved the Jaguar's sleek looks, and was determined to own one despite its less-than-par mechanical reputation. I couldn't find the cherry I wanted in Vegas, so I began searching the out-of-town classifieds at the library. In the *Los Angeles Times* a dozen Jags seemed interesting. I made a list, called the owners, and set up appointments. Joe and I drove out in his new Corvette and spent the weekend looking at Jaguars. On the way, he was bitching that my itinerary was not very well organized.

"Where's your map?" he was asking. "You have to document each appointment you make and mark the precise corresponding location on your map." To shut him up I bought a road map of Los Angeles when we stopped off at the halfway point in Barstow.

The 1974 XKE long-nosed convertible I bought in Pasadena for $12,000 was silver with red pinstriping, a real beauty. Driving it back to Vegas on the interstate, with the cool breeze whipping up my hair as I looked approvingly at myself in the rearview mirror, I thought how nice it was to finally have something courtesy of the casinos, and about how much things had changed since I'd first arrived in Las Vegas two years before. I had gone from sleeping underneath the interstate to cruising it in a convertible Jag.

Cat-and-Mouse

EVERY NOTORIOUS CRIMINAL THROUGHOUT AMERICAN HISTORY HAD his archenemy on the side of justice. Billy the Kid had Sheriff Pat Garrett. John Dillinger had G-man Melvin Purvis, and Bonnie and Clyde had former Texas ranger Frank Hamer. I would meet mine in 1982, though he would not succeed in ending my "peaceful" career as those lawmen mentioned above did to those rather more violent criminals of the past.

But he would try like hell.

The first big adventure of that year was a Saturday night in June and didn't involve casino cheating, just plain opportunistic stealing. We had treated ourselves via a Caesars Palace comp to four ringside seats at the Larry Holmes-Jerry Cooney championship fight in the rear parking lot. After all big fights at Caesars, the casino would be jumping with huge action, and we had plans to deliver our own knockout blows on its tables. The fight itself was boring and one-sided for Holmes, but whatever action it lacked was more than made up for as we filed back inside the casino with the rest of the crowd. We had just entered the main pit when suddenly the unmistakable *pop-pop* of gunshots erupted in the casino. There was no doubt about it, and everybody, patrons and employees alike, hit the floor and scrambled for cover. The whole incident didn't last long, and I was quite surprised how quickly order was restored and everybody got back on their feet.

The four of us gathered in the keno pit to discuss getting the chips we needed for our moves. Joe told me and Duke to go to a craps table and play out an offset to get purple chips. We turned to go, but Jerry stopped us suddenly.

"Don't bother," he said with a mischievous smile on his face. He opened his hand to reveal a fistful of smooth, creamy purple chips.

None of us caught on immediately, so Jerry explained. "You guys didn't think I was gonna let an opportunity like that get away, did you?" He pointed back toward a blackjack table in the main pit, where we'd all hit the deck when the gunshots rang out. "One guy playing purples left his chips sitting on the layout when he dived underneath the table." Jerry shrugged. "So I just took them."

We were all quite impressed that Jerry had the nimbleness of mind to snatch a stack of purples off a blackjack table in all that chaos. It turned out to be a nice six-thousand-dollar bonus. It gave us the rest of the night off. The next day on the news I heard that the Caesars shooting was drug-related and one trafficker had been killed.

Another Saturday night, in October 1982, we were inside the Desert Inn Casino doing blackjack moves. I had become the number-two blackjack mechanic and was taking Jerry's third-base seat at a table where he had just lost three consecutive hands. I won my first hand and put in the ten-o-five. The dealer called the floorman, who immediately called the pit boss. Everything got real negative real quick. Jerry saw the problem developing from where he was standing across the pit and decided to give me a hand. He came around the pit and sat back down in the last vacant seat at the table, making believe he was just another player waiting for the next hand. The pit boss and floorman were discussing the situation behind the dealer when Jerry interrupted them and said to the pit boss, "Why

don't you just pay him already so we can get on with the game."
Sticking his neck out for me like that took a lot of balls. He risked
being tied in with the move. I greatly appreciated Jerry's gallantry,
thinking it was not the sort of thing that Duke would also do.

The pit boss approached the table and got as close to Jerry as
possible, then said to him rudely, "Why don't *you* pay him." Then
he turned his back to us and picked up the phone which was on the
podium right behind table. It would have been to our advantage had
the podium been farther down the pit in a sticky situation like that.
I would've been able to disappear easier without the pit boss seeing
me go. But now he was able to keep me in his sight, looking me
dead in the eye as he talked into the receiver, undoubtedly the surveillance room on the other end. He did absolutely nothing to mask
the contempt he was feeling. Before he hung up, Joe crossed behind
me and distinctly said, "Gallo!"

Without any further ado, I swiped the purples from the betting
square along with the backup chips, stuffed them into my jacket
pocket, bolted out of the chair, and sprinted for the side exit at the
far end of the casino. The dealer panicked and shrieked his protest.
I was about halfway to the exit when I heard the pit boss who'd been
on the phone cry out, "Security! Grab him!"

I plowed into the exit doors, bursting them open with my palms
acting as a battering ram. I ran as hard as I could through the parking
lot, trying to get off the property as fast as possible. I looked behind
me; there were two uniformed security guards chasing, but I had at
least a hundred yards on them. To my right was Las Vegas Boulevard
(the Strip). I debated whether I should cross the street to the other
side. There were throngs of people walking along both sides; I figured it would be easier to disappear along the boulevard. I'd pull the
chips out of my pocket and toss the jacket, blend in with everybody
else.

I started angling for the street, looking for a spot where I could
cut through the endless parade of yellow lights, but the automobile
traffic was just too heavy. I would risk never making it to the other
side if I attempted to cross, so I continued running straight ahead as

fast as I could, weakening slightly but still confident I could shake the security guards, who were bogged down by their equipment belts—and their guns.

Another look behind me and I didn't see them. I slowed down a little.

"Freeze!" a husky male voice suddenly called out.

I turned around as I requickened my stride. Unbelievably, there was a new uniformed security guard right on my heels—ten yards behind. He couldn't have been from the Desert Inn, I thought, as I ran again for my life. He had to be from one of the little motels I had passed en route. Security from the Desert Inn must have radioed ahead.

I kept running.

"Freeze!" the guard ordered again.

I turned around again in midstride. The gap between us had widened—doubled. I felt a surge of adrenaline as my confidence soared. I would outrun this guy, too. A flash from the backroom experience I'd had in Lake Tahoe five years earlier passed through my mind. I didn't want to go through that ordeal again, perhaps face a bust.

"Freeze, or I'll shoot!" the officer demanded.

I didn't stop and wasn't about to—until I heard a loud report from his gun. The fucking guy actually fired a warning shot!

"Freeze, or I'll drop you!"

I turned around, still running, but now panting and out of breath. The security guard was about twenty yards behind and still had the gun in his hand. When he saw me turn around, he squatted into a shooting position, the pistol barrel aimed at my chest. I could see a flicker of light bounce off the metal.

I flung my hands above my head in surrender. It was over. The gunshot unnerved me. I couldn't believe the guy had actually fired a shot. Had I not stopped, would he really have shot me in the back? I was just a fleeing pastposter.

The guard handcuffed me and started walking me back toward the Desert Inn. We were soon joined by the two Desert Inn security guards whom I'd lost at the beginning of the chase. They thanked the guard who had run me down and escorted me back to the Desert Inn in cuffs.

"Shit," one of them said, "you're one hell of a fast mother-fucker."

It was the first time in my life I had on handcuffs.

Inside the back room of the Desert Inn I was cuffed to the back of the chair in which I sat. The two security guards stood over me with a menacing attitude. Within seconds of my arrival there, Desert Inn casino people began pouring into the back room. First came the pit boss, then the floorman, followed by the dealer, and then by a woman and man in plainclothes who I assumed were surveillance inspectors. Fifteen minutes later, two more plainclothes guys came in, and neither one said a word during my entire interrogation. I found out three months later that they belonged to the Hanson Detective Agency. One of them, a tall redheaded guy of about forty dressed in a light-blue denim suit, would become my number one nemesis in the Vegas casinos up until this present day. His name was Steven DeVisser.

During the whole time I was in the back room, all the pit bosses from the entire casino filed in and out to get a look at me. I felt like I was the main attraction in a freak show.

I was interrogated by the plainclothes surveillance couple and then by a black Gaming Enforcement agent who showed up just as they left. It was basically the same routine I had been subjected to in Lake Tahoe five years earlier, except the black guy from Gaming was a real cute-ass, spitting out more bluffs than John Wayne had faced in any silver-screen poker game.

"Now, come on," he was saying in a hushed tone, as if he didn't want anyone else in the room to hear. "We know you tried to pastpost those chips. We got it all on surveillance tape. Why don't you just cooperate with us. We already know who you are from what you did at Caesars up in Tahoe in seventy-seven."

He really thought I'd be thrown for a loop when he brought up the Tahoe incident. I was hardly listening to him. My attention was focused across the room on that Hanson detective, Steven DeVisser, who was glaring at me with his cold blue eyes. I could see he knew that I knew the gaming agent was full of shit. He seemed to be silently berating Gaming's old worn-down approach to someone with obvious backroom experience such as myself. The guy was studying me impassively, but I felt his arrogant confidence, and I sensed at that instant I would have problems with him in the future. He was too cool. He was in a completely different class from all these Gaming lackeys.

"Listen," I said curtly to the gaming agent, "if you had me on tape, you wouldn't be sitting here trying to get me to open my mouth, would you now? Why don't you just stop wasting everybody's time and get on with your paperwork so we can all go home."

DeVisser never took his eyes off me for a second. His partner, a younger guy wearing a lot of cheap jewelry, didn't seem interested in me or why I was there.

The chief of Desert Inn security came into the back room after the gaming agent and his own surveillance crew had finished with me. Before reading me the riot act, banning me officially from the Desert Inn casino, he stated his feeling that he would have liked to take me up to the roof of the Desert Inn Hotel tower and push me off onto the Strip. Finally, I was paraded through the casino for all the pit personnel to see and then cut loose at the main entrance.

If that backroom experience seemed laughable, the back room of the California Club casino downtown three months later, in January 1983, was not. I found myself in real hot water.

Before entering that casino, we'd stopped to have dinner at Binion's steakhouse in the Horseshoe. Though Joe felt bound to honor the agreement made between Benny Binion and the Classon brothers some fifteen years earlier, he permitted himself to enter the steakhouse because its entrance was accessible without having to go through the casino. After the tasty steaks, the four of us passed in front of the Horseshoe's famous display of a million dollars in ten-thousand-dollar bills. On a quirk, Joe suggested that the team pose in front of the display; a photograph of us all in front of the money would make a great memento, he said.

The photographer snapped our picture for five bucks; Joe put it in his pocket, and we forgot about it. A half hour later we were

positioned at the California Club to do a hundred-dollar straight-up
on the wheel with the mix-up claim. Duke put it in; I claimed and
got paid. The whole thing went down without a hitch. After we were
all safely gathered at the meeting place, we went into the Golden
Nugget coffee shop to get some layer cake and coffee. We'd been
there about an hour when Joe decided to go back to the California
Club and cash out the chips. He told us to wait for him there. We
ordered more cake and coffee and continued bullshitting without a
worry in the world.

When Joe still hadn't returned half an hour later, we started
growing concerned. What was taking so long? It was a Sunday night,
and the California Club had been practically deserted when we left
it, so there couldn't possibly be a long line at the casino cage. We
went over all the other possibilities, but there really weren't any.

Something was definitely wrong.

"I'm gonna go check it out," Jerry said after Joe had been gone
an hour. Since Jerry had not been involved in the move or the claim,
it was safe for him to go back into the California Club casino—so we
thought. "If I'm not back in fifteen minutes—" He shrugged. "I
don't know what to tell you."

After Jerry had been gone twenty minutes, Duke and I were
getting skittish.

"What the fuck is going on?" I said. "Joe said the move was
spotless. He hasn't been wrong in six years." I paused a moment to
think, then said, "Has he ever been wrong since you've known him?"

"Not once."

We sat there another fifteen minutes, then Duke got up suddenly.

"Where the fuck you going?" I said, almost in a panic.

"You stay here. I'm taking a cab to the Gingermill. Maybe for
some reason one or both of them ended up at the emergency meeting
place. It'll take me fifteen minutes to get there. I'll page you here
as soon as I'm inside the lounge."

I sat there nervously, fidgeting with the silverware, waiting for
Duke's call or Joe or Jerry's reappearance. When there wasn't any
call from Duke, I realized I was living Agatha Christie's *Ten Little*

Indians. I sat alone in the Nugget coffee shop another hour, trying hard to convince myself that none of this was happening. I was afraid that if I got up and ventured outside, I'd be swallowed up by whatever it was that was collecting my teammates one by one. Finally, at midnight, I couldn't bear the unknown anymore, so I got up from the booth with a long exhalation and walked nervously back through the casino, thinking about an imaginary net dropping over me from above. As I headed toward the taxis lined up along the curb outside the wide-open entrance, I kept stealing glances from side to side, looking for the monster that was going to come snatch me up from behind the slot machines. I was ten feet from the nearest cab and still inside the casino when I found it. Suddenly cutting me off were two uniformed Golden Nugget security guards with a tall redheaded guy wearing a light-blue denim suit whom I recognized immediately. Then I remembered the face and the cold blue eyes from the backroom of the Desert Inn. It was Steven DeVisser, the Hanson agent.

"My name is Steven DeVisser," he said, glaring at me with those cold blue eyes I would come to know so well. "I'm with the Hanson Detective Agency employed by both the California Club and the Golden Nugget. You'll have to come with us back to the California Club to join your friends." He removed a photograph from his jacket pocket and showed it to me. "Do you recognize this?" he asked, delighting in his own sarcasm.

It was the photograph of the four of us in front of the million-dollar display at the Horseshoe.

I was genuinely in shock.

As we walked out into the glittering neon lights on Fremont Street, DeVisser said, "Don't try to run. These guys are a lot faster than you with their radios."

Joe, Duke, and Jerry were already inside one of the California Club back rooms when I arrived. I heard their voices coming from behind a closed door as I was led down a short corridor, past another closed door, to a room at the end. My first thought was that they had all four of us, the whole team—and the photo from the Horseshoe was proof that we'd all been together. By the time I had crossed the street from the Golden Nugget and gotten over the initial shock of the confrontation with DeVisser, I'd deduced that DeVisser had to have taken the photo from Joe, which meant that Joe had been searched. What other incriminating evidence had he had on him?

DeVisser opened the door and rather crudely pushed me inside. Sitting on top of a metal desk leafing through papers in a folder was the black gaming agent whom I'd also encountered in the back room of the Desert Inn. He was wearing a dark blue suit that accentuated his very white teeth. He beamed at me as I was roughly put in the chair next to the desk by the security guards. He put down the folder, and in a musical cadence that highlighted his grin, said, "Long time no see." He was as obnoxious as DeVisser's eyes were ice-blue.

DeVisser motioned the two guards into the hallway and closed the door behind them, then sat in the chair behind the desk, staring me down for an eternally long five seconds. He removed the Horseshoe photograph from his vest pocket and placed it on the edge of the desk by the gaming agent's shoe. He got right to the point. "Your buddy Duke pastposted a black check on roulette wheel number 4 in pit number 1 at or around 8:45 P.M. You claimed the bet, saying you mixed it up with your roulette checks. Very clever. At precisely 9:22 P.M., Joe Classon attempted to cash out thirty-nine black checks at the main California Club cashier. Thirty-five of them you were paid at the roulette table; the other four had already been in your possession, as indicated by the dealer. We know that the checks Classon tried to cash out had to be yours because no other California Club black checks were outside the casino's control at the time, which was verified by a supplementary internal control and casino check count conducted at 9:30 P.M. Jerry Palmer"—he tapped Jerry's face on the photo with his index finger—"was also involved in your little conspiracy, as is evidenced by this photograph." He paused a moment to let it all sink in, then he turned his head toward the gaming agent, cueing him to take over.

"Welcome to the Classon gang," the gaming agent said, climbing off the desk. He paced around the room but avoided looking at me. As he spoke, he alternated his gaze between the ceiling and the floor. At least he spared me the grin and the teeth. "You're all looking at an assortment of felony charges, each punishable by state prison terms of up to ten years. First, we have conspiracy to commit a casino crime. Second, cheating at gambling. And third, fraudulent acts. What makes the case especially excruciating for you is that we have four witnesses who saw everything and are willing to testify against you— testify that they saw *you* take the money off the table, which is the most serious—"

Despite the thought that I was really cooked running through my head, I couldn't help but take note of the black gaming agent's choice of the word *excruciating*. It had to have been rehearsed. The word that did reverberate in my brain, however, was *testify*. Listening to DeVisser detail the chronological order of events in the casino, I had picked up on something that tipped me off to what they were lacking: videotape. DeVisser had said that Duke had pastposted the black chip at or *around* 8:45 P.M. Surveillance videotape keeps an exact running time as it records—to the second. Therefore, neither Duke's move nor my claim was on tape. Judging by DeVisser's exact reference to 9:22 P.M. for Joe's arrival at the casino cage, I ascertained that Joe was indeed caught on videotape by the casino cage surveillance camera, which everybody on *either* side of the casino business knew ran twenty-four hours a day.

However, the word *testify* plugged up any hole in their case made by the absence of videotape. In a jury's mind, eyewitness testimony was even stronger than videotape. It was harder to tamper with. And they had *four* witnesses—holy shit! When entering that back room I had heard other voices coming from behind the second closed door in the corridor, at least one of which belonged to a female. Undoubtedly, their witnesses were gathered in that room, in the process of recounting their rat stories and signing statements. I thought back to Caesars Tahoe and to Veronica, my rat from Sacramento. Had it not been for my cunning little maneuver, my goose would have been cooked there. And now the rat situation appeared much worse, no traps available to shut them up.

I was deep in thought, no longer hearing the gaming agent's words nor feeling DeVisser's diminishing presence, when an uproar suddenly brought me violently back into the room.

". . . prison for a long time . . ." The gaming agent's voice trailed off.

The uproar in the corridor, coming from one of the other rooms, was so loud—so powerful—that it not only penetrated the walls of our room, it also rendered the black gaming agent silent, something I had believed impossible.

It was Joe Classon's voice. I had never heard a human being shout so loud and so intelligibly at the same time. "Nobody in this living world is going to testify against me!" he thundered. "Whatever sorry motherfucker takes a witness stand in front of me in Las Vegas, I'll bury alive in the fucking desert. You tell your witnesses they're dead—all four of them!"

"Shit!" DeVisser cried, as he jumped up and bolted out of the room. The black gaming guy stood motionless in the center of the room, dumbfounded. I thought he was just as rattled as the four witnesses in the other room must have been.

Joe carried on and on and on, shouting his threats. The energy he had to maintain that vocal outburst was incredible. I was thinking, How come they can't shut him up? I was expecting to hear noises indicating a beating, at least *something*. But there were no chairs getting knocked over, no thumping sounds, nothing except Joe's voice. After five full minutes it finally stopped. Even I was relieved. Either Joe got knocked out or they gagged him and dragged him out of the room, or he had a heart attack and died. Whatever the case, that five-minute tongue-lashing was frightening. I'd thought the bawling-out he'd given me in Lake Tahoe for bringing those women rats into Caesars was the eight-point-nine on the Richter scale, but next to this it was nothing.

A few minutes later, while the gaming agent and I were staring at each other in silence, DeVisser returned to the room with a security guard. He had a look of total disgust on his face, and I read it perfectly. The four witnesses they had in the other room had recanted. There wasn't going to be any testimony. Joe had simply scared the shit out of them. I thought back to the people who'd been playing roulette at that table when the move went down. They seemed to be your average Midwesterners, probably God-fearing country folk. Hearing Joe's New York–accented crazed voice in a rage must have made them rip up their witness statements in a panic.

Joe had saved me again. True, he'd made his first mistake since I'd known him—having that photograph on him when we went to work at the California Club—but he once again found the solution to a seemingly unsolvable problem, freeing me from the tiny prison cell into which I was apparently going to be wedged.

DeVisser told the security guard to escort me out to Fremont street and let me go. Before we were out the door, he glared at me with his frosty eyes and said, "We'll be seeing each other again."

I counted on it.

Steven DeVisser had a real hard nut for me ever since that incident at the California Club. After I had been let go by security on Fremont Street, I made a few out-of-the-way turns, circling several blocks before landing back on Fremont Street to hail a cab to the Gingermill where I knew all my recently-released-from-the-backroom teammates would be. Just before I reached the end of one of those blocks, I performed a "security turn" that Joe had taught me. In one brisk movement I whirled around a hundred and eighty degrees without tipping off a would-be pursuer to my about-face. The movement could not be defended against. No matter how good an agent was at following someone, he had to give himself away, because the brain reacted involuntarily to the shock.

The first victim of the security turn was DeVisser. He was a good fifty yards behind me, but he jerked up and stiffened as though someone had stuck a flaming rod up his ass. I took a turn and ducked into a crevice along the building to await my pursuer, who I knew would have quickened his pace once he saw I'd discovered his tail.

When DeVisser darted by, I sprang out of the crevice and shot him a loud "Hey!" He was obviously caught off guard and startled—as well as embarrassed. My success in embarrassing him like that made me his number-one target for casino expulsion throughout the eighties and nineties, and it continues right up to the present day.

"What are you following me like that for, you asshole?" I said, my spirits lifted by his naked capture.

Given the circumstances, he acted rather coolly, without stuttering or losing his composure. "I'm just doing my job," he said, but anger was evident in his icy eyes.

"Well, I'll tell you what, *asshole*, why don't you go looking for a few purse snatchers along Fremont Street and get off my back. Maybe *they* won't pick up on you." I turned and walked away leisurely, knowing he was too humiliated to continue his pursuit. I felt his fury at my back, though. Over the years we would develop a scathing mutual hatred for each other. And as those years went by, I realized how dangerous this guy was. I learned his history, which was quite impressive.

Steven DeVisser went to work for the Hanson Detective Agency in 1973. Unlike his boss, Clint Hanson, DeVisser was not an ex-cop; he was a ranch hand from Texas who had come out to Vegas to seek work in the booming construction business. How he met Hanson and became his ace agent is not known by this author, but I can certainly attest to his effectiveness inside the casinos.

DeVisser's career in Vegas took right off. He began busting casino cheaters at a preposterous rate. In 1974, he corralled a major slot jackpot-fixing team at the Sahara. He spotted them casing their machines. He set them and their wires up for the cameras, filmed their mechanics wiring the one-arm bandits, and finally swarmed all over them with the casino's security force. In 1975, he busted a team of blackjack hole-card readers at the Mint. Each member had a tiny mirror glued onto one of his fingernails. As certain vulnerable dealers slid off their hole card from the pack to tuck it under their up card, the identifiable pips on the corners of the card reflected into the cheaters' eyes as they looked into their mirrors. In 1977, he nabbed a highly profitable team of card-benders at the Flamingo Hilton, where Hanson had established his first field office. Bending was the art of subtly creasing the corners of aces, 10s, and picture cards with your fingernail when you tucked them under your chips in blackjack games, where the cards were dealt facedown to the players, who picked them up and played their hands accordingly. Done properly, the bender would know the value of all those cards the next time they appeared facedown at the top of the dealer's deck, or even at the front of a card shoe, if the bender had mastered his craft to the point of putting the tiny indentation in the middle of the cards. Knowing the value of the *next* card in blackjack is much more powerful than knowing the value of the dealer's hole card, especially when contemplating certain plays such as splitting pairs and doubling-down. If you were bending at the optimal first-base position, and thus the first player dealt to, you automatically increased your bet threefold when you knew the top card was an ace and coming to you because it gave you a 60 percent advantage against the house. Benders could not even lose in the short run with their overall edge of 20 percent once they got all the key cards bent, ten times stronger than the edge the casinos had against honest blackjack players having optimal skills.

In the late seventies, when blackjack card counting became such a phenomenon, DeVisser began identifying the counting teams for the casinos, who systematically barred them from the premises. Card counting was not a crime, but it could very well be said that the hordes of counters who converged on Atlantic City at the time—including Ken Uston—had been expelled from Las Vegas by Steven DeVisser. And as far as the real convicted casino criminals went, those spending their days at Nevada's Indian Springs Prison (where most of the state's casino felons were sent) whiled away a lot of time talking about the "asshole" who had them sent there.

For nearly two decades DeVisser tried assiduously to set me up inside casinos and get my ass shipped off to prison. A few times he almost succeeded—but never quite.

There are times when a casino town becomes so hot that you absolutely cannot work it. One of those times in Las Vegas arrived in February 1983. With the backroom incidents at the Desert Inn and California Club, compounded by DeVisser's almost obsessive determination to put me permanently out of business, I had become one of the most notorious casino cheaters operating in America.

My notoriety became evident at the Barbary Coast one Saturday night in April. We had decided to put me on the bench for a while as far as the blackjack moves were concerned. After Jerry, Duke would now be the number-two man. If needed, Joe would bat third. That was our starting lineup as we cruised the blackjack pit looking for open spots.

Jerry sat down at third base on a table at the extreme end of the pit, farthest from the podium. The shortstop position was also vacant, so I decided to occupy it and play a hand to help create the action on the table that Jerry needed to do the ten-o-five. We had both placed our bets in the betting circles when I noticed the floorman walking toward the table with what appeared to be an eight-by-eleven-inch sheet of white paper in his hand. Jerry was too busy concentrating on Joe's signals from across the pit to notice the floorman's arrival. But my curiosity was aroused. The floorman looked at the sheet of paper, then looked at Jerry, then again at the paper, and finally walked back through the pit to the podium, where he opened the top drawer and deposited the sheet of paper.

The dealer had dealt the cards and Jerry had a pat hand of 20; he was preparing to move in accordance with the chin Joe was giving from across the pit. Meanwhile, I was aware that Joe could not have noticed the floorman carrying the sheet of paper.

Just before the dealer busted out his own hand, making everybody at the table a winner, I leaned over to Jerry and whispered, "Hold up, something might be up."

At that moment, the floorman was walking casually back toward the table, nothing in his hand. He didn't seem concerned about anything. I watched him approach the table, wondering what was up. Jerry was now watching him, too. The floorman looked again at Jerry, and again there was nothing alarming in his expression. He might have been taking a walk in the park. Then he looked directly at me for the first time. His eyes nearly popped out as he froze in his tracks.

Then I understood. The sheet of paper he'd been carrying had a photograph of me on it. It was a flyer distributed by Hanson agent Steven DeVisser to all the casinos alerting them to the blackjack move. Since I was the one who had been back-roomed at the Desert

Inn after an attempted blackjack move, it was my picture appearing on the flyer. In describing the mechanics of the move, DeVisser had included the detail that it was preferentially done from third base. The Barbary Coast was protecting itself by having its pit personnel systematically compare my photo with all males in my age group who matched my general description and sat down at third base. Jerry was a few years older than me, though we appeared around the same age. The floorman had compared my photo with Jerry's face. He had concluded that it was not a match. Then on his second tour through the pit, our eyes made contact and he recognized me as the person he was looking for. What I read from his reaction was, Holy Shit, that's him!

I said to Jerry as I hurriedly got up, "I have a Gallo here. I'm going to the Gingermill."

The floorman, who had been walking quickly back to the podium, undoubtedly to have another look at the photo, saw me get up and went right into a panic. "There he goes!" he yelled out to no one in particular. When he spotted a uniformed security guard, he pointed me out and shouted, "Grab him!"

But I was already gone.

I hustled outside to Las Vegas Boulevard, turned right, and entered the Flamingo Hilton, hurried through its casino, out the far side door into the Holiday Casino, through there and out the side door, finally getting a cab to the Gingermill. When I walked inside the rear entrance of the darkened lounge, I got my second huge surprise of the night. Steven DeVisser and the black gaming agent I now knew so well were sitting in one of the booths having a cocktail. Another detective type in jeans and a button-down whom I didn't know sat with them. They didn't see me, and I did about the quickest about-face of my life and shot back out the door. I trotted toward the curb and found a seat on top of a pornographic promotions newspaper box on Las Vegas Boulevard. From there I could see both the entrance of the Gingermill—in case the gaming agents came out—and the vehicle entrance, where my teammates would eventually arrive in their cab.

What a night, I said to myself as I leafed through *Las Vegas's Hottest Nights*. First I have to run out of a casino when I wasn't even doing a move, and then discover that Steven DeVisser and the enforcement agents of the Nevada Gaming Control Board were using our emergency meeting place to have cocktails.

I wondered just how much of a pain in the ass this guy DeVisser was going to be.

The summers of 1983 and 1984 were particularly hot in Las Vegas. Whatever the temperature of the desert air, the heat we were getting from Hanson inside the casinos was higher. Before the fall of 1984, DeVisser already had me eighty-sixed from more Las Vegas casinos than I legally had the right to enter.

It was in the summer of eighty-four that Joe taught me railing. We went into the Las Vegas Hilton, which had rapidly become one of the glamour casinos in Las Vegas after taking over the property on Paradise Road formerly known as the International, and found a drunken loudmouth braggart at the craps table. With all the casino experience I already had, it didn't take any longer to say the word *railing* than I understood exactly how it worked. I stood behind Joe at the table in my sports jacket with the deepest pockets. Joe periodically passed me off a few green and black chips he was stealing from the mark. When it was over, we had gotten him for $1,100. We were just warming up.

Later that night we ran into a real *monstress* at the MGM. A high-rolling, extremely good-looking blonde in her midforties, dressed in a low-cut top and high-cut bottom, a superbly matched outfit, was proclaiming her satisfaction with a Texan's accent as she hit a hot streak on a craps table. She had easily been the center attraction long before the dice started falling her way. This situation was the ultimate challenge for Joe—what he would call afterward *extreme railing*—because he would attempt to rail this woman while everybody was watching her *and* her chips. In her chip rack built into the table she had swelling rows of black chips, at least $20,000, and it was growing. Joe had to wedge himself in between her and a cigar-smoking fat guy who seemed of irritable disposition, without annoying either of them.

After about twenty minutes behind the woman, Joe managed to edge into position next to her. He ordered a drink and began making typical Vegas small talk. She took to him right away. Joe's personality went into high gear. Soon he had her laughing, jumping higher when she won than she'd been jumping before, kissing his cheeks, then his mouth—the works. All the while he was passing me chips—lots of them. The woman kept winning; Joe kept passing. I was conscious of the possibility that he had gone overboard, that the woman was bound to catch on. At one point during the feast, the woman—while all eyes and ears were on her—ballyhooed and said to Joe with a humorous laugh, "Honey, I've been winning all night, but my rows of chips ain't gettin' any wider." I thought I was going to die when I heard that. The biggest thrill I got from the experience was not the fifty-two black chips I later cashed out at the cage, but the sight of Joe and the lady Texan walking hand in hand to the bank of elevators leading to the rooms. He spent the rest of the weekend with her, and before leaving town she invited him to come visit her Dallas ranch.

He did.

The Other Side of the Road

WHEN WE LANDED AT HEATHROW OUTSIDE LONDON, MY FIRST TRIP abroad, I had no idea of the variety of international adventures awaiting me. When it was over, though, I couldn't wait to go back to Europe. Even before the return flight to the States took off.

The difference between Las Vegas and London casinos might not be day and night, but it is at least sunshine and rain. Whereas inside the behemoth casinos along the Las Vegas sun-drenched Strip you had a bustling atmosphere about the tables and a constant cacophony of slot machine noise, the finer gaming establishments in dreary London were hushed and reserved, and each had only two silent slot machines, and few had even a single craps table. People inside them practiced restraint.

Back in 1986, before the devaluation of the British pound, one American dollar didn't even buy you a half pound sterling, which meant that casino minimums and maximums were considerably higher in London than in Las Vegas. Joe determined that in spite of the losses incurred with the currency exchanges to and from British pounds, we had a very healthy potential in England's private gambling clubs.

That potential, however, was mitigated by certain British gambling regulations and casino procedures. The first adversity we faced was simply getting through the door of a casino. In order to enter a legal British casino, you had to either become a member or have an already existing member sign you in as his guest. Given the fact we were already an internationally known casino-cheating team (despite the fact we had never before worked together in Europe) with names that triggered red flags on computer screens, none of us could ever qualify for membership in a London casino. Our only way to gain entry was to be signed in by a member—who accepted responsibility for our actions once inside the casino.

Joe had a handful of British acquaintances that he'd known in Korea. But before we'd left the States, he had decided not to use them to get us into the casinos. He couldn't reveal our intentions to them and, at the same time, didn't want to risk their memberships. On the plane ride over the Atlantic, I kept bugging him about how we'd get into the casinos. Maybe it was better, I had suggested, that we forgo England and go directly to France. He had told me not to worry, that he'd figure out a way to get us in.

Joe's solution was London's cabbies. A gambling buddy back in New York had once told me that hookers would do *anything* for money; Joe said that cabbies would do *almost* anything. He found a chubby cabdriver sitting inside his big black London taxi outside the Park Lane Hilton, inside of which was the Rendez-vous Club casino. He offered the cabbie £500 to secure a membership in each of six London casinos and to sign us in as his guests twice at each one. In addition, Joe would pay all the membership fees, which amounted to £300. A dozen cabbies outside London's fashionable hotels had already refused Joe's offer, but this chubby fellow wearing baggy pants and dirty shoes got out of his big black cab, shook Joe's hand, and said affably, "You got yourself a deal, old chap." Sizing up the guy who was shaking his hand, Joe decided to throw in a suit so the cabbie could get *himself* into the casinos.

There was an odd law concerning British casinos: once you took out a membership you had to wait forty-eight hours before your initial entry. It was reminiscent of the American "cooling off" statute applied to the purchase of firearms. The member was, however, permitted to sign his guests in along with him the first time he entered the casino; he was obligated to stay inside the casino until all his guests had departed, though that abidance was less strictly observed.

During the forty-eight-hour cooling-off period, we did the Americans-sightseeing-in-London scene. We all piled into the chubby cabbie's black cab (Joe paid the fare as any other client would), and he sped us around to all London's tourist sites. We visited Buckingham Palace, 10 Downing Street, Big Ben, Madame Tussaud's Wax Museum, and to Joe's great liking, Winston Churchill's underground war room. Sandy and Marla, of course, took a tour of the famous Harrod's department store, and when they emerged we were stuck another £1,000. Joe, on the other hand, found a small second-hand shop where he bought the cabbie his suit. The guy was thrilled and asked Joe if he could keep it after we left town. We all got a big laugh out of that, and it was Sandy who asked him, "Who else do you think is going to fit snugly into that suit?"

Once inside a casino in London, an American-style pastposting team encounters certain factors that inhibit it from doing all its home-grown moves. The highest denomination chip we could work with was £100, because at £500 the round chips got bigger, and at £1,000 and up they changed form and nationality, resembling the rectangular plaques seen in French casinos.

Another inhibiting factor was the logistics of their gaming personnel. Their floormen and pit bosses were called junior and senior inspectors. Unlike American casinos, British casinos were supervised with undivided attention. At each roulette table an inspector was perched in a high chair above the layout in front of the wheel, much like laddermen in Vegas baccarat pits. He never took his eyes off the layout. As a pastposter sitting on the bottom of the layout, you felt the intensity of his glare; you even got the feeling he was strategically placed there to keep *you* under surveillance. Doing the straight-up move underneath the piece was too difficult to tempt even Duke. The blackjack move was also out of the question due to the size difference of the chips. We decided our best opportunity resided in the first-section street move, any of the four three-number bets at the top-left side of the layout that paid 11 to 1. We'd do a six-chip switch—three one-hundred-pound casino chips mixed in with three two-pound roulette chips. Since roulette is by far the most popular high rollers' game in Europe, with layouts so pasted by chips that machines had to be invented to sort and restack them for dealers, no setup bet was needed; we'd just use the mix-up claim.

The first London casino we went to was the Palm Beach. The cabbie picked us up at 9:30; we were there before 10:00. We'd left the girls at the hotel for security reasons. As we'd all be signed in by the same member, we couldn't hide the fact we were together, so if we took steam, they'd be immediately linked to us and subject to interrogation.

We were greeted at the entrance by a uniformed valet wearing a tall hat, who held the door open for us as we entered. There was a small reception area where two men in suits sat behind an oval desk, upon which sat the casino guest register. The cabbie was given his membership card, and he promptly signed us in. We walked through a short chandeliered foyer into the casino. Joe gave the cabbie a £100 note, told him to have a good time and get lost.

Inside, I was immediately impressed by the atmosphere. It was dimly lit with dark reddish walls displaying contemporary paintings. There was a bar up a small staircase off the casino floor. Off to another side was the casino cage, small by Vegas standards. In all, the casino resembled a stately men's club but with a decor not quite that masculine. Surprisingly, most of the dealers were women wearing long frilly dresses.

The quietness—especially the lack of slot machine blips and coin-jingling—struck me as soon as I entered. There was only the chorus of hissing wheels and spinning balls. There was practically no conversation among the dapper clientele, who seemed to flow like elegant strangers at a grand ball.

In that regard, we had to be especially careful. Knowing that concealing our togetherness was impossible, we still had to give the impression that we were together naturally and not as coconspirators. These London casino people are sharp, trained in a tradition older than the United States itself. They picked up on scammers quickly, and for some reason held American gamblers either in contempt or with outright distrust. What we had to do was behave naturally without giving the impression that we were *conspiring* to behave naturally.

The Palm Beach had fifteen roulette wheels and six blackjack tables, all of which had bugs hidden somewhere on the surface or bottom (this was commonplace in European casinos). The wheels were all jammed-up with tons of action from a multitude of nationalities. I was able to distinguish the Chinese from the Malaysians, but not the Saudi sheiks from those coming from other oil-rich Gulf States. There was also muted conversation in French, German, and Spanish. Only one blackjack table was going; Jerry bought in for £1,000 and played a few hands with red chips. He openly passed me and Duke the blacks we needed for the move. Assuming we were under observation, it was imperative that nothing appeared clandestine.

It took an hour before Duke, Jerry, and I were able to slide in and around all those Asians, Arabs, and Europeans and reach a roulette table and yet another fifty minutes before we finally hit our bet without someone's chips covering mine and impeding the move. Duke was forced to lay in the chips while standing awkwardly out of position between a heavyset woman spectator and me, and without Joe's giving him the chin. Because of the roulette pit's structural difference and the high chairs behind the wheels, Joe couldn't post himself in Duke's line of sight. So we worked with audio security instead of visual.

The move itself was very difficult. Duke's true brilliance as a wheel mechanic came into evidence at that table. Under the inspector's glare, and without camouflage, he had to do a one-handed switch. It was arduous because the six chips switched in had to replace those switched out perfectly—on the center of the vertical street line and in the middle of the imaginary line cutting through the three winning numbers. If the move-chips were placed even slightly off center, the dealer would know that someone had tampered with the original bet, simply because she never would have let a sloppy bet like that go unattended before spinning the ball.

Duke created his own diversion with his right hand as he put the move in with his left. His right hand threw a twenty-five-pound chip toward the dealer which he purposely made land in the *neighbors box*, a European-style wager in which you bet a group of five numbers that were next to one another—or neighbors—on the black-red-and-green-slotted disk inside the wheel, but not on the layout. These neighbors bets were handled entirely by the dealer. Players did not place neighbors bets themselves because the neighbors box was too far away, in front of the dealer. Instead, they passed their chips to the dealer and verbalized the bets they wanted. The dealer then placed their chips accordingly.

We took advantage of this never-before-seen facet of roulette to distract both the dealer and the inspector sitting above. Because Duke's tossed chip threatened to interfere with the yet-unpaid winning neighbors bets, both the dealer's and the inspector's eyes were instinctively drawn to it, giving Duke the fraction of a second he needed to do the one-handed switch. And he had only one shot at it. Once the move was in, there was no going out to retrieve it if the result was sloppy. By that time, the neighbors distraction would be over, and you would be caught red-handed if you tried to make a last-second adjustment.

What I saw just as Duke disappeared from the table was the six move-chips perfectly placed at the intersection of the vertical street line and the imaginary line cutting through the heart of the numbers 4, 5, and 6, exactly on the spot where I had placed my six roulette chips before the spin.

My claim was very low key. No need for all the hysterics we used in Vegas; we were selling ourselves to a different mentality. Instead of jumping up and down for joy after having crawled around the floor looking for my missing black chips, I just simply said to the dealer in a normal voice as I pointed to the move-chips, "Look at that, I bet £300 on the street by accident and it won. It must be my lucky day in jolly old London."

The dealer's reaction was even lower-keyed than my claim. At first, I wasn't certain she saw my winning bet, which had changed from £12 to £306, but I didn't press the claim as I would have at home. It turned out the dealer had noticed my bet right away, and she paid me £3,366 without uttering a word. The inspector on the high chair didn't blink. It was as though nothing at all out of the ordinary had occurred. Walking away from that table to the cage, I thought, This could be the greatest American coup on the British since the Revolution.

Our second stop was the Rendez-vous Club at the Park Lane Hilton. Inside, the decor was similar to that of the Palm Beach. We found another crowded wheel and went to work. This time, as I was getting paid, the cabbie happened upon the table and noticed the stacks of black chips the dealer was pushing toward me. He let out a "By George, you hit a big one there, chap." It was really funny because the casino was so damned quiet, and when he blurted that out, everyone at the table frowned at me, as if rebuking me for not having taught my chauffeur proper London casino manners. Outside the casino, Joe told the cabbie to tone it down a little if he couldn't just avoid us completely.

We packed it in for the night, picked up the girls, and went for a midnight stroll through Hyde Park before stopping at a café for a final decaffeinated cup.

I asked Joe how long he expected our London excursion to last.

"Until we take steam," he replied. "The slightest steam in any casino, the cabbie's membership is revoked in all of them and we're done."

That steam came two nights later on our sixth London move at the International Sporting Club just behind the Park Lane Hilton. Our second night working London, I had gotten paid £3,300 each at the Ritz Casino, Les Ambassadeurs, and the Golden Horseshoe near Baywater Station. The third night's first payoff at the Sporting Club was our last.

Everything had gone down smoothly as in all the other gambling clubs. Duke put in another flawless move, I made a low-key claim and got the money. Just as I turned to leave the table with the chips and cash out, a debonair fellow in a tuxedo was standing in front of me, offering his handshake as he introduced himself as the president of the casino.

"Mr. Wilson," he said, addressing me by the false name I had scribbled onto the guest register (guests weren't required to show ID). "The membership of the gentleman who signed you in this evening has been revoked. You and your associates will have to leave the casino immediately, and you shall not be allowed to return to our establishment as the guests of any of our other members. If you'll come with me, we'll get your chips cashed out."

I was mildly shocked. What had gone wrong? Where was the steam coming from?

He escorted me to the cage, and I was promptly cashed out. The teller gave me three cellophane-wrapped packets of a £1,000 and loose bills for the rest. Then I was brought into the foyer where Joe and Jerry were standing, having themselves been escorted there by other casino personnel. Duke had already left, and the president of the casino didn't mention him, which made me think that perhaps the steam wasn't coming directly from the move. The cabbie was no longer in sight. Besides the president telling me that his membership had been revoked, he didn't divulge any other details.

Outside the Sporting Club another surprise awaited us—this one a bit more pleasant. It was a chauffeur-driven Rolls Royce. The driver and the casino valet were holding the doors open for us. As we got in, the president gave a stiff smile and said, "Our driver will take you anyplace you want to go—in England."

How was that for class? I thought as we pulled away. Here we are getting booted out of the casino, then chauffeured around London in the casino's Rolls-Royce.

We settled for a ride back to the hotel. We didn't really have the time to take a tour of England, though we did joke about it inside the Rolls. Jerry said humorously, "We can tell Duke we had steam and vaporized to Scotland in the casino's Rolls."

We spent the rest of that evening discussing what could have happened. We tossed around several theories, including intercasino communication about a certain American repeatedly winning a strange unseen bet, a bizarre previously unheard-of cabdriver who suddenly joins six gambling clubs the same day (and whom we'd been ready to tell to join six more), and the always lurking possibility that somehow one or all of us had been identified.

Finally, Joe said it was really no use trying to figure out what had happened. He'd said in the beginning that our London experience would come to an abrupt halt. Even if never caught doing the moves, we'd eventually find ourselves barred for committing another London casino infraction: repetitive winning. We had cleared $35,000, a good start for the European trip that still had France, Italy, Germany, and Holland on the itinerary.

The next morning we found out what had happened at the International Sporting Club. Joe received a phone call from the cabbie—who was calling from jail. While we had been working the roulette table, the accommodating cabdriver was toiling away himself on the other side of the casino. He'd gotten himself arrested for stealing fifty pounds' worth of chips from one of the Arab sheiks' wives at a blackjack table. He asked Joe if he'd mind coming down to the jail to bail him out. He even promised an entire month of free taxi service as a payback for the inconvenience. Joe said to him indignantly, "What are you, kidding! I didn't have you go into all those casinos to rob their clients' chips. You ought to be ashamed of yourself."

The history of casino cheating in France is as tasty as its centuries-old best bottles of wine. During and after the Renaissance, France's nobility, and the rest of Europe's alike, won and lost fortunes in the fabled Monte Carlo casinos with their golden-domed chandeliers and museum-like paintings and sculptures. The English language expression "break the bank" comes from the French *"faire sauter la banque."* Many Frenchmen, as well as gamblers from other European countries with a rich gambling heritage, had different ingenious ideas about how to accomplish just that. The one common trait was that they were always dishonest.

In the early 1800s, the French gaming police was established to combat casino crime among the royalty that gambled in Monte Carlo's princely gaming palace, Le Grand Casino, and later in the other Côte d'Azur beachside gaming playgrounds lining the Mediterranean. To the surprise of these gaming gendarmes, European royalty was found on both sides of the fence. Dukes, barons, and earls could be found not only buying their "chances" at a roulette wheel but also pocketing gold pieces they had furtively removed from the layout when other aristocratic members weren't looking. Generals, polo players, and even a beloved princess had all been caught tampering with spinning wheels to give themselves a little noble edge over the commoners.

One infamous French casino cheat, whose second occupation was that of a carpenter, had once hidden inside Le Grand Casino with a toolbox from his atelier when it closed in the early morning. Alone in the darkness, he lit his torch and went to work filing down the grooves on the inner disk of certain roulette wheels, which resulted in biased roulette balls landing with odds-defying frequency on a few select numbers. He got wealthy, busted, broke, divorced, wealthy again, and remarried, before finally dying broke and divorced in a wooden cell inside a French Riviera prison, ten years after being caught a second time with his torch and toolbox inside Le Grand Casino.

The most spectacular French casino scam ever perpetuated was a lot more modern, taking place in the summer of 1973, long after the demise of the French gaming police. A ham radio buff employed as a roulette dealer at the Casino Deauville on the Atlantic coast built a radio transmitter into a pack of Marlboro cigarettes, embedding the tiny weightless receiver into a roulette ball he snuck into play. His brother-in-law placed the bets while his sister, a sexy, raven-haired temptress, softly pressed an invisible button on the cigarette pack as the ball was spinning, sending it into a controlled dive which resulted in the ball's landing in groups of six numbers with 90 percent accuracy. In a week the Casino Deauville was beaten for five million francs ($1 million at the time).

The owners of the casino could not figure out what was hitting them. First they thought the wheel itself was defective and that somebody had gotten wise to it. They had experts come in and completely dismantle the wheel, examine every working piece integral to the ball's spinning around the disk and the wheel's revolutions in the opposite direction. When the astonished owners were told that the wheel was in perfect balance and that there was not even the slightest imperfection that could produce biased outcomes, they began suspecting the dealer. They watched him secretively from above, but his motion was the same every time; he was doing nothing out of the ordinary to control the movement of the ball. It always made the same number of revolutions before going into its descent.

The scam was truly a marvel, the best I'd ever heard, and neither the ball nor the cigarette pack ever malfunctioned. Like most ingenious scams do, it came apart for a reason that had nothing to do with the scam.

The problem was that the dealer's sexy sister was a bit *too* sexy and drew the attention of the principal casino owner. He wanted to make her his mistress. He had subtly approached her in the casino several times while she was working the gadget. Being a chain-smoker, he was often asking her for a cigarette with his apologies. The raven-haired beauty was cool and able to operate despite the man's presence. She told her husband about his advances, but he replied that the owner's libido couldn't hurt the scam, so they continued.

Finally, the owner—realizing he was going nowhere fast with the temptress—began watching her with a different eye. Why was she so often in the casino, apparently alone? Why did she always stand by the same roulette table without making more than an occasional bet? And most of all, what was the connection between her and that table losing so much money whenever she was in the casino? All the answers came when the owners, at last suspecting some kind of radio interference with the roulette wheel, had an expert debugging crew come in and sweep the casino while the wheel was in action. The next time the principal casino owner asked the temptress for a cigarette, the chief of the Deauville Police Force was there at his side to confiscate the pack and put the lovely lady in handcuffs.

Monte Carlo boasted four casinos in 1986, two of which were American style—Loew's and the Café de Paris. The majestic Le Grand Casino that stood elegantly up the steps in front of the tiny principality's main square was perhaps the most famous casino in Europe (if not, Baden-Baden in Germany was), and there was also the Monte Carlo Sporting Club a bit farther off the square.

Entry to the Monte Carlo casinos differed from those in London. You could walk right into Loew's and the Café de Paris just as you could any American casino. However, at the two French-style casinos you had to pay a small entrance fee, around $10, and show your passport, which they entered into their computer. We had worried about showing our passports. If our reputations had preceded us, we could always be refused entry, so we naturally decided to start with Loew's and the Café de Paris.

We had landed on the Côte d'Azur during the Cannes Film Festival, the busiest two weeks of the year in the Monte Carlo casinos. We were really looking forward to pelting them with the blackjack move, certain they had never seen anything of its like before. Our only problem, we figured, was going to be the crowds in the relatively small casinos. If we had trouble obtaining blackjack seats, we'd have to fall back on roulette moves.

The Café de Paris casino was filled with sun-tanned people getting an early start on the summer season following the festival. There was the usual dotting of celebrities. I recognized a few very famous international actors as well as American professional athletes and European and South American Formula One drivers, in Monte Carlo for the Grand Prix.

The first blackjack move Jerry did with two creamy white twenty-five-hundred-franc chips underneath a red twenty-five-franc chip (about the equivalent of the American ten-o-five) was received courteously with a *"Je suis désolé, Monsieur"* preceding the payment. The second move was done with Sylvester Stallone sitting next to him at the table. I don't know if Sly saw the move or not, but he did shoot Jerry a Rocky Balboa look. The third, with Arnold Schwarzenegger at the other end of the table, definitely went unnoticed by the muscle-bound star, but not by a tiny Russian ballerina standing behind Jerry, who wanted to practice her English with him, and began describing to Jerry what she had seen him do with an assortment of hand and arm movements that were, I imagined, a lot less graceful than what she performed on stage.

There were only twelve blackjack tables in the casino. We attacked them with surgical precision, spreading out around the pit so that one of us could pounce on any chair left vacant by a player leaving the table. All four of us were equipped with the chips needed to do the move. Whoever was closest to the table opening up sat down, although we favored Jerry and held the chair for him if nobody else approached to take it. Sandy and Marla helped out, too. If a chair in front of the women became available, one of them sat down and played a hand until Jerry passed behind to take the seat. After ceding the place to Jerry, the two women roved around the pit, waiting for another opening they could protect until Jerry finished his business at the other table. If Jerry lost three hands in a row at any table, I replaced him while he took the seat that Sandy or Marla was holding. The whole scenario was the casino version of musical chairs—but it was supereffective. Before we left the casino, Jerry had gotten six of the twelve tables; I chalked up three, and Duke—a little bit rusty on the blackjack move—managed to get one paid with a laugh. We went back and got the two remaining tables the next night—before starting our second round.

In Loew's casino it was more of the same. Just below the Café de Paris on the base of a hill, the second American-style casino was bigger and had more blackjack tables and even a craps pit. We went right back to the blackjack attack, hitting them with a dozen moves before we finally took steam when one pit boss told another what had happened on one of his blackjack tables, and was then told in turn by that second pit boss that the same thing had just happened on one of his. My French was not very good, but I did hear the words *les américains* and you didn't have to be fluent to know they were talking about us. We cashed out the chips and headed for Le Grand Casino.

With its high ceilings, red carpeting, Renaissance paintings, and tapestries, the interior of Le Grand Casino was quite impressive, practically regal. In contrast, the dimly lit area by the gaming tables was no feat worthy of Michelangelo. As in any dumpy casino, billowing cigarette smoke filled the room. Surprisingly, the action itself was sparse in comparison to what we'd seen in the two American-style casinos. The big French roulette tables, each with its three croupiers pushing chips of different sizes and shapes around the layout with their little rakes, had only a trickling of players. There were two roped-off American roulette wheels in the casino, opened only on demand. The blackjack tables weren't jumping either. I had the impression that Le Grand Casino of Monaco was really more of a show-and-tell centerpiece than a high-stakes gambling establishment, so we left it alone.

We got in our rented car and drove along the winding and sometimes breathtaking coast to Cannes. There were four summer casinos in the celebrated town, the best-known occupying the seventh floor of the Carlton Hotel. We left the women in a nearby nightclub and took the elevator to the casino's reception area, each of us arriving separately, at ten-minute intervals. There were literally tons of Americans around—with and without the film festival—so we decided to take advantage of that patriotic presence in Cannes to confuse casino personnel if they tried to figure out which Americans were together.

What I saw inside was dazzling, perhaps the real Palme d'Or prizewinning film in Cannes that year. Never before—and I mean *never*—had I seen action like that! If the roulette tables in London had been flooded with big action, the downpour of chips on the dozen layouts inside the Carlton's casino was a veritable deluge. Seated at one of the English-style tables (same as American without the oo) were three Arab sheiks in their customary white robes and headdress. They were spreading large diamond-studded ten-thousand-franc chips straight up on the numbers. I had never been in a casino that accepted that much money on a straight-up bet. At the same table was a threesome of identically dressed Japanese men matching the sheiks bet for bet, blanketing the layout with their version of diamond-studded ten-thousand-franc chips. They all wore dark blue suits, badly tailored by Western standards, and the contrast to the sheiks in pure white made you believe they really were filming a French comedy.

My mind raced a mile a minute as I watched that phenomenal action. Ten thousand francs was at the time the equivalent of $2,000, which meant that each of the Arab and Japanese straight-up winning bets was being paid off at seventy grand! The largest straight-up move we had ever done earned us $7,000. This French Riviera casino would pay ten times that! The move I envisioned was feasible but extremely difficult. As in London, each roulette table had an inspector sitting high above the table. He would have to be taken out by distraction in order for Duke to move underneath the marker. I figured that the table with the sheiks and Japanese offered the best opportunity for a move because our ten-thousand-franc bet would blend right in on the layout. The casino wouldn't want to appear unclassy in front of their superrich clientele by squabbling over one "measly" winning chip that nobody had seen.

The problem was that these diamond-studded ten-thousand-franc chips were larger than roulette chips. We could not put the move-chip underneath the claimer's roulette chips as we'd been accustomed to doing. It would stick out and raise questions even if the move went in cleanly. The only solution was to have Duke lay in a naked capper, just like Mumbles and Wheels did in the old days. Simply lay our oversized ten-thousand-franc chip underneath the winning oversized ten-thousand-franc chip or chips already on the number. The problem with the naked capper was that the total number of chips on the winning number would be increased by one. A seasoned dealer might notice that difference even if there had originally been as many as six or seven winning chips. If there had been less, the one-chip increase would be that much more noticeable. At what minimum number of chips on the winning number would we deem sufficient to try it?

There was yet another worry. Since Duke and I (Joe and Jerry weren't needed to check-bet) would be the only players at the table not belonging to either clan, the Arabs or the Japanese might feel uncomfortable with our being there. Assuming we managed to get the move in, would one of them rat on us? You never knew who your rats could be, as I'd learned in Lake Tahoe with the Veronica experience. Asians tended to almost never rat, as that was part of their culture, but I knew nothing about Muslims. The stonings and hand choppings I'd heard about were punishments meted out for crimes committed *against* Arabs, usually by Arabs. But were their morals as supreme concerning French casinos ripped off by Americans?

There are certain times when even the most sophisticated casino-cheating teams cannot rely on intricate sign languages to communicate inside a casino. Normally, when we entered a casino we had a basic game plan—two or three different moves with which to attack. Once inside, we "called our play" based on prevailing conditions. If we decided to change the original plan, the new play was communicated by flashing each other signs, much like a football team calling its original play in the huddle then changing it with an audible at the line of scrimmage. But when the situation presenting itself was too complex—rendering our quarterback indecisive—a time-out was called to discuss it.

The multitudinous possibilities and their inherent complexities inside the Carlton casino forced us to take a time-out. Joe signaled me to leave the casino. I took the elevator down to the lobby and walked outside onto the *Croisette*. Ten minutes later Jerry appeared, then Duke, and finally Joe.

We all had individual impressions and ideas about what we'd seen inside the casino. After exchanging them excitedly, Joe made the decision.

"We go with the naked capper." He turned his attention specifically on Duke. "Even if there's only one winning chip on the number, you pop in ours underneath."

Duke exhaled the smoke from his cigarette. "What do I do if there're no winning chips straight up on the number? Do you want me to go on a split?"

"Absolutely not," Joe said firmly. "We wait for the straight-up.

As long as you're confident about getting it in there under the piece, we go for the jugular."

"No problem," Duke said, stomping out the butt. "I need the guy on the chair taken out for a full second."

"You got it," Jerry said.

Now Joe turned his attention to me. "This is what it's all about," he said. "New challenges. How long have we been together now, ten years? You have a lot of experience; you're a monster claimer. You never chilled-up once on me. You never committed the cardinal sin of leaving a move on a layout unclaimed. I have enormous respect for you ... as I do for both Duke and Jerry. You're a warrior, and your reward is the opportunity to claim the biggest move of all time." He paused a moment, then said triumphantly to us all, "Now let's go back in there and get these French motherfuckers!"

Jerry handed Duke the ten-thousand-franc chip he'd gotten off a blackjack table. Duke gave it an admiring glance, commented that it didn't have the diamond studding like the Arabs' and Japanese chips did, then shrugged and put it in his pocket. We filed one by one back to the lobby elevators.

I stood two roulette tables away from the target table and watched Duke on the bottom of the layout, wedged in between two sheiks. The sheer sight of that was laughable. The fact that Duke was wearing an expensive Armani suit did not make him look any less ridiculous. The presence of the Japanese only heightened my hilarity. I couldn't help but laugh softly to myself. Surprisingly, I was not the least bit nervous. In fact, I was perhaps the most relaxed I'd ever been when preparing myself to claim an important move. I was comfortable with the feeling that I had *earned* the right to claim this record-setting move. A lot of hard work, sweat, and discipline had gone into my career as a pastposter—not to mention balls of stone. My feeling was that I didn't want anybody else claiming that move but me.

When number 30 came in on the third spin with four winning diamond-studded chips on the number, Jerry stepped right in front of the inspector on the high chair and said loudly, almost obnoxiously,

"Monsieur . . . monsieur . . . s'il vous plaît . . . je ne parle pas le français . . .
Can you explain . . ."

That was all the greatest roulette mechanic in the history of the
world needed. With nerves of steel and unshakable will that made
me proud to be a part of this pastposting team, Duke shot out to the
layout from between the two sheiks, lifted off and held the marker
with his left hand while his right slid our big ten-thousand-franc chip
underneath the four already there, replaced the marker, leaned back
in his chair, and took a deep breath, all before the two stunned sheiks
witnessing the feat could praise Allah. The work Duke had done
with his right hand—picking up four oversized chips and sliding a
fifth underneath with his pinkie, then centering the marker, all in a
single second—was truly incredible.

I appeared at the front of the layout between two of the Japanese, just as Jerry was leaving to follow Duke out the door. *"Merci
beaucoup,"* I said loudly but without hysterics. "It's about time I won
a large bet in France!" There was no need to carry on too much
with the claim; the value of my chip exceeded none of the others
lying on the winning number.

What happened next was the biggest disappointment of my entire pastposting career. It was hard to believe, and when the French
gaming inspector on the high chair told me almost nonchalantly in
broken English that my bet couldn't be paid because I had violated
a French gaming regulation by betting a blackjack chip on a roulette
table, I thought he was either joking because I was an American, or
that his English was incapable of expressing what he really wanted
to say. When it hit me that he *was* serious, that in French casinos
(where rules differed from Monte Carlo) you simply were not allowed
to bet chips bought at blackjack tables straight up on roulette numbers, I went into a silent shock. I could not fathom this disappointment. The inspector explained that casino chips were permitted only
on the outside even-money and 2-to-1 bets.

There was no steam, no stirring—nothing. The inspector didn't
tell anyone else in the casino. The dealer went about his business of
paying the Arab sheiks and the Japanese, each of whom had two
winning chips on number 30. I watched numbly as the dealer pushed

$140,000 in chips, first to the two sheiks at the bottom of the table where Duke had been, and then to two of the Japanese. Finally, I managed to raise my head and look across the pit behind the inspector to where Joe was standing. He was staring at me with a ghastly grimace. He understood what had happened, the minute reason why our giant move was not being paid. I held Joe's stunned gaze with my own frozen version for a full minute, before finally turning away and cashing out the useless ten-thousand-franc chip at the cashier.

Years later, again in France on another pastposting trip, I saw a famous French film (*Mélodie en sous-sol*) in my hotel room that starred Jean Gabin and Alain Delon. Gabin played a lifelong older thief who had just been released from prison and was looking to put down one last big score before retirement. He hooks up with Delon, a clever Young Turk. Together they pull an armed holdup in a Cannes casino attached to the hotel where they were staying, escaping with several million francs. Knowing that the town would be completely bottled up by the police searching cars for the booty, and that they would be prime suspects, the two thieves decide to hide the money in a big duffel bag and stuff it into the chemical reservoir of the pool outside the hotel. A few hours after the early-morning holdup, Gabin and Delon are sitting across the pool from one another, biding their time before their eventual escape. Gabin is wearing sunglasses as he reads the *Nice Matin* detailing the robbery. Two detectives enter the pool area and split up to interview each suspect. The detectives' backs are toward the pool as they stand in front of Gabin and Delon. Suddenly, the duffel bag comes loose and is floating in the pool, the zipper undone by the journey. The bills begin slowly but steadily filtering out of the bag and onto the surface of the water, drifting. Gabin and Delon notice it immediately, but the detectives do not; they continue posing their questions to the two suspects, who are mesmerized by what they see. The money is sucked out of the bag faster and faster and soon covers the entire surface of the pool, but the detectives still don't notice, so immersed are they in their interrogations. Gabin's and Delon's faces express complete and utter shock. They look past the floating money at each other, knowing that their lives are finished by a quirk of fate. All the planning, the execution, and the pressure—literally down the drain because the duffel bag came loose at the precise instant the detectives arrived at the pool. The look exchanged by Gabin and Delon, well known to historians of French cinema, is the same look Joe and I exchanged inside the Carlton casino—also in Cannes.

Despite the bitter disappointment, the trip continued. In Italy we hit the San Remo casino on the Italian Riviera for a few blackjack moves and an *outside* roulette move. In Val d'Aosta, north of Milan, we found the biggest casino in Europe with its sixty American-style roulette wheels and twenty-five blackjack tables. Before we bought chips, Joe asked a boss if the casino accepted casino chips on the inside of roulette layouts. The boss smiled at him and said, "Oh, you must have been playing in France. They have strange rules over there."

We showed the same pit boss our "strange" move on one of his roulette tables—a hundred-thousand-lira straight up. We had been a little leery about working Italy because we'd known that at least one other international roulette pastposting team was Italian. Joe had discussed what precautions we would take if we ran into them again—or their steam.

In Germany, we visited the monumental palace of a casino called Baden-Baden. I don't know if Baden-Baden was more famous than Monte Carlo's Grand Casino, but it was certainly the most magnificent casino I had ever seen. In my opinion, it should not even have been called a casino. The place deserved better; it was an art museum.

Inside, below lustrous chandeliers that hung from towering ceilings, were separate regal gaming rooms whose walls were lined with works of art by the masters. The Teutonic mosaics in one room were as impressive as the Renaissance paintings in another. The Old World ambiance was simply overwhelming for someone brought up on glitzy Las Vegas casinos. Old European wealth was what came to mind. Cruising Baden-Baden's interior, I thought about how Dostoyevsky had gambled there. I'd read *The Gambler* and now understood exactly what he meant by the seduction of an old-money casino.

Out of awe and perhaps a little respect, we let Baden-Baden go. I don't think any of us, including Joe, would have been comfortable working it. However, I was quite content that we had stopped by. I'll never forget how impressed I had been by a goddamned casino.

We continued north to Holland, a country whose gaming industry was beginning to rival England's and France's with the advent of its Holland Casinos Group. What it lacked in originality (the interiors of all seven casinos in Holland were nearly identical) it made up for in terms of action. There was a lot of it in the group's flagship casino in Amsterdam. They accepted black casino chips (100 guilders— about $60) on the inside roulette numbers. We did two straight-ups and got paid—with a tinge of steam. The bummer was that their five-hundred-guilder chips were the French-style bricks, so doing blackjack moves was not practical. We could only work with round chips.

We went on to Rotterdam and did another wheel move—and again got paid with steam. In the Dutch summer resort town of Scheveningen—a name impossible for an Anglophone to pronounce— we found out why we had picked up steam on the roulette payoffs in Amsterdam and Rotterdam. The Italians we were apprehensive about running into in Italy had shown up in Holland. We didn't see them, but their presence was explained to me by the chief of casino security in the back room.

I was claiming another of Duke's wheel moves when suddenly a series of clamoring bells went off inside the casino. It sounded like the Good Humor truck had arrived in the neighborhood. I aborted the claim and picked the black chip off the layout—and tried to get out the door. Nothing doing. Security had me surrounded before I got near it.

In the back room I was treated with a courtesy that went as far as my being given donuts and coffee. The Dutch are a very relaxed and liberal people. The security chief was laughing wholeheartedly at my misfortune to enter his casino on the heels of the Italian team that had been there the night before.

"You Americans are very good at what you do," he said, almost in a congratulatory tone, "but your Italian rivals were here last night doing the same thing."

Not exactly, I wanted to say, knowing he probably would have laughed at that remark.

"We paid them several times before finally wising up to what they were doing."

One question I wanted to ask was, What *were* they doing? But again, I didn't.

"Would you like some more coffee or donuts before I release you? You can't come back to any of Holland's casinos, you know." He said that almost as if it were an afterthought.

We had been in Europe a month and were tired, but Joe insisted on a southern foray into Spain and Portugal. Both the Costa Brava and the Costa del Sol are as breathtakingly beautiful as the French Riviera but, ironically, the ratio of French roulette wheels to American and English wheels was greater than in France itself; thus we were mostly constrained to low-limit blackjack moves. We did find, however, a delightful little Portuguese gold mine in the Estoril Casino near Lisbon. We spent three days there beating their American wheels and eating their seafood meals. We finished the trip in Greece, where I had always wanted to go. Everyone I knew who had visited Greece and its islands raved about the warmth of its climate and the natural beauty of the seascape. We didn't intend to work its small casinos; the trip would be entirely pleasure for a change.

Lying on the splendid beach, Joe was reading an English-language newspaper in which there was an article about the growth of casinos in Turkey.

He put the paper down on his towel and said, "I think we should fly to Istanbul before we go home."

"What for?" I asked.

"The Istanbul Hilton just opened up one of the biggest casinos in Europe."

"Are you crazy?" I was amazed that he could even suggest working Turkey.

"Why?"

"Obviously, you never saw the movie *Midnight Express*."
Sometimes I thought Joe Classon really *was* crazy.

The European road trip was a smashing success. With all the expenses and blown opportunities accounted for, we had still cleared more than $50,000. The expenses were phenomenal. We had started in May and run into peak season in the middle of June. Including the Greek vacation and the two brand-new filled-to-the-gills Louis Vuitton suitcases needed to transport the bulk of Sandy's and Marla's purchases made in the continent's finest shops, we had spent a matching $50,000 at least. But the money aside, I really had a great time, and I think everybody else did, too.

The next overseas road trip we took six months later, during the Christmas holidays and into 1987. Joe called it our Deep South Tour, as if we were a rock-and-roll band in concert. We flew down to Buenos Aires, Argentina, rented a car, and drove to the rich seaside resort of Mar del Plata. There, on the beautiful golden shores of the Atlantic, the South American jet-set crowd gambled inside the continent's largest casino, with its hundred-plus roulette wheels. Unfortunately for us, the wheels were French-style, so we had to settle for making the blackjack rounds. From Argentina, we went north to Costa Rica and Colombia. Costa Rica had a bunch of thriving casinos in and around San Jose, and we hit them hard—perhaps a little too hard. After one particular steamy wheel move, I found myself being chased out of a San Jose casino by a half-dozen security men, and I ran smack into a muscle-flexing military parade. Having probably the stablest government of any Latin country, Costa Rica's leaders liked to show off its military discipline. I ran smack into a smiling Costa Rican colonel, who asked me, "*¿Qué pasó?*"

"*Nada,*" I said, running past him. Then I turned back and yelled to the security guards from the casino chasing me, "*No tienen miedo. No regreso al casino.*" Don't worry, I'm not coming back to the casino. Amazingly, they gave up the pursuit, and the colonel waved good-bye to me and continued his parade. We continued ours into Colombia and Panama.

In Colombia, the drug lords like to gamble, too, which puts a lot of periodic action into its dozen casinos. We *carefully* chose our spots, always a little leery of being mistaken for some of those very same drug lords. Joe said that the Colombian casinos reminded him of the casinos he'd worked with his brother in Cuba. Of course, I couldn't relate to Joe's comparison, but assumed that Batista's long-gone casinos had gotten their prerevolutionary share of the big action spilling over from the States. We did a dozen small wheel moves, then headed to Panama, which was about the same.

We wound up spending three weeks in South America. The profits were nothing like they had been in Europe, but the experience of the travels made the trip worth it. I had a wonderful time learning about Latin cultures inside the temples and museums we visited when not working. Joe enjoyed speaking Spanish, and I struggled along. South American conversation in the outdoor cafés is lively, and we found the people in Central and South America to be warm and friendly, much as they were in Puerto Rico.

After South America, we stayed true to Joe's Deep South tour and flew east underneath the equator to South Africa. There were several large casinos in and around Bophuthatswana, including the internationally known giant resort, Sun City, which had boasted Frank Sinatra in its showroom opening night. We made about $30,000 in the African casinos but ended up losing most of it to scandalous black-market currency traders. We had known before landing at Johannesburg that the African rand was not convertible and could not be taken out of the country in significant amounts. Joe had figured that we could sell the "worthless" rands back to illicit buyers with greenbacks at a loss of only 30 to 40 percent. But that wasn't at all the case. They scalped us at nearly 70 percent. Before doing the deal I had suggested that maybe we'd be better off buying Krugerrands and taking them back to the States where we could sell them at a reasonable price, but Joe declined, saying that we would be fucking with customs and could find ourselves in a big hassle. We ended up blowing as much money as we could—a veritable spending binge— on expensive dinners, champagne, excursions, anything we could do to get rid of the rands without picking up hard goods. What we got stuck with at the end we sold to the black marketeers.

On the way back through the bush to Johannesburg, Joe gave us a history lesson on apartheid. Though we hadn't felt South Africa's policy of racial segregation during our casino tour, Duke had expressed his concerns about driving outside the city while we were standing on the rent-a-car line inside the airport terminal, just after we had gotten off the plane. He was afraid of racial attacks against whites. Before we reached the city, heading back to the airport, we pulled a little practical joke on him. Joe began pressing and releasing the gas pedal with his foot, making the car putt-putt. Then he cut the engine and we all made Duke believe we had run out of gas and would soon fall prey to vicious black bands roaming the bush in search of stranded white tourists. Well, Duke might have been an iron man with no fear in the casinos, but out there in the bush he turned as white as the Dark Continent's whitest snow.

Before returning to the States, we discussed the possibility of adding another leg to the trip, to make up for the disappointment in South Africa. All of us had heard about the supposedly twenty-four-hour nonstop wild gambling action on the island of Macao, less than an hour's hydrofoil ride from Hong Kong. I immediately expressed my objections, thinking about Asian punishment that never fit the crime and always went overboard. Joe informed me (as I already knew) that Macao was actually a Chinese territory under Portuguese administration that would eventually revert back to Mainland China like Hong Kong at the end of the century. Therefore, he said, casino crimes were still punishable by Portuguese law, not Chinese. I told him that I didn't give a shit, that it would be the Chinese meting out that punishment, Portuguese or not Portuguese. Joe came to his senses and we flew back to Vegas, but not before he brought up the Philippines, another Far East gambling mecca I had no desire to visit. I had heard about butt-lashings given there to people with dishonest fingers.

Passage of Rites

NINETEEN-EIGHTY-NINE WAS A VERY EVENTFUL YEAR IN MY LIFE. First, Joe Classon retired—just like that.

I was dining on the terrace of my new apartment when Joe arrived unexpectedly and gave me the news.

"I'm fifty-six years old," he said. "I've been in these goddamned casinos since I got back from Korea. I think I've had enough."

Though I had expected that one day Joe Classon would abandon the road, hearing it so suddenly was a shocker. We'd been together in the casinos for twelve years—longer than the Beatles were together—and now he was leaving, breaking up the team. At least, it wasn't because of a woman.

"You guys will have no problem going down the road without me, provided you don't squabble over who's boss. Personally, I feel you're the most qualified; you have the best leadership qualities of the three of you, but Duke and Jerry will never go for it. There can't be a leader anymore. If I was the general, now you three are all colonels. I'm going to call Duke and Jerry in California tonight and tell them to fly into Vegas this weekend. We're going to have a final sit-down. Sorry for interrupting your dinner."

The last time Joe, Duke, Jerry, and I were all together was at Joe's apartment on Sunday afternoon that weekend in March 1989. The night before, we'd been barbecuing lobsters when Joe said, "Guys, I'm going out with a bang. Tonight at Caesars Palace I am going to do my last move—the rainbow." He was smiling mischievously.

Duke, Jerry and I were all looking at each other puzzled. You never knew what Joe Classon had in mind.

"That's right," Joe confirmed. "The rainbow. It's my final tribute to all of you." He looked at Jerry. "It may be the most special for you because you invented the blackjack move."

"What exactly is the rainbow?" I ventured.

"Exactly that—a rainbow. I'm going to bet five red chips on a blackjack table at Caesars Palace—I wouldn't think of doing it anywhere else, considering how classy Caesars has been all these years. When I win the hand, I'm going to do a five-chip switch. But instead of doing a normal move with the purples, I'm going to do an insane one. The five chips I'm going to switch in will be a yellow, a purple, a black, a green, and a red. So instead of calling that move a sixteen-thirty"—$1,630-total value of the five chips Joe proposed switching in—"why not just call it the 'rainbow.'"

Duke nearly fell off his chair laughing. It was infectious; we all started laughing—Joe, too. But he was dead serious. If Joe Classon told you he was going to walk naked through the Everglades, you had better warn the alligators.

"Joe," I said with affected deference, "I have never respected anyone else in my life the way I do you . . . but you are a fucking nut job."

We finished our lobsters, toasted the rainbow with champagne, then headed over to Caesars Palace, which was filling up rapidly as the doors to the Circus Maximus Showroom had swung open and begun spilling people out onto the checkered carpeting of the main pit.

The floorman who came over to Joe's blackjack table, after being called in by the dealer, took one look at the chip-rainbow sitting in the betting circle and shook his head exaggeratedly, as though he were trying to dismiss the possibility that he had just seen a multi-colored UFO. He then removed a pen from his shirt pocket and with it softly collapsed the chips into a heap, and then restacked them.

"How on heaven's earth did you miss *that?*" he asked the smiling Latino dealer named Eduardo.

"I don't know," Eduardo answered with a shrug. "I must not have slept too good last night."

The floorman left the table to get the pit boss. Not because he was steamed up but because he wanted the pit boss to have a good laugh. The pit boss did have a good laugh and said to the dealer, "Eduardo, if you took that for a twenty-five-dollar bet, that tequila you've been drinking must be pretty strong." He laughed, shook his head, and walked away with the floorman, neither one wanting to get over it.

I had watched the whole thing in amazement. That Joe's rainbow got paid was not exactly stupefying. What I found incredible was that they didn't even question it. There wasn't the slightest doubt in the heads of *three* Caesars Palace casino employees. In spite of more than a decade's experience I had already had at casino trickery, I would have hardly believed that the rainbow could be put over on them so easily—had I not seen it with my own eyes. I wondered how long Joe had had that little move in his head.

Over more champagne back at Joe's apartment, he explained it to me. "It's all psychology, my boy." Joe was feeling good. "Why do you think all this crap works in the first place? Besides the straight-up roulette moves under the piece, all our moves are easy; anybody can do them. It's not the moves that knock them dead, it's the psy-chological effect. It's a progression of influencing people's thought patterns, making them believe what you want them to. The setups, the back-ups, the mix-ups—they're all part of the act. So I go and do a ridiculous move—the rainbow—and it gets paid easier than any-thing you've ever seen. Why? Because it *is* so ridiculous. No one in his right mind would do something so insane—and the casinos know that. Whatever doubts they have are squelched when they ask themselves, 'Would anyone really try to slip in something like that?' "

Joe raised his glass and the three of us followed. "To the rainbow, to the road . . . to my guys." We clinked glasses and drank. Toward the end of the night we all got a little emotional. Joe was hugging all of us, and everybody had tears welling up. The next day we had breakfast together at Joe's apartment, then we went to the airport to see Duke and Jerry off. On Monday Joe and I spent a final day together, mostly reminiscing about the adventures we'd had. On Tuesday, Joe flew to Miami, where he eventually bought himself a condominium near his mother's on the beach.

Joe Classon never came back to Las Vegas.

And I never saw him again.

The second main event of 1989 was the opening of Steve Wynn's first gambling megaresort, the Mirage Hotel. Though Caesars Palace had always been, and always will be, the class of Las Vegas, the Mirage presented it with a serious challenge. Wynn, who already owned the Golden Nugget properties in Las Vegas and Atlantic City, built his new casino intending to attract the world's high rollers. He also attracted the three remaining members of the Classon Pastposting Team.

Joe's mind-boggling rainbow move at Caesars, with the thousand-dollar chip on the bottom, served as more than a colorful way of sending Joe Classon off in glory. The move let us know that the time to start pastposting thousand-dollar chips had arrived. During the Mirage's grand-opening week in the spring of 1989, Jerry and I went through its casino popping in ten-twenty-fives (a yellow underneath a green), and then two-thousand-twenty-fives (two yellows and a green), all off fifty (two greens) and seventy-five-dollar (three greens) original bets. Our success that first week was phenomenal. Our illusions equaled those of the famous German illusionists Siegfried and Roy, who opened the Mirage's showroom. They made their white tigers turn into elephants; we made the Mirage's green chips turn into yellows. True, we didn't make as much money as they did, but we weren't under contract, either. We did end up earning $50,000 that first week at the Mirage, which matched our earnings from the entire 1986 summer trip to Europe.

But our Mirage success was short-lived. The historic opening of the Mirage marked our own history with some very negative events. Duke, who had taken over Joe's role as security for the operation, made an error in judgment after Jerry took steam on a blackjack move. The pit boss had authorized the dealer to pay him but was very upset about it. Afterward, we discussed the situation, and Duke, who'd been the last one out the door, decided that the intensity of the steam was not enough to halt our assault on the Mirage. At first his assessment appeared correct. A few days later we went back there on a different shift and I was paid on two yellow-chip moves without any problems. Duke then felt that Jerry could resume his position as leadoff mechanic, and Jerry agreed. Half an hour after my second payoff, Jerry sat down at a blackjack table and placed his three green chips in the betting circle. I was sitting at the other end of the same table, playing two hands to create action. Jerry's hand won, and he switched the chips and claimed. No sooner had he finished saying, "Hey, dealer, you paid me wrong," than a half-dozen green-jacketed Mirage security guards led by Hanson's Steven DeVisser swarmed over Jerry from behind. They grabbed and handcuffed him right there at the table. DeVisser spotted me right away and smiled as he instructed the guards to take me away as well. Only Duke escaped the dragnet.

I was grilled in the back room and released, but Jerry got arrested and charged with fraudulent acts in a gambling casino, a felony. It was the first bust in our team's history—going back to the days of Mumbles and Wheels. That occurrence enlightened us about casino surveillance's newest tool: twenty-four-hour instant playback. Steve Wynn, determined to thwart the cheaters working from both inside and outside of his casino, had installed the latest state-of-the-art surveillance equipment in the Mirage. Every square inch of casino space was under twenty-four-hour video surveillance, and a phone call up to inspectors in the sky could have the tape from any camera in the casino reviewed instantly, literally in a matter of seconds. In the first month of operations, dozens of dishonest casino employees and cheaters were arrested and charged with felonies.

This new threat from surveillance changed our tactics as the 1990s arrived. Soon all the casinos in Nevada and Atlantic City modified their surveillance systems with such equipment. We were forced to abandon claims earlier. If the claimer wasn't paid right away, there was no dispute; it was simply right out the door. We operated under the assumption that every table was under twenty-four-hour surveillance, that every move was on videotape and could be replayed by surveillance inspectors upstairs and confirmed for pit bosses on the casino floor within seconds. That was too much for us to buck.

Sandy went down to the jail and bailed Jerry out. Jerry was pissed off—not at Duke but at the Mirage—and wanted to go right back out to work. Duke and I both discouraged him. We brought him back to his senses. We didn't know how far the Nevada prosecutor was going to go with the case. To risk a second bust would be madness.

We hired Jerry the best criminal attorney in Las Vegas, Terry Williamson. During discovery, when the prosecutor was obligated to turn over all his evidence to the defendant's attorney, Williamson recovered the surveillance tape from the Mirage. We watched it in the attorney's office. The tape itself was impressive. It came from an overhead stationary camera above the blackjack table. It was black-and-white with a clear image. You could see the table layout and the hands and part of the arms of all the players around it, including mine and Jerry's. The only person's face you saw was the dealer's. The move was clearly depicted on tape. According to Williamson, from seeing the tape, in conjunction with expert testimony from surveillance personnel, a jury could be made to understand exactly what Jerry had done and with what intent. To make matters worse, Williamson—who had strong contacts with Nevada Gaming Control Board people—told us the prosecutor was being pushed to make a conspiracy case against us based on testimony from a certain Hanson agent, who could supposedly prove we had entered the casino together and were already known associates in the business of cheating casinos.

But for $10,000 he'd see what he could do.

I gave Williamson the ten grand in cash. He told us to stay out of the casinos—at least in the state of Nevada—and that he should have the case resolved in a few months.

Meanwhile, the Mirage case also made Jerry a television star— but not in the same way that Caesars Palace was responsible for Joe's ex-wife Ruthie becoming a movie star.

During the months of inactivity while Jerry's case was pending, I hung around the apartment a lot. One night I was watching television and one of the stations ran a brief publicity piece for the nationally syndicated program *Real Stories*, which chronicled interesting happenings from all walks of life. One of the segments that night was about casino surveillance at the new Mirage Hotel and how they catch thieves and cheaters in the act. Of course I watched it. First, there was a piece showing a man-woman team using a distraction on a roulette table to steal chips in the dealer's well. The man created a commotion that got the dealer's head turned to the bottom of the table while the woman picked off clumps of five-dollar chips from the stacks in the well at the top. It wasn't very sophisticated. The next sequence caught a pretending-to-be-handicapped man's surprised facial expression as he was taken away by Mirage security men. They had just caught him performing a burglary on one of the casino's rolling coin carts as he rolled alongside it in his motorized wheelchair. Again, it wasn't too impressive, neither for the burglar nor the Mirage, but it gave me a good laugh.

The third incident, however, piqued my interest. As soon as it came on screen I recognized it. It was the tape that Jerry's attorney Williamson had shown us in his office. And there was an added clip I hadn't seen before: Jerry getting dragged through the casino by Mirage security. His face was easily identifiable. While the tapes were playing on-screen, one of the inspectors at the Mirage was describing what was happening on the voice-over. I heard him make a glaring mistake in his description. He said that the cheater had picked up the three green chips and then "slipped" the two yellow ones underneath. Well, that's not at all what had happened. What Jerry had done was completely *replace* the three green chips with two yellows and a green. He had left none of the original chips on the layout.

First thing the next morning, I called Williamson in his office. I asked him, "In the prosecution's case description, what exactly does it say Jerry did?"

I heard the rumpling of pages through the line and then Williamson began reading from the prosecutor's detailed case report.

"The suspect then pastposted two one-thousand-dollar chips underneath the three twenty-five-dollar chips that he had originally bet, increasing the total amount of his bet to $2,075."

When I heard that last part about the total bet being $2,075, my mind raced in frenzied excitement. I was thinking that perhaps I had found a technicality that would allow Jerry to walk. Maybe I could save him the way Joe had once saved me in the back room of the California Club, when he'd scared off the witnesses and destroyed Gaming's case.

"What chips did they lock up as evidence?" I asked Williamson. That was the key. If the chips locked up did not match the description of the alleged crime, it would be me who had the case—not the Mirage.

"They have three chips in evidence," Williamson said, exactly what I wanted to hear. "Two yellow thousand-dollar chips and one green twenty-five-dollar chip."

I could barely contain myself as I explained the discrepancy to Williamson, who said when I had finished, "You might have something there."

A week later Williamson struck a deal with the prosecutor. Jerry would plead guilty to disorderly conduct, a petty misdemeanor, and pay a $500 fine. No casino or felony conviction would be entered onto his record. The disorderly conduct conviction was no more serious than disturbing the peace by playing your stereo too loud. In effect, Jerry got a walk, and no conspiracy charge against me ever materialized.

We had escaped again. Steven DeVisser lost another battle to me. In his zeal to tie me into a major conspiracy, he had forgotten to oversee the Mirage surveillance department's handling of the case. They put the wrong chips in the evidence bag, and the result was a blown case.

As 1989 continued, I began to gradually wrest control of our operation from Duke, who didn't want to conform to my leadership, but had no choice because Jerry sided with me. Though Jerry never said anything, I sensed that he blamed Duke for his getting busted at the Mirage. Being reduced to a three-man team, we stayed with the blackjack move as our primary source of income. I had often proposed to Duke that he begin sharpening his skills at the blackjack table, but he constantly protested, deeming it foolish to change the rhythm of the Jerry-and-me tandem attacking the tables. His attitude was becoming rebellious, and I began preparing for his eventual farewell.

So Jerry and I continued picking the cherry spots for blackjack moves as 1989 wore down to an end. After so many years in Vegas, I had developed an intimate relationship with the casinos, and even with some of the pit personnel working inside them. What that meant is that I knew each casino so well I could reasonably predict what moves it was good for, with what frequency, and, most important, with what floormen and pit bosses. Contrary to what people unfamiliar with casino cheating might think, the selection of dealers is not that important. The mechanics of the moves and the psychology that Joe had loved so much to talk about took care of the dealers. The trick was to intimately know your floormen and pit bosses. Which floormen paid on their own without alerting their pit bosses? Which pit bosses paid without making a fuss? Those were the important details to remember. Following Joe's procedure, I kept a thorough logbook on casino personnel in Las Vegas. (Boy, would Steven DeVisser like to see that!) In it I charted every move done, down to the last detail. It helped me enormously in deciding which casinos to go into and when.

At the Riviera there was an old floorman of about sixty who must have been working there for at least twenty-five years. Joe had remembered him from the sixties. We referred to him as Grumpy because every time the dealer called him over after one of us did a blackjack move, he'd grimace annoyingly and throw his notepad down on the table with absolute disgust as he ordered the dealer to pay, asking either Jerry or me if we wanted our action "rated."

Grumpy's routine was the same every time. I had begun to notice it after the second move was done on him. True, the expression about going to the well one too many times was a worthy one, but with Grumpy I continued going to the well anyway. After ten, twenty, even thirty moves on his tables, nothing changed. He kept coming over to the table and throwing down the pad, albeit sometimes a little less forcefully than at other times. But his wrath was always directed at the dealers, never us. One time after I'd done a move and was in the process of getting paid, he grumbled to me, "What's the matter with these damned dealers?" as he threw his pad down on the table. So every two weeks, like clockwork, it was "Let's go over to the Riv and pick up our dime [$1,000] from Grumpy."

Caesars Palace was loaded with hospitable floormen. For some reason, many of its casino personnel were ex-athletes who at one time had been on the fringes of professional sports, especially basketball. Not to sound racial, but when you notice the overabundance of tall black men in the pits, you'll get the idea what I'm talking about. Usually, these ex-athlete floormen, some of whom had once starred with the University of Nevada Las Vegas basketball team, were extremely cool and sometimes a bit uninterested—being heavily juiced into their jobs. One of these men, named Cecil, who looked like the boxer Larry Holmes, was a gentleman's gentleman. Every time Jerry or I moved on a table he was supervising, he came over and introduced himself, gave us his card—and made us a comped reservation to see Sinatra, Diana Ross, or whoever was playing the Circus Maximus Showroom. With some floormen that repetitiveness helped us get paid after the initial move. Cecil would say, looking down at our yellow chips on the layout, "How are you, sir? I remember you from before . . . always playing yellow chips." I brought in mechanic after mechanic to Cecil's tables during the nineties. The first five-thousand-dollar blackjack move with a chocolate chip was to be done by the great Pat Mallery on Cecil's table in 1994.

Thanksgiving weekend 1989, Duke quit as anticipated.

So did Jerry. That was the shocker. As I had wrested control of the operation from Duke, drugs had begun wresting Jerry from me. He had gotten into cocaine and crack, and was losing control. He'd become distraught and couldn't work anymore. He said he was going back to his native Missouri, where he would try to live clean for a while. I was sad to see him go but knew that abandoning both Las Vegas and California was necessary for his sanity. He promised to stay in touch.

With the demise of our team in 1989, I nearly quit the casinos myself. In fact, during 1990 and 1991, I didn't do much except hang around Vegas and play poker while watching sports, always in disguise to protect myself from Steven DeVisser. But the following decade brought both a casino explosion—and Jerry out of retirement. He phoned me in January 1992. Said he'd kicked the drugs and was ready to go back to work.

I was happier than ever. Another decade of new casino adventures awaited me, and I wouldn't be going at it alone.

The Gay and Not So Gay Nineties
(A Casino Revolution)

IN THE EARLY 1990S, THE CASINO INDUSTRY IN THE UNITED STATES went through a sort of industrial revolution. In 1992, in Ledyard, Connecticut, the Pequot Indian tribe opened up a casino called Foxwoods—literally in the woods where foxes had been roaming—that soon became the most profitable casino in the world. It produced more gambling revenues than Atlantic City's three biggest casinos combined. The Indians had won a decision in federal court that exempted them from all federal and almost all state taxes on these revenues, giving them, in effect, a license to become untaxed billionaires. This decision, which also granted them the right to operate casinos on their reservations in direct conflict with state laws, led to a massive casino development craze on Indian reservations throughout the country. In addition to that, also in 1992, the state of Mississippi voted in casino gambling, and casinos began springing up along the Gulf Coast and then up in Tunica, a buggy patch of Mississippi swampland less than an hour's drive from Memphis. There was also a riverboat boom at the same time. From New Orleans to Chicago, all the nation's midwestern rivers suddenly had a flotilla of docked and sailing riverboat casinos. By the middle of the decade there were hundreds of American casinos outside of Nevada and New Jersey— all staffed with new and incompetent casino employees.

As the casino industry revolutionized itself, the pastposting business revolutionized right along with it. Suddenly there were a hundred new candy stores for us to enter, wide-eyed and eager, like infants gawking at all the chocolate bars to be had. The potential for us was endless. Jerry and I went to Foxwoods in the fall of 1992. If during Atlantic City's infantile stage in 1978 the casinos paid anything you pastposted on its tables, at Foxwoods you could throw a purple chip across the casino and probably be paid by the dealer whose table it landed on. That's how incredibly unorganized and green these people were. We did nothing but blackjack moves, one after the other. The structure of table limits and the casino chips were identical to Atlantic City casinos. Unfortunately, their thousand-dollar orange chips were bigger than the other chips; if not, they would have felt our double-barreled attack twice as hard. We had even discussed the possibility of ignoring that size difference and moving the big orange chips, but decided against it, refusing to let greed get the better of us.

All in all, that decision to stay with the purple chips did not hurt us. We did fifteen-twenty-fives (three purples and a green replacing four original greens) wherever we could, ten-twenty-fives wherever we couldn't. After a full week of hammering all three shifts we gave them a rest. The bottom line was $100,000 profit. In a casino where you cannot work with chips valued at more than $500, that one-week record will never be broken, no matter how large the team that tries to do so. We had lost track of the exact number of moves done (it must have been close to a hundred), but I'll never forget the amazing accomplishment of only having a single miss—which was caused more by confusion than by steam.

Jerry had moved on one of the real Native American dealers (the overwhelming majority of dealers were not Indians; the casino was run by ex-Atlantic City people and staffed from the surrounding non-Indian population) who had difficulty communicating to the floorman what had happened on his table. Despite the presence of ten purple backup chips on the layout, the floorman couldn't be made to understand what the dealer was trying to tell him—that Jerry had bet three purple chips and a green, not four greens. The floorman understood the opposite. He thought that the dealer had mistakenly paid Jerry three purples and a green instead of four greens. He had taken the dealer's four-green-chip payoff for Jerry's original bet and Jerry's three-purple-one-green-chip move for the dealer's payoff. He looked at Jerry and said with an annoying, squeaky laugh, "If we keep paying off like that, we're gonna go broke fast." Then he did the amazing: he took the three purple chips Jerry had switched in and put them in the dealer's rack, giving him three greens in exchange. The fucking idiot just locked up our move, I said to myself as I watched all that happen in a combination of horror and amazement. And the dealer didn't even notice it, after he himself had tried to make the floorman understand that Jerry had bet the three purples in the first place. Amid all that unbelievable confusion, Jerry wisely let it go, knowing that it was better for us to take the $1500 loss than to stoke the fireball of confusion that was rapidly getting out of hand. We also assumed that Foxwoods was equipped with the same state-of-the-art surveillance systems we had run into at the Mirage in Las Vegas three years earlier. Ten minutes after that debacle, Jerry was at a blackjack table in another pit getting paid the same $1,525.

Though Jerry had not lost any of his effectiveness on the blackjack tables during his three-year layoff, he was not the same guy I had known before. Physically, he was thinner and his face had assumed an oily glow. His temperament had also changed. He had become rash, sometimes indifferent. He would get excited by something, then a minute later forget it. I noticed he was eating less than before, and smoking less pot. Though I never witnessed him doing so, I assumed he was back on hard drugs. I suspected it was speed this time. I didn't risk saying anything to him, for fear that my observations would send him into a rage. I just hoped he could overcome it.

Mississippi was generally the same story as Foxwoods in Connecticut, but it was really humid down there, even in winter. There were four casinos along the coast between Biloxi and Gulfport in early

1993. They didn't have the same big action that we'd seen at Fox-woods, but their ineptitude matched their Yankee rivals step for step.

A funny example of that ineptitude occurred one night at the Isle of Capri casino in Biloxi. We had just finished working the President casino a few miles down the coast, where we had gotten two black-jack ten-o-fives paid. Figuring we would go back there the next day on the afternoon shift, we decided to keep the purples from that casino to avoid having to rebuy them. Now, at the Isle of Capri, Jerry had just lost three blackjack hands in a row and it was my turn to go in behind him. I prepared the move and backup chips in my hand as I sat down on third base, placing three red five-dollar chips in the betting circle. I won the first hand and moved and claimed. Just after doing so, I got ill looking at what I had done. Sitting underneath the red-chip capper were two purple five-hundred-dollar chips from the President casino, not the two from the Isle of Capri that should have been there. I had stupidly gotten the purple chips from the two ca-sinos mixed up. Normally, I was extremely cautious, but somehow I had overlooked that most basic precaution.

My first thought was to grab the chips off the circle and go into a drunk routine, as if I didn't know what I was doing. But it was too late; I had already claimed that I was betting purples and that the dealer had paid me wrong. The dealer didn't crack off the red capper. He just called over the floorman. When the floorman arrived, I went into a drunk routine with a built-in protection disclaimer. I began praising my two favorite casinos, the President and the Isle of Capri. If he noticed the President purples underneath, which I felt was highly probable, I would at least be covered inasmuch as I was a purple-chip player over at the President and enjoyed drinking while gambling. I had only a smidgen of Joe's psychological knowledge, but I remembered his basic teachings about taking control of nega-tive situations. The floorman, a guy in his early twenties who had possibly never dealt a hand of blackjack in a casino himself, figured to be somewhat manipulable. At that point I was not at all thinking about getting paid, only about controlling the situation well enough so that I could escape without further problems.

Casinos never ceased to amaze me. The floorman looked at my

bet and simply told the dealer to pay me. I couldn't believe it. I had switched in the wrong goddamn chips, and they were still paying me! As soon as the dealer put the two purples and red chip next to my errant move under the floorman's eyes, I scooped up all those chips faster than a bird of prey snatched a water snake out of a pond. Nobody noticed anything, and before the floorman left the table he assured me that the Isle of Capri casino was far more hospitable than the President. Considering what had just happened, I couldn't really argue.

After Mississippi, we decided to test the fledgling riverboats. We agreed that we'd only work the ones which were docked. That way we avoided the risk of having to escape in open waters. The first one we boarded looked to be boundless with opportunities, but Jerry suddenly fell ill before we bought chips. It was hot and I noticed he wasn't sweating much, and I was becoming greatly concerned about his drug abuse.

The next day, Jerry decided to return to Missouri, and I sensed that his pastposting days were numbered—this time permanently. If I wanted to continue in the business, I'd soon need a new partner.

But recruiting people for this kind of work is not easy. First, who would believe that pastposting really works? And second, if you convinced someone that it did, what were the chances that that person would have the balls to do it? The pressure of being in the casinos is indeed unique. Being a sneak thief is one thing, robbing the casinos under their noses is another. Even rough-'n'-tough mob guys balked at putting themselves under that kind of pressure. I had once talked with an actual "made" guy about joining the operation, but when he saw a move go down he quipped, "No thanks, I'd rather put a bullet in somebody's head." Of all the people I had worked with or eventually would work with, I was the only person who never entered the casino under the influence of *something*. Joe and Duke had been pot smokers. My next great partner-to-be, Pat, worked best under the influence of alcohol. As glamorous as some of my experiences may sound, it just wasn't an easy business.

Balls

BACK IN THE MID 1970S, JUST BEFORE I DROVE OUT TO VEGAS FOR the first time, I knew a guy my age named Mark Abromowitz, a stalk-thin mad Jewish gambler who smoked more than he ate and was nicknamed Balls for his reckless pursuit of big-time scores without the least bit of fear of what that might cost him. He took all forms of gambling to the hilt. At no-limit poker he'd throw in his whole bankroll on a hand that couldn't beat ace-high. At the track he'd do the same on a 20-to-1 long shot if he believed in the horse. Sometimes he won, more often he lost, but some of his scores were magnificent. At twenty-one years of age he'd probably had more gambling experience than 90 percent of the compulsive gamblers twice his age—and that's saying a lot.

In March 1993, I ran into Balls in Vegas after not having seen him for seventeen years. He was playing $75–$150 seven-card stud at the Mirage (a very expensive game) and going broke fast. We went into the coffee shop after he tapped out. He told me he was stone-broke and had to go back to New York and see if he could hustle up a bankroll. It was then, for the very first time, that I decided to let someone new into my operation. I sensed that Balls, being as fearless as he was at the gambling tables, would be interested in getting some of his money back the hard way—stealing it. One thing I was sure of: he'd understand right away that pastposting really did work. And I needed a new partner.

I took Balls back out to the Mirage casino and showed him a little two-o-five on the blackjack table. When he saw that, he gave me one of his head-slanting nods that I would come to know so well. He did it when he approved or when something impressed him—or both. After I did the second blackjack two-o-five, Balls's nod was a bit more pronounced. "Show me how to do that," he said.

I took him down to Laughlin, a small-getting-big Nevada gambling town ninety miles from Las Vegas, across the Colorado River from Bullhead City, Arizona. I had been there a few times with Joe and Duke, when they'd first trained me in the business. Now, a decade and a half later, I was again entering the Pioneer Club casino to train Balls. As it had been so many years before, the decor of the casino was still pioneering cowboys, and all the dealers and pit personnel dressed that way. I put Balls on a blackjack table and had him do a one-o-five, a little two-chip switch with a black and a red replacing two reds. It was sloppy but he got paid. I took him down the road to the Colorado Belle, where he did three more. I noticed he was moving too fast, too abrupt. He wasn't waiting for the dealers' hands to get out of his way. The impatience in his character was spilling out onto his moves, resulting in sloppiness. I had to get him to calm down a bit. "You have to finish one move before doing another," I told him. "There's no clock in this. Take your time and do it right." It took a dozen more moves, but Balls finally slowed down and mastered the technique.

Back in Vegas, we went to Bally's to do a craps move. I had explained it to him in Laughlin and quickly reminded him of a few details inside Bally's keno pit. He nodded impatiently, saying, "Okay, okay, let's go do it." I put it in and he got paid, but again his impatience caused a little uneasiness in the pit.

At the new MGM, the hugest and ugliest green monster I'd ever seen sprout out of the desert, that impatience at the craps table turned into overaggressiveness and caused quite a hysterical incident.

Balls was standing over my shoulder waiting for me to pop in a ten-o-five on the pass line. I had bet the three red chips, and now the shooter rolled a winner. I bent down to the layout and started my push forward to make the switch, but at the last split second the dealer hesitated as he was cutting into my chips, so I pulled back without switching.

Suddenly, I was being shoved roughly to the side as a body rudely invaded my space. It was Balls lunging into the craps table, claiming, "Hey, dealer, I'm betting purples here! What is this horseshit!" Balls practically fell *inside* the craps table.

The dealer gave Balls a look that could've simply changed his name to Nuts. The boxman's evaluation of the skinny little guy flying into the table wasn't much different. "I'm sorry, sir," he said in an appeasing tone usually reserved for babies, "but there are no purple chips on the layout."

Balls stared down on the pass line. The look he had on his face was comical. He seemed to be the awed witness of an illusionist's disappearing act. Perhaps Balls thought that I was such a good craps mechanic I'd put the move in *underneath* the felt, I reflected humorously. Back in the keno pit, I told him kiddingly, "Oh, there's one thing I forgot to tell you about pastposting: they don't pay invisible chips."

During the summer of 1993, I worked exclusively with Balls in Vegas. We stuck with blackjack and craps moves because roulette was not yet workable with a two-man team. He had finally calmed down and learned that patience was an integral part of the business. We were rolling along nicely until Steven DeVisser finally chased us out of town.

One night, he came out from behind a bank of slot machines at the Excalibur casino with two security officers and had me grabbed up, thinking I had just done a move in the casino. I was taken to the back room and held there until surveillance could run back all the tapes from the tables where I had been sitting. I had another stroke of good luck that night. It was Balls, not me, who had done the blackjack move at the Excalibur, and I hadn't even been at his table because only one seat was available at the time. Once again, DeVisser had to cut me loose, grudgingly.

Just a week later, we ran into him again at the Imperial Palace. We were on our way out the door, not having done anything more than case the casino. DeVisser, again wearing his denim suit, just happened to be entering through the main entrance with two security guards. I called out for Balls to run as I took off in the other direction, figuring I'd let them grab me up down the road while he got away. Protecting Balls was of the utmost importance because he was still unknown to Hanson Investigations. I let DeVisser and one of the guards catch up to me near Harrah's, and they walked me back. Unfortunately, Balls had gone stiff and never got out of the blocks. Evidently, his name didn't apply to escapes. I'd have to remember that.

In the back room, DeVisser kept me and Balls company while surveillance reviewed the casino tapes. DeVisser was practically foaming at the mouth like a starved dog. He was sure he had us dead to rights, knowing that the casino filmed all their table games twenty-four hours. He kept asking, "Why did you run? Why did you run? I'll bet the answer will be on tape." When the surveillance director came into the backroom an hour and a half later shaking his head, DeVisser said with dismay, "You ran *all* the tapes?"

"We went back four hours," the surveillance director said. "Nothing."

"Did you check the baccarat pit?"

"We ran back everything. Neither one of them ever approached a table."

"Shit!" was clearly in DeVisser's eyes. Before they cut us loose I said to him, "To answer your question about why I ran—I just wanted to see if you could keep up with me."

"One of these days your luck's gonna run out," he said, with a frosty glaze in his eyes.

"May . . . be."

That particular back-rooming was disastrous in that it allowed

DeVisser to identify Balls for the first time and to chalk him up as one of my "known associates." Two more run-ins with him in the span of a month and I decided that was enough; I had to get away from him for a while before my luck really did run out. In spite of my wisecracking every time I came across him, I never for a second underestimated the seriousness of his threat, nor did I forget his resolve to put me behind bars.

At the end of September Balls and I flew to Minnesota and rented a car at the airport. We traveled the state, stopping off and beating its Indian reservation casinos for a thousand here and a thousand there. It was really a joke, like taking candy from a baby. However, the trip was more to get away from DeVisser than to make a shitload of money. When we got back to Vegas, Thanksgiving had arrived, and Balls and I celebrated it in a practically empty restaurant, watching football and eating turkey that was a bit dry. I felt a little lonely not having a real place to go for the occasion. I guess that's the price I paid for living my kind of life.

A few days later Balls came by my apartment with a very interesting tale.

"I'm playing stud in the Mirage," he said as he parked himself next to me on my living room sofa, lighting his cigarette, "when this woman sitting across the table comes around behind me and whispers in my ear she wants to talk about something important. I know her several years from the poker rooms in town, so I figure what the hell, and I go take a walk with her outside the casino on the Strip. As soon as we're out the doors, I say, 'What's up?' Listen to what she lays on me. She says a guy she knows back in New York, an optometrist, or an eye doctor or something, developed a solution for marking cards that can only be seen with certain lenses—"

I sighed, rolling my eyes, and cut him off. "So what's the big deal? Reading marked cards with glasses is a shortcut to prison without passing Go. Any pit boss that's ever been to the movies is hip to it. Shit, haven't you ever seen *Casino Royale*?"

Balls blew out a lungful of smoke and grinned for effect. "Who said anything about glasses?"

I looked at him slantwise. "Contact lenses?"

He gave me a big, tilted nod. "Yep."

"Are you shittin' me?"

"Nope. They're specially made to read the solution on the cards."

"Who is this woman?"

"Poker player, bets horses too. She might be even a bigger degenerate than me. Not bad looking either."

"And she just approached you like that? Clear out of the blue?"

Balls shrugged. "We ain't strangers. I've shot the shit with her several times. In fact, we know a bunch of the same people from the tracks in New York. She probably figures she can trust me."

"What's her name?"

"She told me once but I forgot." Balls said that as if it didn't matter. It probably didn't.

I couldn't help but chuckle. "Some broad whose name you don't even know wants to turn you on to marking cards. Sounds a little fishy to me."

"That's what she said."

I quickly got suspicious and was about to tell Balls to tell whatever-her-name-was that he wasn't interested. But then I got just as quickly intrigued.

Marking cards is as old as poker itself. There are several ways to do it, and I'd heard of just about all of them. Most of the time glasses and liquids were not involved. That was more or less movie stuff. Skilled professional card markers practically always marked cards by putting tiny nicks or scratches on them that only they would distinguish. Some used their fingernails (especially women), others did the trick with minuscule tools concealed in rings. These methods were better than using dyes and glasses because the lenses could never be normal-looking and had to be shaded in order to create the proper light flows needed to read the dye off the cards. Anybody wearing shades while playing blackjack or poker inside a casino was immediately suspect, especially if he was winning at a table too long.

But contact lenses? This was the first I'd heard of it. Though at that moment I never considered involving myself in such a scam, I wanted to hear more about it.

"If she's got access to this solution and the contact lenses, and she's already a gambler, what's she telling you for?" I skeptically asked Balls.

"She's probably just looking to be the middleman and get a piece of the action."

"Or maybe just con you out of some money."

Balls shook his head firmly. "That wouldn't pay off for her. She's been around this town a long time; she's got a rep to protect. If she sold me the solution and it was bullshit, she'd have to stay out of the poker rooms. Hardly possible."

Maybe he was right about that. "Did she mention a price?"

"No. And I didn't ask because I didn't want to seem too interested right off the bat."

"What about this optometrist guy? If he's got the solution and the know-how, why the hell is he advertising it? Isn't he better off just keeping his mouth shut and going out and marking cards himself?"

Balls dragged on the cigarette. "Maybe he just ain't got the balls to do it. Maybe he's got too much to risk, if he's still in business."

I nodded reflectively. "Well, how did you leave it with her?"

He spread his palms, the cigarette dangling from his lips. "Nothing, really. I see her practically every time I go into the Mirage. You want me to set up a meet with her?"

"Lemme think about it?"

Over the next few days I thought about it hard. One of the first things I had learned from Joe was *never* scam the casinos with something that could leave a trail of physical evidence. This was the First Commandment of casino cheating and the main reason Joe had never gotten involved in slot-machine scams using equipment. Both he and his brother Henry had been approached numerous times back in the fifties and sixties to work with slot gangs rigging jackpots. They'd always refused. One casino bust with hard evidence against you, and there was no wiggle room. You were gone.

And as invisible solutions go, they are indeed invisible, but that doesn't mean they leave no evidence. Even if casino cops could never pull the contact lenses off your eyes to match them up with the marked cards, they surely could put the cards through certain infrared detection devices and watch them light up. That much I knew. And what about smell and feel? I didn't know much about that but assumed any liquid capable of illuminating cards might have both, either of which would spoil the whole deal.

Despite the obvious negatives, I was overcome with curiosity. That and the fact we were practically frozen stiff in Vegas because of DeVisser's heat gave me the time to indulge myself. I'd been thinking about blackjack, not poker.

"Set up a meet with her," I told Balls the next time he came over.

"Where?"

"Someplace outside, far away from the Strip." The last thing I needed was a meeting inside a casino and another run-in with DeVisser. I thought of possible places, then asked. "Does she have a car?" Balls nodded. "Then set up a meet at Red Rock Canyon."

"Red Rock Canyon? That's all the way out in the fucking desert!"

"You got a better idea?"

Late the next afternoon, just as the sun was setting, we met her at pretty Red Rock Canyon, surrounded by impressive reddish-orange rock formations that jutted into the valley. Balls spotted her sitting at a picnic table at a scenic overlook, so we joined her on the opposite bench. Her name was Dawn. She was in her thirties and quite attractive, with a big personality that matched her chest, which protruded from the halter-top above her jeans. You didn't find too many good-looking degenerate female gamblers, but they were out there.

After the introductions and smiles I got right down to business. "Why do you need us and why does this optometrist in New York need you?" I asked her with undisguised suspicion.

"The guy wants nothing to do with the casinos," Dawn replied simply, with been-around coolness. "He developed the solution and just wants to sell it." As an afterthought she said, "By the bottle."

"Yeah, okay. So where do you fit in?"

She smiled as she opened her handbag. She took out her contact lens case and prescription glasses and set them both on the table.

"I've been blind for a long time," she said. "The guy happens to be my optometrist."

Balls and I laughed. She was very expressive and funny as well.

"And he knows I'm a gambler," she went on. "So what better person for him to approach."

Balls and I shot each other a glance, and he nodded at me as if to say, "I told you there was something to this."

"What do you know about the solution?" I asked Dawn. "Do you have any of it?"

She shook her head. "I don't have the five grand he wants for a bottle. That's why I'm here talking to you."

"Five grand!"

She nodded. "He said one bottle the size of perfume samples will mark a thousand cards. Only a little dab with the finger is necessary."

I pictured a perfume sample in a department store, which prompted me to say, "That's not a bottle, that's a tube." But the thought that a thousand cards were approximately twenty decks raced through my mind. In a high-limit house you could make a fortune at blackjack marking that many cards.

"Is there any special technique for applying the solution to the cards?" I asked her.

Suddenly she wised up. "Look, all your questions are for naught unless you're really interested and are gonna put up the cash."

"*You* look," I snapped back at her, as Balls just looked on. "I gotta know who and what I'm dealing with before I know if and when I'm interested. I don't know who the hell you are or jack shit about you, and unless I completely trust you, nothing is going to happen between us."

She gave me a piercing look and a kind of seductive smile. "Well, until we pay him for a bottle, we're not gonna know much of anything," she said smartly. "All he told me is that the solution has no odor and it disappears without a trace within an hour."

When she said that, a giant "wow!" rang through my head, though I kept a straight face. Now I was hearing about reading marked cards through contact lenses with a solution that disappeared in an hour! Nothing beat evaporating evidence.

"If I'm interested, how do we proceed?"

Dawn put her lenses and glasses back in her handbag and took out her cigarettes and lit up.

Not another smoker, I thought disparagingly, but who didn't smoke in poker rooms?

"You tell me, I tell him, and he decides how to arrange delivery and payment," Dawn rattled off. She sounded like a goddamn drug dealer, I mused, but at the same time I appreciated her street smarts. I didn't want to be dealing with someone rash and stupid. And I also liked her. It had been awhile since I had some good female company; Dawn excited me on the spot. Thinking that, I also thought of another no-no: Don't mix business with pleasure. I was reminded of what had happened so many years before when I did exactly that with a certain Veronica up at Lake Tahoe.

"We'll be in touch." I smiled at Dawn across the table, not really sure why I had said "we."

Balls and I rushed back to my apartment and discussed it.

"Could be the best scam ever," he said. He picked up a deck of cards that had been lying on the coffee table and dealt out a hand of blackjack to himself and an imaginary dealer. "Imagine the scores we'd make on splits and double-downs knowing the value of the next card off the top of the deck." He turned the rest of the cards over to expose their faces, continued playing with the same perfect knowledge we'd have with accurately marked cards.

"If the solution disappears in a hour, it's big," I agreed. "That's the key. The evidence must disappear, and I mean without a trace. Just because it supposedly disappears from sight does not mean it can't be brought up again like latent fingerprints after the fact. Know what I mean?" I knew I was perhaps taking it too far, but marking cards had never been my bailiwick, and as such I wanted to cover all angles.

We continued another hour with the pros and cons. Finally Balls said, "So do we invest the five grand?" He was really asking if I'd invest the five grand. Whatever money Balls had earned with me up to that point had already been distributed to Dawn and her peers at the Mirage's poker tables.

"I think so," I said with a slow nod and pursed lips. "Just one thing, though. Neither you nor I go anywhere near a blackjack table in a casino carrying that stuff. Not for a long while. We're going to let our little friend Dawn mark the cards."

The next day I met Dawn alone at a café in the Fashion Show Mall on the Strip. I gave her an envelope with five grand cash in it and told her to buy a bottle from the optometrist and have him send it to her apartment, not mine (for security reasons). After a quick lunch and a few drinks, we got in my Jag (I still had it) and drove to a Fed-Ex office near the airport. In the parking lot she skillfully taped the bills in little clusters to the pages of a magazine. It was evident she'd done that before. Then she went inside and shipped out the package to the optometrist in New York.

"Best way to send cash," she said cheerfully as she climbed back into the Jag and closed the door. We both laughed as I nosed it with the top down into the breeze dusting Sunset Road.

While we waited for the solution to arrive, also by Fed-Ex, Balls hung out at the Mirage losing more money while Dawn hung out with me at my apartment. We spent half the time in bed, and I began feeling real good about her and this card-marking affair. But I was still not considering allowing Balls or myself to touch the stuff in a casino. That would not happen until I was absolutely sure about her and her product. It all seemed too good to be true, and too timely.

The package arrived at Dawn's apartment three days after she sent the money. She went home to fetch it and immediately brought it right over. The three of us sat on the carpeting around my coffee table; the deck of cards still lay there. Dawn opened her handbag and removed two contact lens cases and a very narrow two-inch-long object wrapped in brown paper, obviously the solution. When she undid the wrapping, I noted the tube indeed resembled a perfume sample, just a little longer but the same coffee-bean width. The solution inside was crystal clear.

"He supplied two pair of lenses," she said. "They're good for about fifty hours of wear."

"How much to replace the lenses?" Balls asked, exactly what I was thinking.

"A thousand dollars."

"Is that each lens or the pair?" I asked.

Dawn smiled. "If it's not the pair, I'll kill the son of a bitch," she said, making us laugh.

The lenses were shaded green, maybe just a little too green, and I wasn't thrilled about that. First thing I thought of was people staring at them, saying, "Look at those phony green eyes he's got." But worse was that pit bosses might see that phoniness in a different light.

Dawn noticed me inspecting them in their case. "Colored lenses are more popular than clear ones these days," she said with authority. She was probably right. I didn't let it bother me too much.

Balls and I popped in the lenses. Not expecting saline solution to come with the package, I'd gone out and bought some. It took us a few minutes to get used to the lenses in our eyes. Sure enough, the room took on a dull light-green hue, and it seemed a little misty, almost as though I were looking through a night scope. I jerked my head from side to side, as if trying to speed up the ocular adjustment. Dawn watched and waited.

I had absolutely no experience with marking cards, so I applied common sense. I knew that cards were usually marked in the center, not on the corners as most people believed. That was because the corners of cards were always bent or damaged by the players and dealer repeatedly handling and shuffling them. The center of the cards stayed intact. Since Dawn had said that only a small dab was necessary, I'd do just that. The little tube had a screw-on cap and I unscrewed it. As soon as it was open, I rushed it up to my nostrils. I wanted to get a fast whiff of the stuff before the air penetrated it and weakened any smell. But there wasn't one, a first good sign.

As I readied myself to apply the solution to one of the cards, a sensible thought struck me, and I couldn't believe I hadn't thought of it before. If the lenses and the solution proved viable, then how would we carry it and use it while actually sitting on the blackjack table in a casino? You couldn't exactly take it out of your pocket like you were removing a handkerchief to blow your nose. If the eye in the sky didn't catch you, surely the dealer would. This would be a problem, and I'd start worrying about it as soon as this first little experiement was a completed success.

I tilted the tube with my right hand and let one tiny drop leak onto my left index finger. I was satisfied that the dripping was perfectly controllable and that the solution had no stickiness. Then I dabbed the back of the top card on the deck that was already lying face down on the coffee table. Balls and I waited anxiously. Nothing was immediately discernible on the card, and I rapidly got the feeling I was being had. I looked contemptuously at Dawn, whose eyes locked with anticipation on mine.

Suddenly a very pale bluish-greenish tinge appeared and took form on the card. It was the size of a partial fingerprint. Balls and I stared down at it in disbelief, as if we were observing a butterfly changing back into a caterpillar through a microscope.

"Holy shit!" he said.

My astonishment remained silent. Dawn smiled her satisfaction.

We kept the lenses in our eyes and waited for the solution to disappear. After just a few minutes it became fainter. In a half hour it was completely gone. A half hour!

In my head I quickly did some simple math and summed up that the thirty minutes between marking and evaporation was a perfect time span, allowing enough hands to be played before having to mark the cards again, while assuring a quick destruction of the evidence after we left a particular table or the casino. When undertaking a dangerous scam such as this, you didn't want to stay at any table longer than half an hour anyway. Long exposure was risky and went against everything I'd previously done in casinos.

A final rub over the area where I'd applied the solution revealed no difference in feel from the rest of the card. Everything as far as the performance of the lenses and solution was concerned appeared perfect.

For several days I wrestled with the problems of transport and application in a live casino. Since Dawn had agreed to be the first to try it, we concentrated on how she could work it. Being a woman naturally gave her feminine advantages. She already had the handbag and makeup cases to start. She could be looking into her little pocket mirror while on the table, dabbing on some rouge or makeup. Which is how we decided to do it. Dawn would carry the solution in her cosmetics case and work from it at the table.

After more experimenting, we found that one drop of solution was enough to sufficiently mark three cards. So if Dawn managed to get a drop on each fingertip of both hands, she'd be able to mark thirty cards before having to reapply the solution, more than half a deck. Normally, when dealers dealt blackjack from their hands and not out of a card shoe, they used two decks. Thus, theoretically, Dawn could mark ninety of the hundred-and-four cards with three applications of the solution. We decided this would be sufficient. I chose to go for three applications rather than a fourth one that would be needed to mark all the cards. For the experiment, the making of money was not important. We only needed to see how well the solution held up and how quickly it disappeared in the casino. Naturally, we didn't expect any changes inside the casino. Air was air.

We drove out to the Nevada Landing casino in Jean, Nevada. It was twenty-two miles from Vegas and happened to sit right next to a minimum-security state prison, whose inmate population did consist of some convicted casino cheaters. My sole reason for going out to Jean was that Hanson agents rarely were seen there, so DeVisser would not stumble upon us and get the lucky break of his life having us filmed and busted.

Balls and I sat at the opposite end of a two-dollar blackjack table from Dawn. I was truly amazed by her performance. She marked the cards like a real pro. Her movements were naturally feminine and she didn't go into her handbag any more than the two other women at the table did. When she was done and the dealer shuffled up the cards, I got up from the table and walked into the men's room. Inside, I popped in the lenses. I had decided not to wear them while actually sitting at the table. I was taking absolutely no chances. If anything went wrong, neither Balls nor I could be tied to Dawn—provided we had nothing in our eyes or anywhere else on our bodies that could be connected to her marking the cards.

I came out of the men's room and crossed the casino back to Dawn's table. Balls, as instructed, had already gone out to the car in the parking lot. I stood behind another woman on the table and looked at the backs of her cards as she tucked them beneath her chips. Clear as day, I saw the same blue-green tinge from the solution. I signaled Dawn to get off the table and join Balls in the car outside. Forty minutes later, I passed by the table again and looked at the backs of the cards. The markings were gone.

During the following week, I pondered when and where we'd proceed with this new card-marking business. There weren't that many casinos left in Vegas that dealt blackjack from the hand (card shoes had long since taken over, mainly to prevent players from touching the cards). There were more of them up in Reno, and in Atlantic City and the rest of the world there were none. I finally decided that the best bet was Reno. We'd fly up there Friday night and work the town for the weekend, completely on an experimental basis. There'd be no bet increases when we knew we'd receive an ace off the top of the deck on an upcoming deal. Nor would there be any outrageous plays that might tip off the pit that we had advance knowledge of the cards.

On the Thursday afternoon before our scheduled departure, I stopped off at the home of my surveillance friend Donnie. I usually did that at least once a month to get the casino lowdown, or just before taking a trip out of town. If anything was "hot" about Reno, Donnie would know it and warn me off.

As soon as he appeared at his front door, I greased him up with a hundred.

That hundred ended up saving my life.

"I got two nice cassettes to show you," he said with a giggle.

We settled in on the sofa after he shoved the first tape into the VCR. It started out as an overhead color shot of a blackjack dealer with a lone woman player at his table. The woman was seen putting a small stack of green chips on the table, evidently wanting to change them into reds. Then the camera zoomed in on the small green stack.

"Look closely at that stack of green chips," Donnie said.

I looked closely but noticed nothing.

The dealer placed a tall stack of red chips on the layout in front of him, then slid it to the woman. He put the small stack of greens into his chip rack, at the front of a tube holding black chips. That was not uncommon, and I still hadn't noticed any move on the dealer's part. The camera now zoomed in on those green chips sitting in the black-chip tube.

"They're not chips," Donnie said, and he froze the image with the remote. "Look at them closely now."

I still could not distinguish anything unusual about those green chips, and chips were my business. "I still don't get it," I said.

"You will in a second." He fast-forwarded the video. When it resumed, the woman was placing her stack of red chips on the layout in front of the dealer. She'd played a few hands we missed on the fast-forward and now wanted to change her reds back into greens. The dealer's hand went into the black-chip tube to grab the same green chips she had arrived at the table with. The camera zoomed right in on his hand as he grabbed those chips. Like Donnie had said, they were not chips at all. It was a hollow green cylinder that looked like a small stack of green chips and had a bottom base that moved inward on springs. Just before the dealer removed it from the rack, he lightly pressed the top end of the cylinder to activate the springs on the bottom which sucked up black chips. Then he slid it back to her and she left the table with her little green cylinder containing five blacks, $500.

Donnie replayed it twice, and on the second viewing I actually saw the tube of black chips diminish when the dealer pressed on the device.

"Twice a day and they clear a grand in the dark," he said. "They just got too greedy."

"Not bad," I commented. "What's next?"

Donnie got up and popped in the second tape. It was from an overhead camera above a filled-up blackjack table, also in color. I immediately recognized the yellow logo screened into the green felt of the table: the Treasure Island casino. I could identify any Vegas casino from a quick look at a table, dealer uniform, or even a floor carpet pattern. Probably faster than anyone in the world.

I figured this next tape would show a player capping extra chips onto his bet or some other move less spectacular than what I'd seen on the first tape.

I was wrong.

"Hanson busted a paint team three weeks ago," Donnie said as the dealer on the screen pitched out the cards to the players. "Watch the two women with their handbags."

I immediately concentrated intensely on that table. A "paint team" was a card-marking team. Dyes or solutions were called paint.

"The best one ever in this or any other town," he added. "Their paint disappears a half hour after they put it on the cards."

I was completely astounded by what my ears were hearing. And then an instant later, I was stunned beyond comprehension when my eyes took in Dawn on the screen. The image was not totally clear, but there she was sitting in the middle of that table on the screen. No doubt. I even recognized her handbag. It was the one she had used to mark the cards in Jean.

"You see the two women painting the cards with their finger-tips?" he asked.

I was in such a state of shock I couldn't reply.

Donnie perceived my consternation. "You *know* these people?" he asked.

"How many of them are in on it?" I finally managed to respond.

"The whole table."

"Who busted them? Which Hanson agent?"

"DeVisser, of course."

The revelation washed across my brain like a storm.

"Thanks a lot, buddy," I whiffed at Donnie as I blew off his sofa and out the front door. I got in my car and headed right to the Mirage to find Balls in the poker room. During the ten minutes it took to get there, everything unraveled in my head, in successive tidal waves.

The whole thing was a setup engineered by DeVisser. The de-tails were sketchy, of course, but what I surmised was that Dawn and her gang had been busted marking cards, then DeVisser had entered into some kind of deal with her to get me set up in exchange for a break with the DA. Had to be. Since he'd already ID'd Balls at the Imperial Palace, he must have known from general surveillance that he was a regular at the Mirage poker room. So he used Dawn to approach him there, knowing that Balls would go directly to me. This was huge!

Before I went inside the Mirage I found a pay phone and called Donnie. "How did DeVisser bust them if their paint disappeared?" I asked him.

"They went to the well too many times," he explained. "One of the pit bosses at the Treasure Island got suspicious because they kept winning and making exotic plays, like doubling-down on weak hands and splitting weak pairs against the dealer's ten up-card. They finally pulled the cards right off the game and put them under some kind of special light, and there it was."

They must have done it quick, I thought as I walked past the white tigers on display in the Mirage corridor. At least within a half hour.

I grabbed Balls right off the poker table and whisked him out of there. He protested.

"Let's go!" I said hurriedly. "We got a problem."

"Where we going?" he asked as I practically dragged his little body through the main casino toward the exit.

"Out of town."

"Again! We just got back."

"Well, we're leaving again, buddy."

Dawn came over that night and rang the doorbell. I yanked it open, and she started to step inside. I blocked her path and said as chillingly as I'd ever said anything in my life, "Get the fuck out of here, you motherfucking bitch, and don't let me ever see you again!" I slammed the door in her face.

I never saw Dawn again. Donnie told me later that she and her teammates had all gone to prison for three years each. DeVisser must have been real pissed off and figured she fell in love with me and broke down and told me about the setup. I knew the guy had an extremely hard nut for me, but I never would have imagined the lengths he went to nab me. And I wondered whether Dawn had felt anything at all for me, or whether she had just given me her ass to save it.

Before I went to sleep that night, I flushed the solution and both pairs of contact lenses down the toilet. It was back to work for me. I learned a vital lesson. Joe had been right. Never trust anyone outside your "family," and don't work scams that leave evidence.

Thank God for Donnie.

In December Balls and I took a four-month road trip that started in Mississippi, went through the islands in February and March, and ended up in Atlantic City in early April. In the Taj Mahal poker room Balls introduced me to Pat Mallery, with whom he had once worked in the quasi-legal sports telemarketing business. He said that Pat had the gift of gab and might be interested in becoming the missing link in our operation. Pat was a short, stout Irishman with a great personality and a radiant smile that enhanced his olive complexion (dark Irish roots). I immediately felt drawn to him. He was a gifted scammer with the rap to go with it. Balls had already told him basically what we did, and when Pat and I spoke for the first time, we held each other in mutual respect, one guy who'd been around talking to another. Pat said he was tired of sports-touting and was very interested in joining our "gig."

We lunched in the Taj coffee shop, where I demonstrated the mechanics of the blackjack move with the chips sitting among the plates and silverware on the table. Pat understood the theory but had some difficulty believing that casinos paid thousand-dollar moves at a rate of 90 percent. Seeing the doubt in his eyes, I paid the check and said to Pat, "I think you need to see a little demonstration in the casino. Let's go." I had Balls go up to a blackjack table and bet two reds, having told him to switch in a five-o-five with one purple. I kept it simple and prayed he didn't have a miss. I liked Pat immensely and didn't want him thinking I was mouthing off about something full of shit.

Balls did the five-o-five and got paid in a flash.

"Did you see that, Pat?" I said with bravado.

"I saw it," he said, shaking his head approvingly.

We hit it off right away. I knew that Pat could be huge in the casinos.

"It's your turn," I said, handing him the chips. "Don't forget about the backup chips."

"Which table do you want me to go on?" he asked.

"I don't really care," I said smiling largely. I knew that the Taj Mahal was entirely clean.

Pat nodded, walked down the pit with me and Balls in tow. He looked over the tables and chose one with its third-base seat open. He bet the $10, won the hand—and did nothing. He made another bet, won the hand, and still sat there like a donkey. He got up and walked toward me.

"What's the matter?" I said.

"Nothing," he said quickly, without stopping. He continued through the pit and found another table with third base open. He sat down and made the ten-dollar bet, which lost. He got up with the annoyed facial expression I would come to know so well and went to another table. He won the first hand and switched the chips and claimed. When I saw the dealer's reaction and the berating look he gave Pat, I knew immediately that something was *terribly* wrong with the move. I looked down on the layout in front of Pat and saw what. Pat had put the move in upside down. The purple chip was on top, glaring at the dealer. Not even a real Indian dealing blackjack on one of Minnesota's reservations would have been fooled by that.

The last person to notice what Pat had done was Pat. The dealer was telling him to take it down the road, but Pat kept arguing, that strict Irish stubbornness that I would also come to know so well on display. I had to go right up to the table and say to him, "Let's go, Samuel. The bus is waiting to take you back to the institution." At least that crack softened up the dealer and may have prevented a worse disaster.

Outside on the boardwalk, Pat was annoyed that Balls and I couldn't stop laughing at him. "What was that Samuel crap?" he demanded.

"You still don't know what the fuck you did on that table, do
you?" I said.

"I put a move in. That's what I did," Pat said firmly.

"Yeah, you put a move in, alright," Balls said comically, hunched
over and ready to collapse from the laughter. He was laughing so
hard Pat grabbed him by his hair to get him to stop. The sight of Pat
yanking on Balls's hair only made us both laugh harder.

"If one of you guys don't tell me what the hell you're laughing
at, I'm gonna kill you both right here on this boardwalk."

"You know what?" I said, still cracking up. "You're a fudd. You're
a real live fudd."

Finally, Balls explained to Pat that he had put the move in upside
down. Pat started laughing, too.

"You're right, Johnny," he said to me. "I'm a fudd."

"*Johnny?*"

From that moment on, Pat called me Johnny, and soon enough
I started calling him Johnny. Sharing that moniker became the foun-
dation of our friendship.

I suggested that Pat do a few one-o-fives with black chips to
sharpen up a little before going back in with the purples. He agreed.
We spent a few days training on the blackjack move, then took Pat
into Trump Plaza, where he claimed a fifteen-o-five in the first-
column box at a dealer-helper roulette table, which I had switched
in before the dealer paid. Pat collected the $3,010 and was now a
made member of the pastposting team.

Pat Mallery soon became the team. To recount all the stories
about what he did in the world's casinos, I would have to write another pastposting book. But to make it short, I can say that not only
did the mad dark Irishman from rural Massachusetts become the best
blackjack mechanic-claimer I had ever seen, he was also the most
amazing person I'd ever met, and according to him, he was crazy.

Pat and the Chocolate Chip Cookie

THE SMALL RURAL MASSACHUSETTS VILLAGE THAT PAT MALLERY came from had a reputation that preceded itself not only for its own police officers but for relatives of its inhabitants drinking on the other side of the ocean in Ireland. It came from an old eighteenth-century insane asylum tucked away in its rustic hills. During the American Revolution, inmates either escaped or were let go from the institution to join the insurgents, and they poured down the hill and mingled merrily with the "normal" folk. There were marriages, new generations, still more new generations, and then some. If Pat had traced his family tree, he would have found that his maternal great great great great great great great grandfather had been one of the escapees who had rolled down that hill and married his great great . . . grandmother. Like all his nutty peers, that ancestral inmate had passed down the boozing, brawling, and general unruliness through the bloodlines. Over the centuries that insane institutional blood may have thinned a bit, but every villager still had a little of that craziness running in his veins. That's why the police, firemen, hospitals, and bars were always extremely busy.

Before his seventeenth birthday, Pat had already burglarized
every house in his village *at least* once and held up the same Sunoco
service station attendant three times with the same fake pistol and
Frankenstein mask. At summer clambakes, he cheated his fellow
villagers at poker and craps with marked cards and loaded dice. The
funny thing was that everyone knew Pat was the culprit repeatedly
victimizing them and didn't care. Everybody just liked him too
much—even the village police chief, whose maternal great great . . .
grandfather was Pat's maternal great great . . . grandfather's best
friend at the hillside insane asylum the winter George Washington
was on his way to Valley Forge.

People in all walks of life think about what would be for them the
ultimate. A heart surgeon at Johns Hopkins might fancy the successful implantation of a functioning electronic heart in a human being
as the ultimate. Or a farmer growing watermelons in China might
dream about the ultimate seedless watermelon without sacrificing the
sweet juicy taste. For me, as a pastposter, the ultimate was pastposting
five-thousand-dollar chips—the ultimate as well as the highest denomination chips available in American gambling casinos. They were
like the five-hundred-dollar bills Monty Hall used to give away to
screaming ladies on *Let's Make a Deal.* In circulation but not really.

I had often thought about the possibility of working with five-
thousand-dollar chips. Inside the classier casinos in Vegas, I had seen
them in dealer's racks at higher-limit tables catering to big action. In
Caesars Palace, the classiest of all casinos, their "chocolates" were
on all the blackjack tables in the main pit at the front of the casino
and on all the craps tables throughout. The move I had envisioned
for Caesars using the chocolates was a "fifty-one," a chocolate chip
underneath a hundred-dollar black, switched in for an original bet of
$200, two blacks. The thought was massive—clipping the casino for
$4,900 a pop—and what if that move ever got stepped up to a "ten-
o-one"?—*two* chocolates under a black, replacing an original bet of
$300, three blacks. That would be a $9,800 profit on a single black-

jack move, and it was possible because some of the tables at Caesars had ten-thousand-dollar limits.

In order to dare that monster, I figured, two things were vital. One, I had to have big action in the casino to support it. Two, I had to have the perfect guy to do it—a person who really sold himself as a chocolate-chip player. I already knew that the black chips alone gave high-roller credibility. A guy betting $200 a hand at a hundred-dollar-minimum table next to a guy betting $5,000, may have been betting $4,800 less than his neighbor but was still sitting at the *same* table, and was therefore also considered a premium player. But chocolate chips were reserved for a catered few. The person moving them had to be polished in every sense of the word. It was much more than just the move. It was his presence at the table, his posture, how he sat, how he held his head. It was not only the way he looked but the way he looked at you. When pit bosses came up to the table, *they* had to be affected by the guy on third base looking at them, had to feel it was they who were being scrutinized. It was not just *what* he said to those pit bosses that counted but *how* he said it. The conversation didn't have to be intelligent; it only had to be right.

The heavyweight championship fight at Caesars Palace between Evander Holyfield and Michael Moorer on April 22, 1994, certainly satisfied the first vital condition of having big action in the casino. Championship fight nights at Caesars always brought in mega–high rollers from all over the world. Chocolate chips would be spread out generously over green felt throughout the casino.

Pat Mallery would satisfy the second vital condition: He was beyond any doubt the perfect guy for pastposting five-thousand-dollar chips.

In a single night Pat Mallery went from fudd to the Pastposters Hall of Fame. When he sat down at his first blackjack table at Caesars Palace, as the crowds were pouring back into the casino from the rear parking lot where the outdoor championship bout had been staged, Pat had only had about fifteen blackjack moves under his belt. Just before, he had been at the Cleopatra's Barge cocktail lounge off the passageway between the front and rear casinos, having a few beers to "warm up." He'd given me the signal that he was ready to go.

Seeing Pat at that table, I was convinced I was looking at the quintessential chocolate-chip player. He was wearing a two-thousand-dollar dark-blue Armani suit with a blazing red tie, a two-thousand-dollar hairpiece that he called his dooflicky and filled out his thinning hair, and a pair of light-brown tinted Porsche sunglasses that rounded out his "costume"—including dress shirt and Bally shoes—to around $6,000, not including the gold watch and rings he wore on his manicured hands. The suit, hairpiece, sunglasses, manicure, and one of the rings had all come from Caesars' shops.

The biggest blackjack move Pat had done successfully while I trained him in Atlantic City was a five-o-five. To get the ball rolling for this fight night, we agreed that he'd start off with a two-thousand-twenty-five, switching in two yellow chips with a green capper for a seventy-five-dollar original bet of three greens. Pat put the move in perfectly, claimed, was acknowledged by a floorman's nodding head, and got paid. The relaxed manner in which he talked with the dealer, accompanied by his soft natural laugh, was the best table demeanor possible for a casino grifter. He made dealers feel both comfortable and apologetic when they paid him wrong.

I was eagerly ready to witness the first fifty-one blackjack attempt, but Pat decided to stop back at Cleopatra's and have another beer beforehand. I didn't object. It was not a question of nervousness or needing to calm himself. I was to learn that alcohol was Pat's fuel; when it was running through his veins, it charged him up. While 99 percent of the population became obnoxious slobs when consuming the amount of alcohol Pat did, Pat became smoother and friendlier, his already confident walk metamorphosed into a dance. He glided around casinos. To watch his behavior and attitude under the influence was truly remarkable. If you tested his blood, the result would say he was legally drunk, but the level of his self-assuredness wasn't measurable.

When I first saw a fifty-one lying in the betting circle next to the two black chips one of Cecil's dealers had paid Pat, I could not believe the complete "fusion" of the Caesars five-thousand-dollar chocolate chip with its black hundred-dollar chip. You could practically not distinguish the difference when the chocolate was on the bottom. Even the speckling on the sides of the two chips appeared similar, albeit a slightly different color. The chocolates were speckled with a medium yellow, the blacks had a shade of light green. Although matching chip colors were not that important in our business, this uncanny chocolate-black marriage at Caesars was an added bonus.

Pat had two chocolate backup chips in front of him on the layout as he delicately touched the dealer's arm and said softly but powerfully, "Wo, wo, wo! You slightly underpaid me here!" Then he laughed easily and pointed to the $5,100 in the betting circle.

"I did at that," the tall light-skinned black dealer said simply, without hesitation or any sign of uneasiness. He immediately picked up the two blacks he had paid Pat, put them back in his chip rack, removed the plastic lammer that covered the tube of chocolate chips and peeled off the top chocolate, placing it with a black chip next to Pat's move-chips in the betting circle. Now there was ten-thousand-two-hundred-dollars' worth of Caesars chips sitting in the circle and another ten thousand by the table cushion in front of Pat, a total of six chips.

Balls and I looked at each other in shock. We couldn't believe that the dealer had paid Pat so fast, without even letting the floorman, Cecil, know what had happened. He didn't even announce, "Chocolate out," to inform Cecil there was a five-thousand-dollar player at his table. True, a lot of dealers in Caesars were heavily juiced in with jobs about as secure as the pope's, but not even mentioning a five-thousand-dollar winning bet that hadn't been seen? That was flagrant contempt of Nevada Gaming Control Board regulations. The thought of how successful we were going to be with Pat moving chocolate chips at Caesars boggled my mind. I just prayed that Steven DeVisser wouldn't show up at an inopportune moment and ruin it.

Pat immediately asked the dealer to change a chocolate chip into five yellows as was dictated by our script. Then he bet back $1,100, a yellow and a black, and made a separate black-chip bet for the dealer, placing it in front of his own bet at the edge of the circle. Betting for the dealer served us psychologically. Any negative reactions that might have been creeping toward the front of his brain would hopefully be pushed backward. Dealers appreciated players betting for them and frowned upon high rollers who didn't. Keeping the dealers on our side after a big move was extremely important.

The dealer made a twenty-one and beat Pat and himself, but thanked Pat very much for the try. At that point Cecil arrived on his own at the table. He looked Pat over, took in the costume, the Porsche glasses, the chocolate and yellow chips lying regally in front of him, was instantaneously sold and smiled approvingly. He had to be thinking Pat was one of the super mega-high rollers in for the fight.

Pat quickly turned his charm on the floorman, chatting and laughing and, more important, cutting off the means of communication between floorman and dealer, realizing that those first few seconds of their coming together were vitally important and had to be controlled. Pat and I had never discussed that subtlety, but now as I watched him doing just that, completely controlling the situation, I appreciated his brilliance. He was the consummate con man. He had all the virtues essential to rocklike credibility.

Pat's next bet was reduced to $600. We had to be careful with these large bet-backs because a little bad streak could wipe out the entire profit from the move, and at the same time we didn't want Pat getting up too soon after getting paid the $5,100, which might bug the dealer, and then the floorman if he'd been told that Pat's winning chocolate had been unseen. The bet-back scheme after a chocolate-chip move had to be played out as long as possible. The first bet would always be $1,100. Then at least two following bet-back hands of $600 were necessary unless there was steam on the move. In that case, Pat would leave as soon as he felt it, or I signaled him. If he got lucky and won a few bet-backs, he'd naturally stay at the table longer and play out the streak, always capping his bets with a black chip that conformed to the move. Each situation was unique and therefore handled according to the vibes coming from the pit. When graduating to the ten-o-one move with two chocolates being switched in, the bet-backs increased along with it. The first one would be $2,100, the follow-ups $1,100, again with a single black chip on top.

Pat won the first six-hundred-dollar bet and lost the next two, then left the table after receiving Cecil's business card and comp for a party of four to the show. Cecil and the dealer chatted a few minutes about Pat, but there was no mention of his bets. And that's just it—they talked about *him*, not his bets, which is what made Pat the greatest of all time. When he beat you, his incredible personality took your mind off it. You didn't know you just got beat, and if you did, you might—at least more with him than anyone else I'd known—forgive and forget. Watching him work, I understood quickly why everyone he had ripped off at the village clambakes returned voluntarily to get ripped off again.

With Pat there was no stopping in the keno pit after every move. As soon as he was finished at one table, the trail started up again as he led me and Balls through the pits looking for the next. If, along the way, he wanted to pass me off excess chips or needed more blacks because he'd lost a few hands in a row, we'd make the exchange furtively en route. To describe what happened the rest of that fight night at Caesars, the word that comes to mind is "rampage." That's exactly how Pat went through its casino. He sat down, bet, moved, claimed, chitchatted, laughed, toked the dealer, got back up, stopped off at Cleopatra's or another casino lounge for a beer, tugged on his ear to let us know he was ready again, and found the next table. After the fourth fifty-one had been paid, Pat signaled me that he wanted to go outside and get a little air.

We were in front of Caesars in the warm night breeze, standing on the porch by the imposing marble-white statue of Julius Caesar near the intersection of the Strip and Flamingo Road. Pat had a glass filled with beer in his hand, Balls the cigarette in his.

"How'm I doin', Johnny?" Pat asked cockily.

I laughed. "I've seen worse." Looking at Pat wearing the Porsche sunglasses outside at night was humorous.

"This is what you call a cocking, Johnny. I'm a little cocked up right now, but you wouldn't call me the village idiot, would you?"

"Not exactly."

"Johnny," Pat continued as he wavered around the statue, "you remember that fudd in Atlantic City?" He started exaggeratedly shifting his head from side to side as though he were looking for somebody. "I can't seem to find him. Do you know what happened to him, Johnny? Do you know where the fudd is hiding?"

Pat was putting on a little sideshow for me and Balls outside Caesars, and we loved it. The more he went into his routine, the more we laughed. The guy was gifted. I thought he really could have been a movie star. I told Balls as Pat was twirling around the statue saluting Julius that it was too bad I hadn't run into him fifteen years earlier. Balls gave one of his agreeing nods.

"You know what, Johnny," Pat said, downing his drink, "I'm getting sick looking at both you guys. Don't you think it's time we went back in there and paid Julius another little visit?" He put his glass down on the ledge of the statue, looked up and saluted Julius a final time, then led us back inside the casino. Balls and I followed behind, cracking up. To think that only three weeks earlier Pat hadn't even known that casino pastposting existed. Now *he* was leading us through the world's greatest casino, doing the biggest blackjack moves ever as if he were picking dandelions from his front lawn. I was having so much fun watching Pat I hardly thought about counting the money.

By the time that first chocolate-chip night was over at Caesars, Pat had done seven moves, including the monster of all monsters, the first ten-o-one—two chocolates underneath a black for a $10,100 payoff. The closest thing he had to a miss all night was when a young pretty floorwoman said to him flirtatiously after the dealer told her that he hadn't seen his chocolate chip underneath, "You slipped one in on us." There was absolutely no accusatory note in her voice; she was just being personable and friendly. Later on, we had a good laugh about it: if only she had known, he really did "slip" one in on her.

When we got into the car in the Barbary Coast garage, my pockets were bulging chips everywhere. I had to climb in gingerly, pressing my pants pockets closed so no chips would fall out. Pat refused to hold any of the chips. "You count them up later, Johnny. I just want to get a pizza." I passed a fistful of chips carefully to Balls, who lumped them into his jacket pocket and got behind the wheel. Balls would become our designated driver. In the future, when we went on road trips through the Midwest and South, Balls demonstrated that behind the wheel of a car he was the same monster Pat was in the casinos. The guy could drive two days without stopping to take a piss—so long as he had his cigarettes.

Back in my apartment Balls and I emptied out all our pockets and let the rattling chips spill over the kitchen table. Pat was working on the pizza we'd picked up at Pizza Hut, completely ignoring the spiraling little multicolored suns invading his space. He was drinking milk now instead of beer, moaning and complaining that he was dizzy and his stomach hurt from all that alcohol. It was still funny listening to him. Even when he was feeling sick Pat entertained.

Balls and I arranged the chips into stacks of chocolate, yellow, purple, black, green, and red. The greens and reds we had accumulated from hands Balls and I played when saving open third-base seats for Pat. I counted up the total twice. There was $52,880 in Caesars Palace chips sitting on my kitchen table. We had started with $15,000, so we had a fight-night profit of $37,880—the largest score I had ever been part of for a single shift inside a casino. And that was the first day!

"You know something, Johnny," Pat said, chewing the remaining crust from his pizza. "I don't want either one of you guys doing these blackjack moves anymore. You really taught me good, and now I'm the best, so what I propose is that from here on in I do all the moves myself and we cut up the money evenly three ways. Do either one of you guys have a problem with that?"

The mad Irishman from Massachusetts also had class.

After that first night with Pat at Caesars, I lost control of my team. But I was neither surprised nor upset. Watching Pat on those blackjack tables, I realized that I was just going along for the ride. I was swept up by the whirlwind he created. Unlike Balls, Pat was already a seasoned grifter when I met him. Once he knew the move, he no longer needed my guidance. In fact, after his first chocolate payoff, Pat didn't need me or Balls for anything. He could have simply walked with the knowledge I had given him and gone out on his own. And I had been expecting him to. But he didn't. I guess for him also the camaraderie meant something. I felt a great pleasure to be working with people who weren't dominated by greed.

The morning after the fight-night barrage, Pat leased a Mercedes convertible and rented an apartment. He picked me and Balls up with the top down, and we cruised along I-15 under the clear blue sky with its bright yellow sun, heading to the Levitt's Furniture show-room downtown. As we passed the backs of the Strip casinos lining the interstate, Pat yelled his praise in the direction of Caesars, ya-hooing and promising the casino through the air that he'd be back that evening. Inside Levitt's, Pat didn't waste any time browsing. He asked a salesman to come along and began marching him and us up and down the aisles, through all the departments. "I'll take this bed," he instructed him, "that dresser, these tables, those chairs, both the sofa and love seat . . ." Then we drove over to Circuit City, where he purchased two Sony TVs and a top-of-the-line stereo system. The bill for Pat's day of shopping came to twenty grand. Since we hadn't yet cashed out the Caesars chips, Balls and I put everything on our credit cards. Pat didn't have one and said he'd reimburse us as soon as we cut up our first "package." He loved referring to paydays as packages. I told Pat I wasn't worried about loaning him the money for the furniture. Balls wasn't exactly spitting up blood about it, ei-ther.

That night, as Pat had promised on the interstate, we went back to Caesars. The casino was as busy as it had been after Friday night's fight. The crowds were still in Vegas, and Saturday night might prove even better because there wouldn't be a fight to interrupt the action on the tables. After two more chocolate moves were paid, including the second ten-o-one, Pat signaled us outside to the statue.

"I noticed the guy sitting next to me looking at me funny while I was claiming," he said. "Like he was going to rat me out. Balls, I want you to do something for me on the tables. Just as I'm getting ready to move, come up to the person sitting on my right and ask him what time it is. Come over his right shoulder so that he turns his head away from me."

I didn't think that such a detour was necessary; rats were rare.

But if Pat wanted that to add to his comfort, I had no objection. Besides, it was his show now. I might as well let him run it.

So that's how it was with Pat's blackjack moves from then on. Just as Pat was putting in moves, Balls was leaning over the person on Pat's right asking what time it was, drawing the person with the watch's attention away from Pat. We often kidded Balls about being the best-paid time-asker in the country.

That second night at Caesars Pat got five of the giant moves paid, and we picked up another thirty grand. We went back a final time on the Sunday day shift where Pat got paid three more times. We made an astounding $80,000 for the weekend.

There were two predicaments I considered while looking at the nearly $100,000 in Caesars Palace gaming chips on the kitchen table as I took my Monday morning coffee. One of them was rather pleasant. All those chips! How were we going to get them cashed out? Casinos had certain individual policies as well as uniform gaming regulations they had to adhere to when it came to cashier cage operations. The first and foremost was the IRS cash transaction reporting law, which stated that anyone cashing out $10,000 or more (or buying in) within a twenty-four-hour period had to fill out federal forms at the cage, which were then passed along to the IRS. Even if you made four separate cash-outs of $2,500 during the twenty-four-hour period, you were subjected to that law. And the casinos enforced it strictly. Every casino's nightmare was the huge seven-figure fines that accompanied IRS violations. We had to be *extremely* careful about this. Even the slightest suspicion would put tails on us, investigations, a barrel of problems in addition to what we had to guard against already.

Another worry was casinos' internal controls regarding cash-outs. Using Caesars Palace as an example, when you were at the cage presenting any purple or higher denomination chips for payment, you were routinely asked if you had any markers. That alone posed no problems, because once you said no, the teller never pressed the issue. The problem was that if you presented $2,500 or more in chips, the teller asked you where you had been playing, asking, in effect, where did you get these chips? Your answer was then verified by the teller, who called the pit you said you'd been playing at right in front of you and described you for the pit boss on the other end of the line. You were only paid if the teller received approval from that pit boss. If there was a problem, the teller would hold you up while the pit boss came right to the cage and looked at you. If there was a further problem, such as the pit boss saying he never saw you at the pit, you could be subjected to an interrogation in the back room. With all the money laundering and scams going on inside them, as well as the pressure from the IRS, casinos were obligated to ask a few questions once in a while. But we could not afford to be on the receiving end of those questions. Since it was only the claimer who would have been recognized in the pits, neither Balls nor I could ever tell the teller at the cage where we'd been playing—because we never played. Therefore, we could never cash out more than twenty-four-hundred-ninety-nine dollars' worth of chips at a time. And had the claimer, in this case Pat, gone to the cage with only the chips from a single chocolate move and payoff, he would have still been over the ten-thousand-dollar limit and forced to show ID and fill out forms.

The solution to all these problems was the adoption of a strict cash-out procedure that had to be adhered to with the same rigor as the moves themselves. All three of us would participate in cashing out the chips. Normally, a claimer never cashed out, just on general security principles, but with the advent of chocolate-chip moves, there were just too many large-valued chips to cash out. Balls and I couldn't handle it alone. Pat's participation in cashing out resulted in a 50 percent increase in chips-to-cash production.

A hundred thousand dollars in Caesars chips to be cashed out at less than $2,500 a pop meant at least forty-one trips to the cage. There were two cages in Caesars Palace, as there were in most of the big casinos. That helped matters significantly, but we still couldn't "get rid" of all those chips easily without eventually picking up steam for repetitive large cash-outs (without ever paying off markers), considering the fact we were never seen buying in. I knew that casino cages were under constant twenty-four-hour video surveillance. What I didn't know is how often the tapes were reviewed and by whom. My surveillance friend Donnie didn't know, either. That information was secret. I had heard rumors that the FBI and DEA routinely reviewed casino cashier tapes for investigative purposes concerning money laundering. It was also probable that the IRS reviewed those tapes, too, checking up on the casinos' adherence to its cash transactions reporting laws, and netting a few tax evaders who showed up at the cage with more money in chips during a twenty-four-hour period than their tax returns said they earned in a year. One thing I was certain of was that we had to be extremely careful at the cage. It is the most dangerous place inside a casino.

The three of us repeatedly went into Caesars on all three shifts when we weren't pastposting and took turns very carefully cashing out amounts just under $2,500, often on different teller lines right next to each other. Obviously, we never cashed out the chocolates; they got broken down into yellows and purples at the craps tables. If the casino was busy enough, we would hit both cages. All three of us making a trip to both cages could cumulatively cash out $15,000 on a shift. But we couldn't cash out on all the shifts. The graveyard shift during the early morning hours was usually stone dead. The biggest action was often the noise of the vacuum cleaners on the carpeting. We might sneak in and catch them asleep for a single cash-out of less than $2,500, but that was it.

It was during the Caesars rampage that I decided to rent a safe-deposit box solely for five-thousand-dollar chips. I kept three or four chocolates from Caesars in the box at all times. As we started working other casinos with five-thousand-dollar chips, I added a reserve of their chocolates to my box as well. Since Pat proved to be a compulsive spender on life's luxuries, and Balls blew off most of his money gambling on poker and sporting events, I was forced to hold those chips with my own capital, meaning for each chocolate chip I had in storage, Pat and Balls had been given a packet of $5,000 cash. I wasn't too thrilled about that, but with the supreme importance of keeping the team together in my mind, I was forced to do things clearly not equitable for me.

The second predicament I found myself in—or rather, put myself in—concerned my retired partner Joe. During the years I worked with him, Joe had been innovative when he had to be, but his imagination stopped along the creativity line where mine kept on going. He never would have conceived the use of five-thousand-dollar chips in the casinos. He would have believed it far too risky and an invitation for big problems. Now that we were operating with them at a success rate superior to any color chip we had used before—up to that point there had not been a single miss—I felt obligated to notify Joe about that giant leap we had taken. That was not the dilemma, however. What troubled me about keeping Joe abreast of my activities was how much did I owe him? My loyalty to him could never be diminished, not by the arrival of Pat, not by any woman—not by anything. But did that loyalty stretch to give Joe a piece of the profits that were now coming in in an abundance never before seen? Balls and Pat clearly owed Joe nothing, and in flopping the perspective, they didn't owe me anything, either. But with me and Joe it was different. Had he not come into the Four Queens that night in 1977, I might still be there dealing mini-baccarat instead of writing this book—or worse. For that I owed him. But Joe had retired on his own initiative; he had made that decision voluntarily, telling me it was my turn to take over and lead the warriors into the casinos. He had never mentioned further compensation for himself. However, a part of me felt that he was entitled to a sort of casino pastposters' pension. I wrestled with the conflict for several weeks, torn between loyalty and money. Finally, remembering what Joe had taught me and always reinstilled in my head, not to be greedy, I called him and told him what was going on in Las Vegas.

"You're moving chocolate chip cookies," Joe said with a laugh. "That doesn't surprise me at all. It shows me you're doing a good job where I left off."

"Joe," I said hesitantly, "there's something we have to discuss. We're making a lot of money out here . . . me, Pat, and this other guy Balls, who doesn't do much besides asking people what time it is. I don't know how long this is going to go on before we have a miss—and you know as well as I do that a miss on a chocolate chip is gonna cause problems—but I was thinking that maybe I ought to . . . throw you a little something. You deserve your end because you taught me everything I know."

Joe's voice changed; it became soft and the most tender I had ever heard it, even more so than when he had given us that 1978 New Year's Day speech about how happy he was with Duke, Jerry, and me. "I love you like a son," he said. "And I appreciate you thinking like that about me. I can see that I did indeed teach you well. You're not a greedy person and that, my son, is the most important thing about money. As far as your offer is concerned, thank you very much, but no. Remember, I retired of my own free will. I made a nice living in the casinos, and I had a lot of good times with you and the boys. But it's over for me now. All I want from your operation is that you continue to run it well."

So Joe ended up once again solving my problem.

During the spring and early summer of 1994, we continued working the blackjack tables in Las Vegas with chocolate chips. We added the MGM, Hilton, and Mirage to our list, but none of them matched up to Caesars. Balls and I finally got the chance to do chocolate moves one night when Pat was too tired to get cocked up. We both got paid, but after seeing Balls put in what he considered a sub-par move, Pat had seen enough. He had Balls drive him back to his apartment so he could put his costume on and "have a few cocktails." Whenever Pat said he was going to have a few cocktails, the translation was: The casinos are in trouble.

Pat had developed a ritual that proceeded his going out to work. It involved cocktails and Frank Sinatra. When working the swing shift (his favorite and most productive shift) during the prime hours of 10:00 P.M. to 2:00 A.M., he began his preparations at around eight o'clock. His apartment had become the center of operations; we always met there. Just before eight o'clock, he'd say, "All right, fellas, you got to go now. Why don't you stop on by at around ten o'clock and pick up the other guy living in this apartment" (meaning the cocked-up version of himself). Then, with us out the door, he turned on Sinatra, mixed himself a hard drink, and chased it with a few beers, in order to get himself cocked-up, as he coined the term. He waltzed around the apartment, singing along with Frank, while at the same time "going over his life." Just what that meant, I assumed, was a great reflection on who he was and where he had come from. One thing I did know was that you didn't ask Pat too many questions about his "ritual." It was a sacred thing for him and made everybody a lot of money. Sometimes after a night's work he would say, "I bet you guys would just love to witness my ritual, right Johnnies?" Once in a while he pluralized the Johnny.

Toward the end of his ritual he began putting on what he called his costume—the suit, tinted glasses, and dooflicky. When we returned at ten o'clock, he'd be in high spirits. He'd always say, "Let's go boys. Balls, get me over to that casino. There's a gig there tonight. You guys know what the gig is? It's me. I'm the gig. Get the gig over to the gig."

And that's how it went.

Just before I met Pat Mallery, I was starting to think that the blackjack move was dying out in Las Vegas, especially with the big-denomination purple and yellow chips. Balls and I had both had a few steamy misses in Vegas before heading on the eastern road trip that eventually led to recruiting Pat. Steven DeVisser at Hanson was tracking our movements, constantly hassling me and Balls in the casinos, derailing us. Our pictures were being delivered to the casinos with the same regularity as its weekly magazines.

But Pat Mallery had put us back on track. He completely revamped the move. In defiance of DeVisser's casino warnings, Pat bombed away every weekend for two solid months in Las Vegas. Ironically, some of DeVisser's warnings may have worked in Pat's favor. Knowing all our chocolate-chip moves were clean, DeVisser's descriptions of our MO had to have been alerting the casinos about purple and yellow chips being pastposted on blackjack tables, not chocolates. Surveillance people filtering those warnings down to casino employees on the floor are not very imaginative; it's not their job to be. If they're warned about yellow chips, they assert that same warning down on the floor. They don't say, "And watch out for the same guys doing the blackjack move with chocolates." Inversely, on the floor, a floorman or pit boss hearing from a dealer that someone had bet an unseen winning chocolate chip underneath a black didn't make the connection, either, because that scenario didn't mesh with a yellow under a green or a purple under a red, the two pastposts they had been warned about by surveillance. A long time could pass before the casinos realized that chocolates went with blacks just as well as yellows did with greens and purples with reds. We could be into seven-figure profits before they made the connection. Those little distinctions created huge gaps in their internal security controls—and we always slipped through them.

Since Pat's arrival in Las Vegas, we were having better luck with DeVisser. Whereas before, it was always him spotting either Balls or me before we saw him and could get out of the casino, now the tides were turning. Three times since we started working the chocolates I spied DeVisser in casinos without his seeing me, and we were able to flee the camp before the wily Hanson agent could cause any trouble. The key result was that DeVisser never got a look at Pat. As long as that remained the same, Pat could run around the casinos blasting in chocolates while casino personnel were looking at photos of me and Balls and worrying about purples and yellows.

By the end of June 1994, Pat had worked over Las Vegas to the tune of $800,000. He had done 130 fifty-ones as well as 21 ten-o-ones, all without a miss. I must tell you humbly that such an accomplishment is absolutely astounding. When I look back at it now, thinking about casinos with all their state-of-the-art surveillance equipment—which gives them an aura of invincibility—and all their personnel who are supposed to be wise to pastposters' tricks, I shake my head and say to myself, "Did all that really happen? Did I train a guy and a few weeks later witness him going from blackjack table to blackjack table, switching in five-thousand-dollar chips *after* he got paid, claiming the dealer made a mistake with the payoff, and ultimately convincing dealers, floormen, and pit bosses that they *had*—one hundred and fifty-one straight times? Just impossible."

Chocolate chip move number 152 was a miss—just barely. We were in Caesars and Pat was at a table with a dealer he'd already beaten twice and his floorman once. After a hundred and fifty-one moves, we were getting into the third round with some of the dealers at Caesars.

There was no problem with the dealer. He was beat for the third time. He went into his rack and took out the chocolate to pay Pat. He had the chip in his hand, and his arm actually moved forward to place it in the betting circle next to the chocolate Pat had switched in. But at the last fragment of a second possible before that chip would have touched the green felt, the dealer stopped and called the floorman, a very tall guy in his late thirties with a thick crop of pre-mature gray hair. He just wanted to advise the floorman that a choc-olate chip was being paid out, properly doing his job.

The floorman's initial reaction was just an approving nod of his head. The dealer placed the chocolate chip down on the layout next to Pat's move-chip. Pat's arm was in the process of reaching out to pick it up when something clicked in the floorman's head. As Pat's hand dipped onto the layout to grasp the chip, it landed on a strange object whose feel of rough flesh and hard bone made Pat's hand send a message to his brain that he wasn't touching a smooth chocolate chip.

The floorman had reached into the betting circle and scooped up the chocolate chip the dealer had paid before Pat could get to it. "I don't want to pay that without calling surveillance," he said. He put the chip back in the dealer's rack and walked briskly to the podium and picked up the phone.

I squeezed my eyes shut in disgust when I saw that, knowing that our magnificent run was over. I reopened them quickly. Now the business at hand was to get Pat safely out of the casino. Not waiting to further reevaluate the situation, I called out, "Chester!"

Pat did not hesitate. He swiped his own chocolate chip off the betting circle with his backup chocolates and abandoned the claim and the table.

The dealer cried, "Sir, you can't leave just yet!"

The floorman on the phone heard the dealer's voice and turned back toward the table to catch a glimpse of Pat turning a corner by a bank of slot machines, on his way to the front entrance where he would do his disappearing act. The floorman broke his connection on the phone and immediately dialed security's extension (he'd been talking with surveillance). I heard him say excitedly, "Blue suit and brown sunglasses!"

The chase was on. Pat had about two hundred feet to go to the doors. If caught, we'd have a real disaster. Right off the bat, we'd lose the $20,000 in chips Pat had on him; Caesars would lock them up as evidence. Then Pat would be in jail with a high bail, charged with at least one gaming felony, and who knew what other trumped-up charges he'd be facing once Hanson's Steven DeVisser tied him and the crime to me. With attorney's fees and lost productivity, we could be looking at a $250,000 loss.

But Pat already had something working in his favor as he headed for the doors. His disappearing act did not wait until he was outside Caesars Palace; it started inside, just as he turned that corner around the bank of slot machines out of the floorman's view. From his waistband he pulled out a folded-up shopping bag, flapped it open. He then threw the suit jacket and tinted glasses inside the bag. His escape route was not a beeline to the exit. Pat took a thirty-second detour into the men's room fifty feet from Caesars' main entrance. Inside one of the stalls, off came the suit trousers and the hairpiece with the tape that held it in place. The practically bald guy emerging from the men's room was quite sporting in the tennis outfit he had been wearing underneath the suit. When he finally did walk calmly out the main entrance of Caesars Palace, a foursome of security officers shot through the doors looking for a shadow.

Pat got into a cab and told the driver to take him to the Gingermill.

An Irishman in France

WHAT REALLY BOTHERED PAT MALLERY ABOUT NICE, FRANCE, IN August 1994, was twofold. First, he didn't like its pebbled beaches. Lying on one now, under the hot sun and very warm, dry Mediterranean air, he just couldn't get comfortable. A French kid selling beignets approached him, thinking he had a sale, but Pat asked him for a pillow. A couple of pretty and topless French girls lying near us understood English and giggled, so Pat bought the girls beignets and made everybody happy.

The second thing disturbing Pat was that the Irish bars in Nice were just not the same as back home; there weren't enough fistfights, and if there had been, people cussing each other out in French wouldn't have sounded right.

But in the casinos Pat felt right at home. The splash he made at the Café de Paris casino on the Mediterranean coast, where I'd been with Joe's team seven years earlier, was like a second Allied landing on Omaha Beach, which was fitting because everywhere along the Côte d'Azur and the rest of France, the French were celebrating the fiftieth anniversary of the Liberation. Pat really brought the house down.

We'd gone to a bar near our Nice hotel where Pat had gotten cocked-up pretty good before rolling into the streets to finish his cocking with a band of drunken Frenchmen who were doing their best to listen to an American rock band tuning up a Liberation party. In the casino, filled with its usual international assortment of beautiful, rich, and suntanned people, it was Pat who stole the show. Everybody, including the rich and famous, was watching *him*.

Pat had on his usual costume, the dark suit and tinted Porsche glasses. What Jerry and I had done in that same casino during my first European pastposting trip, Pat did all by himself. He glided from table to table, popping in and claiming moves as he laughed, danced, and joked with everybody, taking for granted that *tout le monde* spoke English, and even those who didn't had no trouble relating to Pat. The dealers, floormen, and pit bosses were all his audience, wondering who this *Américain* putting on such a spectacle as he hobnobbed with their jet-set clientele could be, all the while indifferent to his winning five-thousand-franc bets that nobody ever saw.

In the middle of the show Balls began panicking. While Pat was waltzing up to another table, chatting in English to a Frenchwoman he now had in tow—who was responding in French—Balls pulled me aside and said, "He's bringing too much attention on us. We're gonna end up getting busted."

I didn't share that opinion at all, so I reassured Balls. "He's in complete control of the situation; he's doing his thing. Pat loves that attention; he thrives on it. Don't worry for a second that he doesn't know when to turn it off."

Pat sensed that Balls was panicking, and played off big on it when Balls was seated next to him on a blackjack table he'd just moved on. He patted Balls on the shoulder while a ranking pit boss was leaning on the table and said cheerfully, "Where you from, partner?" Pat knew that Balls was shitting bricks about being connected to him and got a big kick out of it. I was standing at the other side of the table, getting off, too.

"Puerto Rico," Balls responded in a fake Puerto Rican accent, not wanting the pit boss to know he was American. "I come from San Juan."

"Puerto Rico?" the pit boss said.

Pat turned to the bit boss and said loftily with another pat on Balls's shoulder, "That's my partner Jorge from San Juan, Puerto Rico."

Balls was turning red, more like—no balls.

"San Juan," the pit boss said, and when he continued his sentence we all realized he was talking to Balls in Spanish, *"yo conozco San Juan muy bien. Bienvenidos, amigo!"*

Pat was absolutely dying looking at Balls's face. So were the people clustered behind the table, not exactly understanding why they were laughing, but it was contagious. The whole casino was enveloped in laughter emanating from that table. Pat egged the pit boss on. "My friend Jorge doesn't speak English or French."

"No problema. Podemos hablar español como el quisiera." We can speak Spanish as he'd like.

Balls went, *"Sí, sí. Tengo que ir al baño,"* and hurried off to the bathroom. Pat and I were smiling at each other, enjoying the moment. That Balls managed the Spanish phrase about having to go to the bathroom made us both laugh even harder.

From Monte Carlo we went to London. We couldn't find any more cabbies willing to join the casinos to sign us in as guests, so Pat stood outside the entranceways in his suit, pitching whatever he had to in order to get us in. At the Victoria Club, London's largest casino, he convinced a member coming out that his long-lost brother whom he hadn't seen in ages was inside gambling and that he wanted to surprise him at the roulette wheel. He introduced me and Balls as two more of his brothers. We got in, Balls popped a straight-up on the number for Pat, who got paid but with steam—from both the casino and the member, who noticed nothing brotherly going on at the bottom of the victimized roulette table.

At the Stakis casino on Russell Square, Pat flirtatiously invited an exiting woman member back inside the club with a dinner offer. For dessert, she unknowingly check-bet and watched us clip the establishment for £3,500. We got into a third casino but were tossed out before we could buy chips. Evidently, the steam from the move at the Victoria had caught up with us.

In Amsterdam we spent more time in the red-light district than in the casinos. None of us went inside the women's windows, but we did look around a lot. From a pay phone on one of those narrow streets I dialed Jerry's number in Missouri. I wanted to see how he was doing. I don't know why I chose to call him from Holland; maybe because I'd thought of that first European trip I'd been on with him, Duke, and Joe.

I got a recording that his line had been disconnected and that worried me, so I called his girlfriend Sandy.

I received a shock. She told me Jerry had died, a cocaine-induced heart attack. I was numbed upon hearing that. Jerry had been more than a partner; he'd been a close friend. My relationship with him had always meant more than how I felt about Duke. I still miss him.

We flew to Dublin, Ireland. Pat had suggested that leg of the trip. There were no casinos in Ireland; he just wanted to see his "roots." Ireland is a fabulously beautiful country, and I was glad to have gone there. In the Irish pubs wherever we went, Pat got along splendidly with his "cousins," and we were all welcomed by some of the nicest but rowdiest people in the world. We stayed there for two weeks before flying back to New York. From JFK we took a chopper down to the Resorts Steel Pier in Atlantic City. Outside the Taj Mahal on the boardwalk, Pat said to me, "Johnny, remember the fudd you found here a few months ago?"

I nodded. I knew where he was going.

"Things have changed a little bit since then, haven't they?"

I nodded again.

"Now I'm gonna go inside this Taj Mahal and show Donald Trump a thing or two. Are you in for that gig?"

"I wouldn't miss it for the world."

What Pat really wanted to do was move the bigger thousand-dollar orange chips under twenty-five-dollar greens, but he settled for doing fifteen-twenty-fives with three purples. I was watching him get paid on his first table when a well-built older man with a full

pate of startling silver hair leaned over to Pat and whispered something in his ear. I had the feeling I had seen the man before but just
couldn't place him. Just as fast as he'd appeared, he walked away.
My eyes followed him down the pit until he was out of view. Then
I eared Pat from the table, signaling him to come out on the boardwalk. I wanted to discuss what had just transpired. As Pat got up, I
could tell by his expression that whatever that man had said affected
him, too.

"Johnny, that was weird," Pat told us on the boardwalk. "The
guy said to me, 'Did my brother show you that move?' "

It clicked immediately. I thought I'd seen the man before because of the strong resemblance to his brother Joe. He was undoubtedly the one and only Henry Classon, the person who had taught Joe
everything *he* knew about cheating the casinos.

"He said that if you want to meet him, you can page him under
the name Chester Gallo in the Taj poker room."

"If *I* want to meet him? He knew you weren't alone?"

"He said, 'You and your partner.' Who the hell is that guy?"

"*That guy* is indirectly responsible for us being here right now,"
I said candidly. "He's Joe Classon's brother, Henry."

I had told Pat and Balls a lot of the stories that Joe had told me
over the years. They had both been intrigued by pastposting's colorful history. When Balls asked, "Are you going to go see the guy?"
I responded, "Absolutely."

I walked back into the Taj Mahal and picked up the first house
phone just inside the boardwalk entrance. I asked the operator to
connect me to the poker room, then asked the person answering there
to page Chester Gallo. I found it amusing that Henry had chosen the
name Chester Gallo; he knew that I'd know its significance immediately. I was also thinking, as I waited on the line, that the move
Joe had always so desperately wanted to keep hidden from Henry
was now out of the bag.

"Chester Gallo speaking," the voice said, bringing me back from
my thoughts. Just hearing those few words I detected a similarity to
Joe's voice.

"The guy you saw do the blackjack move," I said, "I'm his

partner. I'm the one who learned it from your brother, Joe."

I met Henry Classon alone five minutes later in the Taj coffee shop. We sat in a booth and drank tea with cheesecake. Up close like that, the resemblance to Joe was striking. I guessed Henry was at least five years older, although Joe was no doubt destined to age identically. In talking with Henry, I had the impression he was a little coarser around the edges than his baby brother but still shared certain personality traits with him. Like Joe, Henry was very well spoken and seemed to have that same unshakable will that natural-born leaders always had. It turned out that the blackjack move that Joe had so arduously tried to keep hidden from Henry had been uncovered just a few months after Jerry's historic, pioneering jaunt through the Aladdin in Las Vegas.

"I saw that young kid with black hair doing it in Vegas more than twenty years ago," Henry was saying. "I spotted my brother in the casino—I think it was in the Sands—and I hid behind a slot machine and watched what they were hatching. It was the old craps move being done on the blackjack table. I have to hand it to my brother for coming up with the idea to make the transition."

"It wasn't Joe's idea," I corrected Henry. "The kid you saw is dead now—overdose. His name was Jerry and *he* invented the black-jack move."

"Yeah, but he was working under Joe," Henry said, surprising me by what I interpreted as his sticking up for his brother's creative-ness.

"Yeah, you're right. Joe always had a way of bringing out the best in people."

"You know, I haven't spoken to him in twenty-five years."

"I know. He told me all about you . . . about Ruthie . . . even about Mumbles and Wheels."

Henry laughed softly remembering his long-ago mentor Mumbles. I noticed that his tone of voice had become nostalgic. Joe had once described his brother as mean and having a vicious streak in him, which I didn't doubt, but I had the impression that Henry Classon was not all that bad and even regretted the lousy things that had transpired between him and his brother.

"But every time I was in a casino doing that blackjack move and took steam, I knew that I'd just missed him. You know, the move was so good there was always enough to go around for everyone. Still is."

I doubted that Henry knew we'd been doing it with chocolate chips. I had the urge to tell him but didn't.

"Is Joe still working?" he asked out of curiosity, not concerned about the competition.

"No. He packed it in five years ago. What about you?"

"I don't do much of the pastposting anymore. I spend most of my time traveling the country playing poker. With all the casinos sprouting up everywhere, you don't even have to cheat anymore. The suckers are on both sides of the Mississippi now, north and south of the Mason-Dixon line too. If I'm not playing cards, I'm either railing someone at a craps table or picking up stray bets. Did Joe ever show you the opportunities with sleepers?"

"He spoke about it, but we never did it." I told Henry about the experiences I had railing with Joe. He burst out laughing when he heard that his brother had spent an entire weekend in bed with a rich woman from Texas he'd just finished railing. "You should've seen her. She was a real looker to boot."

"That's a real Classon for you," he commented.

In all, I enjoyed my little sit-down with Henry Classon. I was even a bit saddened about his breakup with Joe, though, had it not occurred, I most likely never would have met a Classon. Before I left, Henry asked me if I was still in touch with Joe.

"I don't speak to him very often, but I did a few months ago. He's living near your mother's old condo in Miami Beach."

"Can you do me a favor next time you do?"

"Sure."

"Tell him that I'm sorry for having hit him that time in Puerto Rico."

I called Joe that night and told him Henry was sorry.

———

From Atlantic City we flew north of the border to welcome the new
Canadian casinos in Montreal and Windsor. We beat the hell out of
them but made less money because the Canadian dollar was worth
only seventy cents and no extraordinary limits could make up the
difference.

Southward bound, we found the Midwest riverboats. Some
tugged out, others stayed docked while you played on them. I was
never much thrilled about working riverboats because of the obvious
problems with escape. Even when docked, it was a long way from
the boat down at the dock to the parking lot, usually up a hill—and
there was always only one way on or off the boat, a narrow gangway
in which we'd have no room to maneuver if we were being chased.
Despite my concerns, Pat and Balls wanted to go aboard, and they
overruled me two to one.

The best riverboat at the time was the Empress, about an hour
outside Chicago near Joliet. It was a "sailer" and presented all the
usual riverboat problems. We arrived just as it was getting dark at
about 8:30 P.M. We cased the Empress while she was still docked.
We observed heavy action with a lot of purple and yellow chips in
play. However, I was still leery about working it, but both Pat and
Balls figured I was being too cautious.

"You can never be *too* cautious," I said to them at the entranceway to the boat, indicating the narrow gangway leading to the terminal above. "Even if we work her when she's docked, look what
we're up against if we gotta escape. What the hell do we do if we
take steam in the middle of the fucking river?"

"Jump," Pat said.

"Be serious, will you! They got holding tanks on these shit heaps.
If somebody rats us out or something, there's no way out. They stick
you in the tank until the boat docks, then turn you over to the cops
on land."

"If we stick with the blackjacks, it's pretty safe," Balls said.

He was right about that. Rarely did we have a rat on blackjack
tables, especially since Balls was always asking the person next to
the mechanic what time it was. But what if we did? "You guys really

think it's worth the risk just to pick up a couple of grand?"

"We're already here," Pat said. "Let me do the blackjacks. We'll be alright."

I let myself be convinced, and Pat did the first blackjack move at a table on the upper deck when we were about fifteen minutes into the cruise. Before you could say, "Overboard," we had our rat. A young girl wearing an Empress windbreaker who appeared to be barely of gambling age had come up behind Pat at the last second to read the posted table-limits plaque sitting on the layout to Pat's left. I saw her coming, but it was too late to call off the move. Just as Pat was claiming, the girl cried in a terrible, screechy voice, "He switched the chips! Look in his pocket! He put some chips in his pocket!"

She had seen everything.

I got sick looking at that girl, who was thinking that she'd done such a good deed. I think the ignorance of people ratting us out riled me up more than anything else about the business.

Pat was sick from looking at her too—and he told her so. He grabbed his chips as he got up from the table, stuck his head right in her face, and screamed, "You motherfucking scumbag bitch! I hope you die!" It was so ferocious that I thought he really might kill her. The only comparable outburst I'd ever heard was when Joe went off on the witnesses in the back room of the California Club, threatening to kill anyone who testified against him. Pat then sped away from the table toward the door leading onto the outside deck, heading I didn't know where. The rat was crying from fear.

I said to Balls fatalistically, "We're done now." Extremely rare were the occasions when I said to someone, "I told you so." But that's exactly what I said to Balls.

General pandemonium broke out on the top deck of the Empress. Uniformed security officers were running around everywhere, several out the same door that Pat had just raced through. Balls and I watched the developing circus, and when the same security officers walked back inside the cabin through the same door—without Pat—we looked at each other and realized we were both thinking the same thing.

It was a security guard's radio that confirmed it. Amidst the crackling voices the two words "He jumped" were clearly audible. I hadn't taken Pat seriously when he'd said he'd do just that if necessary, but as that thought swam around in my head, Pat Mallery was swimming fully clothed somewhere in the dark, murky waters of the Des Plaines River.

"I knew he was gonna do it," Balls said with a laugh.

I nodded. "I *should have* known he was gonna do it."

For this kind of emergency we had what was called the emergency-emergency meeting place. It was not a place but a telephone voice-mail depot. Since we had not yet checked into a motel, it was not possible for Pat to contact us directly, nor was it possible for us to know where he would end up. Back in Las Vegas, we had secured a voice mailbox for which all three of us had the code to pick up the messages. If and whenever we got separated while on the road, the message phone in Las Vegas was our sole means of communication.

Balls and I hurriedly debarked the Empress once she was docked, got into the car, and drove to the nearest restaurant. Once there, we ordered soft drinks and checked the voice mail in Vegas every fifteen minutes, hoping to hear from Pat soon. Neither one of us was worried that he might have drowned; the river was not very wide at the point where he'd jumped. There was the much more distinct possibility that he could have been picked up by the police harbor patrol, assuming that the Empress security staff had surely alerted whatever authority was charged with capturing swimming criminals.

The message I received with relief on the fourth call was, "Yeah, it's me, Johnny. My little dip in the drink is over. I'm in the lobby of the Holiday Inn in a town called . . . yeah, what's it called . . . yeah . . . Harvey . . . That's it . . . Harvey . . . like Harvey Wallbanger. You should've seen the look the desk clerk gave me when I walked in. I told him it was hot outside and that I sweat a lot. . . . Okay, Johnny, see you soon."

We picked up Pat at the Harvey Holiday Inn, which took us forty-five minutes by car. Pat recounted his adventure. He swam a mile, which was more like two because of the current—and because he was holding the chips in his right hand as he alternated between the backstroke and crawl. He'd been afraid that they would drift out of his pocket in the water. He finally ended up on shore near a marshy industrial area that smelt like shit. He walked a half mile and luckily came across a phone booth where he could call using a credit card. Knowing it would be difficult to persuade a cab company to send one of their cars to an out-of-the-way industrial zone at that time of night, he fabricated a story over the phone that he had worked late and his car refused to start. When the cabbie arrived, he became suspicious as hell when he saw Pat sopping wet in a suit. Pat gave him a soggy hundred-dollar bill and told him to keep his mouth shut and drive. Pat did stink a little when we picked him up at the Holiday Inn, so he took the T-shirt and shorts we had brought, went into the men's room in the lobby, washed up, and changed. He left the suit and mud-caked shoes behind in one of the stalls. We got back on the highway and drove toward the Empress. We checked into the motel closest to the riverboat, and the next morning Balls and I reboarded to cash out the chips. Then we headed to Indiana and another riverboat.

The experience aboard the Empress taught us one thing: As in the movies, a *great escape* is always possible.

Taking Savannah to the Ball

IT WAS ABOUT A MONTH LATER THAT PAT AND I DEVELOPED THE SA-vannah roulette move, far and away the greatest casino chip move ever invented, and one that would keep Steven DeVisser busy for years to come. Ironically, Balls had left us just a week before our first Savannah test in downtown Las Vegas. He'd decided to open his own sports-betting service. After a lengthy discussion, Pat and I decided to keep Balls in the dark about Savannah. There was no thought of greed involved. Only two people were needed to do the move, and it was he who decided to leave us. I had no inner conflict concerning Balls as I'd had about Joe's retirement.

As soon as Pat and I returned with Savannah from that experi-mental trip to Reno in August 1995, we began preparing our lucky lady for the grand ball. I had never been filled with such excitement and anticipation in my entire life. The thought of taking free ten-thousand-dollar shots at casinos was just too much. Bet a chocolate chip on a 2-to-1 shot, get paid ten grand if it won, lose twenty bucks if it lost. Who would ever believe it!

There is only one casino in the world where I would consider dropping the first chocolate-chip bomb on a roulette table: Caesars Palace in Las Vegas. Throughout my twenty years in the casinos, as you've probably realized by now, Caesars had always been the cherry, the sweetheart. Back in the early seventies, when Joe's team had been doing blackjack moves with black chips, it was in Caesars where Jerry ventured the first use of a purple. In 1989, it was again in Caesars that Joe first used one of their yellow thousand-dollar chips to do his unforgettable rainbow move. And it was Pat, of course, who did the first blackjack pastpost with a Caesars five-thousand-dollar chocolate the night Michael Moorer won the heavyweight championship from Evander Holyfield in the Caesars Palace rear parking lot on April 22, 1994.

Caesars is—was since the day it opened in 1966—and always will be the class of Las Vegas. It is the king of kings. It is the casino where the true world heavyweights of gambling come to blow their money. It does not matter how many behemoth megaresort casinos get built by Steve Wynn or any other casino mogul. Caesars Palace can never be outdone when it comes to class and action, not by an American casino, not by Baden-Baden, Le Grand Casino of Monte Carlo, or any other casino in Europe or the rest of the world. Caesars Palace is mystical; for me, it is the iconic casino. I love it. Truthfully, one day I'd like to be buried there—if old Julius will have me.

It was a busy Saturday night on Labor Day weekend 1995. I put on a lightweight summer suit for the occasion. After all, we were dealing with five-thousand-dollar chips. I had to act the part of a legitimate high roller; I had to dress it as well. Though I could never project the presence of my great partner, Pat, I needed to resemble his chocolate-chip appearance at Caesars as much as possible. He was casual in a Caesars T-shirt, which made his beer belly stick out a little, swimming trunks, and a matching Caesars ball cap. In view of our contrasting appearances, nobody would think we were together.

I strolled through a blackjack pit that had two roulette tables at the end. Pat followed me in the same direction across the double-rowed pit. I stopped in front of a jammed-up roulette game with a short Japanese dealer named Soko. She was wearing glasses with lenses as thick as Coke bottles. Watching her was comical. She was so small she had to reach way over to grasp the chips at the bottom of the table. When she looked up at me, I got sprayed by the light reflecting off her glasses. Thinking she could neither see the chips clearly nor reach out far enough to grab them effectively, I couldn't resist. To break the ice on this move I needed every advantage possible, no matter how unfair.

I signaled Pat that I'd found the table I wanted, grazing my chin subtly with my thumb and index finger. He moved in and took his position by the wheel as I squeezed in between two Chinese men sitting at the bottom of the table. Having Chinese around you was ideal because they never ratted. It was part of their culture to mind their own business and never cooperate with police or any other authorities unless their own blood was threatened.

Soko was finishing paying the winning bets from the last spin. I looked up by the wheel, saw Pat ensconced in position. He gave me a chin that let me know he was ready. However, I was nervous. I was doing something new for the first time and for a considerable amount of money. If the bet lost and I froze up, five grand would be down the drain.

Soko removed the piece from the layout, and the Chinese and other gamblers around the table began placing their bets. The difference between the tables here and those up in Reno was not the volume of action but the amount of money the roulette chips spread all over the layout represented. In Reno, roulette chips usually represented half dollars or dollars. At Caesars their preferred value was often $5 and $10, and it was not uncommon for a high roller to plaster the layout with green twenty-five-dollar casino chips, or even hundred-dollar blacks.

My hands had become sweaty, and I had some difficulty cutting the three red chips off the chocolate. I wanted to get the bet down cleanly the first shot, because in the event of a surveillance situation later, I didn't want to be seen on camera manipulating the chips as though they had to be laid down in some precise fashion. A sharp surveillance guy might get wise to the move if he saw me on tape.

All he had to do was realize I'd intended to hide the chocolate and from there figure out the rest. At least that was my thinking at the embryonic stage of the move, before its unbelievable power dawned on me. It never would have occurred to me at the time that casino surveillance would *never* figure out the simplicity of Savannah.

I put the chips back in my jacket pocket and rubbed my hands along the sides of my trousers, trying to dry my hands as best I could. When I removed the chips again, I managed to get them down in the first-column box but wasn't too satisfied with the placement. I had cut the reds off the chocolate a bit too far. Looking down at them, the effect was like the jaws of a shark. Suddenly, the Chinese guy on my left leaned back in his chair and looked up at me with a furrowing eyebrow. I thought I detected a slight smile outlining his lips. I was certain he saw my chocolate chip and appreciated its value. But did he sense I planned on swiping it off if it lost? At first, that thought unnerved me, but then I chided myself for being ridiculous, at the same time reminding myself that Chinese don't rat.

I looked again at Pat, who glanced at my bet and gave me another chin to indicate it was well enough placed from his point of view, which wasn't that much different from the dealer's. He was sending the message that from where he stood he could not see the chocolate chip.

I still had second thoughts and might have reached out to fix up the chips, but it was too late. Soko had spun the ball. I felt my neck muscles tightening as the ball revolved around the cylinder. And it was rolling slowly; it was going to drop terribly soon. I had forgotten to ready myself for a slow spin. When sizing up the little Japanese dealer, I hadn't thought about the corresponding small lapse of time there'd be from the beginning of her spin until the moment the ball dropped into one of the number slots on the wheel.

I barely had time to swallow the bile rising in my throat before the click-clack of the dropping ball reverberated in my head. Then Pat was shouting loudly, "Damn it!" as Soko's eyes were coming back from the spinning cylinder, the piece wrapped up in her hand as she reached toward the layout to place it. She put it on number 00, then her two hands began working their way in unison toward my bet. She had an easy sweep to make because there were no winning bets on the layout. All she had to do was sweep off all the chips, not having to worry about inadvertently removing winners off the layout, which slowed a dealer's progress. Generally, the casino cleaned up when the numbers 0 and 00 came out. Many gamblers considered those numbers bad luck and therefore never bet them.

I hesitated a fraction of a second before my left hand shot out and grabbed the chips. There was no doubt about my tardiness. When timing is everything, a fraction of a second can be an eternity. Thinking I was caught red-handed, I fumbled putting the four chips in my left jacket pocket, worried about dropping the chocolate on the floor. In that instant of my own ineptitude, I completely disregarded what I'd considered to be my advantage in Soko's nearsightedness, and even feared that she might have seen the chocolate chip. My eyes jumped directly to Soko as soon as the chips were finally in my pocket. She was still sweeping losing chips off the layout. She didn't look up at me, didn't react at all—nothing! I couldn't believe it. As late as I'd been, she hadn't seen me snatch up the chips.

My head turned to Pat. He was giving the chin to reassure me that Soko hadn't seen anything. I took in a deep breath, blew out the air, and settled down. The two Chinese men began rattling away in Chinese. I was sure they were talking about me and what they'd just seen, but neither one turned his head to look up at me. I kept my eyes glued on Soko for ten seconds. She was busy restacking the chips in her working bay, putting the fresh stacks in her chip well. She wasn't giving me the time of day. Satisfied that I had indeed snatched that chocolate chip cleanly off the layout, I backed away from the table and walked off.

Ten minutes later Pat showed up where I was waiting in the sports book at the Barbary Coast casino.

"Johnny, you were a little late over there," he said, smiling. "It looked like you were playing chicken with the dealer. I wasn't sure who was gonna pick the chips up first."

"I was a little nervous," I admitted. "And I got taken by her slow spin."

"Don't worry about it," he reassured me. "It was clean."

"I think those Chinamen saw me."

"*Saw* you?" Pat laughed from the gut. "Johnny, if they had tickets to the show at Caesars tonight, they've probably already ripped them up."

We shared a laugh and went over to the bar next to the sports book. The Barbary Coast was hopping like all the other Vegas Strip casinos on Saturday night. We had to wait a couple of minutes to get drinks, so we talked a little strategy. We agreed that if everything appeared clean after a pickup, it would no longer be necessary to leave Caesars. We'd arrange an internal meeting spot off the casino floor where I would wait for Pat. If any steam came down after I left the table, he'd come over immediately and flash the signal to get out. Should I win the bet and get paid, I'd automatically come back over to the Barbary Coast sports book.

We gulped down our drinks and headed back across Las Vegas Boulevard to Caesars. We both were eager to get back in there. The cocktail had done me good. I was now exuding confidence, all the jitters gone. I would find another table, put the bet right down, pick it right back up if it lost, get paid the ten grand if it won. Nothing was stopping me now.

Cruising the pit, I passed by Soko's table. The two Chinese men were still there, and when one saw me he nudged the other almost childishly, and they both looked at me and laughed. Pat had been right. I must have given them all the entertainment they'd needed for the night. I would've loved to take another shot on Soko's table but simply couldn't because of general security principles. If I did and my bet won, and a pit boss decided to go to the video to check its legitimacy, I'd be running the risk that they'd rewind the tape back far enough to catch the sequence where I raked off the chips earlier on the same table. That would be a real stupid way to give up our newly discovered move.

I found another beauty of a dealer on a roulette game in the main pit near the front entrance. I joked to myself that if I had to get out quick, I couldn't have been in a more advantageous location. The dealer was an older guy named Ray. You would've sworn he was an ex-boxer. He had one of those punched-in noses and was kind of ugly, but in spite of all that gave the impression of being a "sweetheart" dealer. He was helping people place their bets, explaining corresponding payoffs, smiling continually. I would have guessed it was fifty-fifty that Ray was dealing in the Caesars casino the night they opened its doors in 1966.

This time I got the bet down without my hands sweating, and the three red chips were cut perfectly off the chocolate. One thing about cutting the chips like that: when they were cut right, I knew it. A sudden click went off in my head, like a safecracker feeling the tumblers give way just before the vault pops open.

Ray spun the ball, and it was one of those spins where the ball goes around and around, then gets stuck along the rim and refuses to drop into the bowl. That can be really exasperating when you're trying to break the ice with something like this. Ray was forced to retrieve the ball and spin it again. This time it dropped into the number-4 slot, a winning outcome, but then bounced out, ricocheted around the wheel and finally found a loser, where it stayed put. Pat had stayed focused on the wild ball and was now yelling, "Damn it!" at the soonest possible instant. I was equal to the task. My hand shot out and grabbed the chips long before Ray had even turned his head from the wheel. The rest of the people at the table had no reaction, though I hardly looked at them.

Mumbling an expletive, I turned away, not looking back at anything. I was pleased with my performance and had complete confidence in Pat to report back the details. The only negative there was not winning the bet. But that would surely come with a little patience.

Pat was just a couple of minutes behind me in the Caesars keno pit. He gave me a chin, then tugged slightly on his earlobe, urging me to come back into the pit and find another table. Obviously, the last pickup had gone so well it wasn't necessary to discuss anything. Once back on the prowl through the pits, I gave Pat the ear, indicating that I wanted him to follow me through the long corridor toward the far end of the casino.

I pulled up to the bottom of another roulette table in the back pit of Caesars by its sports book. I placed the bet, lost, and raked off.

The dealer caught me, scolded me, and I put back four reds in the first-column box, killing the steam. At another wheel, as the ball was spinning, the shift and pit bosses arrived to carry out their shift-changeover chip-count, and I was forced to pull off the bet at the last instant.

We found ourselves back in the keno pit, tired, the whizzing sound of eighty keno balls flying haphazardly inside their giant bowl on the counter guarding our silence. When the last of twenty winning balls was finally sucked through the vacuum tube, Pat said, "Maybe we ought to pack it in, Johnny. We can come back tomorrow on the day shift."

He was probably right. If I wanted to continue that night, Pat would not have objected. Our relationship was very special in that regard. Though we had only been together a relatively short time, we already understood each other fraternally, and always looked out for each other's ass. We were the perfect team, just the two of us. More types of moves may have been workable with Joe's four-man team, and it did have great coordination but not that perfect mesh that is possible between two great partners. I imagine if you talked to cops they'd give you a similar opinion.

"Yeah, you're right, Johnny," I agreed. "I'm exhausted. I don't want to fuck up. Let's go back to your apartment and watch a movie."

We didn't watch any movie. The television was on, but it didn't keep us from talking about Savannah. Pat was sitting on the couch eating a chicken sandwich while I sat on my customary recliner wolfing down a Sara Lee pound cake.

"Those dealers in Caesars are really something," Pat said. "How the hell do they keep their jobs?"

It was true that half the dealers working Caesars Palace could never get a job in one of the dealer break-in joints downtown on the basis of dealing skills alone. Practically all the dealers at Caesars were juiced in. To work there you had to know somebody; if not, you had to be extremely lucky to happen on a rare occasion when they suddenly needed dealers. During the casino's heyday in the seventies, many Caesars dealers were actually earning fortunes, especially in the baccarat pit. One Caesars four-man crew walked away with tokes of a hundred and fifty grand each on a New Year's Eve when a band of wealthy Mexicans beat the casino for more than ten million.

A lot of Caesars personnel had been there since the casino's inception and were well past retirement age. Since they had the casino juice, nobody could criticize them or tell them it was time to trade in their dealing aprons for seats around the canasta table. A couple of the real old-timers I'd noticed in the pit had to be pushing eighty. All this worked in our favor. Since the dealers often had more power in the casino than the floormen and certain pit bosses, they often didn't bother letting them know what was happening on their tables. A dealer at Caesars could pay an unannounced winning chocolate chip without saying so much as a word to anybody. Nobody questioned the integrity of the dealers working Caesars. The job paid well and carried prestige. It was rare to find a bad apple over there stealing from the inside.

"The only way a dealer quits Caesars," I told Pat, "is by dying or hitting the lottery, and even a dealer winning the lottery is no cinch to quit his job."

The following Sunday afternoon we drove directly to the Barbary Coast, parked the car in its garage, and walked across the boulevard to Caesars. It was a real scorcher outside. We were both dressed in shorts and Polo shirts. I wore the ball cap; Pat left his at home.

Inside, the casino wasn't crowded. Many guests were either out cooling off in the pool or watching sporting events in the race and sports books. Sparsely populated casinos were not ideal, but I was anxious to get a bet down and a payoff. In spite of the lack of big action, there were a few good wheels in the main pit up front, and all the pit bosses seemed relaxed as they usually were on Sunday afternoons.

I found a tall, chubby Latino named Guillermo dealing to a group of Europeans on a lively roulette table with a few legitimate black-chip players. One guy was betting blacks straight up on the numbers while one of his two decked-out female companions was stacking green casino chips on odd. The rest of the layout was sufficiently covered by an assortment of roulette chips. The only problem was that there were too many people—women—packed around the table. I had the impression that each of the European gamblers not only had a wife or girlfriend with him, but a mistress, too. I tried to twist and turn into my position at the bottom of the table, but one of the black-chip gambler's girlfriends was standing against it, impeding my approach. Here I had to be careful because I didn't want to make a scene with the girl and the gambler. I had to somehow gently nudge her just enough to open up a space from where I could maneuver without rubbing her the wrong way—or the right way, which might make the guy think I was trying to bird-dog his girlfriend. Creating an uneasy atmosphere around the table could cause the gambler or one of the girlfriends, or somebody else at the table, to rat me out if I ended up grabbing the bet off the layout.

I tried the best I could to squeeze into position, but it was in vain. The threesome was having too much fun, and now they were holding hands and touching each other as they spoke French and sipped their cocktails. The worrisome thought of accidentally knocking over their drinks when they rested on the edge of the layout entered my mind.

With all these negatives, it seemed best to find another table, or simply wait until the French at the bottom left. But usually, when you waited for conditions to suit you in a casino, it didn't work out the way you wanted. A couple of bad spins and the players could be wiped out. Then suddenly you had an empty table, and you didn't want to go head-up against the dealer, hoping he didn't see your chocolate chip when it sat on the bottom of the *only* bet on the layout, or that he didn't notice it if you got caught raking when it lost. This was just too much to buck. With exactly that in mind, I made a rash decision. I took a few steps to my right, skirting the threesome, and positioned myself against the inside corner of the table, at the last allowable spot next to the dealer. I then placed my $5,015 inside the third-column box, which was located on the bottom right of the layout. I made the tiniest adjustment when cutting the three red chips off the chocolate to compensate for the angle change between

the dealer and the chips now sitting in the third-column box instead
of the first-column box.

Pat had a surprised expression on his face, but he understood. I
gave him a chin with my brows furrowed, silently asking him, "Is
this okay with you?"

It was not automatic. Identifying into which column a winning
number fell was not nearly as simple as red or black, or odd or even.
Red or black was simply visual. Odd or even required a first-grade
education, but with columns you had to invoke your brain's memory,
or actually make the match with your eyes, which took longer. The
first column we had both already memorized since we'd been working exclusively on it from the inception of the move. But I could not
expect Pat to have the third column memorized any more than I had
myself. There was, however, a built-in simplifying factor for the third
column: all its numbers were divisible by 3. I had no idea about Pat's
mathematical skills, or if he even recognized that simple math was
applicable to our situation, but nevertheless, he was now chinning me
with a shrug that said, "Why not."

I left the chips in the box and steeled myself in concentration as
Guillermo spun the ball. It made several revolutions around the
wheel, then fell dead in the number-3 slot. Everything was perfect.
The ball didn't bounce out, and Pat had the easiest of calls because
number 3 was in the top row, the first number in the third column.
It was also, of course, divisible by 3.

He remained silent.

I exploded. All that pent-up energy came rushing out of my body.
I let out a thunderous "Yes!" and followed it up with a monster claim.
"I hit the big one!" I shouted, clapping my hands with an assortment
of exaggerated gestures. It wasn't all an act, however. I was genuinely both thrilled to death and immensely relieved. Our number had
finally come in. The tension had been building up in me that whole
weekend. "I just love Caesars Palace," I carried on. "That's ten
grand in the *third* column for me, Guillermo . . . ten thousand dollars!"

Guillermo looked down at my bet, casually lifted off the three
red chips, flinched momentarily when he saw the chocolate under-

neath, put the reds back down next to it, then reached into his chip well and delicately peeled off two Caesars five-thousand-dollar chips from the handsome chocolate stack sitting behind the red, green, black, purple, and yellow stacks of chips in the well. He put the chocolates on the layout in front of him and announced, "Chocolate going out," to let the pit personnel know he was paying out chocolate chips. Finally, he placed the two chocolates next to mine in the third-column box.

"Are these yours also?" he asked me, indicating the three red chips sitting in the box next to the chocolates.

I was in seventh heaven. A clean ten-thousand-dollar payoff! "No, Guillermo," I responded loftily. "They're yours."

"Thank you, sir."

He paid himself $30, pocketed that plus the three red chips I had bet, picking up a forty-five dollar toke for the spin.

We cleared ten grand. I picked up the three chocolate chips and admired them in my hand, appreciating them as a jeweler did precious stones.

During all that hoopla I'd completely forgotten Pat was even there. When I finally did look over at him, he was smiling profusely and giving me chins, telling me everything was superclean. The floorman came over to take a look at me. There was no misgiving in his eyes whatsoever. He just wanted to catch a glimpse of Caesars' newest chocolate-chip roulette player.

Before leaving the table, I placed two of the chocolates in the middle of the layout and asked Guillermo to change them into ten yellow thousand-dollar chips. This would facilitate our cash-out procedure later. Working Savannah with the chocolates, we'd have to take the same cash-out precautions we'd taken when Pat romped through Caesars doing the blackjacks. If we were not prudent at the cage, they could pick up on us and discover our new move through surveillance.

I think the best feeling I ever had in my life was leaving that roulette table with a fistful of yellow chips from Caesars Palace. I let them jiggle in my hand, delighted in their sweet rattling music as I crossed through the main casino and eased down the passageway toward the back entrance and out the door. I had purposely taken the long route out of the casino because I didn't want the floorman, or any other personnel who'd been in that roulette pit, seeing me walk right out of the casino after having made the winning five-thousand-dollar bet. I never turned my head but assumed I was being watched. Just before leaving the table, I'd said loudly so that everyone in the pit heard, "I think I'll try my luck at baccarat." I did pass and stand briefly by the baccarat pit, which was in full view of the main pit where I'd won the ten grand. Anything and everything to keep up appearances.

I kept listening to the chips rattle in my hand as I crossed Las Vegas Boulevard, thinking the sounds made by the expensive chips were actually more elegant than those made by five-dollar reds when you jiggled them in the same fashion. Maybe I was nuts, but the high I felt was immense.

Pat was all smiles when he entered the Barbary Coast to give me the details. "You were fabulous, Johnny!" He gave me a big handshake.

"Nothing came down after I left?"

Pat shook his head. "The floorman came up to the dealer right after you were gone and asked him if he'd ever seen you before. Then he looked at the stacks of chips in the dealer's well and wrote something down on his pad."

"Oh, that's nothing," I said knowingly. "He was just taking note of the ten yellow chips I walked with."

Whatever doubts I'd had about Savannah were all rubbed out now. The move was perfection, undoubtedly the best cheating move involving casino chips ever conceived. It was the culmination of a gifted cheating-casinos career. And it was so deliciously simple. Sure, there were scams out there I didn't know about; someone somewhere probably had something better that didn't involve the manipulation of gaming chips. But one thing I was absolutely sure about was that Savannah had the best payoff-to-risk ratio in the business. Professional slot machine cheaters using computer chips and remote control to rig jackpots on today's sophisticated machines make more money than us—but incur much more serious risk. Even first-timers caught rigging slot machines in Nevada got five-year prison sentences with no probation.

But the most important element of the Savannah move, what made it so strong, was the people doing it, Pat and I. We never had to worry about one of us cracking under pressure if questioned. There was never the slightest chance that one would give up the other. Not only did we know our business, we knew the law. Getting caught was one thing, going to prison was another. Most people in prison get there for what they do *after* the crime. If it wasn't about a murder or a real serious drug offense, you had a fair chance of avoiding prison just by keeping your mouth shut when confronted by the authorities. You'd be surprised to discover how many people pulled off the best casino scams only to be conned in turn by Nevada Gaming agents into giving them up. I'd estimate that 80 percent of casino scammers, relatively intelligent people, didn't even know the two basic rules for staying out of jail: Keep your mouth shut; and if you have to open it, only utter the word *attorney*. Many inside scams in which cheaters worked together with casino personnel came apart and sent the participants to prison because one person got pressured inside the casino security room and gave everyone else up, wrongly believing he would be sentenced to a long prison term if he didn't.

There was a big baccarat scam in Las Vegas in the mid-1990s that served as a perfect example of people who should have ended up millionaires but instead went to prison broke. A tight-knit band of Chinese from Hong Kong recruited three Vegas dealers who were also from Hong Kong and were working the baccarat rooms in three different major Strip casinos. Their scam was ingenious in its simplicity—as all good scams always are. All they did was keep track of the cards coming out of the baccarat shoe, then used that knowledge to destroy the casino on the next shoe. Since baccarat has set rules, there are no player decisions like hitting and standing, as in blackjack, and nothing can alter the prearranged sequence in which the cards are going to fall out of the shoe. So by keeping track of the cards from one shoe, the Chinese scammers knew how to bet with one hundred percent accuracy on the hands dealt from the following one. And as such they could continue cyclically through the shoes until their dealers were relieved. The key was that the order of the cards being prepared for each new shoe could not be disturbed. That's where the Hong Kong dealers came in. By perfecting the art of the false shuffle, or at least well enough that the cameras above the tables couldn't prove shit, they laid winning hands on their associates for a month before the casinos, finally realizing that the same players kept winning against the same dealers, yanked the Hong Kong trio into the back room. The three casinos had been beaten for a total of five million. Gaming agents reviewing the surveillance tapes put the move together and began making their case. But the surveillance video could not prove that the dealers were perpetuating false shuffles. Without that irrefutable proof, the casinos had absolutely nothing against anybody. Knowing that the Hong Kong group, including the dealers, were going to escape forever to the Kowloon Peninsula, the Nevada Gaming Control Board Enforcement agents told them exactly how their scam worked, and tried to coerce them into believing that the proof against them was on the surveillance tapes. Well, two of the dealers didn't go for the bluff, but the third one obviously didn't know the word for *lawyer* in English and cracked under pressure and gave it all up. The result: the Chinese canary got to leave the country on a deportation order while the other two dealers and the rest of the crew got to stay in the United States for terms ranging from five to twenty years—all because one dealer couldn't keep his mouth shut. If he had, they all would have walked with their five million and the beaten casinos would have been left to lick their wounds. It never paid to enter into a conspiracy with people working inside the casino. The one time that I had ripped off a casino from the inside (the Four Queens scam), *I* was the dealer. The only person I had to worry about cracking in the back room was me—and that possibility never existed. But when you work with other people on the inside, you're asking to wear the chrome bracelets.

Pat and I would never go down the way those Chinese did. If we were ever going to end up in prison for cheating casinos, it was not us who'd make them the key to throw away. They'd have to get us solely on the evidence, without any cooperation from the guilty parties.

During the fall of 1995, we blitzkrieged Vegas with the chocolate-chip Savannah move. One weekend we got paid nine times in nine different casinos, walking away with ninety grand. When we went cold and couldn't hit a winning bet on any of the columns (we'd begun working all three columns), we made a procedural change. We began placing our chocolate chips in the even-money 19 through 36 box at the bottom left side of the layout. The distance from the dealer was a tad shorter, but frankly it didn't matter. Our bet placements were just so good that dealers never saw the chocolate chip underneath the reds.

Arriving at that decision was not cut and dried. Mathematically, in the long run, we'd be giving up 25 percent of the money. However, the long dry spells we dreaded would be reduced, since the 19 through 36 bet had almost a 50 percent chance of winning. And if for some reason Savannah ended up having a short lifetime, that betting change might prove more profitable overall.

Pat had a brazen idea to maximize the number *and* the amount of the payoffs. One night over a beer while we were barbecuing lobster tails, he suggested the previously unthinkable. "Why not put *two* five-thousand-dollar chips underneath the reds in the casinos that take $10,000 on the even-money bets?"

I couldn't help laughing. It was so ridiculous it would probably fly. I pulled Pat's glass out of his hand and kiddingly smelled its contents. "What do you got in this glass, Johnny?"

Pat shrugged playfully and said, "I don't know, Johnny, I'm just trying to improve the move."

"Stick to cooking those lobsters."

At that moment, I obviously didn't know that in the coming months we would not only be hiding two big chips under the reds— but three. In Atlantic City and elsewhere in the country where casinos didn't have five-thousand-dollar chips, we ventured the use of double and triple-chip hiding. In Las Vegas, we eventually graduated to the double-chocolate Savannah and had success with ten-thousand-dollar payoffs on the 19 through 36 box. In order to accomplish that, it was necessary to constantly distract the dealer from the time we placed the bet until the roulette ball dropped into a number slot.

The caller at the front of the wheel had the additional responsibility of keeping the dealer engaged in conversation, so he wouldn't have a chance to look down and case our bet. With the double-chocolate underneath, we couldn't depend on chip camouflage alone.

The highest posted outside-payoff limit I'd ever seen in Las Vegas was at the Desert Inn, where you were allowed to bet $10,000 on all the 2-to-1 propositions. We went for the twenty-thousand-dollar prize by hiding two chocolates on the columns several times but never had the luck to win a bet.

Meanwhile, we did just fine with the 19 through 36 bets at five grand a pop. One weekend Pat would call; I would rake and claim; then the next we switched roles. We'd gotten another sixty Savannahs paid during the rest of that fall, 1995. Then the steam started coming. More and more often, pit bosses began going to the eye in the sky before paying us. Word was bouncing around Vegas that a "wheel team" was hitting the roulette games heavy with chocolate checks.

I called my surveillance buddy Donnie at his home.

"What the fuck are you guys doing?" he asked in his laughingly conspiratorial way.

"We're starting to get serious heat on the wheels," I said.

Donnie chuckled. "Well, you should be. You've been putting down chocolates all over town and the video's backing you up. They know it's you and your buddy Pat, but they haven't identified him. They can't figure out what you're doing. What the fuck *are* you doing?"

The consternation in Donnie's voice made me laugh. Donnie knew all our moves except Savannah. I figured he thought we'd been pastposting as in the old days but with a little more gusto. There was no reason for me to let him know otherwise.

I was already aware before calling him that everyone connected with casino surveillance had identified me and my unknown partner in their tapes. Each time pit bosses went to the sky to verify our bets, we got filmed while waiting. It was impossible to avoid that. By that time, I was already known by the Nevada Gaming Control Board and dozens of other casino regulatory bodies around the world as one of the most innovative international casino cheaters in the business. But that in itself didn't matter. What made the difference was the length of time it would take before they put the whole thing together. Constantly seeing the same two guys on the tape had to tell them something was going down, even when the video evidence legitimized the bets. Even if my name *wasn't* connected to the tapes, they'd still have to be awfully suspicious.

Knowing that Savannah's life might be nearing the end of the line, I decided to implement something that had been in my head for a while—if, of course, Pat agreed. Remembering his crazy suggestion about hiding two chocolate chips underneath, I said to him, "Johnny, remember we talked about putting two chocolates underneath the reds?"

"You didn't want to do it," he reminded me.

"I still don't. But there might be another way to get the same effect." Pat was all ears, so I continued. "Suppose that instead of putting another chocolate underneath, we put it on a second bet. For instance, we put one bet on the first column like we used to and another on the 19 through 36 like we're doing now. If they both win, we pick up fifteen grand. If only the column bet wins, we pick up five grand—ten for the win in the column minus the five lost on the 19 through 36. If the 19 through 36 wins and the column loses, we break out even."

"We don't pick up the loser and leave the winner?" Pat asked.

"No. It's not worth the risk. If the dealer sees us pick up the loser, we can't claim the winner. Then we're caught with our pants down when they spot the chocolate lying on the bottom of the winner while we tried to pick up the loser. No, the only time we pick up is when they *both* lose."

Pat whistled at the boldness of the move.

"We might as well milk it to the end," I said with a coy smile. "Nothing lasts forever."

We decided to give Vegas a rest until New Year's Eve, to let the town cool down for a while. During that break we discussed strategy for the two-bet scenario and ultimately decided we'd stay with the same MO—the caller at the top by the wheel and the raker, who'd rake off both bets himself, at the bottom. The only change we made was to the bet itself. Two red chips would be placed on top of the chocolate instead of three, to facilitate the double rake-off, in that the total number of chips handled would be less.

Pat went home to Massachusetts for Christmas; I stayed in Vegas. New Year's Eve we'd give them a final pummeling with the modified Savannah. In the interim, I hung around the Horseshoe poker room and played a little Texas hold 'em, watched the college bowl games in the sports book when I got sick of the cards. I always wore my ball cap and zeros when pulling prolonged casino exposure like that. Keeping a low profile anywhere inside a gambling establishment was mandatory. DeVisser patrolled poker rooms, too, though I'd never seen him inside the Horseshoe. I never knew if it was one of Hanson's client casinos (it was rumored to be one of the few majors that wasn't), but I felt much safer there than at the Mirage.

When Pat returned to Vegas two days before New Year's Eve, we began practicing picking up the two bets. There wasn't much difference. After experimenting with both one and two hands, I felt more comfortable doing it with only one. Although there'd be two bets to pick up, by placing each in the neighboring extremities of their respective boxes, the actual distance between them was less than two inches, therefore, I could scoop them both up in practically the same time I'd been scooping up the single bets all along. It would just be a tad more complicated getting the six chips back in my pocket and replacing them on the layout with the six reds. We were confident that the dealers would continue missing the chocolates on the layout while casing the bets, despite the second one's presence. Again we were right.

We arrived at the Las Vegas Hilton at ten-thirty New Year's Eve. The Hilton was another of Vegas's classy big-action joints. The casino was already going strong; we had our choice of three or four good wheels, each invitingly flashing its red, black, and green numbers like a rainbow.

An old-timer named Benny was dealing a roulette game, and

another female old-timer was working behind him as a helper. With Savannah, the presence of helpers created no additional problems. They never saw the chocolate chips underneath, nor had a helper ever caught us raking off chips. In fact, their presence behind the dealer was a positive. In situations where a pit boss was suspicious about our winning a five-thousand-dollar bet, he had to wonder, How could they have beaten *two* dealers on a wheel? From time to time such pit-boss reasoning may have saved us an eye-in-the-sky inquiry. To what extent the helper's presence actually did favor us was immeasurable.

The casino was extremely noisy, and the din was exacerbated by a brass band playing in the elevated bar lounge just off the casino floor. I cleared my throat as I approached the roulette table. I knew I'd have to strain my vocal cords in order to be heard when it was time to claim.

I wedged myself between two couples who were rowdy college kids wearing UNLV football jackets and ball caps. I thought I must have looked funny among them in my suit as I reached inside the jacket pocket to ready the chips. Just as I put down the two bets, the band gave a flourish and started a new number, as if to signal the beginning of our show.

Benny spun the ball on cue, really letting her rip. The guy was no slouch, despite his many years in the casino. It was one of the longest spins I'd ever witnessed, and as the ball went around and around, Benny cased and recased the layout, never giving either of my bets more than a passing glance. I had the comical thought that ten—even twenty—identical bets could have been placed out there without a single chocolate chip being exposed to the dealer. The whole damned table could be filled with an army of rakers ready to swipe off the losing bets in unison at the caller's command.

"No more bets," Benny announced deliberately, waving his long arm across the layout to halt the betting. One of those dumb college kids who'd been drinking too much and letting his cigarette ashes sprinkle the bottom of the layout was still ignorantly betting his chips; he received a sharp rebuke from the old dealer. I reflected that if I ended up getting caught raking off my bets, there'd be a real scene, judging by Benny's countenance.

But we had a stroke of luck. Our first attempt at the double-Savannah (as we christened it later) was a double-winner. Number 31 came in, a 19 through 36, *and* a first-column winner. I went through my song and dance, claiming at the top of my lungs over the music that I had just won $15,000. Benny looked down at my bets, nodded, and smiled coolly at me. I was convinced he saw the chocolate chip on the bottom of each bet. He swept off the losers and the helper passed him a stack of five-dollar chips. He took the red stack and cut it into my two bets, paying me $30 for the first-column bet, $15 for the 19-through-36 bet. He hadn't seen *either* of the chocolate chips, and that was a disaster, because now I had to change the claim and revert to the old dealer-you-made-a-mistake claim. How ironic it was that the dealer actually did pay me wrong, and I had to go into that old claim to salvage the situation.

"Whoa!" I hollered belligerently. "Benny, I'm betting five-thousand-dollar chips and you paid me off in reds. What's going on here!"

Benny looked down at my bets and at the chips he'd paid me, then looked back up at me and said curtly, "Don't be an asshole, sonny."

I couldn't believe my ears. I wondered if he now saw the chocolates and figured I took a shot and slipped them in there after he paid me, or if he still didn't see them at all and just mistook me for a wisecracking asshole. The five-thousand-dollar chips at the Hilton were actually shaded more gray than chocolate and blended in so perfectly with their five-dollar reds you really could miss one underneath, even when you were told it was there. All casino chips had a particular design speckled onto their sides, different for each denomination. Whoever had designed those five-thousand-dollar chips for the Hilton must have forgotten the design he'd used on the fives. They were glaringly similar, as though the pattern had been tailor-made for Savannah.

No way was I abandoning that claim. I pressed onward. "Benny,

you don't seem to understand. I bet $5,000 on each box." I pointed
to both sets of chips on the layout, bringing my index finger as close
as possible without touching them. In that situation, touching them
was a no-no. Doing so could put the idea in his head that I had
tampered with the chips while his back was turned. "You don't see
my five-thousand-dollar chips there?" I asked with genuine incre-
dulity. I avoided using the word *chocolates*, which would have made
me seem too casino-wise.

Benny looked down at my bets again, then back at me as if I
had donned a cape and mask and was telling him the earth was flat.
"What are you trying to pull here? There are no five-thousand-dollar
chips on the layout."

"Look again," I said, practically pleading.

"I *am* looking. You have two bets of $15."

At that point I had to take another glance at my bets. Was it
possible that somehow I'd fucked up and never got the chocolate
chips down on the layout? Could that wonderful color combination
have fooled me also?

Suddenly the helper, who hadn't said a word during the entire
confrontation, came to my rescue. "Benny," she said timidly, "I think
there's a chocolate check underneath"—she poked her head down
the layout with squinting eyes—"both his bets."

Benny finally lifted off the two red chips on the 19 through 36
bet. When he saw the chocolate, he went into shock. His body literally swayed as he stared blankly at the chocolate chip. For a moment, I thought the poor guy was going to tumble or have a stroke
or something. The helper had to tell him to lift the reds off my first-
column bet. When he saw the second chocolate, he went stiff and
started to look terrible. The color drained from his face and his mouth
sagged. I began feeling nervous looking at him. I was hoping the
floorman would arrive quickly, almost like a corner man praying for
the referee to step in and save his fighter from a further shellacking.
Finally, the helper called over the floorman, perhaps saving Benny's
life.

The floorman was a young guy not yet out of his twenties. Benny
still couldn't talk, so the helper explained the situation for him. The

floorman didn't ask any questions. He went immediately down to the pit to get the ranking pit boss. They returned to the table together. By that time Benny had regained a little of his composure. At least now he could talk, and I was relieved to notice the color returning to his face.

The pit boss was in his midfifties and had one of those hawk faces with a hooked nose and small beady eyes. I got the impression he was the type of guy who wouldn't trust the pope. He looked suspiciously at me, then at my chips on the layout. What he saw with those beady eyes were my two original bets of $5,010, a chocolate with two reds on top, and the three sets of three red chips Benny had paid me. I would have been better off had Benny put all those chips he'd paid me back in his chip well. Had he done so, the pit boss would have only seen my original bets. His view would have been a lot "cleaner."

"How could you not have seen both those chocolate checks?" the pit boss asked Benny rather crudely, without much respect for his age.

"I thought the bottom checks were also red," Benny answered weakly.

The pit boss turned his hawk face on the helper. "Did *you* see those chocolate checks before he spun the ball?"

"No."

The pit boss turned into a ball of steam. "Alright, hold this up a minute." Without looking at me, he turned on his heels and started back into the pit. At that point I had to get assertive. Any other approach would have been to show weakness.

"What's the problem?" I called out loudly to the pit boss's back.

He turned smartly back toward me. "I'm sorry, sir," he said with cold politeness. "I'm going to have to verify that your bets were there before the dealer spun the ball."

I immediately went into my being-insulted routine. "What do you mean, verify that my bets were there?"

"That's casino policy, sir. All winning bets of a hundred dollars or more not called out by the dealer must be verified by surveillance before they can be paid." He went to the podium, picked up the telephone, and called surveillance. Then he began talking heatedly with another pit boss who had the air of being one of the higher-ups. From the intensity of their conversation, I guessed they'd already heard about the unseen winning chocolate chips showing up on roulette layouts. And now there were *two* of them less than two inches apart on the same layout.

I gritted my teeth and took a deep breath. I knew I was in for a battle. Getting them to pay me the fifteen grand when they knew they had got beat risked being drudgery.

I looked over to where Pat had been standing; he was gone. He'd receded into the background and was watching the situation develop from another pit across the casino. I understood. We both knew this was one of those times when surveillance started filming close-ups of everyone around the wheel as soon as they got the call from the pit boss on the floor. There was no need for Pat to pull the same exposure as me.

The atmosphere around the table grew quiet, except for the college group, who continued bantering away. They seemed amused by the situation. Benny and the helper stood stiffly, Benny nervously fiddling the number marker while the helper repeatedly steepled a small stack of roulette chips in her working bay. Neither one dared look at me. In their eyes I must have looked like a leper.

Five minutes went by, then ten, then fifteen. Usually surveillance verification didn't take longer than ten minutes. Surveillance systems worked just like your home VCR. All the operators had to do was rewind the tape and play back the action in question. They might look at it several times, examining everybody at the table to see whether they could put something together, but I knew in this case there was nothing to see on the tape besides my legitimate bets.

After twenty minutes, there were four pit bosses huddled in very animated conversation in the middle of the pit, each one shooting glances in my direction. I began to understand what was happening. They were stalling. The surveillance operator upstairs had notified them that the camera above the table did not record the events. That happened frequently, for various reasons. They could have been filming something else with that camera, its tilted lens panning to catch action on or around a nearby table as well as inside the pit. Without surveillance verification, somebody in the pit would have to make a decision on his own.

Finally, after a half hour had gone by, the casino shift boss approached me from behind. He was not one of the bosses who'd been engaged in that conversation inside the pit. He introduced himself without offering his hand. "Sir, excuse us for the delay, but matters like this take a little time."

He was full of shit. They'd decided that without videotape to indicate otherwise, I had no doubt taken advantage of their two old-time dealers and popped in two chocolate chips after the ball dropped into the number-31 slot. They figured they would make me sweat awhile, make me crack under the pressure. I noticed two uniformed security guards milling behind the table, part of their little bluff. What the Hilton bosses didn't know was that I was prepared to stay there till next Yom Kippur. My bet was legit; I had committed no crime whatsoever. That was the strength of Savannah.

The shift boss let two hours go by. I now stood alone with the two dealers. Because of the ongoing holdup of the game, neither Benny nor the helper could be relieved; they were required to stay there until it resumed. The other players had all cashed out their chips and left the table. No doubt I was feeling the heat, but I had to stay there under the gun. If I backed off and left, there was a chance they'd bust me trying to leave the casino. When midnight struck and people all around the casino began raising their glasses to toast the new year, our table remained eerily silent. Benny and the helper were also feeling the heat. Their jobs were on the line.

When the shift boss finally did reappear, he came up from behind the dealers inside the pit and was accompanied by the young floorman. He then surprisingly shook my hand and ordered Benny to pay me $15,000. He said that he couldn't pay my five-dollar chips because they'd pushed my bets over the five-thousand-dollar limit. I claimed that I'd bet them for the dealers; he said he was sorry but the limit was the limit. I had the feeling because of the little smirk he gave me that he already knew that line about betting the reds for the dealer.

Benny obediently placed three chocolate chips next to my bets. I saw that his fingers were trembling. The shift boss and floorman stood behind him and watched hawkishly. I could feel both the shift boss's contempt and the floorman's embarrassment. I certainly realized that we were done in the Hilton for a while, so I pushed the three chocolates toward Benny and asked for a chip-change. That seemed to annoy the shift boss even more, and I knew the reason why. He'd been undoubtedly waiting for me to go over to the casino cage and cash out the three chocolates. Had I done that, the casino could have hassled me with all those IRS reports concerning cash transactions of $10,000 or more. Obviously he didn't think someone smart enough to be beating the casinos at their own game was also cool enough not to walk into federal heat.

Benny cut me out fifteen yellow thousand-dollar chips. Before I left the table, I noticed Benny's forehead was dripping rivulets of sweat. I felt a little sorry for the old guy, but business was business. Anytime I felt a twinge of guilt, I reminded myself that the casinos were the biggest thieves in the world. Normally, after getting paid on a move, I tipped the dealer a handful of red or a few green chips, depending on what I had left in my pockets. But this time, both to compensate Benny and to celebrate the first double-whammy Savannah, I tossed him a black chip. Then I went to the cage and placed nine yellows on the counter. The remaining six we'd cash out another time.

The female teller smiled and asked where I'd been playing.

"You must be the only person in the whole casino who doesn't know," I said with a chuckle. She didn't appear to understand my wry humor, so I told her I'd been playing roulette. She picked up the phone and called the pit. "I have nine yellows," she said into the phone.

I turned around to face the roulette pit where I'd spent the last two hours. From where I was standing I could see the hawk-faced pit boss nodding with the phone to his ear. I imagined he was really teed off having to verify my action, and even more so upon hearing that I was only cashing out nine of the yellow chips. The teller hung up, took two $5,000 packets of hundred-dollar bills from her drawer, removed ten bills from one, and finally counted out the nine grand and pushed it across the counter. I crammed the wad of cash into my pocket and left the casino, thoroughly enjoying the thought that I had spitefully cashed out only nine yellow chips under their noses. There was nothing they could do except watch me walk out the doors with a triumphant smile on my face.

I headed immediately to meet Pat at the Gingermill. The $15,000 had been paid, but the steam inside the Hilton was awesome. Having had two hours to prepare their follow-up course of action, there was a high probability I'd be followed by plainclothes Hilton security or gaming agents, so I invoked escape procedure. After walking quickly out the main entrance, I jumped into a cab whose driver I instructed to go to Caesars Palace. Just as the cabbie turned into the Caesars entrance, I threw him a twenty over the seat and bolted out of the cab. Then I ran half-speed across Las Vegas Boulevard, dodging traffic, jumped into another cab at the Flamingo Hilton and headed back up the Strip in the opposite direction to the Riviera. Dropped off at its side doors, I walked a hundred yards back down the road to the Gingermill. Impossible that a tail could have stuck with me.

Pat was seated on one of the plushy couches bordering a little circular fire-island that sprouted a low flame. I let myself sink into the cushion next to him.

"Johnny, that was a long one," he said.

"You might say our hourly rate's going down a bit, but I never doubted for a minute I was getting paid. They were trying to bluff me out the door."

A sexily clad waitress came over to take our drink order. Pat ordered me a Perrier water and a beer for himself. When she was gone, he said, "Do you think we're done with Savannah in Vegas?"

"Not yet. They're still paying her. When—and it will happen—they refuse to pay a chocolate chip, in spite of the fact their video tapes show it was a legitimate bet, we'll know that we're all done in Vegas. But until that happens, we might as well keep attacking."

The next afternoon we tried our luck at the Aladdin—another problem. No sooner had Pat laid down his bet than the dealer reached down the layout and swiped the reds off the chocolate, set them aside on the layout, and immediately alerted the floorman. The floorman went into a panic, running through the pit to report the chocolate bet to the pit boss. I flashed Pat the signal to get out of there. He withdrew his bet and we both hurried out of the casino, knowing that the heat on Savannah was intensifying.

Again at the Gingermill, Pat said, "Johnny, we're ending up in here too often, and I'm starting to get sick looking at all these hookers."

He wasn't kidding. Barely lunch time and the overdressed hustlers were already out trying to separate men from their chips. "We definitely got heat," I acquiesced. "But we still haven't had a miss."

Pat was mildly astonished. "You want to do *another* one?"

I shrugged. "I want to see what they do when that chocolate pops up a winner again. Look, we don't know how long this thing's gonna last. It's been the greatest move I've ever seen, but once it's over . . . it's over. We might as well string it to the end."

Pat thought I was a little nuts, but he agreed to give Savannah one last shot before a vacation.

We chose the Rio, a new Brazilian-themed casino off the Strip that was fast becoming a favorite among Mexican and South American high rollers. The young woman dealer in the front pit did not crack Pat's bet, nor did she see the chocolate on the bottom. When he got caught raking it off after it lost, she had no reaction at all that would indicate steam on the move inside the Rio. Since we had never been paid on a chocolate chip in that casino, we decided to try again an hour later.

Pat put his second bet down at a roulette table on the other side of the casino. The dealer didn't pay any specific attention to it, but when it won, Pat was subjected to the same pressure I had undergone at the Hilton. But this time the result was different. After an hour in the steam bath, the shift boss came over to Pat and told him flatly that the Rio refused to pay his bet because it was suspicious in nature, and that if he wanted to take the matter up with the Nevada Gaming Control Board, he was free to do so.

It looked like the stunning Savannah had suffered a premature death in the valley of Las Vegas dolls. But in fact, Savannah was like a cat—she still had eight lives to go.

After the miss at the Rio we took Savannah on the road. We showed her off in Atlantic City, Connecticut, Mississippi, Louisiana, in the Caribbean, and on the midwestern riverboats. Because five-thousand-dollar chips couldn't be used outside of Las Vegas, we began hiding two and sometimes even three five-hundred or thousand-dollar chips underneath the reds. The caller at the top of the wheel had to keep the dealer distracted during the whole time the bet rested on the layout so that the purples or yellows wouldn't be discovered. In that regard we couldn't be perfect. About 5 percent of the time, dealers saw the big chips underneath before spinning the ball. When that happened, the raker just lifted them off, saying he didn't intend to bet the big chips. We seldom took steam for that. Another 5 percent of the time with the use of multiple big chips, the dealers saw them while the ball was spinning. In that case, we were forced to take the legitimate gamble, which didn't hurt us at all. In fact, we were lucky sons of a bitch when forced to gamble legitimately. I would say that we actually won more than we lost.

Savannah just seemed to be one helluva lucky lady.

And she's still very much alive and well.

The End

In the spring of 1996, we found a new gold mine for Savannah: Australia. Down Under now had twelve casinos, two of which were among the biggest in the world: the complex at Darling Harbor and the Crown Casino in Melbourne. Most of the wheels in Australia were the old double-deckers that were common in Reno, where you had one roulette wheel in the middle of two tables. Only one dealer spun the ball while the other one at the adjoining table listened for the call. That second dealer's inactivity resulted in our getting seen more than usual picking up the losing bets, but overall it had no effect on the number of payoffs we received. Pat couldn't resist reverting back to the old blackjack move in some of the better casinos because Australia had never seen it before. We spent two months in the beautiful island country, appreciating its kangaroos, geological sites, water sports, lobster, and, of course, its casinos.

During the late 1990s and into the twenty-first century there were so many new casino openings in North America we couldn't keep track. New Orleans had reopened Harrah's French Quarter casino. Three casinos were now operating in Detroit, and we "motored" right to them. The Mississippi, Missouri, and Illinois rivers were jammed with riverboat casinos. In Indiana, Caesar's World floated the world's largest riverboat casino, the four-deck monster it named Glory of Rome. And the Indian reservations kept pace with the riverboats. There was a second large Indian casino in Connecticut, and a new Minnesota gaming corporation, Grand Casinos, already had two large Indian reservation casinos in its home state, in addition to a half-dozen more docked on riverbanks in Mississippi and Louisiana. In Canada, there were now large casinos in Niagara Falls, Hull, and a second in Montreal. The casino in Windsor had expanded, making the Detroit-Windsor trip even more worthwhile. And Atlantic City now had its Hilton, and more monsters were planned to rise up around the Marina.

Overseas, casino expansion progressed as well, though not at the North American rate. Australia continued building giant casinos that not only rivaled the monsters in Vegas, they surpassed them. Casinos were becoming so huge you could honestly get lost inside them faster than you could in giant airport terminals. In Central and Eastern Europe, casinos were busting through skies once enveloped by prohibitive communism. There were already a dozen in Moscow alone. When I saw on the news that Yasser Arafat had opened a Palestinian casino in Gaza, I at once called Joe and asked him if he wanted to give it an old Jewish shelling (I was kidding).

When we stayed in Vegas, there was a new formation of giant mega–resort casinos lining the Strip. The mid-1990s introduced the Monte Carlo, the Stratosphere, and New York–New York casinos. By the end of the decade, there was Steve Wynn's new flagship, the Bellagio, as well as the Paris, the Venetian, and the Mandalay Bay, to be followed by the new Aladdin. Savannah welcomed them all to Las Vegas. She was the perfect move to go up against all the new casinos' sophisticated surveillance systems. Each time the inspectors went to the surveillance tape, they surprisingly found that the bet being claimed by the claimer was legitimate. In the summer of 2001, during the writing of this book, Savannah celebrated her sixth birthday, still not having been cracked by either Las Vegas's multimillion-dollar surveillance systems or the supposedly intelligent casino sleuths operating them. The only way those "experts" are going to uncover Savannah's secret—how so many purple, yellow, and chocolate chips keep popping up invisibly and legitimately on roulette layouts (and now also on blackjack layouts)—is by reading my book.

Before I wrote it, I had another blockbuster idea that nearly put it on the back burner. I'd been thinking of attempting a single million-dollar move that I called the "Super Savannah." This was doing the same basic Savannah move on a number straight up, instead of on the 19 through 36 and column boxes on the outside. The only place in the world it was feasible was at the Horseshoe in Las Vegas. As old Benny Binion used to boast, you could bet any amount you wanted in his casino. Since the Horseshoe had ten-thousand-dollar chips, I envisioned hiding three of them under five one-dollar casino chips on a number at the bottom of the layout, and raking it all off when it lost. $30,000 straight up on a number paid $1,050,000. And the Horseshoe would have to pay it when it won, since it had no table limit you could exceed.

I eventually abandoned the idea because the odds on hitting any particular number were thirty-seven to one, which caused procedural problems. We'd have to keep placing the bet and raking off until it won, and to avoid any possibility of surveillance backtracking through their tapes and matching a rake-off to the big payoff, we could only place the bet once a week. Which meant that we could literally wait years for the number to come in, if unlucky. After discussing it at length, Pat and I decided it just wasn't worth it.

But another reason influenced my nixing of the Super Savannah even more. I was starting to think a lot of retirement as I reflected about my life. I had been ripping off the casinos for a quarter of a century. Not as long as the thirty-five years Joe had put in, but a hall of fame career just the same. I had enough money to live comfortably for the rest of my life. But more influential on my decision than that was fatigue. I was tiring. The constant traveling around the world might seem glamorous, but it really knocks you out. And I'm going to let you in on a little secret. Despite my balls of stone in casinos, I'm scared to death of airplanes. Always have been. I just managed to block it out while with my partners.

And, of course, there was Steven DeVisser. He'd been chasing me for nearly twenty years, just dying to bust my ass. I always knew in the back of my brain that if he ever got me, I'd end up getting sentenced to the max, which is ten years in a Nevada state prison. After bucking that all this time, I figured maybe I ought to heed an old gambler's proverb and quit while I was ahead.

In the spring of 2000, I packed it in—at least temporarily. Pat and I were in his apartment watching *Geraldo Live* when he said to me, "You know, Johnny, I bet Geraldo would love to see what we do and put it on his show. We ought to write a book about it or something. What do you think?"

I had once before thought of writing a book about the history of cheating casinos. Listening to Joe's stories about himself and his brother, about Mumbles and Wheels, I'd imagined that they all would make interesting literary characters. My own experiences, I figured, were also worth writing about. But what really pushed me over the hump to recount my life inside the casinos was Savannah. I just could never get over how something so simple, so elementary, could repeatedly fool the world's casinos. Its simplicity had to have been the result of a four-decade-long evolution of human genius and dedication, which had started with Mumbles and continued evolving along with Henry, Joe, and me, and will undoubtedly continue along the road to the next stroke of genius that enables enterprising cheaters to rip off casinos, regardless of how much money is spent on state-of-the-art surveillance systems to stop them.

When Pat first posed that question about writing a book on our experiences, I responded that it wasn't a bad idea, though I doubted sincerely that Geraldo, or anyone else for that matter, would believe it. "We'd have to take Geraldo on a casino tour," I told Pat. When I decided I really did want to write this book, and that I was putting myself into retirement to do so, Pat was flabbergasted.

"You're gonna give up all our moves in a book? What are you, crazy, Johnny?" He reminded me that if Miami Beach ever opened casinos we'd make a fortune.

"Why not?" I said. "The way I see it, if my book ends up putting us out of business because it wised up the casinos, that'll have meant it became a bestseller and made a bundle. I won't need the fucking casinos anymore. On the other hand, if I can't sell the book, I can go right back into the casinos and continue doing the moves. Either way, the book can't hurt me."

"What about *me*, Johnny?"

I laughed. I'd been expecting Pat to ask that question. "Don't worry, Pat," I said humorously but sincerely. "You won't be left out in the cold. If my book sells enough copies to cut short your pinching-pastposting career, I'll put you in the pastposters' workman's compensation fund. Balls, too." I also told Pat that if there had been a Pastposters' Hall of Fame, he would have been inducted in the same fashion Babe Ruth was at Cooperstown. When I said that to him, I actually had tears in my eyes.

And so that's how I retired. In the summer of 2000 I packed a bag and flew off alone to the French Riviera, my happiest discovery on the international road, and began work on my autobiography. During the year I spent there writing this book I did not once enter a casino. But gazing into the blue Mediterranean from my balcony when breaking between chapters, I thought so often of the inspiring adventures I'd had in the world's majestic casinos.

The casinos—I love them all.

And please—whoever one day finds my dead body, see to it that I'm buried at Caesars Palace in Las Vegas.

Of course, before I throw this European portable computer in the garbage, I must include a where-are-they-now epilogue to make the story complete.

Joe Classon still lives in Miami Beach and fools around with the stock market. I speak to him every six months. I didn't tell him that I wrote this book. I prefer to send him an autographed copy as a surprise birthday present. I hope he approves of my writing, being a man of letters himself. He'll probably have a lot of criticism about my lack of literary skills.

Henry Classon is still railing and picking up sleepers in casinos when not playing poker. I last saw him in the MGM Grand in Las

Vegas in February 1996. He was railing a guy on a craps table. Nine months before that, in May 1995, I'd seen him on opening night at Harrah's New Orleans temporary casino near the French Quarter. He was picking up sleepers on a roulette table. As far as I know, he didn't see me either time. He was too busy plying his craft.

Duke must still be living with Marla or someone else in Oregon. I've lost contact with him but am sure he's no longer in the ripping-off-casinos business. If I were still a betting man, I'd bet my last chip that he's flourishing in the marijuana business.

Raul and Rosa Garcia still live in Las Vegas. Raul sells cars and occasionally works with Pat and Balls. Rosa is a housewife who also occasionally works with Pat and Balls. The Garcias now have four children. The eldest, Raul Jr., also works with Pat and Balls during college breaks. He's already claimed a dozen bets, so I'm told.

Steven DeVisser still works for Clint Hanson. I haven't seen him since the spring of 1999, when he was jeering me in another Vegas casino back room. I did, however, see his picture in a gaming magazine nearly a year later, and in it I was shocked to see that he wasn't wearing the blue denim suit. The accompanying article was about his new instant photoidentification system for quickly rooting out casino cheats in the Hanson client hotels. His car had been equipped with a computer link to all the surveillance rooms in Vegas. Any surveillance operator watching a suspicious person in the casino was then able to feed DeVisser the image from the overhead cameras directly to his monitor built into the dashboard. If the image was a hit, the cagey Hanson agent could then speed over to the inquiring casino and set up the unsuspecting cheater. I think I'll send DeVisser an autographed copy, too. Do you think he'll like the way I portrayed him? Regardless, it is accurate.

Pat and Balls are still living in Vegas, working Savannah in the casinos there and around the world. Balls didn't fare well in the sports-touting business and returned to us in 1997. Despite what they say, I'm sure they both want this book to become a bestseller.

My friend Donnie, believe it or not, is now an enforcement agent with the Nevada Gaming Control Board. He often comes into contact with Steven DeVisser, and sometimes they discuss me. Of course,

DeVisser has no idea that Donnie knows me personally. I sure hope that Donnie doesn't lose his job or get in any kind of trouble because of this book. If he does, I'll have to add him to the list of people eligible for pastposters' workman's compensation.

And finally, the Gingermill lounge is still catering to its "preferred" clientele, certainly to Pat and Balls every time they have an emergency in Las Vegas.

I returned to the United States after finishing this book and now live in California. The writing of it brought me two pleasures. The first was all the delicious private smiles I shared with nobody while remembering the moments as I wrote them. The second was that it made me an honest citizen.

Was it all worth it—my pastposting career? You bet. I made a good living for more than two decades, traveled the world, staying in the best hotels and eating in the best restaurants, and I never went to jail for any of the thousands of felonies I committed in casinos. But when speaking about being rich, I am exactly that, because I can never put a price on all the experiences I own. They are absolutely priceless. I am totally fulfilled by the life that I've led and extremely glad to have been part of a small but special breed of people who have the wit and the balls to do what we did.

What does the future hold for pastposting and all cheating-the-casinos-by-manipulating-the-chips businesses? I'd say it's quite rosy. Cheaters will always evolve with the casinos, implementing new versions of the same old moves. Throughout this book I talked constantly about "steam" inside the casinos. Cheating moves done in casinos create steam. That steam has a limited life and dies out with the passage of time. Once it is dead, you can go right back into the same casinos and do the same moves until new steam is created. That reality always fascinated me. If you remember the incident I recounted about the Barbary Coast, where there was so much steam on the blackjack move that floormen were comparing every young white male sitting on third base to my photograph, you didn't forget the floorman who spotted me sitting at a table next to Jerry and then flipped out and called for security. A few months later, I did the same blackjack move and was paid amicably by that same floorman. The steam cycle will continue that way forever.

There are certain psychological factors about the makeup of a casino that favor cheaters. Start with the chips: the little clay multi-colored disks represented money but still were *not* money. It is just a little bit easier to give away chips than money, especially when it's not *your* money the chips represent.

Practically all casino jobs are monotonous. Despite the glamour one sees from the outside, for the people behind the tables, an eight-hour shift is a real grind. The dealers have a robotic function; their job is not much different than a roadway toll collector's. In fact, both a casino dealer and a bridge toll collector are obliged to inhale a lot of smoke, albeit that smoke coming out of a car's exhaust has a different flavor from that at the end of a cigarette. When you stick people into a dead job like that, their brains are not being nourished, and they quickly lose interest. That loss of interest translates into a don't-give-a-shit-attitude. I know all this firsthand. Remember, I was once a casino dealer.

And what do floormen do? They spend their eight-hour shifts watching the dealers. How exciting can that be? Constantly on their feet, they pace up and down their pit like prisoners in their cells. All without much interest. A good example of floorman ennui was my little mini-baccarat scam done at the Four Queens. If you remember, I managed to fix the cards while the floorman, who was supposed to be watching my lacing procedure, had his ass to the table and his eyes on a broad.

A final element that works against the casinos is the never-ending war of attrition. As the years go by, dealers, floormen, and pit bosses—like everybody else—retire and die off, to be succeeded by younger replacements. A lot of the knowledge that had been tucked away inside those old-timers' brains is never passed down to the young bloods, which in effect creates new, virgin casinos—or at least new virgin parts of old used-up casinos. As long as there is natural evolution, there will always be cheaters battling to survive inside the casinos.

Let the casino wars go on.

A final word: In no way is this book meant to be a how-to-cheat-the-casino manual. As easy as some of the moves I've described may seem, not just anybody can go out and do them. If you get caught cheating in a casino, you could have a very serious legal problem. The FBI now investigates organized interstate casino cheating, which is considered a federal racketeering offense and accordingly falls under the RICO statutes.

I hope you enjoyed reading the book, but please, leave the actual cheating to Pat and Balls.

And to me—if ever I decide to go back inside a casino and pop one in for old times' sake.